CHRISTIAN
HISTORY

Fascinating

Facts *of the* Faith

365
DAILY
READINGS
FROM
CHRISTIAN
HISTORY

Fascinating
Facts *of the* Faith

Your Inspirational
and Entertaining Guide to the
Who, What, When, and Where
of Christianity

BARBOUR
PUBLISHING

© 2008 by Barbour Publishing, Inc.

Writing and compilation by Rebecca Currington, Susan Duke, Matthew Kinne, Vicki J. Kuyper, and Patricia Mitchell in association with Snapdragon Group℠.

ISBN 978-1-60260-013-3

Bible translations used are noted on page 373.

Published by Barbour Publishing, Inc., P.O. Box 719, Uhrichsville, Ohio 44683
www.barbourbooks.com

Our mission is to publish and distribute inspirational products offering exceptional value and biblical encouragement to the masses.

ecpa Member of the
Evangelical Christian
Publishers Association

Printed in the United States of America.

Introduction

Methodist pastor Ralph Washington Sockman once said, "The hinge of history is on the door of a Bethlehem stable." How true! The birth of Jesus Christ changed *everything*.

The history of Christianity has been inextricably woven into the history of the world. This book, *Fascinating Facts of the Faith*, highlights those significant Christian threads that have become part of the tapestry of world events. Read this book for an entire year, and you'll walk away with an amazing overview of Christian history—the good, the bad, and, occasionally, the off-the-wall.

Each week, you'll read about a man of the faith, a woman of the faith, an important site, a groundbreaking event, a notable book, a favorite song, and some miscellaneous entry that just doesn't seem to fit elsewhere. As you read, you'll see a bigger picture emerging, characters interacting, and events playing on and against each other. You'll see threads of compassion, martyrdom, forgiveness, hardship, courage, remembrance, accomplishment, enlightenment, and truth. You'll learn that our church history is not without blemish. Controversies, wars, and regrettable choices all prove one thing—Christians are only human, too. But you'll also see that we serve a powerful God, who moves in and through the affairs of mankind.

We hope you'll enjoy reading this book as much as we enjoyed putting it together. We've learned a lot—and you will, too. Happy reading!

THE PUBLISHERS

In the fourth century, oration, rhetoric, and philosophy were lofty pursuits requiring years of study in speech, writing, and persuasion. Augustine was up to the challenge.

At the age of seventeen, he traveled to Carthage to study the great masters. From there, he went on to Rome, where he hoped to make a name for himself in the mighty Greek tradition of Plato and Aristotle. But he failed to find the truth and inspiration he sought. Finally, disillusioned and weary, Augustine settled into a teaching position in Milan.

Perhaps the influence of Augustine's Christian mother made him long for something more. Whatever the cause of his discontent, it was in Milan that Augustine met Ambrose, the first Latin church father from a Christian family. The young man was drawn to Ambrose's beautiful, allegorical preaching, and soon was persuaded to become a Christian. The transformation was so complete that, at the age of thirty-one, Augustine abandoned his career in rhetoric, resigned from his teaching position, excused himself from an arranged engagement, and returned to his North African home to commit himself completely to serving God.

Men of the Faith

Augustine
(354–430)
Orator, theologian, philosopher, and writer

Augustine could have led a quiet, monastic life—but his writing soon drew him into the spotlight. His brilliant views on grace quashed several prevalent heresies, and many readers were touched by his book, *Confessions*, the first real spiritual autobiography. Augustine is probably best known for *The City of God*, in which he established that God has a master plan and imposes His hand on every aspect of human history.

Augustine's name has popped up in some unexpected places. The Christian rock band Petra recorded a song entitled "St. Augustine's Pears," based on the young Augustine's experience of stealing pears from a neighbor's tree. There are also songs about Augustine by Bob Dylan and the alternative rock band Switchfoot, and he's even mentioned in the Rolling Stones song "Family."

FACT

Study to shew thyself approved unto God,
a workman that needeth not to be ashamed,
rightly dividing the word of truth.
2 TIMOTHY 2:15 KJV

As a teenager, Gladys Aylward dreamed of traveling the world to share her faith in Jesus. She worked and saved her money, believing that God would provide an opportunity. When she was thirty years old, it came: Gladys learned of an older woman missionary in China who was seeking an assistant.

Gladys's heart must have been filled with excitement as she packed her belongings and began a long journey across England, Europe, and eastern Russia. After traveling by boat, train, bus, and mule, she arrived in Yangchen, China, and found her mentor, Mrs. Larson. The missionary and a Christian Chinese cook were ministering at an inn for muleteers. Gladys gladly joined them as they shared food, shelter, Bible teaching, and God's love.

After Mrs. Larson died, Gladys settled in Yangchen. She learned the language and immersed herself in the culture. Eventually she became a Chinese citizen and was well known to the local Chinese official. Quietly and faithfully, Gladys worked with the city's prisoners and lepers.

Women of the Faith

Gladys Aylward
(1902–1970)
Missionary to China

When the Japanese attacked China in World War II, Gladys fled Yangchen for shelter in Sian with one hundred orphans in tow. After a nerve-racking, twelve-day journey through the mountains, the group was halted by the Yellow River, with no way to cross. A Chinese officer, who heard Gladys and the children praying and singing, arranged a boat for their crossing.

A simple teenage girl with a heart's desire to share her faith played an extraordinary role in the evangelization of the nation of China. Gladys Aylward's story is immortalized in the book *The Small Woman* by Alan Burgess.

FACT

Gladys's march to Sian with her bevy of orphans became a film—*Inn of the Sixth Happiness*, starring Ingrid Bergman—in 1958. However, Gladys was troubled by the fact that screenwriters fabricated a love interest—a Eurasian soldier—for her character. She felt the love scenes between the two sullied her reputation.

And everyone who has left houses or brothers or sisters
or father or mother or children or fields for my sake
will receive a hundred times as much
and will inherit eternal life.
MATTHEW 19:29

The Church of the Holy Sepulchre, also known as the Church of the Resurrection, is said to rest on holy ground. Tradition says the structure sits on Golgotha or Calvary—the place the New Testament describes as the site of Jesus' crucifixion. The church originally had three parts to commemorate the death, burial, and resurrection of Jesus.

Though it is now within the walled Old City of Jerusalem, in Jesus' time, the site would have been outside the city—where crucifixions were carried out. Nearby was a cemetery many thought included a tomb prepared for a wealthy Jew named Joseph of Arimathea. The New Testament says Joseph offered a burial place to the Lord (Matthew 27:57–60).

In AD 325, Constantine I, the first Roman emperor to embrace Christianity, gave his mother, Helena, the task of restoring Jerusalem's Christian holy sites. The two toured the city and discovered that pagan temples had been built over what were believed to be Calvary and Jesus' tomb. The temples were destroyed, the stones carried away, and a magnificent basilica constructed. The Church of the Holy Sepulchre dates to about AD 333 and also covers a cistern where Helena is said to have found portions of the cross. A stone that some believe to be part of the boulder that sealed Jesus' tomb is also displayed.

Important Sites

The Church of the Holy Sepulchre
Jerusalem

As Jerusalem changed hands over the centuries, the church was destroyed and rebuilt several times. Today's version—less grandiose than the original—was built in 1099 by the Christian Crusaders. Each year, thousands of Christians visit this curious conglomeration of altars, chapels, columned courtyards, and architectural styles.

> After Jerusalem's occupation by Tslah A-Din in the year of 1187, the Holy Sepulchre Church was given for safekeeping to two Moslem families who still own the church and hold the keys.
>
> FACT

The angel said to the women,
"Do not be afraid, for I know that you are
looking for Jesus, who was crucified.
He is not here; he has risen, just as he said.
Come and see the place where he lay.
Then go quickly and tell his disciples:
'He has risen from the dead.'"
MATTHEW 28:5–7

T he fire of the Holy Spirit fell on us." That's the picture painted by those attending the Azusa Street Revival, which took place in Los Angeles in the early 1900s.

William J. Seymour, an African-American preacher, became pastor of the Azusa Street Mission in April 1906. The mission was nothing more than an abandoned church building with apartments upstairs and a stable for horses below. It measured about forty by sixty feet.

Seymour, whose preaching stressed the gifts of the Holy Spirit, gave special attention to speaking in tongues (or *glossolalia*) as a sign that believers had been baptized in the Holy Spirit. The worship was devout and intense. People "fell back" under the power of God, and at times, worshippers would break into spontaneous singing in unscripted harmonies. Some claimed miracles and healings.

Groundbreaking Events

Azusa Street Revival

Outpouring of the Holy Spirit

For the next three and a half years, the crowds continued to visit Azusa Street, staying around the clock despite the hot, smelly, fly-infested surroundings. As many as fifteen hundred people reportedly jammed the old stable, covering windows and doors and stifling every trace of a breeze. But the worshippers were undeterred.

Some claimed the meetings seemed to run themselves while Seymour knelt, deeply engrossed in prayer. The revival was multiracial and multidenominational, and featured the poor and women prominently. Many who visited Azusa Street carried the flame of revival back to their own congregations, starting the modern Pentecostal movement.

> FACT
>
> Some observers told newspaper reporters that the presence of God was so heavy on the Azusa Street Mission that people were knocked to the ground blocks from the mission building itself.

[Jesus said,] "You will receive power when the Holy Spirit comes on you;
and you will be my witnesses in Jerusalem,
and in all Judea and Samaria,
and to the ends of the earth."
Acts 1:8

Categorized as historical fiction, *Ben-Hur: A Tale of the Christ* was a phenomenal success, quickly surpassing Harriet Beecher Stowe's *Uncle Tom's Cabin* as the bestselling American novel. It remained so until the publication of Margaret Mitchell's *Gone with the Wind* in 1936.

Ben-Hur is a tale of betrayal, revenge, and salvation that provides a credible glimpse into the geography and culture of the ancient world. The story concerns the life of Judah Ben-Hur, a rich Jewish prince and merchant in first-century Jerusalem. One day he encounters a childhood friend, Messala, who is now a commanding officer of a Roman legion. At first the two are glad to see each other, but eventually they clash over political issues. Messala betrays Judah, and the young prince is forced to serve as a galley slave on a ship, while his mother and sister are imprisoned. Upon Judah's release, he seeks revenge, taking on his betrayer in a wild chariot race in which Messala is mortally wounded. Only after Judah encounters Jesus and witnesses His crucifixion does he find redemption and forgiveness.

Notable Books

This book has been adapted for both stage and film. After *Ben-Hur*'s release in 1880, it became a Broadway play in 1899. Silent film versions were made in 1907 and 1925—the most expensive silent film ever made. In 1959, the feature

Ben-Hur: A Tale of the Christ
By General Lew Wallace (1880)

film starring Charlton Heston was released—the most expensive color film of its time and the first to win eleven Oscars. A musical version was released in 1999, followed by an animated film in 2003 with Charlton Heston as the voice of Ben-Hur.

A rumor persists that a stuntman was killed during the filming of the chariot race in the 1959 movie version of Ben-Hur. The rumor also alleges that the director, William Wyler, left the fatal accident in the final cut of the film despite the widow's objections. No evidence has been produced to support this claim, but many still believe MGM engaged in a cover-up.

FACT

Forgive whatever grievances you may have against one another.
Forgive as the Lord forgave you.
COLOSSIANS 3:13

This simple yet profound song first appeared in the novel *Say and Seal*, in a scene of a Sunday school teacher singing words of encouragement to a dying boy. The book's author, Susan Warner, asked her sister Anna—who regularly wrote hymns as part of a ministry to cadets at nearby West Point—to create a song for her story. Later, when Anna's simple poem was set to music by composer William B. Bradbury (who also wrote tunes for hymns such as "My Hope Is Built" and "He Leadeth Me"), "Jesus Loves Me" became a national and international favorite.

Songs of the Faith

"Jesus Loves Me"
Words by
Anna B. Warner and
David Rutherford McGuire (1860)
Music by William B. Bradbury (1871)

The second stanza of Anna Warner's original work is rarely found in hymnals—the lines refer to the dying boy of Susan's novel. Many modern hymnals include two additional stanzas written in 1971 by an Anglican priest, David McGuire. He based his contribution on the story of Jesus and the children in Matthew 19.

A story involving this sweet tune holds that when John F. Kennedy's World War II patrol torpedo boat (*PT-109*) was rammed and sunk in the Solomon Islands in 1943, island natives rescued the crew. Faced with a daunting language barrier, the natives began to sing "Jesus Loves Me"—a song they had learned from missionaries—and the Navy crew joined in enthusiastically.

Jesus loves me! This I know,
For the Bible tells me so.
Little ones to Him belong;
They are weak, but He is strong.

Refrain:
Yes, Jesus loves me!
Yes, Jesus loves me!
Yes, Jesus loves me!
The Bible tells me so.

FACT

Recording artist Whitney Houston sang a version of this simple Sunday school song in her movie *The Bodyguard.*

This is love: not that we loved God, but that he loved us and sent his Son as an atoning sacrifice for our sins.
1 JOHN 4:10

On December 24, 1968, an estimated one quarter of the earth's population heard the Bible's account of creation, thanks to astronauts of the Apollo 8 mission. Mission commander Frank Borman, command module pilot James Lovell, and lunar module pilot William Anders used the occasion of a live television broadcast from space to read Genesis 1:1–10 (KJV):

In the beginning God created the heaven and the earth.

And the earth was without form, and void; and darkness was upon the face of the deep. And the Spirit of God moved upon the face of the waters.

And God said, Let there be light: and there was light.

And God saw the light, that it was good: and God divided the light from the darkness.

And God called the light Day, and the darkness he called Night. And the evening and the morning were the first day.

And God said, Let there be a firmament in the midst of the waters, and let it divide the waters from the waters.

Miscellany

And God made the firmament, and divided the waters which were under the firmament from the waters which were above the firmament: and it was so.

Apollo 8
Moon mission

And God called the firmament Heaven. And the evening and the morning were the second day.

And God said, Let the waters under the heaven be gathered together unto one place, and let the dry land appear: and it was so.

And God called the dry land Earth; and the gathering together of the waters called he Seas: and God saw that it was good.

Apollo 8's primary mission was to circle the moon (which the astronauts did ten times over twenty hours), scouting earth's satellite for the planned lunar landing of the Apollo 11 mission. Borman's team took numerous photographs of the moon as well as the earth—including the first image of the "earthrise," a dramatic view of our planet never seen before.

The orbiting Genesis reading thrilled some. Borman said later that Pope Paul VI told him, "I have spent my entire life trying to say to the world what you did on Christmas Eve."

Famed atheist Madalyn Murray O'Hair filed suit against NASA to ban federal employees from such public "prayers." Courts eventually denied her argument.

FACT

Since the creation of the world God's invisible qualities—his eternal power and divine nature—have been clearly seen, being understood from what has been made, so that men are without excuse.

ROMANS 1:20

Andrew Murray knew early in life he wanted to be a minister: He planned for it, prepared for it, prayed for it. But it wasn't until he was involved in his theological studies that he actually met Jesus and was converted. He told his parents, "I have cast myself on Christ."

This complete surrender brought with it a deep commitment to prayer and Bible study, resulting in an intense preaching style. Murray preached that Christians are free to believe and experience the grace of God every moment of their lives since God has provided everything necessary to produce rich, productive, meaningful lives. He only asked for a wholehearted commitment, confidence in the Spirit's anointing, and understanding of the power of prayer. Some considered him a forerunner of Pentecostalism.

Men of the Faith

Andrew Murray (1828–1917)

Minister, author, and ambassador of prayer

Murray, who ministered primarily in South Africa, was the author of two hundred fifty books, a hugely popular speaker, and the father of nine children. Among several organizations he founded was the Huguenot Seminary, a school that trained young women for work in education. When the school opened, the building was found to be already too small for the number enrolled. A wing had to be added immediately.

Though he tried to align his insights with those of the Dutch Reformed Church of South Africa with which he was affiliated, Murray received criticism for his views on free will. Nevertheless, he remained a respected member for sixty years.

FACT

Andrew Murray was the first president of the Young Men's Christian Association (YMCA). He believed that laughter and fellowship were two of life's most important activities.

How rich is God's grace, which he has given to us so fully and freely.
EPHESIANS 1:7–8 NCV

The life of Elizabeth Hooton—a middle-aged, married, English woman of comfortable circumstances—was said to have been remarkably normal until the day she met Quaker preacher George Fox. When she came upon him sharing his faith on a street corner in Nottingham, England, she listened with great interest and immediately adopted the Quaker faith as her own. A few short years later, this simple wife and mother found herself arrested and imprisoned for preaching the gospel. Choosing to follow the example of the apostle Paul, she saw her imprisonment as an opportunity to suffer for Christ's sake.

After her release from prison and the death of her husband, Hooton determined to go to Boston to aid Quakers who were undergoing severe persecution. She set sail at the age of sixty.

In Boston, Elizabeth was soon in trouble again. Jailed along with other Quakers, she fully expected to be hanged. Miraculously, a change in the political climate led to her release. While preaching from place to place, Elizabeth endured numerous beatings with spiked whips and spent time in dark, foul dungeons. Finally, bloody and torn, she was put on horseback and sent into the wilderness, where it was assumed she would succumb to wild animals or treacherous conditions. Once again she survived. At the age of seventy, Elizabeth returned to London to work for the relief of Quaker prisoners and to broadcast the tales of their suffering.

Women of the Faith

Elizabeth Hooton (1598–1672)

First Quaker convert, Quaker preacher, and martyr

Elizabeth Hooton died just a week after leaving England for the West Indies, where she had hoped to encourage a small colony of exiled Quakers.

Hooton is memorialized on one of 77 panels of the Quaker Tapestry, which illustrates the history of Quakerism from the seventeenth century until present day. More than 4,000 men, women, and children from 15 countries embroidered the panels—25 inches wide and 21 inches tall—which tell the story of the Quaker movement over its 350-year history. The tapestry is housed in Kendal, England.

FACT

Who will separate us from the love of Christ? Will hardship,
or distress, or persecution, or famine, or nakedness, or peril, or sword?. . .
No, in all these things we are more than conquerors through him who loved us.
ROMANS 8:35, 37 NRSV

The Romans were a surly lot. Mess with them and you were apt to end up in a disgusting, damp, smelly prison—indefinitely. Offenders weren't sentenced to prison to pay for their crimes; they were thrown in prison until their *real* sentences could be carried out. It is believed that both Peter and Paul were held in Mamertine Prison in Rome prior to their executions.

Located on the east side of the Capitoline Hill, Mamertine Prison is adjacent to the Roman Forum beneath the Chapel of the Crucifix. Constructed in the seventh century BC, originally the prison was a vast network of dungeons under the city's main sewer. By the time Peter and Paul spent their days underground, the prison consisted only of a small building with two cells, one on top of the other. These cramped, miserable spaces must have been particularly cold, damp, and drafty due to their proximity to the sewers. No wonder Paul asked Timothy to "come to me quickly...[and] bring the cloak that I left...at Troas" (2 Timothy 4:9, 13). He must have been wet and chilled to the bone.

Important Sites

Mamertine Prison

Rome

The lower room, where the condemned were thrown, is round and made of pepperino and mortar. Today, a plaque hangs on the wall of the upper chamber, listing the names of some of the more famous prisoners, martyrs, and their persecutors. To one side is a red marble altar, and to the left of that stands a column said to be the one to which Peter and Paul were tied when they converted their guards to Christianity.

FACT

The cross on the altar in the lower chapel is upside down in honor of the apostle Peter, who tradition says was crucified upside down.

[Paul wrote] *"This is my gospel, for which I am suffering even to the point of being chained like a criminal. But God's word is not chained."*
2 TIMOTHY 2:8–9

In the seventh century, Muslims took control of Jerusalem and ruled generously for more than four hundred years. They allowed large numbers of Christians to make pilgrimages to the holy places there. In the eleventh century, all that changed. The Seljuk Turks took over Jerusalem and visits no longer were allowed.

At the same time, Frenchman Urban II became pope and began to search for a strategy to repair a long-standing rift between the Eastern Orthodox Christians and the squabbling princes of the West. When Alexis of Constantinople asked for help fighting against the Muslim Turks, Urban instantly saw an opportunity to unite all Christendom by establishing a common enemy.

Urban played it up big, preaching loudly against "an accursed race utterly alienated from God" that had invaded Christian lands, and sending his representatives across Europe to recruit knights for the liberation of Palestine. Each crusader wore the Crusader's cross—a large red cross with four smaller crosses between the arms. As Crusaders made their way from Europe toward Jerusalem, they left a bloodbath of epic proportions in their wake. Assured by Urban that slaughtering infidels was a service to God with eternal benefits, they killed everything and everyone in their path.

Groundbreaking Events

The Crusades
Fight for the Holy Land

In total there were seven crusades—all eventual failures. The Crusaders' conquest of the Holy Land was not permanent; they did not deter the advancement of Islam, nor did they heal the schism between East and West.

> Like today's Muslim extremists, the Crusaders believed they were fighting a *jihad* or "holy war."
>
> FACT

[Jesus said,] "I tell you who hear me: Love your enemies, do good to those who hate you, bless those who curse you, pray for those who mistreat you."
LUKE 6:27–28

Author Richard Booker says that for years after becoming a Christian, he tried to find life in the pages of the Bible. He really did believe that it was God's Word, but it seemed dry and disorganized. Where was the order, the logic? How did the Old and New Testaments fit together? They seemed to be two separate unrelated documents under one cover. He gave up and put the Bible back on the shelf.

As his hunger for God grew, Booker says, the Holy Spirit urged him to take his Bible down from the shelf and begin again. This time, he found the book of Leviticus. With the Holy Spirit leading him, he began to see God's order in the Bible; the individual pieces began to come together and make sense. As he studied the Old Testament, he made a startling discovery—it was a picture of Jesus. The Old Testament told what would happen—the crucifixion and resurrection of Jesus for the forgiveness of sins. The New Testament tells that it did happen. The covenant between God and humans in the blood of Jesus is the "Scarlet Thread" that runs through both Testaments, touching every single book in the Bible.

Notable Books

Miracle of the Scarlet Thread
By Richard Booker (1981)

The *Miracle of the Scarlet Thread* traces the story of God's blood covenant with humans through both the Old and New Testaments, becoming the consummate primer on the subject. Readers see that we're not in covenant with an organization; we are in covenant with a person! With the scarlet thread of the blood covenant, biblical loose ends come together, and God's order emerges.

FACT

Highly acclaimed by theologians, *Miracle of the Scarlet Thread* is considered standard reading for individual believers, churches, Bible schools, and study groups around the world.

After supper [Jesus] took the cup, saying,
"This cup is the new covenant in my blood;
do this, whenever you drink it, in remembrance of me."
1 CORINTHIANS 11:25

The first stanza of this beautiful and powerful hymn was published anonymously in the *Gospel Magazine* in 1779 with a tune by William Shrubsole. The next year, eight additional verses were published in the same magazine under the title, "On the Resurrection, the Lord Is King."

The author was eventually determined to be Edward Perronet, the son of an Anglican vicar. His family, closely associated with the hymn-writing Wesleys, were Huguenot refugees who immigrated to Switzerland in 1680.

Clearly, Perronet intended his verses, now known as the "Coronation Hymn," as a tribute to the kingship of Christ. He used phrases from the book of Revelation and the Lamentations of Jeremiah to establish the image of a mighty Lord and King.

Songs of the Faith

"All Hail the Power of Jesus' Name"

Words by Edward Perronet (1779)

Music by Oliver Holden (1793)

The song's history carries an interesting story. While in India, Rev. E. P. Scott sought to evangelize a certain inland tribe known for its brutality. Though warned, he ventured on until he found himself surrounded by a group of warriors with spears pointed ominously in his direction.

With nothing in his hand but a violin, he closed his eyes and began to play and sing this mighty hymn. When he dared to open his eyes again, he found that the spears had dropped. The members of the tribe later listened enthusiastically as he told them about Jesus.

All hail the power of Jesus' Name! Let angels prostrate fall;
Bring forth the royal diadem, and crown Him Lord of all.
Bring forth the royal diadem, and crown Him Lord of all.

Six years after this hymn was anonymously published in the *Gospel Magazine*, it reappeared—again anonymously, but accompanied by an acrostic poem. The letters spelled out the name "Edward Perronet."

FACT

O LORD, our Lord, how majestic is your name in all the earth!
PSALM 8:1

Heavy metal is an extreme variation of rock music that gained popularity in the 1960s. It was characterized by heavy sound achieved by a highly amplified distortion of guitar and drums. Hearing this discordant sound might make many conclude that such music is not for Christians. However, by the 1970s and '80s, Christian bands, such as Resurrection, Jerusalem, and Stryper, appeared on the scene.

In the 1980s, however, heavy metal descended into the depths. Though it stayed mostly underground, a new variety known as black metal took the stage. This extreme form of music was characterized by an aggressive and abrasive sound achieved with the use of heavily distorted guitars, harsh vocals, fast-paced rhythms, and unconventional song structures.

Miscellany

Christian Heavy Metal

In addition, the bands held a strong anti-Christian worldview, which they incorporated into their music by way of Christian-hating lyrics, satanic images, and pagan themes. But again they would be challenged.

In 1994, the black metal group named Horde invaded the metal scene. Horde released an album called "*Hellig Usvard*," which means "holy unblack," for Nuclear Blast Records. The album contained overtly Christian lyrics. Great controversy ensued. The record label received death threats and demands that the names of the band members be made public.

Horde disbanded after one album, but their audacity spawned courage in the hearts of others, and new unblack metal bands soon appeared. Bands like Antestor and Crimson Moonlight carry Jesus to dark places where few would dare to go.

FACT

Many Christian musicians who embrace heavy metal music say they simply make it their own, creatively reflecting their faith in Christ.

Even in darkness light dawns for the upright,
for the gracious and compassionate and righteous man.
PSALM 112:4

In Akron, Ohio, a simple epitaph marks the grave: A. W. Tozer—A Man of God. It seems a fitting inscription for the man who preached that we must simplify our approach to God by stripping down to the essentials.

Tozer's commitment to simple faith was evident in his home life as well. Though they had seven children—six sons and one daughter—to care for, he and his wife, Ada, made a pact never to pursue money or material things. Instead they agreed to trust God for all their needs. Even at the height of his success as an author, he never owned a car, preferring to travel by bus and train. The family must have found this more than sufficient, for Tozer once wrote, "I have found God to be cordial and generous and in every way easy to live with."

Men of the Faith

A. W. Tozer (1897–1963)
Pastor and author

Tozer became a Christian when he was seventeen after an encounter with a street preacher. Five years later, he accepted his first pastorate—a small storefront church in Nutter Fort, West Virginia. Though he never received a formal theological education, Tozer spent forty-four years in the pastorate of various churches. He is best known, however, for his marvelous writing.

Two of his books—*The Pursuit of God* and *The Knowledge of the Holy*—are considered Christian classics. They admonish Christians to return to an authentic Bible-based position of deep personal faith and holiness. Compilations of his powerful sermons are also popular with those who are seeking a deeper relationship with God.

Having achieved great success as a Christian author, Tozer gave most of the royalties from his books to those in need.

Make it your ambition to lead a quiet life,
to mind your own business and to work
with your hands, just as we told you.
1 Thessalonians 4:11

As the mother of eight children, Anne Bradstreet had little time to pursue her passion for writing poetry, but she made the most of what she had, drawing from what she knew best: marriage, children, nature, family, and faith.

A child of wealth and privilege, Anne was born in a castle in Northampton, England. Her father served as steward for the earl of Lincoln. She married early, at the age of sixteen, to Steven Bradstreet, who also served as a steward in the Puritan household. In 1630, she and her husband sailed for America.

Life was difficult in Boston. Many returned to England, but Anne chose

Women of the Faith

Anne Bradstreet (1612–1672)

America's first poet

instead to draw from her strong faith and deeply imbedded creativity. A devout Puritan, she filled her poetry with life, passion, and humor that cut across the stereotype of Puritans as cold, prudish, and humorless. Anne wrote mostly for herself, her family, and a few close friends, never intending her poetry for publication. She said she feared suffering the same fate as her close friend, Anne Hutchinson, who was banished from the community for publicly giving voice to her enlightened views.

Eventually, a family friend arranged to have some of Anne's poetry published in England. She contributed much to those Christian poets, authors, and artists who would follow, demonstrating that these pursuits are not frivolous, but rather God-given gifts.

FACT

Anne Bradstreet's accomplishments are even more compelling when we consider she never was completely well. She survived smallpox as a child, lived with a painful inflammatory joint disease, and is believed to have died of tuberculosis.

Every good and perfect gift is from above, coming down from the Father of the heavenly lights, who does not change like shifting shadows.
JAMES 1:17

The *Schlosskirche*, or Castle Church, of Wittenberg, Germany, is noteworthy not for the grandeur of its architecture, the size of its pipe organ, or the brilliance of its stained glass. People are drawn from around the world to this cathedral because of its doors. They were made famous by the sixteenth-century theologian, Martin Luther.

While studying to become a monk, Luther decided to visit Rome. Once there, he was shocked by what seemed to be religious indifference among the clergy, as well as the growing practice of paying indulgences to the church. An indulgence was like a get-out-of-Purgatory-free card, where people could literally pay for their sins with money. Then they didn't worry about suffering any eternal consequences.

On October 31, 1517, Luther nailed a list of ninety-five theses on the doors of Wittenberg's Schlosskirche. In this religious treatise, Luther voiced his objection to how the church was mishandling God's Word. He attacked the practice of paying indulgences, citing scripture that proclaimed salvation solely through God's grace, not human efforts. Soon Luther's theses were translated from Latin into German, printed, and circulated throughout Europe. Within a few short years, "Lutheranism" spread through Germany and then into northern Europe.

Important Sites

Wittenberg Cathedral

Wittenberg, Germany

The original wooden doors of the Schlosskirche were destroyed by fire in the mid-1800s. Today, doors of bronze are in their place, bearing the Latin text of Luther's famous declaration. Inside these doors lies Luther's tomb. His voice may have been silenced by death, but his message continues to be heard today throughout the world.

The doors of mainline Protestant churches are often painted red because that was the original color of the doors on the Wittenberg Cathedral. Red doors on a church infer that the congregation follows in the theological footsteps of the Reformation.

FACT

It is by grace you have been saved,
through faith—and this not from yourselves,
it is the gift of God—not by works, so that no one can boast.
EPHESIANS 2:8–9

The Great Awakening was not one continuous revival; rather, it was several revivals in a variety of locations that went so far as to influence changes in doctrine and social and political thought.

The First Awakening (1730–1740) was sparked when preachers like George Whitefield arrived from England, where revival was already underway. Around the same time, preacher Jonathan Edwards from Massachusetts was putting forth the theology of "total dependence" on the transformative emanations of the Holy Spirit. The revival, or renewal, as some prefer to call it, swept the American Colonies, bringing people back to a greater intimacy with God.

Groundbreaking Events

The Great Awakening

American revival

One important result of this revival was its impact on the hearts and minds of the colonists. They became emboldened to believe that they were not at the mercy of the Church of England. Several decades later, they realized that they were also not compelled to honor the authority of the English monarchy. They could install their own means of governance. A common vision of freedom emerged that gave rise to the Declaration of Independence.

The Second Awakening (1800–1830) did for the unchurched what the first awakening had done for church members. It firmly established the concept of personal salvation through repentance and dependence on Christ.

The Third Great Awakening (1860–1900) was literally interrupted by the Civil War. It produced the Social Gospel Movement and worldwide missionary work.

The Fourth Great Awakening (1960–1970) gave rise to megachurches and parachurch organizations that emphasized the gifts of the Holy Spirit.

FACT

Though the two had doctrinal differences, Charles Wesley so admired George Whitefield that he prepared a hymn especially for his funeral entitled, "Servant of God, Well Done." It was published in 1759 as "An Hymn on the Death of the Rev. Mr. Whitefield."

I will give you a new heart and put a new spirit in you; I will remove from you your heart of stone and give you a heart of flesh. And I will put my Spirit in you and move you to follow my decrees and be careful to keep my laws.
EZEKIEL 36:26–27

Lavishly produced and illustrated with a number of woodcuts, *The Book of Martyrs* provides accounts of the persecutions of Protestant Christians—most from England. The first part of the book deals with early Christian martyrs; the second with those persecuted under the reigns of Henry VIII and Edward VI; the third with the reign of Mary Tudor—Bloody Mary, as some have referred to her.

Since many of the victims of these poignant stories are listed in official registers only with name and occupation, no corroborating documentation exists. This has caused some historians to question the accuracy of Foxe's claims. That certainly didn't keep the book from becoming a favorite with readers, however. It was especially popular with Puritans and Low Church families, probably because of its intense style and colorful dialogues. Before long it was—along with the Bible—being chained to the lectern in churches, where it would be accessible to the people.

Notable Books

The Book of Martyrs
By John Foxe (1563)

Though the work is commonly known as *Foxe's Book of Martyrs*, the full title is *Actes and Monuments of these Latter and Perillous Days, Touching Matters of the Church*. Foxe based his book not only on documents and reports of the trials but also on personal accounts of friends and families of the martyrs. Although Foxe reported all that was told him, many feel he was purposely misled at times, even by some who wished to discredit his work. Four large volumes were printed just in the author's lifetime, and the book continues to have great influence to this day.

The original *Book of Martyrs* was enormous—an astounding 2,300 pages—and its production by printer John Day was the largest publishing project ever completed in England until that time.

FACT

Be faithful, even to the point of death, and I will give you the crown of life.
REVELATION 2:10

Johnson Oatman was a busy man. While carrying out his responsibilities as a Methodist minister, he also ran a thriving mercantile business, served as an administrator for a large New Jersey insurance company, and wrote the words to five thousand hymns over his lifetime. "Count Your Blessings" is generally considered to be his finest.

The music was written by well-known gospel hymnist Edwin O. Excell, who first published it in his songbook for young people in 1897. Born in Stark County, Ohio, Excell left home at the age of twenty to become a singing teacher. He traveled around the country, setting up music schools. He composed the music for more than two thousand songs and published fifty songbooks.

Songs of the Faith

"Count Your Blessings"

Words by Johnson Oatman (1897)
Music by Edwin O. Excell (1897)

Once published, "Count Your Blessings" quickly became a favorite both in America and abroad. During the time of the great revival in Wales, it was said to be sung at almost every service. While reporting on a revival meeting in the area, the *London Daily* said the hymn was introduced enthusiastically with these words, "In South London, the men sing it, the boys whistle it, and the women rock their babies to sleep on this hymn."

When upon life's billows you are tempest tossed,
When you are discouraged, thinking all is lost,
Count your many blessings, name them one by one,
And it will surprise you what the Lord hath done.

Refrain:
Count your blessings, name them one by one,
Count your blessings, see what God hath done!
Count your blessings, name them one by one,
And it will surprise you what the Lord hath done.

FACT

Johnson Oatman also wrote notable hymns "Higher Ground" and "No Not One."

From the fullness of his grace we have all received one blessing after another.
JOHN 1:16

Westinghouse started the first radio station in Pittsburgh, Pennsylvania, in 1920, using the call letters KDKA. The company's radio sets were becoming popular, and the station needed programming to keep the trend alive. As the station scrambled for program ideas to fill the airways, someone suggested the broadcast of a church service to test the feasibility of broadcasting from a remote location. One of the engineers belonged to Calvary Episcopal Church in Pittsburgh, so arrangements were made for the first Sunday evening in 1921. It was a hit and the program became a regular.

In the Chicago area, preacher Paul Rader was broadcasting his radio show from a rooftop, using a single telephone microphone. When he noticed that Chicago's WBBM was off the air on Sundays, he asked to use the studio. For fourteen hours each Sunday, he filled the airways with the sounds of preaching and a brass quartet. Using special, Sunday-only call letters, WJBT became the station "Where Jesus Blesses Thousands." By 1928 there were sixty

Miscellany

Christian Radio Broadcasting

religious radio stations. New rules by the Federal Radio Commission reduced that number to thirty, but those that survived were strengthened.

Most Christians saw Christian radio as far more than godly entertainment. It was viewed as a tool in their quest to disseminate the gospel to as many people as possible by whatever means possible. Donald Grey Barnhouse was the first to buy time on a national radio network, which made him in essence the first radio preacher. The first missionary radio station, HCJB, established in Quito, Ecuador, in 1930, was also the first radio station in the entire country.

Some evangelical Christians opposed the introduction of Christian radio broadcasts, arguing that the Bible calls Satan the "prince of the power of the air" (Ephesians 2:2 KJV).

What you say can mean life or death.
Those who speak with care will be rewarded.
PROVERBS 18:21 NCV

Those who knew him as a child often described Andrew van der Bijl as a daredevil—a bent that followed him into adulthood. When he joined the Dutch Resistance against Nazi occupation during World War II, he was said to have engaged in a number of pranks and acts of sabotage against German soldiers.

When the war in Europe ended, Andrew joined the army, fighting the Japanese in the Dutch East Indies (now Indonesia) until the horrors of war rendered him cold and depressed. Eventually, he was injured and barely avoided losing his leg. Looking for ways to pass the time during his hospital stay, Andrew began to read the Bible—from cover to cover—and soon surrendered his life to God. "A bullet made an end to my sports ambition," he later said, "but put me on the track to Jesus." After leaving the hospital, Andrew earned a degree at a seminary in England.

Men of the Faith

Brother Andrew
(b. 1928)

Missionary and Bible smuggler

Andrew planned his first trip behind the Iron Curtain after reading about a Communist youth festival in Warsaw, Poland. He sought permission to go as a missionary, and surprisingly his request was granted. While there, Andrew slipped away and witnessed with his own eyes the desperate plight of many behind the Iron Curtain and noted that there were few Bibles. He recognized he could do little to change the conditions—but he could bring them Bibles.

Brother Andrew's first smuggling mission was into Yugoslavia. There he began the custom of praying, "Lord, please make seeing eyes blind." On countless missions since, he and his fellow smugglers moved quickly through checkpoints with cars full of Bibles and tracts.

FACT | Andrew's organization has been responsible for smuggling millions of Bibles to Christians in more than sixty countries since the 1950s.

Jesus answered, "It is written: 'Man does not live on bread alone, but on every word that comes from the mouth of God.'"
MATTHEW 4:4

In Colonial America, men dominated the publishing industry, but Hannah Adams managed to earn a living as a writer. She became the first American woman to do so and earned a reputation for scholarship and writing prowess on both sides of the Atlantic.

At seventeen years of age, Hannah's father announced that he was bankrupt. His five children would have to fend for themselves. She had learned some Greek and Latin from one of her father's boarders, and when he learned of her situation, the boarder encouraged her to combine what she had learned with her fondness for study. The idea hit a chord, and Hannah set out to do just that. Her most famous work, *View of Religious Opinions*, was published in 1784. It provides a comprehensive survey of the various religions of the world, including a section on Christian denominations, a brief overview of paganism, Mohammedanism, Judaism, and Deism, and an overview of the other religions of the world. It was a success both in England and America.

The title was later changed to *Dictionary of Religions*. This project was followed by *A History of New England*, *Evidences of Christianity*, *A History of the Jews*, and *Letters on the Gospels*—all of which continue to be respected as significant literary works.

Women of the Faith

Hannah Adams
(1755–1832)
Author

During her life, she ventured only a few miles from her home in Boston, yet, she made worthy contributions to an emerging American democracy and created a wealth of information on world religions.

Hannah Adams established the first evangelical mission to Palestine— and she did so almost single-handedly.

FACT

Religion that God our Father accepts as pure and faultless is this: to look after orphans and widows in their distress and to keep oneself from being polluted by the world.
JAMES 1:27

It's hard to believe a rock could be so revered—especially one in such bad shape. But Plymouth Rock, traditionally believed to be the site where the Pilgrims disembarked from the Mayflower after their sixty-five-day sea voyage from Plymouth, England, is venerated as a memorial to those who were courageous in the face of religious persecution.

The people we traditionally call "pilgrims" referred to themselves as Puritan Separatists. They "separated" from the Church of England because they believed the church was not fulfilling the work of the Reformation Martin Luther had set in motion. Facing ongoing persecution, 102 Puritans chose to sail to the New World to start a British colony—all this in the hope that they would be able to freely live out their faith.

Their dream came at a high price. The Mayflower was overcrowded and the seas were rough. On the crossing, two people died and two babies were born. But many of the Pilgrims were sick when they arrived at the end of December 1620. By spring, more than forty of their small group had perished. But working together with the Wampanoag Indians, the Puritans carved out a home where their faith could thrive. Years later, their leader William Bradford wrote, "Thus, out of small beginnings. . .as one small candle may light a thousand, so the light here kindled hath shone unto many, yea in some sort to our whole nation, let the glorious name of Jehovah have all the praise."

Important Sites

Plymouth Rock

Plymouth, Massachusetts

FACT

Plymouth Rock has been moved several times, cracking and breaking apart in the process. Throughout the years, people have also chipped off pieces to take as souvenirs. It's believed that only about one third of the original 20,000-pound rock remains enshrined in Plymouth, Massachusetts.

Who shall separate us from the love of Christ?
Shall trouble or hardship or persecution or famine
or nakedness or danger or sword?
ROMANS 8:35

The infamous emperor Nero—great-grandson of Caesar Augustus—took control of the empire when he was just sixteen years of age. Perverted by power and ambition, he is alleged to have killed his mother, even though she married and possibly murdered his predecessor in order to gain him the empire. One of his grand schemes was to tear down about a third of Rome in order to build a series of palaces to be called the Neropolis. The Senate objected, but Nero got a lucky break.

In AD 64, a fire broke out in the shops and tenements surrounding Rome's mammoth chariot stadium—the Circus Maximus. The flames raged for ten days, leveling two-thirds of the city. Fires in the tenement areas of Rome were common, but this one was different. It was reported that Nero had the fire set intentionally and then sent thugs to keep citizens from fighting the fire. True or false, the result was the same—Nero got what he wanted. When the city was rebuilt at public expense, he seized the land needed to build his palaces.

Groundbreaking Events

Fire Ravages Rome

Hoping to quell the rumors, Nero looked for a scapegoat and found one. He blamed the fire on an obscure Jewish sect called the Christians. Authorities rounded them up; some were crucified, others fed to wild animals at the Coliseum games, others used as human torches. Similar persecution, though sporadic, lasted for two and a half centuries. Interestingly, this persecution is thought to have been the greatest impetus for the growth of the early church.

Legend has it that Emperor Nero fiddled while Rome burned. Other accounts say he was away from the city at the time, visiting one of his seaside resorts. One historian insists that Nero was seen running wildly throughout the city, urging his soldiers to get the flames under control. It's possible that all three accounts have some truth.

FACT

Consider it pure joy, my brothers, whenever you face trials of many kinds,
because you know that the testing of your faith develops perseverance.
Perseverance must finish its work so that you may be
mature and complete, not lacking anything.
JAMES 1:2–4

The phrase *"What would Jesus do?"* has become an icon of pop culture, but its origins date back more than a century. Charles M. Sheldon, a Congregational minister, coined the phrase in a series of sermon stories prepared for his congregation in Topeka, Kansas. As a ploy to increase attendance at the Sunday evening services, Sheldon began reading one sermon story per week. These explored moral dilemmas concerning poverty, deprivation, and inequality encountered in everyday life. Each ended with a dramatic cliff-hanger. The strategy was a huge success. The crowds came pouring in, eager to hear the next installment.

While Sheldon was reading his stories to his parishioners, they were also being published as a serial in the *Chicago Advance*, a religious weekly newspaper. Sheldon later put the story into book form and entitled it *In His Steps*. The result was a compelling novel about a group of people from a Chicago church who agree to base all their actions and choices for one year on the question, "What would Jesus do?" They find they are unable to settle for easy choices, instead opting for difficult but spiritually rewarding projects in service of others. The message of this book is said to have been the inspiration for the advancement of the social gospel, as well as a catalyst for change in the lives of many thousands of believers.

Notable Books

In His Steps

By Charles M. Sheldon (1896)

Some recent reviewers have complained that the book is stuffy and poorly written. Whether their assessments are true or not, no one can dispute the popular success of *In His Steps*. An estimated thirty million copies have been sold in the century since its original release.

FACT

Due to a technical error in filing, the copyright for *In His Steps* was deemed defective and the book passed immediately into the public domain. It was subsequently published by dozens of publishers. The author received only minimal royalties from one publisher who stated it was simply the right thing to do.

Follow my example, as I follow the example of Christ.
1 CORINTHIANS 11:1

Originally, the first line of this great hymn was "Crown Him with crowns of gold," which proved to be quite popular in the United States. With the gold rush still fresh in singers' minds, this must have seemed particularly appropriate.

Matthew Bridges, an Anglican, wrote his version at the age of fifty-eight, shortly after converting to Catholicism. He named it, "The Song of the Seraphs." More than twenty years later, Godfrey Thring wrote six additional verses and added them to those of Bridges, making twelve verses in all. Each celebrated a different aspect of Christ's kingship, providing a musical teaching on His person and ministry. Since that time, both their names appear with the song in hymnals, even though they most likely never met.

Songs of the Faith

"Crown Him with Many Crowns"

Words by Matthew Bridges (1852)
and Godfrey Thring (1874)
Music by George J. Elvey (1868)

Crown Him with many crowns, the Lamb upon His throne.
Hark! How the heavenly anthem drowns all music but its own.
Awake, my soul, and sing of Him who died for thee,
And hail Him as thy matchless King through all eternity.

Crown Him the Lord of life, who triumphed over the grave,
And rose victorious in the strife for those He came to save.
His glories now we sing, who died, and rose on high,
Who died eternal life to bring, and lives that death may die.

Crown Him the Lord of lords, who over all doth reign,
Who once on earth, the incarnate Word, for ransomed sinners slain,
Now lives in realms of light, where saints with angels sing
Their songs before Him day and night, their God, Redeemer, King.

Praised for its simplicity and singability, the melody for "Crown Him with Many Crowns" is entitled "Diademata."

FACT

His eyes are like blazing fire, and on his head are many crowns.
REVELATION 19:12

Speculation abounded in the years leading up to 2000. Christians took a renewed interest in Bible prophecy and dug into the study of the end-times. Were we coming to the end of the age? Was the return of Christ imminent? Were we entering the Great Tribulation period? Similar questions ruffled the feathers of Christians as they approached the end of the first millennium as well, but this time those questions were firmly nested in an unusual, never-before-experienced technological marker.

In the second half of the twentieth century, computer technology exploded. By the 1990s, computers controlled many aspects of our everyday lives—communications, electricity, transportation, finance, medicine, employment, governmental functions, to name just a few. When technology experts announced that a faulty date-storage system on most computers could process the date 2000 as the date 1900, causing the computers to shut down completely or experience significant errors, the media ran with it—and Christians took notice.

Miscellany

Y2K

Computer threat to
the new millenium

Many Christian books, newsletters, and Internet Web sites popped up sounding the alarm. Even some mainstream Christian groups began to advocate preparation, such as hoarding cash, stockpiling dried grains and canned goods, equipping homes with alternate sources of electricity, and storing water. Around the world, companies and organizations upgraded their computer systems, hoping for the best.

But when the clock struck 12:00 a.m. on January 1, 2000—nothing happened. Across the nation and the world, computers pulled up the new year just as they should, leaving Christians to wonder whether the problem never was a real threat or good preparation averted a disaster.

FACT

On the Focus on the Family radio program, Dr. James Dobson made the following comment regarding Y2K: "Is it possible that we are sliding into the end-time events that I have read about and heard about in my childhood and in my family and my reading of the book of Revelation and other places in the scripture?"

[Jesus said,] "Surely I am with you always, to the very end of the age."
MATTHEW 28:20

Children of the Irish working class often were fostered by others, but rarely by a priest. In this case, however, the mother of the infant, who was christened *Colum* (Latin for "dove"), had dreamed her son would become a man of God, so the child was assigned to a priest named Finnian.

The young boy took a keen interest in his religious studies, often reciting the Psalms before the neighborhood children. No one was surprised when he became a monk—and one of some standing, having been credited with several so-called miracles.

Around the year 560, Columba faltered, however. During his study sessions with Finnian, he secretly made an unauthorized copy of his mentor's psalter. When Finnian learned of this, he demanded the copy, but Columba refused to part with it. The matter was brought before the high king, who ruled in Finnian's favor. But again, Columba refused to part with his precious copy of the book of Psalms. In desperation, Columba enlisted his countrymen to defend his right to the manuscript, and a

Men of the Faith

Columba (521–597)
Missionary to Scotland

bloody battle ensued. The king was defeated and many were killed. Conscience-stricken, Columba asked his confessor for advice. "You must win as many souls for Christ as there were lives lost in the battle," he was told. A short time later, Columba and twelve of his followers sailed for the Scottish island of Iona.

Once on the island, Columba established a monastery and began evangelizing the Scots. His efforts were greatly successful, and he is credited with playing the principal role in the Christianization of Scotland.

Columba lived out the remainder of his life on Iona. As an act of contrition, he never allowed himself to return to his beloved Ireland.

FACT

Go and make disciples of all nations,
baptizing them in the name of the Father
and of the Son and of the Holy Spirit.
MATTHEW 28:19

Aimee Elizabeth Kennedy, born in Salford, Ontario, Canada, was the daughter of James Morgan Kennedy and Mildred Ona Pearce. At the age of eighteen, Aimee met and married Robert James Semple, a Pentecostal missionary from Ireland. Unfortunately, Robert Semple died of dysentery during their first evangelistic tour to Europe and China. Their daughter was born less than a month later.

Aimee returned to the United States and worked with her mother at the Salvation Army. Two years later, she married Harold McPherson, an accountant, and gave birth to a son. The months that followed were difficult for Aimee. She suffered from postpartum depression and prayed that God would heal her. When she recovered, Aimee committed herself to a life as a traveling evangelist. She began to hold wildly successful tent revivals along the East coast and across the South of the United States. Unfortunately, this led to the collapse of her second marriage.

Women of the Faith

Aimee Semple McPherson (1890–1944)
American evangelist

Eventually, Aimee settled in Los Angeles, where she raised funds and built the Angelus Temple in Echo Park. The 5,300-seat facility was filled to capacity three times a day, seven days a week. In this place McPherson formed the International Church of the Foursquare Gospel in 1927. During the Depression, she was active in creating soup kitchens, free clinics, and other charitable activities. She died in 1944 of an accidental overdose of barbiturates.

FACT

In 1926, Aimee McPherson disappeared while swimming with friends at Ocean Park Beach. Thinking she had drowned, friends and family were shocked when she staggered out of the desert just across the border from Douglas, Arizona, claiming to have been kidnapped, drugged, tortured, and held for ransom. Her story was later discredited when witnesses reported seeing her in Mexico with a friend—a married man who had disappeared on the same day.

Until I come, devote yourself to the public reading of Scripture, to preaching and to teaching. Do not neglect your gift.
1 Timothy 4:13–14

God can use anything to draw people to Himself—even Swiss immigration laws. In the 1950s, an American couple named Francis and Edith Schaeffer were missionaries in Switzerland. But the Swiss government informed them that if they didn't buy property they'd be deported. So the Schaeffers bought a Swiss chalet.

The Schaeffers named their new home *L'Abri*, which is French for "the shelter." Their vision was to open their chalet to traveling students as a shelter from the secular pressures of the twentieth century. The students who took the Schaeffers up on their offer stayed anywhere from a week to several months. Anyone with an interest in studying Christianity and its relevance to modern life was welcome, both Christians and non-Christians alike.

By the 1970s, L'Abri became a combination retreat center, commune, and seminary. There were no fixed courses or lectures. Students spent half of their days in individualized study, reading books and listening to recorded lectures based on their interests. The rest of their time was spent working around the property, cooking, cleaning, or doing maintenance work. Schaeffer wanted students to experience what it meant to live out what they believed in a Christian community.

Important Sites

L'Abri
Switzerland

What began as a place where students could openly discuss their philosophical and religious beliefs grew into a worldwide academic evangelical organization. Although Francis Schaeffer died in 1984, L'Abri currently has residential study centers in the United States, Canada, South Korea, England, the Netherlands, and Sweden—in addition to its original location in Switzerland.

Francis Schaeffer and his L'Abri movement were credited with inspiring Christian evangelicals and fundamentalists to return to political activism in the 1970s and '80s, particularly in the ongoing legal debate over abortion.

FACT

Be inventive in hospitality.
ROMANS 12:13 MSG

As nose rings and tattoos are today, so long hair and hallucinogenic drugs were in the 1960s. Parents didn't even want to think about them. But kids—they gravitated right to them.

The hippie counterculture of the late sixties birthed crowds of spaced-out, street-living, guitar-strumming runaways. Among the disheveled souls, however, emerged revitalized Christians, often fresh from the local detox unit, who had found Jesus. They believed they stood at the cusp of a "Jesus revolution" and that the end-times were imminent. They preached on street corners, gathered a following, worshipped in jeans and T-shirts with swaying bodies and raised hands in coffeehouses, and grouped together in communes reminiscent, they imagined, of how the first Christians lived in the earliest years of the church. The Jesus Movement promised the best of both worlds: an antiestablishment statement today and eternal salvation tomorrow.

Groundbreaking Events

The Jesus Movement

Counterculture movement

The newly evangelized hippies' brand of religion was as far from the mainstream Protestant church of their upbringing as their lifestyle from their parents' middle-class values. Having personally "found Jesus," worshippers shunned organized religion for meetings marked by extemporaneous outpourings of praise and prayer, speaking in tongues, emotional "second blessing" baptisms, and personal spiritual experience.

Mainline ministers noticed the difference in worship styles and many added young ministers to their staff as "hippie liaisons" and incorporated more freedom of expression in their services. Members of the Jesus Movement who later cut their hair, married, and moved to the suburbs down the street from Mom and Dad tended to find their spiritual home in Pentecostal, charismatic, and evangelical congregations.

FACT

The Jesus Movement consisted largely of Baby Boomers, kids born after World War II. They grew up living the American Dream—house, refrigerator, television, car. As they came of age, however, the threat of nuclear war and the perceived hypocrisy of middle-class manners drove many to chuck it all for the streets of major cities and beach communities.

All the believers were together and had everything in common.
ACTS 2:44

Using a specific interpretation of certain passages in 1 Corinthians, 1 Thessalonians, and the book of Revelation, authors Jerry Jenkins and Tim LaHaye created a story about the disappearance of millions of people from the earth. Frantic survivors, including airline pilot Rayford Steele, his daughter Chloe, pastor Bruce Barnes, and young journalist Cameron "Buck" Williams, search for their friends and family members only to conclude that they had been taken in the Rapture—the event marked by the coming of Jesus to snatch up His own, quietly and dramatically, as the scriptures say, like "a thief in the night."

The success of the first book—*Left Behind: A Novel of the Earth's Last Days*—led to a dozen sequels, concluding with *Kingdom Come: the Final Victory* in 2007 and three prequels: *The Rising, The Regime,* and *The Rapture.* Readers have received all of the books with much enthusiasm.

Even though a great many Christians hold to the teaching of the Rapture as scriptural, there are a variety of theories concerning when the Rapture will actually take place. Some hold that it will happen before the period described in scripture as the Great Tribulation. Others feel the Rapture will occur midway through the tribulation or after it ends.

The series has been criticized for many reasons including its pre-tribulation stance. The controversy seems to have done little to hurt sales, however, and could be credited for at least a portion of the phenomenal success of the books even with non-Christians.

Notable Books

The Left Behind Series
By Jerry B. Jenkins and
Tim LaHaye (1995)

Rayford Steele, the airline pilot in the Left Behind series, was borrowed from a real-life incident in coauthor Tim LaHaye's life. While on a flight, LaHaye noticed the captain, who was wearing a wedding ring, flirting with the senior flight attendant, just as Steele does in the first scene of the first book.

FACT

Listen, I tell you a mystery: We will not all sleep,
but we will all be changed—in a flash,
in the twinkling of an eye, at the last trumpet.
For the trumpet will sound, the dead will be
raised imperishable, and we will be changed.
1 CORINTHIANS 15:51–52

Imagine how it must have felt to be separated from your loved ones and taken far from your native land—against your will. Is it any wonder that African-Americans living as slaves in America embraced Christianity? It provided the promise of hope and freedom from bondage in the life to come.

Unlike free men, those living under the fist of slavery had no time for a convenient faith. It was to them a port in the storm, a lifeboat in the ocean, a vibrant part of everything they did. It had to be. One of the results of their passionate faith was a body of African spirituals—simple, poignant, and faith-filled—that remain with us today.

All that's known of this beautiful, almost childlike melody is that it is of African-American Christian origin. Perhaps it was sung by weary, frightened voices on board slave ships or later as slaves labored side by side in the fields. The song's message of simple surrender to God's loving care is certainly consistent with the slaves' experience. And it is still capable—even these many years after the abolition of slavery—of rendering a tender, heartfelt emotion for those who raise its lovely strains to heaven.

As is the case with other African-American Christian folk songs, this one is meant to be sung by one or many singers and lends itself well to both unison and harmony.

Songs of the Faith

"God Is So Good"

African-American Christian folk song

God is so good,
God is so good,
God is so good,
He's so good to me!

He cares for me,
He cares for me,
He cares for me,
He's so good to me!

FACT

Gene Shay, cofounder and host of the Philadelphia Folk Festival, said, "In the strictest sense, [folk music] is music that is rarely written for profit. It's music that has endured and been passed down by oral tradition.... Also, what distinguishes folk music is that it is participatory—you don't have to be a great musician to be a folk singer....And finally, it brings a sense of community. It's the people's music."

Give thanks to the LORD, for he is good; his love endures forever.
1 CHRONICLES 16:34

Chaplains serving aboard military vessels date back to the eighth century, when they provided some engineering and medical assistance to the crew as well as pastoral care. Since World War I, the role of the military chaplain has been more carefully defined. Now chaplains serve in every branch of the military, providing spiritual insight and conducting religious services at sea or in the field.

Chaplains can now receive rank based on years of service and promotion. Their uniforms identify their rank and religious affiliation. Endorsement by a religious affiliation is vital; they cannot serve without it.

Designated noncombatants by the Geneva Convention, chaplains do not have the right to directly participate in combat. Since World War II, U.S. chaplains are to be unarmed and accompanied by an armed chaplain assistant when in combat. Many other nations leave the issue to each individual's conscience. If captured, chaplains are not to be considered prisoners of war and are to be returned to their home country unless they choose to stay in order to minister to other prisoners. Just the same, many chaplains have been killed on the battlefield. The U.S. Army and Marines lost scores of chaplains during World War II.

Miscellany

Military Chaplains

The Chaplain's Medal for Heroism is the highest honor given to military chaplains. Awarded to those who have died in the line of duty, it so far has only four recipients—the chaplains of the USAT *Dorchester*, which was torpedoed in 1943 by a German U-boat. All four chaplains aboard the transport ship drowned after giving their life jackets to others.

In the United States a chaplain is often referred to as "padre." In Britain, nicknames such as Devil Dodger, Sky-Pilot, and God-Botherer are common.

FACT

I thank my God through Jesus Christ for all of you, because your faith is being reported all over the world.
ROMANS 1:8

Although Handel's *Messiah* is considered one of the greatest compositions of all time and revered as the pinnacle of worship music, Handel, the man, was often at great odds with the church of his day. His first English oratorio, *Esther*, was met with derision by the church. They found it vulgar that the words of God would be spoken in a theater. One minister even claimed it was the work and will of Satan. The bishop of London banned the work from being performed. Handel defied the church and performed it instead for the royal family, who loved it.

Men of the Faith

George Frideric Handel (1685–1759)

Composer of *Messiah*

Handel's next religious work, *Israel in Egypt*, was met with similar disdain. Christians went so far as to tear down playbills posted in the streets. All of this angered the devout Handel, who often became irritated by his contemporaries.

Handel was hopeful that his next work, *Messiah*, would fare better. His wealthy friend Charles Jennens commissioned him to write the music to a libretto about the life of Christ and His redemptive work for mankind. Though depressed, Handel decided to accept the work. In twenty-four days, Handel had composed 260 pages.

On its premiere in London, the name was changed to *A New Sacred Oratorio* to quell cries of blasphemy over its original title, *Messiah*. The king arrived and was so moved by the opening refrains of the "Hallelujah Chorus" that he stood upon hearing it. Handel produced the work thirty times before his death on the day before Easter in 1759.

> FACT
>
> J. S. Bach is reported to have said, "[Handel] is the only person I would wish to see before I die, and the only person I would wish to be, were I not Bach."

For to us a child is born, to us a son is given, and the government will be on his shoulders. And he will be called Wonderful Counselor, Mighty God, Everlasting Father, Prince of Peace.
ISAIAH 9:6

Hrotsvit—pronounced "rotsveet"—was a nun of exceptional literary prowess. Encouraged to write by her abbess, she produced a wide range of works, including poetry, religious legends, historical epics, and plays, which are considered to be an exceptional example of Christian drama. Little is known of Hrotsvit's early life, but she is thought to be from a noble family because of her affiliation with the royal abbey of Gandersheim in eastern Savony.

Women of the Faith

Hrotsvit von Gandersheim (935–973)
Poet, author, and playwright

In the 950s, the Ottonian Renaissance began in the Ottoman Empire. In 962, King Otto I ruled as emperor over Germany, Austria, Switzerland, and northern Italy. With the encouragement of the king, writers and artists came from all over Europe to the king's court, making it a remarkable place. Young girls were often educated at the abbey, and it is generally believed that this was the case with Hrotsvit, the rich environment feeding her extraordinary talent.

Around the year 973, Hrotsvit organized her writing into three books. The first contains her earliest work—five legends (simple stories), a preface, and a letter of dedication to the Abbess Gerberga, King Otto's niece. The second book contains a preface, a letter to her patrons, and six plays. The third book contains three letters of dedication (one to Gerberga, one to Otto I, and one to the future Otto II) and two epic poems.

Perhaps Hrotsvit's stories and plays are so greatly loved because each one demonstrates the inexhaustible love and forgiveness of God, who offers reconciliation to even the worst of sinners.

In her writing, Hrotsvit often expressed her political opinions, even to the point of admonishing Otto and his noblemen that it is the duty of Christian rulers to defend and extend the church.

FACT

Since you are eager to have spiritual gifts,
try to excel in gifts that build up the church.
1 CORINTHIANS 14:12

In the early 1600s, much of what is modern-day Europe faced a seemingly unbeatable foe: the Black Death. As the bubonic plague swept the countryside, one small town in Bavaria boldly called on the only one they knew who could stop this indiscriminate executioner. They called out to God.

In 1633, nearly every family in Oberammergau had lost someone to the plague. So its citizens joined together and vowed that if God would spare their town, they would honor Him by performing a "Play of the Suffering, Death and Resurrection of Our Lord Jesus Christ" every ten years until the end of time. As the number of deaths radically diminished, plans for the Passion Play began to take shape. In 1634, on a stage erected on the still fresh graves of the town cemetery, Oberammergau performed its first Passion Play. Every decade for the last three centuries (except in 1870 and 1940 during times of war) has seen the Passion Play grow in scope and popularity.

Important Sites

Oberammergau

Bavaria

The now world-famous Passion Play is performed in years that end in a zero. The pageant involves over two thousand actors, whose good moral standing is as crucial as their acting talent. Hundreds of musicians and stage technicians also take part in the production. Anyone involved in the musical extravaganza must have lived in Oberammergau for at least twenty years. Performed in an open-air theater before an audience of more than five thousand, the play lasts more than six hours and is repeated five days a week from May through September.

FACT

Every ten years, on the Ash Wednesday a year before the Passion Play is to be performed, the "Hair Decree" goes into effect. All the men in Oberammergau involved in the performance begin to let the hair on their heads and faces grow out.

If my people, who are called by my name, will humble themselves
and pray and seek my face and turn from their wicked ways,
then will I hear from heaven and will forgive their sin and will heal their land.
2 CHRONICLES 7:14

J im Elliot was a gifted writer, speaker, and teacher. In fact, he excelled in most everything, including sports. Those who knew him, however, pointed to extraordinary spiritual depth as his defining characteristic. Everyone expected him to one day contribute to the advancement of the American church. But Elliot had something different in mind.

After much prayer, Elliot felt called to the mission field, specifically South America. Through a friend, formerly a missionary to Ecuador, he learned of the fierce Auca tribe deep in the jungle and unreached by the gospel. The Aucas had a murderous history—two Shell Oil employees had fallen into their hands and were killed.

In 1955, while ministering to the Quichua Indians, Elliot saw a chance to reach the Aucas when Nate Saint, a missionary pilot, spotted an Auca village from the air. For several months, the men dropped gifts from the plane in an attempt to befriend the villagers. In January of 1956,

Groundbreaking Events

Missionaries Massacred
Ecuador (1956)

Elliot, Saint, and three others landed on the beach near the village. Two days later, all five of the brave, young missionaries were attacked with spears and killed.

In the years that followed, other missionaries, including Jim Elliot's wife, Elisabeth, and Nate Saint's sister, Rachel, reached out to the Aucas, and many came to Christ. *Life* magazine featured a ten-page article on the incident, and Elisabeth Elliot's books *Shadow of the Almighty* and *Through Gates of Splendor* chronicled her husband's life and ministry. The story of the five missionaries to the Aucas stirred the hearts of many and created a boon for Christian missions around the world.

In 2006, a movie entitled *End of the Spear* was released. It told the story of pilot Nate Saint and followed his son's journey back to Ecuador and a reunion with the Aucas he had known as a child in the years Nate's sister, Rachel Saint, ministered among them.

FACT

Because of the service by which you have proved yourselves,
men will praise God for the obedience that accompanies
your confession of the gospel of Christ.
2 CORINTHIANS 9:13

How to plumb the depths of prayer has engaged Christians ever since Jesus first invited His disciples to pray. Spiritual leaders of every generation have offered their experiences and insights on prayer to encourage believers to consistently spend one-on-one time with the Lord.

During the Civil War, Methodist minister Edward McKendree Bounds was arrested and later released by Union troops. He served as a chaplain with the Confederacy until the end of the war, when he went on to minister to Methodist congregations in Tennessee, Alabama, and Missouri.

Bounds was known for his rigorous Bible study and deep prayer life. He is said to have spent the early morning hours of every day in intercessory prayer.

Notable Books

The Complete Works of E. M. Bounds on Prayer
By E. M. Bounds (1990)

During the last two decades of his life, Bounds wrote a series of books on the spiritual life. The authenticity of his experiences shone through his words; Bounds was a man who practiced what he preached. His many books drew a devoted following.

Bringing together under one title his eight classic books on prayer, *The Complete Works of E. M. Bounds on Prayer: Experience the Wonders of God through Prayer* examines various principles of prayer under individual topics such as: the essentials of prayer, its necessity, possibilities, power, purpose, and reality; and how prayer becomes a potent weapon in the hands of a "prayer warrior." His timely message urges Christians to practice the principles of prayer for a richer and fuller prayer life.

> **FACT**
>
> E. M. Bounds wrote: "In any study of the principles, and procedure of prayer, of its activities and enterprises, first place, must, of necessity, be given to faith. It is the initial quality in the heart of any man who essays to talk to the Unseen. He must, out of sheer helplessness, stretch forth hands of faith."

Let us then approach the throne of grace with confidence, so that we may receive mercy and find grace to help us in our time of need.
HEBREWS 4:16

T his may be the one and only hymn William R. Newell wrote. Better known as a Bible teacher and evangelist, he served for a time as assistant superintendent of Moody Bible Institute in Chicago. Newell possessed an amazing gift of Bible exposition and drew large audiences in Chicago, St. Louis, and Toronto for his citywide Bible classes. His commentaries are still widely used, especially the ones on Romans, Hebrews, and the book of Revelation.

As Newell tells it, he was on his way to teach a class one day when he was suddenly overcome by the magnitude of what Christ had done for him on the cross. The words to the hymn "At Calvary" came to his mind in a rush. He hurried to an empty classroom and wrote them down on an old envelope.

Newell showed his lyrics to Daniel Brink Towner, who was the director of music at Moody at that time. Towner was an accomplished composer who put music to more than two thousand hymns. Towner

Songs of the Faith

"At Calvary"

Words by William R. Newell (1895)
Music by Daniel B. Towner (1895)

quickly saw the song's potential and sat down to compose. Within an hour, the hymn was put to music. It was published in 1895.

Years I spent in vanity and pride,
Caring not my Lord was crucified,
Knowing not it was for me He died on Calvary.

Refrain:
Mercy there was great,
And grace was free;
Pardon there was multiplied to me;
There my burdened soul found liberty at Calvary.

Daniel B. Towner is also the composer of the great hymn "Trust and Obey."   FACT

When they had come to the place called Calvary, there they crucified Him,
and the criminals, one on the right hand and the other on the left.
LUKE 23:33 NKJV

"God made me fast, and when I run, I feel His pleasure." While Eric Liddell's quote from the film *Chariots of Fire* describes delight only a dedicated runner could relate to, *Chariots* has captured the hearts of diverse audiences for over twenty-five years. The British film won an Oscar for Best Picture in 1981 and numerous other awards.

Chariots of Fire is based on the experiences of Harold Abrahams and Eric Liddell, two Cambridge University undergraduates who competed in the 1924 Paris Summer Olympics. Abrahams, a nonreligious Jew, overcame anti-Semitism and proved himself an exceptional sprinter. His nearest competitor was Eric Liddell, also an exceptional sprinter. The story follows the two athletes and contrasts their motivations to compete and win. Abrahams ran to achieve the acceptance and status winning would confer on him. Liddell ran for the God-given pleasure of running. Win or lose, he planned to leave for his father's mission in China upon graduation.

Miscellany

Chariots of Fire—the Movie
The Eric Liddell story (1981)

Liddell resolved not to run on Sunday in honor of the Sabbath. This meant he couldn't run in a race in which he excelled. He ran another race on another day instead. In the movie, Abrahams won but found no lasting satisfaction in his victory, while Liddell discovered joy not dependent on winning, but on being faithful to the dictates of his religion and following God's purpose for his life.

While the screenplay contains several inaccuracies of fact and circumstance, it tells compellingly the real story of Liddell's struggles and perseverance. The film's stirring music and uplifting themes of resolve, integrity, and character along with its Christian message continue to resonate with viewers.

FACT

William Blake penned the following lines in the poem "Jerusalem" from his epic work *Milton*:

Bring me my bow of burning gold:
Bring me my arrows of desire:
Bring me my spear: O clouds unfold!
Bring me my chariot of fire.

Those who hope in the LORD will renew their strength. They will soar on wings like eagles; they will run and not grow weary, they will walk and not be faint.
ISAIAH 40:31

William Carey was born in the small village of Paulerspury, England. His parents, weavers by trade, encouraged his curiosity and natural gift for learning languages, which became apparent when he taught himself Latin. When William was fourteen years old, he apprenticed with a shoemaker and learned Greek as well. Not long after, William added Hebrew, Italian, Dutch, and French to his list of conquered languages. One might have expected him to become a foreign ambassador or diplomat, but another flame was burning in Carey's soul—the fire of evangelism.

When he was still quite young, Carey joined a local association called Particular Baptists, and became acquainted with many contemporary Christian luminaries. In time, he was given the pastorate of a small Baptist church.

Men of the Faith

William Carey
(1761–1834)
Father of modern missions

While serving there, Carey published his seminal missionary manifesto, *An Enquiry into the Obligations of Christians to Use Means for the Conversion of the Heathens.* Consisting of five parts, the first part is a theological justification for missionary activity. In the second part, Carey outlined the history of missionary activities. The third part had tables listing areas, populations, and religious statistics, for every country in the world—the first compilation of its kind. The fourth section answered objections that others had about sending missionaries. Finally, the fifth part asked for the formation of a Baptist missionary society and described how it could be partially supported.

With his written works and his principles and bylines for the missionary lifestyle, he inspired, motivated, and provided priceless models for countless others who chose to preach and live the Great Commission.

While working as a missionary in Serampore, India, William Carey translated the Bible into Bengali, Sanskrit, and many other languages and dialects.

FACT

[Jesus] said to them, "Go into all the world and preach the good news to all creation."
MARK 16:15

From the moment she was born, delivered by her father—a missionary doctor in Jiangsu province, China—Ruth seemed destined for a life of Christian service. Growing up, her father often told her stories about the 1900 Boxer Rebellion. She considered the commitment and sacrifice of the martyred Christians and Chinese converts a noble expression of faith and looked to them as her heroes. Although she witnessed and shared the hardships of her parents' missionary work, she felt called from childhood to a life of helping others.

At the early age of twelve, Ruth read about Amy Carmichael, a single woman who gave her life to missions, and felt the first stirrings of her personal call to evangelism. She dreamed of serving as a missionary in Tibet.

Women of the Faith

Ruth Bell Graham
(1920–2007)

Author and wife of evangelist Billy Graham

When she met a farm boy named Billy Graham, however, she found his commitment mirrored her heart for evangelism to the point that she was willing to support him in ministry even if it meant setting her own dream aside.

Through the years, Ruth remained faithful on the home front, relying on God to help her raise four children, while praying, encouraging, supporting, counseling, and doing research for her husband. She was also a prolific writer, publishing fourteen books and a collection of poems.

Her world-famous husband reflected in his autobiography, "The secret of Ruth's survival was in her commitment—not only her marriage commitment before God of her love for me, but also her ministry commitment of the two of us to the Lord's purpose for our lives together."

> **FACT**
>
> Ruth Bell Graham wrote: "Let us accept each day as the Lord sends it, living obediently and faithfully, not fearing what may come, knowing that the glory ahead will obliterate the grim past, and praying we may be able to say to our Lord, 'We are honored to have served. . .under difficult circumstances.' "

Commit to the LORD whatever you do, and your plans will succeed.
PROVERBS 16:3

Along the Eastern seaboard in the early 1700s, the fledgling British colonies were quickly sliding away from their religious roots. Many people lived on small farms or plantations miles away from their neighbors. Church membership dropped as families became more self-sufficient and didn't want to travel a long distance to attend church. Among the dwindling group of still-staunch Puritans, there was concern that the younger generation was becoming too "frivolous" and that morality was on a downhill slide. Then a wave of religious fervor rolled over the colonies. It became known as the "Great Awakening." Enfield, Connecticut, was at the epicenter of the revival.

In July of 1741, Calvinist Congregationalist minister Jonathan Edwards traveled to Enfield to preach at a local church. He'd previously preached "Sinners in the Hands of an Angry God" at his own church in Northampton, Massachusetts, with little response. But the Enfield church was different.

When people heard Edwards (who has been described as "monotone" and "boring") preach on Deuteronomy 32:35, their emotional response to his "fire and brimstone" message was overwhelming. People wept, swooned, went into convulsions, and even barked like dogs. So many people committed their lives to God that Edwards preached the sermon several times. His words were also printed and distributed around the countryside. As a result, a revival took place throughout the churches of New England.

Important Sites

Enfield, Connecticut
Epicenter of the Great Awakening

Today, "Sinners in the Hands of an Angry God" is frequently used in high school and college English classes as a classic example of Puritan literature.

Due to a surveyor's error, Enfield was originally settled as part of the colony of Massachusetts. Though the error was corrected in 1695, the citizens didn't pursue legally becoming part of the colony of Connecticut until 1750.

FACT

It is mine to avenge; I will repay. In due time their foot will slip; their day of disaster is near and their doom rushes upon them.

DEUTERONOMY 32:35

Digging through rubble brought about by the Six-Day War of 1967, Israeli excavators in Jerusalem discovered the ruins of much earlier devastation—the Roman sack of Jerusalem in AD 70. In the crumbled rooms of a long-buried house were found a severed arm, overturned furniture, and shattered pottery, all marks of brutal, horrific events.

Thirty years after Jesus' crucifixion on a hill outside the city walls, Jerusalem was embroiled in civil strife and open rebellion. Rebels incited riots, leading to bloody battles between mobs of rioters and the Roman guards stationed in the lightly garrisoned city. In addition, three Jewish sects fought violently among themselves for power and dominance, plunging the city into anarchy, famine, and starvation.

In the spring of AD 70, Titus Flavius Sabinus Vespasianus encamped outside Jerusalem with the Roman army. Members of the warring factions, now united in common cause, poured out of the city and routed the Romans. Delirious with their initial success, the rebels refused to give up their fight, even though a lasting victory over the more powerful and better organized Roman army was an unrealistic dream.

Groundbreaking Events

Titus Destroys the Temple

In August, Titus ended the war by attacking Jerusalem. In the melee, his soldiers set fire to the temple. They watched as melted gold and silver flowed in rivulets down stone walls; then his soldiers proceeded to tear apart the stones to get at the precious metals. Literally, not one stone was left on another. The only remnant of the temple is a retaining wall, the Western Wall. Also called the Wailing Wall, it is a gathering place of prayer for Jews the world over.

FACT

The site of the temple, the Temple Mount, lay in ruins until 638, the time of the Muslim conquest. Fifty years later, the Muslim shrine known as the Dome of the Rock was built, along with a mosque called *al-Aksa*. Both stand on the site to this day.

Jesus left the temple and was walking away when his disciples came up to him to call his attention to its buildings. "Do you see all these things?" he asked. "I tell you the truth, not one stone here will be left on another; every one will be thrown down."
MATTHEW 24:1–2

*Q*uo vadis, Domine?" the apostle Peter asks the Lord. According to an early Christian legend, the apostle Peter, exiting Rome at the height of Christian persecutions, meets the Lord, who is walking toward the city. Peter inquires, "Where are You going?" Jesus answers, "I am going to Rome to be crucified again." Upon hearing His Lord's reply, the apostle returns to Rome where he is later crucified.

Quo Vadis, first published in Polish in 1895, quickly became an international bestseller in its many translations. Henryk Sienkiewicz set his historical novel in first-century Rome under Nero's cruel and decadent reign. Romance develops between a pagan officer, Vinicius, and a young Christian woman, Kalina, a hostage of the Romans. Deception and subterfuge ensue, leading to Vinicius's meeting Peter and Paul and his eventual conversion. *Quo Vadis* vividly depicts the brutal persecution of Christians and their endurance under extraordinary fear and hardship. In the novel, the parallel between the sufferings of Christians under Roman rule and the privations endured by Poles under Russian domination was not missed by Sienkiewicz's countrymen.

Notable Books

Quo Vadis
By Henryk Sienkiewicz (1895)

Stage adaptations of the novel appeared as early as 1900, followed by an operetta, a panoramic painting based on the story, and the first film version in 1912. MGM's 1951 *Quo Vadis* was a monumental and a monumentally expensive undertaking with a cast of sixty thousand. The movie proved so profitable, however, that Hollywood studios embarked on a series of biblical extravaganzas. In 1985, Italian television aired a miniseries loosely based on the novel.

To research material for *Quo Vadis*, Sienkiewicz relied heavily on Tacitus's *Annals*. He toured Rome, visiting museums and studying the social and religious customs of ancient Rome, along with food, clothing, art, and occupations of the time. Critics have discovered few if any anachronisms in the story.

FACT

Simon Peter asked him, "Lord, where are you going?"
Jesus replied, "Where I am going, you cannot follow now, but you will follow later."
JOHN 13:36

Just a small boy living in eighteenth-century England when his father died, Robert Robinson was denied the love and encouragement of a strong father figure in his early years.

He soon fell in with a group of unsavory characters and might have become a lifelong criminal had it not been for an unusual event.

The boys often harassed a drunken gypsy woman who was known to tell fortunes. When the boys pressed her to tell theirs, she pointed a bony finger at Robert and told him he would live to see his children and grandchildren. Somehow God used her words to strike a chord of hope in Robert.

As a result, the young man went to hear the Methodist preacher George Whitefield and came under conviction. For three years he struggled against it, but finally, at the age of twenty, he gave his heart to God.

Two years later, he wrote this beautiful hymn, "Come, Thou Fount of Every Blessing." It is thought to be an autobiographical sketch acknowledging Robinson's tendency to wander from God's love and care and his need for daily grace.

The hymn is set to an American folk tune known as "Nettleton," attributed to the evangelist Asahel Nettleton, in the early nineteenth century.

Songs of the Faith

"Come, Thou Fount of Every Blessing"

Words by Robert Robinson (1757)

Music: American folk tune:
"Nettleton" (early 19th century)

Come, Thou Fount of every blessing, tune my heart to sing Thy grace;
Streams of mercy, never ceasing, call for songs of loudest praise.
Teach me some melodious sonnet, sung by flaming tongues above;
Praise the mount, I'm fixed upon it, mount of Thy redeeming love.

FACT

This hymn recently met with newfound popularity when the David Crowder Band included it on their album *All I Can Say* and their live recording *Our Love Is Loud*.

Grace and peace to you from God our Father and from the Lord Jesus Christ.
ROMANS 1:7

How could I ever think, to wed
A man who's always drunken;
Who really has so large a head,
It looks like a ripe pumpkin.

A swell-headed, bottle-toting gentleman in the illustration accompanying this poem from an 1860s woodcut looks like a poor marriage prospect, and that's the point. Choose for yourselves, men: the bottle or a bride.

The temperance movement in the United States began to take shape in the late eighteenth century after the publication of Dr. Benjamin Rush's moral thermometer. The Philadelphia physician illustrated degrees of drunkenness by beverage and its effects. According to the moral thermometer, pepper in rum, the worst beverage, led to suicide, death, and the gallows. Water, the best beverage, brought health, wealth, serenity of mind, reputation, long life, and happiness.

By the mid-nineteenth century, temperance organizations attracted men and women of all races, classes, and religious leanings with around one million members. Vocal temperance advocates lobbied for federal and state restraints on the increasingly profitable alcohol trafficking business. In 1851, Maine lawmakers declared the entire state of Maine "dry." Other states followed with laws limiting or prohibiting alcohol sale and consumption.

Women proved a formidable force within the temperance movement. In 1874, they organized the Woman's Christian Temperance Union (WCTU), advocating total abstinence from alcohol because of its destructive effects on health and family life. The WCTU and other all-female organizations became the political "training grounds" of several later prominent suffragists.

Miscellany

The Temperance Movement

America

The movement lost popular attention during the years of the Civil War, though its influence continued through the Prohibition Party in the early twentieth century.

In the late 1800s, T. S. Arthur's temperance book, *Ten Nights in a Bar-Room*, ranked second only to *Uncle Tom's Cabin* in sales. The narrative describes three alcoholic husbands. One ends up in the poorhouse, and another dies in a barroom brawl. The third changes his ways and vows never to touch the bottle again.

FACT

Let us behave decently, as in the daytime, not in orgies and drunkenness,
not in sexual immorality and debauchery, not in dissension and jealousy.
ROMANS 13:13

Francis Bacon was born with the genes for learning. His father was a high official serving Queen Elizabeth and his mother was a woman of keen intellect. Young Francis was so intelligent that his formal schooling bored him, and he was able to poke holes in the theories and practices that passed for the day's scientific inquiries.

When Francis's father died, youthful privileges were stripped away and the family fortune dwindled. Francis returned to school with a renewed sense of purpose—to become a barrister, which would afford him the ability to fulfill his three life objectives: discovery of truth, service to his country, and service to the church.

A devout Christian, Bacon divided knowledge into philosophy, or natural knowledge, and divinity, or inspired revelation. He knew that knowledge of God could only come by special revelation, while knowledge of the physical world came by inductive study. He published these thoughts in essay form with his work *The New Atlantis*.

Men of the Faith

Francis Bacon
(1561–1626)

Establisher of the scientific method

While working with King James in a series of legal jobs, Francis Bacon published his most famous work, *Instauratio Magna* (Great Revival). Within its pages, he summed up the extent of learning and the deficiencies in human understanding. He also proposed a new way to develop scientific thought, based on experimentation and inductive reasoning. This gave rise to the scientific method, which is still the standard for experimentation used in universities and research centers today.

FACT

Since the 1800s, many scholars have suggested that Bacon was, in fact, the author of *Don Quixote*, attributed to Miguel de Cervantes, and other literary works and plays commonly thought to be written by Shakespeare.

It is the glory of God to conceal a thing:
but the honour of kings is to search out a matter.
Proverbs 25:2 KJV

T hough she had no formal education, Abigail Adams was an intelligent, well-read woman with a strong sense of faith. Those qualities served her well. In the foundational years of America, her husband's political career as a state legislator and delegate to the First and Second Continental Congresses demanded his energy and forced him to be away from home much of the time for more than ten years. Abigail remained at home where she raised their children and opened her door to sick and hungry people escaping Boston.

At age thirty-two, during a brief reunion with her husband, Abigail became pregnant with their sixth child. This time when her husband left for political service, it was with tears in his eyes. Their little girl was stillborn. Abigail (also known as Nabby) was alone again when two of her children became deathly ill with smallpox. Again, her husband was away serving on the committee to draft the Declaration of Independence.

Women of the Faith

Abigail Adams (1774–1818)

Documenter of America's foundational years

Despite these difficulties, some suggest that Abigail Adams should be known as the mother of our country. A keen observer of her surroundings, she witnessed the Battle of Bunker Hill from a hilltop near her home. Because she was so close to the battle, she was able to give firsthand reports of the American Revolution to her husband and other leaders creating a new government. In fact, a great many of the political characters and historical events that occurred during the foundational years of America were well documented in more than two thousand faith-based letters Abigail wrote to her husband, sisters, and friends.

John Adams became the second president of the United States, which made Abigail the first president's wife to live in the White House after the U.S. Capitol was moved to Washington, D.C.

FACT

Whatever is born of God overcomes the world.
And this is the victory that has overcome the world—our faith.
1 JOHN 5:4 NKJV

Before God caught Moses' attention with a burning bush, before Moses received the Ten Commandments, before Moses ever stepped on Mount Sinai's holy ground, this peak in Egypt was already known as the "mountain of God." Though some biblical scholars believe the actual location of the biblical landmark to be Jabal al-Lawz in Saudi Arabia, tradition has long linked this mountain on the Sinai Peninsula to Moses.

For the last one thousand years, pilgrims have made the journey across the inhospitable, volcanic landscape of the Sinai Peninsula to Jebel Musa (as Mount Sinai is known in Egypt). The 7,498-foot mountain is considered a sacred spot by Muslims, Jews, and Christians alike. In AD 330, Helena (the mother of Roman Emperor Constantine) built a chapel at the foot of the peak where it was believed Moses saw the burning bush. In 530, the Byzantine emperor Justinian fortified the chapel against invaders and built the Church of the Transfiguration. It still survives as part of the monastic complex of St. Catherine's, which is believed to be the oldest monastery in continuous existence.

Important Sites

Mount Sinai

Middle East

Behind the monastery, the 3,750 "steps of penitence" lead visitors up a steep ravine to the mountain's peak. On Mount Sinai's summit is a mosque and a Greek Orthodox chapel. The chapel was only erected in 1934, but it was built on the foundations of a sixteenth-century church. Though the chapel is closed to the public, tradition holds that it contains the rock from which the Ten Commandments were cut.

FACT

In 1975, more than three thousand ancient manuscripts were accidentally discovered behind one of the walls of St. Catherine's monastery.

The LORD descended to the top of Mount Sinai
and called Moses to the top of the mountain.
So Moses went up.
EXODUS 19:20

While watching gruesome Roman spectacles in which Christian slaves were brutally killed for the enjoyment of the audience, Tertullian was struck by the victims' courage in facing death. Though a pagan, he wrote a treatise in their defense. Subsequently, he converted to Christianity himself.

A prolific and influential writer, Tertullian was the first to write Christian books and religious texts in Latin, the language of the Roman Empire. He addressed doctrinal debates, controversies, and heresies of the day in a hard-hitting, no-holds-barred and often witty style. Later church fathers held his work in high esteem, especially St. Cyprian, theologian and bishop of Carthage in the early third century. Through St. Cyprian, Tertullian's

Groundbreaking Events

Tertullian
Pioneer of Christian Books

writings profoundly influenced Christian theology in the West and the formation and language of doctrine in both the Roman Catholic and Protestant churches.

Tertullian's most famous work, *Apologeticus*, defended Christians against popularly held opinions that they were unwilling to contribute to civil society and plotting to subvert secular authority. Another work of lasting influence, *Adversus Praxean*, defined the biblical doctrine of the Trinity, which was being creatively explained by various teachers of the time. In this and other scholarly treatises, Tertullian established terms of doctrine still in use among theologians today.

Religious books, tracts, and scholarly texts have nourished and enriched the church throughout the centuries. Christian writings have served to clarify scripture, edify and instruct believers, and pass on the teachings and truths of the faith and the witness of Christian experience to each succeeding generation.

The writings of Tertullian and his contemporaries reveal which books of the Bible were commonly recognized and used for reference and teaching in the first centuries of the church. Though Tertullian most often translated scripture directly from the Greek, evidence points to his possession of a Latin Bible.

FACT

The discerning heart seeks knowledge, but the mouth of a fool feeds on folly.
PROVERBS 15:14

Readers today may not be aware that the book they hold in their hands, *With Christ in the School of Prayer*, debuted more than a hundred years ago. Still in print, Andrew Murray's classic exposition continues to gather devoted readers with its message of hope and confidence in the power of prayer.

Murray, a minister in the Dutch Reformed Church in South Africa, found his congregations sadly lukewarm in regard to prayer. He realized that for most believers it was routine, ineffectual, and shallow. In *With Christ in the School of Prayer*, Murray aimed to light a fire in the prayer lives of believers by designing thirty-one lessons around the prayers of Jesus Christ recorded in the Gospels. He framed each study to bring readers to a fuller realization of God's work in their lives. In the book, Murray invites believers to communicate with God not to gain favor with Him, but in order to joyfully surrender to His will and purpose.

Notable Books

With Christ in the School of Prayer
By Andrew Murray (1885)

Murray's spiritual insights frequently ran afoul of orthodox Reformed theology. Nonetheless, he held to his conviction that each believer should expect and would receive the fullness of the Holy Spirit.

While the language of the original appears dated to the modern reader, Murray's short, concise chapters appeal to contemporary taste. His fervent passion for his subject comes across through real-life examples familiar to anyone who has grappled with what it means to pray. In Murray's words, fellow believers hear and learn from the vibrant voice of passion, experience, wisdom, and faith.

FACT

Andrew Murray wrote, "If there is one thing I think the Church needs to learn, it is that God means prayer to have an answer, and that it hath not entered into the heart of man to conceive what God will do for His child who gives himself to believe that his prayer will be heard."

[Jesus said,] "This, then, is how you should pray:
'Our Father in heaven, hallowed be your name.'"
MATTHEW 6:9

Inspired by the Gospel account of Jesus calming the raging Sea of Galilee, "Jesus, Savior, Pilot Me" was written specifically for sailors in terms they would easily understand. It includes the mention of charts, compasses, and the need for a competent pilot to guide through troubled waters.

Edward Hopper, the hymn's author, was the pastor of a small church in the New York harbor area, known as the Church of Sea and Land. In 1880, Hopper was asked to write a new hymn for the special anniversary of the Seamen's Friend Society. Instead, he read this hymn, already widely known. It was not known until that day, however, that he had authored it. A man of humble, gentle spirit, Hopper had written all his works anonymously. He was determined that all the credit would go to God. Hopper wrote this one was written while he was ministering at his sailor's mission in New York City.

Songs of the Faith

"Jesus, Savior, Pilot Me"
Words by Edward Hopper (1871)
Music by John E. Gould (1871)

Jesus, Savior, pilot me over life's tempestuous sea;
Unknown waves before me roll, hiding rock and treach'rous shoal;
Chart and compass come from Thee: Jesus, Savior pilot me.

As a mother stills her child, Thou canst hush the ocean wild;
Boist'rous waves obey Thy will when Thou say'st to them, "Be still."
Wondrous Sov'reign of the sea, Jesus, Savior pilot me.

When at last I near the shore, and the fearful breakers roar
'Twixt me and the peaceful rest, then, while leaning on Thy breast,
May I hear Thee say to me, "Fear not, I will pilot thee."

FACT

In 1888, at the age of seventy, Edward Hopper's prayer expressed in the third stanza of his own hymn was fulfilled. He was found dead sitting in his office chair. His pen was in his hand. He had been working on a new poem on the subject of heaven.

[Jesus] got in the boat, his disciples with him. The next thing they knew, they were in a severe storm. Waves were crashing into the boat—and he was sound asleep! They roused him, pleading, "Master, save us! We're going down!". . .Then [Jesus] stood up and told the wind to be silent, the sea to quiet down: "Silence!" The sea became smooth as glass.
MATTHEW 8:23–26 MSG

Whatin claymation is this? Gumby and Pokey, move over and make room for Davey and Goliath. The animated clay figures developed by Gumby creators Art and Gloria Clokey stepped into American living rooms in 1960.

Now a classic television series, *Davey and Goliath* began as fifteen-minute episodes designed to teach Christian values to children. Faith-based stories featured small-town kid Davey Hansen and his talking dog, Goliath. Goliath, whose voice remains unheard by anyone but Davey and the audience, acted as Davey's faithful conscience. Action and dialogue expanded on issues of character, responsibility, and faith in God in an imaginative and entertaining way. *Davey and Goliath* was ahead of its time in children's programming by delving into substantive topics of race relations and near-death experiences. The original small cast of Davey, his dog, and family members expanded to an assembly of more than twenty assorted claymations.

Miscellany

Davey and Goliath
American television

The Lutheran Church in America (now ELCA) produced the award-winning program and its numerous specials. For twenty years, *Davey and Goliath* drew fans throughout the United States and abroad. Several cable stations across the country still air episodes.

While dear to the hearts of baby boomers who grew up with the Saturday morning show, *Davey and Goliath* is attracting new fans among today's young people. Davey and friends have appeared at recent ELCA church gatherings and the characters are featured in church materials for Vacation Bible School. In 2003, a one-hour documentary, *Oh Davey! History of the Davey and Goliath Television Series*, was broadcast on network television across the United States and Canada.

FACT

Davey and Goliath has become a pop-culture icon for nostalgic Baby Boomers. Screenwriters picked up on the phenomenon, leading to *Davey* references in numerous television shows, commercials, and films. Licensed *Davey* products—from bobble heads to T-shirts—remain popular items.

Reject the wrong and choose the right.
ISAIAH 7:15

Though William Booth was born into a relatively wealthy British family, he soon learned what it was like to be poor. His father, Samuel, made some bad financial investments and the family descended into poverty. By the time William was thirteen years old, Samuel was bankrupt. Since his father could no longer afford his school fees, the boy was forced to become a trade apprentice. Though he showed an aptitude for it, William disliked his trade—pawn brokering—and instead, took to preaching, specifically open-air evangelism.

William strongly believed that poverty was the devil's weapon—lack of money and occupation driving men to drink and women to the streets. He was convinced that a person's economic status determined the direction his or her life would take. Hence, he felt a strong obligation to do something about it.

In 1865, William and his wife Catherine opened the Christian Revival Society, later renamed the Christian Mission, and then the Salvation Army. It offered repentance, salvation, and Christian ethics to London's poorest and neediest residents. The group flourished, and some even described it as having an almost circus-like atmosphere. The poor witnessed to the poor, and thousands were converted. London's *Times* described the Salvation Army by turns as ridiculous, heroic, subversive, heretical, noble, and duplicitous. William was nonplussed and expanded his vision to nations and colonies the world over.

Men of the Faith

William Booth (1829–1912)
Founder of the Salvation Army

Today, the Salvation Army operates in 111 nations and is one of the largest distributors of food and humanitarian aid in the world.

William Booth was much more than a figurehead administrator. He personally established Salvation Army missions in fifty-eight countries and British colonies.

FACT

Treat others the same way you want them to treat you.
LUKE 6:31 NASB

The parents of baby Frances Jane Crosby, born March 24, 1820, became alarmed when they noticed their tiny infant's eyes were red and inflamed. A doctor wasn't readily available, so when Frances was six weeks old, her parents took her to a practitioner who was later exposed as a quack. After his prescribed treatment, the infection gradually healed, but the damage to little Frances's eyes was permanent. She was blind.

Fourteen years later, Frances traveled by stagecoach to the New York Institute for the Blind. She described the day as the happiest of her life. Miss Crosby spent two decades at the Institute. When her own schooling there was complete, she stayed on as a teacher. Nationally recognized as "The Blind Poetess," she was called upon many times to write and recite a poem for visiting U.S. presidents and other dignitaries.

Women of the Faith

Fanny J. Crosby
(1820–1915)
American hymn writer and poet

In 1858 Frances (better known as Fanny) married a fellow teacher and blind musician, Alexander Van Alstyne, and they left the institute to begin a new life. Sadly, their only child died in infancy. Fanny's life work was redirected in 1864 when William Bradbury encouraged her to write Sunday school hymns.

Fanny Crosby perceived her blindness as a gift from God. She even believed the practitioner's mistake became a prelude to her writing nearly nine thousand hymns. "Blessed Assurance" and many other beloved hymns became favorites at D. L. Moody's revivals and are still being sung in congregations today.

FACT

Fanny Crosby never earned more than four hundred dollars per year and gave away anything not needed for basic living. She spent countless hours ministering in street missions and the slums of New York, where she also lived.

I have learned the secret of being content in any and every situation.
PHILIPPIANS 4:12

Early in the fourth century AD, soon after Constantine legalized Christianity, believers began tracing Jesus' last steps through Jerusalem as a pilgrimage of remembrance for His sacrifice. They journeyed on foot from where Christ was condemned to the hill where He died. As they walked, they worshipped, prayed, and imagined. Two thousand years later, this tradition continues.

Every Friday afternoon at three, modern-day pilgrims who travel from every corner of the world gather together to walk the *Via Dolorosa*, which is Latin for "the Way of Grief." Franciscan friars, who have served as caretakers for the street since the thirteenth century, lead the contemplative procession. Though no one knows for sure the precise route Christ took through the streets of Jerusalem on the day He died, the Via Dolorosa leads pilgrims on a symbolic journey through fourteen different "stations." Each stop along the route represents a significant moment in Christ's journey toward the cross. The last five stations are located inside the Church of the Holy Sepulchre. They include contemplative stops to meditate on Christ's being nailed to the cross, taking His last breath, being taken down from the cross, being buried, and then rising on Easter morning.

Important Sites

Via Dolorosa
Jerusalem

During Easter Week, thousands of pilgrims pack the streets of Jerusalem for the devotional walk, which begins in the Muslim Quarter and ends at the Lion's Gate. Many pilgrims choose to carry crosses on their backs in remembrance of the One who carried a cross for them.

In the Middle Ages, the Via Dolorosa was divided into two rival routes, due to a theological split in the Roman church. Churches to the west of the city walked the westward route, while those to the east followed the eastward path.

FACT

---

*[Jesus] said to them all: "If anyone would come after me,
he must deny himself and take up his cross daily and follow me."*
LUKE 9:23

Origen was a highly accomplished and widely recognized biblical scholar and teacher of the early third century. In the Christian church, he is considered the father of systematic theology and allegorical interpretation of the Bible. While these terms may be unfamiliar to many, Origen's profound thought and scholarly contributions influence Christianity to this day.

The term *systematic theology* applies a particular method of analysis of theology, that is, the study of God's Word. To study what the Bible says about heaven, for example, scholars using systematic theology organize every mention of heaven throughout the Bible into the category *heaven*. All topics in scripture are categorized in this way for the purpose of analysis and explanation.

Groundbreaking Events

Origen Teaches Systematic Theology and Allegorical Interpretation of the Christian Bible

The Jewish philosopher Philo (c. 15 BC–AD 50) applied the allegorical method of interpretation to Hebrew scripture. With this method, scholars search for allegorical meanings, that is, what the word stands for, as opposed to its literal meaning. Origen admired Philo and used the allegorical method to explain scripture from a Christian perspective.

The allegorical method of biblical interpretation versus a literal interpretation of the Bible divides Christians today. When a particular passage challenges human reason, poses a mystery, or appears to contradict another passage, many Christians will search for a symbolic meaning to explain it. Other Christians, however, will not, but accept the passage as fact the way it stands, unless it's clearly meant to be allegory, such as prophetic events, certain Psalms, and Jesus' parables.

FACT

Origen's tome *Hexapla* compared six different versions of the Old Testament taken from various sources. The work was a highly influential text in Christian biblical scholarship. Though the original volume was destroyed in the seventh century, fragments of copies exist in various libraries and museums.

I meditate on your precepts and consider your ways.
I delight in your decrees; I will not neglect your word.
PSALM 119:15–16

Despite its hefty moniker, *A Practical View of the Prevailing Religious System of Professed Christians* by British parliamentarian and reformer William Wilberforce became an instant bestseller.

Commonly known as *Real Christianity*, Wilberforce's book urges Christians to engage themselves in the push for social change, most particularly for the abolition of the British slave trade. He believed that vital, authentic Christianity compels believers to actively enrich the society in which they live by eradicating social ills and injustices.

He took on a formidable challenge. A booming business in eighteenth-century England, the slave trade lined the pockets of many of Wilberforce's peers. Ordinary people knew little about the pernicious business being conducted abroad, and those who did cared little about what was taking place on distant shores. Wilberforce realized he would need to do more than attempt to legislate against slavery. He would need to convince both leaders and the public of the basic injustice of slavery and moral corruption of a society

Notable Books

Real Christianity
By William Wilberforce (1797)

that condoned it. He wrote *Real Christianity* to effect a change of thinking among his countrymen.

Real Christianity succeeded in its mission. It brought the abolitionist argument to the forefront of public discussion with its clear, articulate prose and influenced leaders and decision-makers of the day. His work inspired American luminaries Henry David Thoreau, John Greenleaf Whittier, Ralph Waldo Emerson, Harriet Beecher Stowe, Abraham Lincoln, and many others. Wilberforce University of Ohio, the oldest African-American college in the United States, continues his legacy, along with other Wilberforce-inspired groups devoted to social reform and renewal.

For twenty years, Parliament voted down Wilberforce's proposed bills to end the slave trade in Britain. The governing body finally abolished slave trafficking in 1807 by an overwhelming vote. In 1833, in Wilberforce's last days, slavery was abolished throughout the British Empire.

FACT

There is neither Jew nor Greek, slave nor free,
male nor female, for you are all one in Christ Jesus.
Galatians 3:28

With its harvest theme and celebratory music and lyrics, this beloved hymn is a Thanksgiving favorite. The author, Rev. Henry Alford, was born in London in 1810. He became an Anglican minister and is described as an eloquent preacher, a sound biblical critic, a man of great learning and taste, and one of the most gifted men of his day. It was also said of him that he was an affectionate man, full of good humor.

Songs of the Faith

"Come, Ye Thankful People, Come"

Words by Henry Alford (1844)
Music by George J. Elvey (1858)

In addition to his abilities as a scholar, preacher, and songwriter, Alford excelled as an author, having written fifty books, including a four-volume exposition of the New Testament.

Some say that Alford's Thanksgiving hymn is based on Psalm 126:6, while others say it was taken from the Parable of the Seed in Matthew 13. It is clear that the first stanza deals with the literal harvest here on earth, while stanzas two and three portray the spiritual harvest of precious souls gathered into God's Kingdom. The fourth stanza is a prayer for the Lord's return.

Come, ye thankful people, come, raise the song of harvest-home
All is safely gathered in, ere the winter storms begin.
God, our Maker, doth provide, for our wants to be supplied.
Come to God's own temple, come, raise the song of harvest-home.

Even so, Lord, quickly come, to Thy final harvest-home.
Gather thou Thy people in, free from sorrow, free from sin.
There, forever purified, in Thy presence to abide.
Come, with all Thine angels, come, raise the glorious harvest home.

FACT

At the age of sixteen, Alford wrote in his Bible, "I do this day, as in the presence of God and my own soul, renew my covenant with God, and solemnly determine henceforth to become His, and to do His work as far as in me lies."

He who goes out weeping, carrying seed to sow,
will return with songs of joy, carrying sheaves with him.
PSALM 126:6

For your shopping convenience, we're open seven days a week." Among the few notable exceptions? The quick-service restaurant chain Chick-fil-A. In defiance of the trend toward extended hours, Chick-fil-A eateries close on Sundays to allow employees worship and family time.

In 1946, Truett Cathy opened his first restaurant, the Dwarf Grill, in a suburb of Atlanta, Georgia. He pioneered food service in mall locations during the enclosed-shopping craze of the 1960s and 1970s and then opened his first free-standing Chick-fil-A in 1986. The following years saw additional Chick-fil-A and Truett eateries pop up throughout the South on college campuses and in medical centers and airports. In the early 2000s, the mouths of many transplanted Southerners watered to find Chick-fil-A locations in cities throughout the rest of the United States.

Miscellany

Chick-fil-A

Closed on Sundays

In addition to expanding locations, Chick-fil-A broadened its menu to meet consumer demand for healthier fast-food choices, lighter options, and gourmet coffees. While the company has kept pace with changing demographics, shopping destinations, and taste preferences, it has not wavered from its Christian founder's closed-on-Sundays policy.

The company reports strong earnings despite an increasingly competitive marketplace. One of the largest privately held restaurant chains, Chick-fil-A showed $1.975 billion in system-wide sales in 2005, and has received numerous industry awards as well as a devoted following of Chick-fil-A fans. Just don't get cluckin' for a big plate of Chick-n-Strips after church on Sunday. They're closed.

Truett Cathy, founder of Chick-fil-A, says, "Our decision to close on Sunday was our way of honoring God and directing our attention to things more important than our business. If it took seven days to make a living with a restaurant, then we needed to be in some other line of work. Through the years, I have never wavered from that position."

FACT

"Remember the Sabbath day by keeping it holy."
EXODUS 20:8

In 1921, out on the flat ranchlands of northeastern Oklahoma, Mary Lee Bright, heavy laden with child, was told her life was at risk. Few thought that both she and her baby would survive. Mary prayed only for the safety of her unborn child. She promised God that if she gave birth to a healthy child, she would dedicate that child to His glory and service. On October 18, God gave her a perfectly normal baby boy, whom she named William.

Young William enjoyed the rugged way of life on the ranch, and his eager, ready-to-do-anything attitude endeared him to many. He intended to join the military, but an ear injury sustained during a high school football game kept that from happening. After college William—or Bill, as he was now called—accepted Christ at Hollywood Presbyterian Church and decided to enter ministry full-time.

While a seminary student at Fuller Theological Seminary, Bright felt the call to reach others for Christ. He began by sharing Christ with students on the campus of the University of California, Los Angeles (UCLA). From those small beginnings, Bill and his wife launched Campus Crusade for Christ (CCC). Over the next fifty years under Bill Bright's leadership, CCC opened operations in more than 191 nations worldwide. Their pamphlet *The Four Spiritual Laws* is the most widely disseminated religious booklet in history. Though it began as a campus ministry, Bill Bright's organization now reaches out to every segment of society—students, inner cities, governments, prisons, families, military personnel, executives, musicians, athletes, and many others.

Men of the Faith

Bill Bright
(1921–2003)

Founder of Campus
Crusade for Christ

FACT

Based on the Gospel of Luke, the film *JESUS*, which Bright conceived and funded through CCC, has been translated into a thousand languages. The most translated film in history, it also is the most widely viewed film ever produced. Estimates suggest more than five billion people have seen the film.

The Son of Man must be lifted up, that everyone who believes in him may have eternal life.
JOHN 3:14–15

At age fifty, Cornelia ten Boom found herself in the middle of a national crisis that changed her life forever. As war ravaged Germany she prayed, "Lord Jesus, I offer myself for your people. In any way. Any place. Any time."

Within days of Cornelia's prayer, she and her family, living in the Netherlands, became an integral part of an underground rescue mission. Offering refuge from racial persecution to all who knocked on their door, her family's home soon became a safe hiding place.

In February of 1944, a trusted friend told the Gestapo that the ten Booms were harboring fugitive Jews. The entire family was arrested and imprisoned in the Ravensbruck Concentration Camp, where Corrie lost her father, a nephew, and eventually her beloved sister, Betsy. Before Betsy's death, the sisters spent much of their time ministering God's love through His Word to the other inmates. At great risk, they smuggled in Bibles and translated the Dutch Bible into German.

Women of the Faith

Corrie ten Boom (1892–1983)
Missionary and evangelist

Due to a clerical error in 1945, Corrie ten Boom was released. She later learned that one week after her release, all other women her age had been executed in the gas chambers. "I knew my life had been given back for a purpose. . . . I was no longer my own," Corrie stated.

In 1945, Corrie set up a ministry for the war-damaged people of Holland in Bloemendaal—a donated mansion. She later renovated a German concentration camp and opened her own father's house for refugees.

Corrie ten Boom traveled to more than sixty countries, sharing her story of love, forgiveness, and restoration, and published eighteen books. *The Hiding Place* sold in excess of a million copies and became a movie seen by more than fifteen million people.

FACT

Yet he did not waver through unbelief regarding the promise of God, but was strengthened in his faith and gave glory to God.
Romans 4:20

Jordan's Oil—that's what Jordanian tour guides have nicknamed the ancient city of Petra. It's true that Petra brings in more tourist dollars than any other attraction in Jordan. But Petra is more than a tourist attraction. It's also a site sacred to Christians, as well as Jews and Muslims.

Petra and its environs have long been linked with Bible history. *Wadi Musa*, just outside of Petra, is believed to be the spot where Moses struck a rock with his staff and water began to flow. For hundreds of years, nearby *Jebel Haroun* (Arabic for "Mount Aaron") has been a destination for pilgrims of various faiths who have come to visit the shrine where Moses' brother Aaron supposedly is buried. Herod the Great, who ordered the "slaughter of the innocents," grew up in Petra. It's also

Important Sites

Petra

Jordan

believed that Petra was the last stop for the three wise men who traveled to Bethlehem to worship the newborn Messiah. And for many Jews, Petra is believed to be where the Jewish people will flee when the Antichrist appears and Jerusalem falls.

The city itself includes more than eight hundred monuments, many carved directly into the red rock cliffs. At one time, archaeologists believed Petra was simply a "city of tombs." Though more than four hundred caves have been found, no human remains have ever been uncovered. Across the street from the Great Temple (which was the size of two football fields), pilgrims can still visit a Christian basilica famed for its intricate mosaics.

FACT

The Treasury of Petra, featured in the 1989 film *Indiana Jones and the Last Crusade*, got its name from the large urn carved into its façade. It was believed to hold great riches, though none have ever been found.

After Jesus was born in Bethlehem in Judea, during the time of King Herod, Magi from the east came to Jerusalem and asked, "Where is the one who has been born king of the Jews? We saw his star in the east and have come to worship him."
MATTHEW 2:1–2

In the aftermath of World War I, a soldier was digging a trench in a remote part of Syria. His shovel uncovered a vibrantly colored fresco beneath a mound of sand and mud. Little did the soldier realize he had taken the first step in uncovering the long lost "Pompeii of the desert." Soon an expert archaeologist was on the scene, and excavation began in earnest.

Historians had known of the city of Dura-Europos for years, thanks to ancient literary sources. But its location had remained a mystery. In ancient times, the city was located on a road that followed the Euphrates River and was a trade route. For a time it was a Roman outpost. When the Persians laid siege in AD 256, residents of Dura piled dirt around the city's walls for extra fortification and to make the city less conspicuous. In the process, some of the houses built next to the city walls were buried. Shortly after this effort, the five-hundred-year-old city was abandoned.

Groundbreaking Events

Discovery of the Earliest Known Church
Syria

The discovery of Dura provided a glimpse into the worship of Christians in early centuries, as well as to adherents of other religions. Archaeologists uncovered several places of worship, including a Christian house-church. Hidden among a cluster of private homes was a house that had been converted into a church. From the outside, it would have looked like a typical home. Once inside, however, Christians would have seen the symbols of their faith on the walls and recognized that this building had been set aside for a holy purpose.

The Christian community in Dura appears to have enjoyed a great amount of tolerance and freedom to practice their religion. In addition to the church and baptistery, archaeologists located several temples dedicated to Greek and Roman gods and the oldest synagogue ever found.

FACT

I rejoiced with those who said to me,
"Let us go to the house of the LORD."
PSALM 122:1

Are you going to Vanity Fair? Overseen by Beelzebub, the fair and its tempting wares waylay all travelers on the road of discipleship. *The Pilgrim's Progress* maps the route of the pilgrim, Christian, as he makes his way from the City of Destruction to the Celestial City.

Christian, troubled by the world's meanness and selfishness, yearns for inner peace impossible within the confines of the City of Destruction. Guided by Evangelist, his journey takes him across a landscape dotted with traps and snares. Mired in the Slough of Despond, he struggles to get rid of the burden of fear, doubt, and despondency that weighs him down. He goes through the Valley of Humiliation, the Mountain of Death, and the dungeon of the Castle Doubting. He visits rest stops like the Palace Beautiful and the Delectable Mountains. Obstinate, Discontent, and Atheist challenge him; Help, Hope, Interpreter, and others support him in his difficult path to the Celestial City.

Notable Books

The Pilgrim's Progress
By John Bunyan (1678)

John Bunyan, a Puritan preacher, refused to worship in the state-authorized Anglican Church. During one of his several stints in the dungeon as a guest of His Majesty, Charles II, he began to write down his "dream." The first part of *The Pilgrim's Progress* appeared in 1678 and became an instant success. The second part, published in 1684, met with equal acclaim. The book's first editions were cheaply produced, intended for mass consumption. Not until a hundred years later were deluxe editions printed, these embellished with elaborate illustrations and sumptuous bindings.

The Pilgrim's Progress is widely considered the most important allegory ever written in any language.

FACT

John Bunyan opens *The Pilgrim's Progress* with these words: "As I walked through the wilderness of this world, I lighted on a certain place where was a den, and laid me down in that place to sleep; and, as I slept, I dreamed a dream."

Humble yourselves, therefore, under God's mighty hand,
that he may lift you up in due time.
Cast all your anxiety on him because he cares for you.
1 PETER 5:6–7

Born in Yorkshire, England, Frederick W. Faber began his career as an Anglican priest, but converted to Catholicism three years after his ordination. Recognized as a man of true faith by both Catholics and Protestants alike, Father Faber was even memorialized by the evangelical author A. W. Tozer. In *The Pursuit of God*, Tozer wrote: "Father Faber's love for the Person of Christ was so intense that it threatened to consume him. It burned within him as a sweet and holy madness and flowed from his lips like molten gold."

It seems that Faber was concerned that Catholics had no collection of hymns as could be found in the Anglican church. Therefore, he made it his lifelong mission to write hymns of the faith for that purpose. He wrote 150 hymns in all, including "Faith of Our Fathers."

Many today assume Faber's hymn is about America's founding fathers. In fact it is not, nor was it written about the early church fathers. The author was actually commemorating those Catholics martyred during the reign of Henry VIII in the early years of the Church of England. The hymn's

Songs of the Faith

"Faith of Our Fathers"
Words by Frederick W. Faber (1849)
Music by Henri F. Hemy (1864)

refrain, as it is now often sung, was added by James G. Walton in the songbook he published in 1874.

Faith of our fathers, living still
In spite of dungeon, fire, and sword:
O how our hearts beat high with joy
When-e'er we hear that glorious word!

Refrain:
Faith of our fathers! Holy faith!
We will be true to thee till death!

The Protestant adaptation of the hymn, which includes a rewriting of the third stanza, is often sung in U.S. churches in celebration of Memorial Day.

FACT

Faith is being sure of what we hope for and certain of what we do not see.
HEBREWS 11:1

"What do you feel is the most important factor in changing a man spiritually, from immaturity to maturity?"

For the stereotypical macho American male, such a question might elicit little more than a dismissive grunt. But when football coach Bill McCartney asked fellow Christian Dave Wardell the same question, Wardell replied, "Discipleship."

Wardell and McCartney founded Promise Keepers in 1990 around the concept of discipleship for men. They envisioned a nationwide revival of men who would take a stand for Jesus Christ, each man committing himself to seven promises: honor Jesus Christ; pursue meaningful relationships with other men; practice moral purity; build marriages on biblical values; support his local congregation with time and resources; strive for unity across racial and denominational lines; and make a positive difference in the world.

Miscellany

Promise Keepers

Liberal Protestant denominations generally do not support Promise Keepers' decidedly conservative evangelical brand of Christianity, and progressive women's organizations decry the all-male meetings and conferences. The latter fear the influence of Promise Keepers will work to reverse rights won by women in the last several decades.

Since its founding, Promise Keepers has attracted untold numbers of men through conferences, books, Bible-study resources, church outreach, the Internet, and radio broadcasts. Unlike most organizations, Promise Keepers does not keep a membership roster. Its gatherings, however, often attract hundreds of thousands of participants. Its 1997 rally, Stand in the Gap, on the National Mall in Washington, D.C., drew upward of seven hundred thousand men. Similar responses in other cities across the nation show the ideals of Promise Keepers continue to resonate with America's Christian men.

FACT

Conferences, held in sports stadiums, are two-day, male-only events. Speakers offer personal testimonies, Bible teaching, and man-to-man encouragement to participants to fulfill their roles as godly husbands, fathers, brothers, and friends. Promise Keepers urges participants to form local Promise Keepers groups for mutual growth and support.

What God promised our fathers he has fulfilled for us,
their children, by raising up Jesus.
ACTS 13:32–33

Despite creating such a beloved, often translated Christian allegorical work as *The Pilgrim's Progress*, British author John Bunyan faced a life of difficulty and obstacles. First, he had little schooling. His formal education lasted only two to four years, he served as an apprentice in his father's tinker's trade, and he also spent some time in military service. Second, his youth appeared not to be one of piety, but of abandonment, where he indulged in profanity and other behaviors considered sinful at the time. For a while, he was racked with fear over having committed the "unpardonable sin." Some even believed he suffered psychotic illnesses. Only after becoming an enthusiastic believer while immersing himself in the Baptist Church did he feel free from his mental and spiritual burdens.

These trials became the basis for his great work *The Pilgrims Progress*. As he began to write, he also preached, and this, too, became a contentious issue in his life. He fiercely disagreed with the Quakers and at one point was indicted for preaching without a license. When he refused to stop preaching, he was thrown into prison. For twelve years he was confined, and there he wrote a large part of his definitive work. Only after

Men of the Faith

John Bunyan
(1628–1688)

Author of *The Pilgrim's Progress*

Charles II issued the Declaration of Religious Indulgence was Bunyan finally released. But Bunyan began to preach again, causing Charles II to retract his declaration and throw Bunyan into prison again. Despite these circumstances, Bunyan was able to finish his masterpiece.

An uneducated, mentally anguished criminal wrote *The Pilgrim's Progress*, the second most translated book of all time behind the Bible.

Sir Walter Scott was convinced that John Bunyan was of gypsy descent because his father was a traveling tinker—a mender of pots and pans. But historians seem to indicate that Bunyan's father's occupation was more that of a village blacksmith.

FACT

Give your burdens to the LORD, and he will take care of you.
He will not permit the godly to slip and fall.
PSALM 55:22 NLT

The beginning of Catherine Marshall's writing career was not an easy one. When her first husband, Peter Marshall, chaplain for the U.S. Senate, died suddenly from a heart attack, Catherine was left to raise their nine-year-old son alone. Later, she felt compelled to write a biography of her beloved and highly respected husband that would include some of his prayers and sermons. Unknown to Catherine at the time, that first book launched a writing career that would span the next thirty-four years.

At age forty-four, Catherine's life took another turn when she married a man with three children. In order to establish a new home and life, she placed on hold the writing of a novel she'd been working on for more than a year. Catherine and her new husband, Leonard LeSourd, editor of *Guideposts* magazine for more than twenty-eight years, soon realized they made a great writing team. Catherine's writing and Leonard's editing developed into a wonderful working relationship that be-

Women of the Faith

Catherine Marshall
(1914–1983)

Inspirational bestselling author
and novelist

came an integral part of their lives. Together they created plots and ideas for novels, and even coauthored a book entitled *My Personal Prayer Diary*.

Inspired by her mother's story and mission to teach poor children in the Appalachian Mountains, Catherine took nine years to write her first novel. Published in 1967, *Christy* was hailed as Catherine's greatest writing accomplishment and eventually became a popular television series.

Despite many personal trials, including the death of two grandchildren and her own physical challenges from debilitating emphysema, Catherine consistently inspired and motivated others to the same deep intimacy with Christ she cherished.

FACT

Catherine Marshall wrote, "No matter how late the hour, no matter how desperate the moment, we cannot despair; the joy and the riches [God] has promised stretch like a shining road into the future."

The LORD is the stronghold of my life.
PSALM 27:1

On August 28, 1963, more than two hundred thousand people culminated their March on Washington for Jobs and Freedom at the Lincoln Memorial. Here celebrity speakers including Sidney Poitier, Marlon Brando, and Joan Baez addressed the incendiary topic of the day—civil rights. But it was the words of a Baptist minister that would long be remembered as those that changed the course of history, words that forever linked the hope of racial equality with the phrase "I have a dream. . . ."

Using the style of a black Baptist sermon, Martin Luther King Jr. called on "all God's children, black and white, Jew and Gentile, Protestants and Catholics" to join together as one, their unity a living testament to the words of the negro spiritual, "Free at last! Free at last! Thank God Almighty, we are free at last!"

Important Sites

The Steps of the Lincoln Memorial

Washington, D.C.

King's speech was regarded as a turning point in the legal fight against racial discrimination, inspiring the 1964 Civil Rights Act. In the wake of King's speech, he was named Man of the Year by *Time* magazine in 1963. In 1964, he was the youngest person ever to be awarded the Nobel Peace prize. And in 1968, he was assassinated.

On August 22, 2003, the concluding paragraph of King's "I have a dream" speech was inscribed on the granite approach to the Lincoln Memorial. It's a reminder that on these steps a Baptist minister courageously carried on the fight for racial equality that Lincoln had so valiantly fought, and died for, a century before.

A monument under construction on the National Mall forty years after King's assassination is the first to give tribute to an African-American. It is situated on a four-acre site near the Lincoln Memorial.

FACT

As for me, I watch in hope for the LORD,
I wait for God my Savior; my God will hear me.
MICAH 7:7

Constantine the Great was the first Roman emperor to convert to Christianity. Along with the emperor's conversion came freedom of worship for Christians throughout the Roman Empire, in addition to legal rights and lavish financial support for the growing church.

Born Flavius Valerius Constantinus at Niš in present-day Serbia, Constantine was the son of an officer, who later became Constantinus I, and a commoner mother, Helena. Like others of his class and culture, Constantine was a devoted follower and worshipper of the sun god Sol, who was believed to be the companion of the Roman emperor.

The account of Constantine's conversion to Christianity begins in the year 312. On the eve of a battle with a major contender for power, Constantine had a dream. In his dream, he heard Christ command him to inscribe XP (the first two Greek letters of the word *Christ*) on his army's banners. In addition, he saw a vision in which the Latin words *in hoc signo vinces* ("in this sign you will be the victor") shone superimposed on a cross. The emperor promised to convert if he won the battle. Win he did. He legalized Christianity, then issued the Edict of Milan, which proclaimed religious freedom to all, including Christians. His personal conversion followed, though slowly. He was baptized shortly before his death in 337.

Groundbreaking Events

The Conversion of Constantine

As the first of a succession of Christian emperors, Constantine set the foundation for the growth and expansion of the medieval Christian church throughout the vast Roman Empire.

FACT

While the Christians enjoyed freedom from persecution, state sponsorship of the church brought its own problems. Constantine, and succeeding emperors, often used the church to further imperial policy. These rulers imposed the state's ideology on the church and appointed to positions of power those churchmen willing to support the party.

The word of the Lord spread through the whole region.
ACTS 13:49

If a weekend has ever left you feeling as if you've been to hell and back, meet Dante Alighieri. He's been there, done that.

Dante's allegorical poem, *La Divina Commedia*, or *The Divine Comedy*, describes his fantastical trip from the underworld to paradise. Cast as a man wandering away from the Truth, the poet begs for spiritual guidance. God responds by sending Virgil, considered the most moral of the poets of ancient Rome, to show His lost child the nature and outcome of sin. On Good Friday, Virgil and Dante set out on their journey. Virgil takes Dante through the nine circles of hell, where he meets a range of historical and fictional personages, each one representing a particular sin or virtue. Then, as dawn breaks on Easter Sunday, Beatrice, Dante's lady love, takes over from Virgil and guides Dante through the nine spheres of heaven.

Numbers held mystical meaning for most people of Dante's day. His epic poem's organization was no accident. *The Divine Comedy*, written in rhyming triplets, is composed of three canticles of thirty-three cantos each, with one extra in the first canticle, to total a hundred cantos in all. The number three, a sacred number, signifies the Trinity, and the number ten, completion (intensified as 10 x 10). Sinners fall into one of three vices, where lurk the seven deadly sins (a limitless number). Paradise is blessed by three types of Divine Love, those divided into the three theological and four cardinal virtues, seven in all.

Notable Books

The Divine Comedy
By Dante (1321)

Some would say the story has never been told in more dramatic fashion.

[Jesus said,] "Do not be afraid of those who kill the body but cannot kill the soul. Rather, be afraid of the One who can destroy both soul and body in hell."
MATTHEW 10:28

Considered the quintessential Irish hymn sung in English-speaking churches, "Be Thou My Vision" has been part of Irish monastic tradition for centuries.

Dallan Forgaill, thought to be the author of the lyrics, was a sixth-century monk martyred in 598 by pirates who invaded the island monastery where he lived. During his life, he was widely known as the chief poet of Ireland. Tradition has it that Dallan studied so intently that he became blind from reading and writing poetry.

Songs of the Faith

"Be Thou My Vision"

Words by Dallan Forgaill (sixth century)

Music: Irish folk song: "Slane" (unknown)

The text of the hymn was translated from Old Irish into English by Mary E. Byrne in 1905. Oddly, she chose to keep the Elizabethan language.

"Be Thou My Vision" is sung to the Irish folk song, "Slane," which tells the story of Slane Hill where in AD 433 St. Patrick lit candles on Easter Eve in defiance of the pagan king Loe-gaire.

The context of the hymn is a prayer proclaiming Christ as our model and ideal. Each stanza begins with an aspect of His provision as: my vision, my wisdom, my true word, my great Father, my inheritance, my treasure, and my heart of my heart. The first and last stanzas are given here.

Be Thou my Vision, O Lord of my heart;
Nought be all else to me, save that Thou art
Thou my best thought, by day or by night,
Waking or sleeping, Thy presence my light.

High King of heaven, my victory won,
May I reach heaven's joy, O bright heaven's Sun!
Heart of my own heart, whatever befall,
Still be my Vision, O Ruler of all.

FACT

"Be Thou My Vision" has become a popular song performed by contemporary Christian musicians such as Rebecca St. James, Ginny Owens, and Jars of Clay.

My eyes are fixed on you, O Sovereign LORD; in you I take refuge.
Psalm 141:8

P lease, won't you be my neighbor?" The genial Mister Rogers's invitation has proven irresistible ever since the PBS premiere of *Mister Rogers' Neighborhood* in 1968. It remains the longest-running program on public television.

Host Fred Rogers oversaw a creative and visually simple town populated by assorted neighbors and puppets to capture the imagination of his preschool-aged audience. In measured cadence, Mister Rogers helped his young charges understand themselves and the world around them. Rogers's carefully paced, close-up conversations with children conveyed a sense of one-on-one friendship. When he invited viewing children to join in the dialogue, *Mister Rogers' Neighborhood* may have been the first children's show to anticipate interactive television.

Rogers's conversations touched on children's concerns and experiences. He helped children develop healthy self-esteem as they learned about their experiences and about how to get along with family, friends, and classmates. In ways designed to appeal to young children, Rogers taught lessons in cooperation, persistence, and patience, while at the same time encouraging children to think independently and use their imaginations. His emphasis on individual character formation, traditional values, and learning readiness earned him the respect of early-childhood educators and Christian parents.

Miscellany

Mister Rogers and His Neighborhood

American television

In today's fast-paced environment, long, thoughtful conversations with friends and leisurely strolls through the neighborhood may seem like a lost ideal. Yet for young children, the deliberate slowness of *Mister Rogers' Neighborhood* allows them to absorb, enjoy, and respond. And perhaps for viewing parents, the show reminds them to slow down and smell the roses (or pick the dandelions) growing in their own backyard.

Fred Rogers died in 2003 at his home in Pittsburgh, Pennsylvania.

Mister Rogers said, "You've made this day a special day just by being you. You are the only person like you in this whole world. And people can like you just because you're you."

FACT

Jesus said, "Let the little children come to me, and do not hinder them, for the kingdom of heaven belongs to such as these."
MATTHEW 19:14

When Chuck Colson was a boy, his family temporarily moved into a renovated bat-filled barn. After Chuck and his father opened fire on the beasts with .22 shotguns, he wrote about that event for a class assignment. The professor gave him an A and said he should become a writer. He did—but not until thirty years later when he was an inmate in a federal prison.

When Chuck was eight years old, he watched his father accept a degree from Northeastern Law School. Chuck himself attended Browne & Nicols, a well-known private school in Cambridge, Massachusetts. After attending Brown University and George Washington University, Chuck became a valued aide to President Richard Nixon. With fierce loyalty to the president, he would say and do anything to protect his chief executive. In the end, Colson found himself morally compromised, and he went to prison in 1974 following the Watergate scandal.

Men of the Faith

Charles (Chuck) Colson (b. 1931)

Founder of Prison Fellowship

Just prior to his imprisonment, Chuck Colson gave his life to Christ. In prison, Colson didn't see human waste but, instead, the brotherhood of his fellow prisoners. In 1976 after serving eight months of his one-to-three year sentence, Colson founded Prison Fellowship. Because many people in Washington doubted Chuck Colson's conversion to Christianity, he wrote his testimony and the story of his imprisonment in his book *Born Again*. Since that first book, he has produced more than twenty others with worldwide sales of more than ten million copies in circulation.

FACT

In 1993, Chuck Colson was awarded the Templeton Prize for Progress in Religion, the world's largest cash gift (more than one million dollars), given each year to the one person who has done the most to advance the cause of religion. Colson donated the prize, as he does all speaking fees and royalties, to Prison Fellowship.

"I, the LORD, have called you in righteousness. . .to open eyes that are blind, to free captives from prison and to release from the dungeon those who sit in darkness."
ISAIAH 42:6–7

T he oldest of seven children, Amy Carmichael was born December 16, 1867, in Millisle, Northern Ireland, to devout Presbyterian parents. When her father died in 1885, she was adopted and tutored by Robert Wilson, founder of the Keswick Convention.

As a child Amy was considered tomboyish and poetic. She never married. After hearing Hudson Taylor speak at the Keswick Convention in 1887 about missionary life, Amy was convinced her life's calling was to the mission field. Despite a nerve disease and severe weakness in her body that often required complete bed rest, Amy was committed to her calling.

In 1892, after hearing the words, "Go ye," Amy fully believed she was ready to serve in the mission field; but the China Inland Mission rejected her as a missionary because of her physical frailty. Regardless of the report, Robert

Women of the Faith

Amy Carmichael (1867–1951)

Missionary to India / Founder of Dohnavur Fellowship

Wilson sent her to Japan as a Keswick missionary. Within that first year, Amy's health problems worsened. During times of great physical weakness, when she felt like a failure as a missionary, Amy remained dedicated to her calling.

Commissioned by the Church of England's Zenana Missionary Society in 1895, she arrived in India, where she found her lifelong vocation and remained for fifty-six years. She was dedicated to saving many young women from forced prostitution. She also founded Dohnavur Fellowship in Tamil Naduto, a sanctuary and rescue mission for hopeless, suffering children. Selflessness, commitment, and an example of one whose sole existence was devoted to her beloved Lord and Savior were the marks of Amy Carmichael's life.

A prolific writer, Amy Carmichael produced thirty-five published books including *His Thoughts Said. . .His Father Said* (1951), *If* (1953), and *Edges of His Ways* (1955).

FACT

"Therefore go and make disciples of all nations."
MATTHEW 28:19

Though underground cemeteries have been found throughout Asia Minor, Egypt, Tunisia, and Malta, the word *catacombs* has become almost synonymous with the funereal tunnels of Rome. This maze of galleries and chambers, up to five levels deep, was carved out of the soft volcanic rock outside the city walls of Rome. (Burials were not allowed within the city walls.) Forty different catacombs have been discovered in the environs of Rome, one as recently as 1959.

Both Christians and Jews, who did not believe in cremation like many Romans did, were buried here. Rectangular niches, called *loculi*, line the narrow passageways of the Roman catacombs. The bodies of canonized saints, martyrs, clergy, as well as common citizens, were wrapped in linen, placed in sarcophagi, and then slid into these niches. The loculi were then sealed with a stone slab. The walls of the catacombs were decorated with brilliant-colored frescoes, the most popular subject being Jesus' raising Lazarus from the dead.

Despite the persecution of Christians during the first three centuries, the Romans held these catacombs as sacrosanct and did not disturb them. On occasion, Christians gathered there to celebrate communion or the anniversary of someone's death. In the seventh century, visiting the catacombs became a popular pilgrimage for European Christians. The catacombs were even part of an ancient *itineraria*, or tourist guidebook, describing the sacred sites of Rome. However, by the tenth century most of the bones had been moved to churches for veneration as relics. Soon after, the tombs were all but forgotten.

Important Sites

The Catacombs

Rome

FACT

Contrary to popular belief, early Roman Christians did not use the catacombs as a hiding place from those persecuting them. This is simply a story line made popular in novels and film.

Jesus said to her, "I am the resurrection and the life.
He who believes in me will live, even though he dies."
JOHN 11:25

The age of mass communication opened when Johann Gutenberg's Latin Bibles rolled off the press. Or perhaps more accurately, were lifted off the press. Regarded as one of the most important inventions in history, the movable-type printing press made it possible to produce thousands of books in a short amount of time—a far cry from the laborious and time-consuming task of copying each individual page by hand.

Large books, such as the Bible, required some fifty thousand pieces of type. While printers already used wood or metal blocks to reproduce images, Gutenberg was the first to devise a way to move letters around and reuse them once a page had been copied the desired number of times. Gutenberg's metal blocks produced sharp and clear letters and images on rag cotton linen paper or vellum animal skin.

Groundbreaking Events

The First Printed Bible, Produced by Gutenberg
Mainz, Germany

Published in Mainz, Germany, Gutenberg's Bible was bound in multiple volumes, each with three hundred pages. The text was printed in Latin—the prevailing language of the church, government, and scholarship. The majority of books to follow, however, including Bibles, were written in commonly spoken languages. Before Gutenberg's death in 1468, printers in cities throughout the Continent and the British Isles had eagerly entered the profitable business of producing books, pamphlets, tracts, and posters.

Fewer than fifty original Gutenberg Bibles are known to exist today. Appraisers estimate that a complete Gutenberg would fetch more than thirty million dollars if offered for sale, making it one of the most valuable books in the world. Original Gutenberg Bibles, and sometimes individual pages, can be found in the collections of public institutions and private libraries.

The Library of Congress's copy of the Gutenberg Bible—one of three "perfect" copies known—has been photographed digitally. Now anyone with a CD player can page through a book formerly off-limits to all but select scholars and rare book collectors.

FACT

I do not write to you because you do not know the truth, but because you do know it.
1 JOHN 2:21

With the exception of the Bible, no Christian writing has enjoyed more popularity over so long a time—five hundred years—as *Of the Imitation of Christ*. And yet, its unique appeal comes not from brilliant original writing, but rather a delicate balance of ideas and phrases from the Bible and the writings of early church leaders and medieval mystics. Together they form a mosaic that stands as an unforgettable guide to spiritual aspiration.

Written in Latin early in the fifteenth century, this book has now been translated into more than fifty languages. Its meditations on the life and teachings of Jesus have influenced millions. *Of the Imitation of Christ* is actually four books rather than one. Its components are as follows:

Book One: *Thoughts Helpful in the Life of the Soul*
Book Two: *The Interior Life*
Book Three: *Internal Consolation*
Book Four: *An Invitation to Holy Communion*

The work encourages a life of devotion to Jesus Christ and discourages dependence on the human intellect. Topics include freedom from worldly inclinations, preparation for prayer, the benefits of prayer, communion, and how these things contribute to a devout life.

Notable Books

Of the Imitation of Christ
By Thomas à Kempis (1418)

Though the name Thomas à Kempis is on the manuscript, actual authorship is still in question. Because he was a quiet scribe who lived an uneventful life in a monastery in the diocese of Utrecht, many believe that Thomas à Kempis simply copied and edited the work from older manuscripts, possibly those of Gerard Groote, since the work seems to be a summary of his writings.

FACT

Thomas à Kempis's real name was Thomas Haemmerlein. He was originally from Kempen, near the Rhine, about forty miles north of Cologne. He died quietly at the monastery on July 26, 1471.

Therefore, holy brothers, who share in the heavenly calling, fix your thoughts on Jesus, the apostle and high priest whom we confess.
HEBREWS 3:1

Originally penned in Latin, both the words and music of the hymn *"Adeste Fideles"* were the work of Englishman John Francis Wade. This came as quite a shock when it was revealed just after World War II. Many had thought that the song originated with St. Bonaventure.

The hymn was also known for a while as "the Portuguese hymn." This error is attributed to the Duke of Leeds. In 1795, he heard the hymn being sung at the Portuguese Embassy in London and assumed it had been written in Portugal.

But when English scholar Maurice Frost found seven transcripts written by hand and signed by Wade, authorship at last was documented.

Wade was a Catholic priest and calligrapher as well as a skilled musician. He loved to preserve old pieces of music through detailed drawings and manuscripts and send them to Catholic churches throughout Europe for congregations to enjoy. He also wrote new hymns

Songs of the Faith

"O Come, All Ye Faithful" (or *"Adeste Fideles"*) (1760)

Words and music by John Francis Wade

and distribute them. *"Adeste Fideles"* would become the best known of his works.

"O Come, All Ye Faithful" was first published in English by Frederick Oakeley and William Thomas Brooke in 1852.

O Come, all ye faithful, joyful and triumphant,
O come ye, O come ye to Bethlehem.
Come and behold Him, born the King of Angels!

Refrain:
O come, let us adore Him,
O come, let us adore Him,
O come, let us adore Him, Christ the Lord.

Yea, Lord, we greet thee, born this happy morning;
Jesus, to thee be glory given;
Word of the Father, now in flesh appearing!

"O Come, All Ye Faithful" is one of the few traditional religious carols to land on the pop charts. It reached the top ten three times and has been called by some the greatest carol ever written.

FACT

"Arise, shine, for your light has come, and the glory of the LORD rises upon you."
ISAIAH 60:1

Were the Founding Fathers Christians or not? You decide.

The Founding Fathers—men who put together the Constitution and whose names appear on the Declaration of Independence—were highly educated men of deep ethical sensibility. Their religious affiliations reflected the rest of the American population. The majority of the men belonged to Protestant denominations and four were preachers by profession. Two were Roman Catholics. Many actively practiced their religion, attending church regularly and serving as lay leaders in their congregations.

Yet the personal beliefs of a good number of the Founding Fathers strayed quite far from orthodox Christianity. They had trouble with concepts that prove stumbling blocks to this day: the identity of Jesus Christ; the physical reality of miracles as recorded in the Bible; and the authority of church creeds and doctrines. More than a few were Deists, believing in the existence of an all-powerful God, but not in a personal God and not in Jesus as a divine Savior. Some of the Founding Fathers embraced Freemasonry, which accepted the religious as well as the nonreligious as members so long as they professed belief in a Supreme Being.

Miscellany

Beliefs of America's Founding Fathers

Their differing views on the truths of the Christian faith, however, never emerged as a point of argument in the formation of the government. All agreed that each person should possess the right to worship (or not worship) according to his or her conscience. Certainly Christian ethics and principles played a significant part in the moral and ethical underpinnings of the secular nation's founding documents. And Divine Providence ruled over all.

> **FACT**
>
> John Adams wrote: "The general principles upon which the Fathers achieved independence were the general principles of Christianity.... I will avow that I believed and now believe that those general principles of Christianity are as eternal and immutable as the existence and attributes of God."

The fool says in his heart, "There is no God."
PSALM 14:1

Born a slave in Talbot County, Maryland, Frederick Douglass was separated from his mother while still an infant and raised as an orphan. However, his slave master's wife took an interest in him. Noticing his obvious intellectual promise, she broke the law and taught him the alphabet. From there, young Frederick learned to read by watching the white children around him.

After successfully escaping slavery and moving north to New York, Douglass officially won his freedom when British sympathizers paid off the slaveholder who still legally owned him. He was finally free to pursue the business of abolishing the American slave trade. Douglass joined various abolitionist organizations, read their weekly journals, and befriended leaders of the movement. In time, he was able to secure his own speaking engagements, and even began writing his first autobiography: *Narrative of the Life of Frederick Douglass, an American Slave.*

By the time of the Civil War, Douglass was one of the most famous black men in the country. After President Lincoln issued the Emancipation Proclamation, Douglass worked tirelessly to secure the equality that document promised.

Douglass served in several important political positions and

Men of the Faith

Frederick Douglass (1818–1895)

American abolitionist and statesman

was nominated vice-president of the United States. At that point in U.S. History, no African-American had ever gained such power. An example and credit to all human beings, Frederick Douglass proved to the United States and the world that a person can rise to greatness even from the lowest circumstances.

Frederick Douglass wrote, "I would unite with anybody to do right and with nobody to do wrong."

FACT

Stand fast therefore in the liberty wherewith Christ hath made us free, and be not entangled again with the yoke of bondage.
GALATIANS 5:1 KJV

The inner life of the spirit captivated Frances Ridley Havergal. As a child, she wrote poems of remarkable depth and fluidity and was published in several highly regarded religious periodicals. Her philanthropic work began when, as a schoolgirl, she formed the Flannel Petticoat Society to provide clothing for children of poor families. While her life's mission consisted of telling others about Christ and encouraging faithfulness to Him, she actively tended to temporal matters as well.

Havergal's own life was marked by a series of heartbreaking losses. When

Women of the Faith

Frances Ridley Havergal
(1836–1879)

Poet, songwriter, and philanthropist

Havergal was eleven, her beloved mother passed away. Havergal later recounted her anguish as she watched her mother's funeral procession leave the family home and turn in the direction of the churchyard. When she came of age, the man with whom she fell in love did not share her faith. Rather than marry an unbeliever, she chose to remain unmarried. Throughout her life, Havergal endured long periods of ill health.

Troubles and trials neither weakened her faith nor dampened her spirit. Rather, she accepted personal hardship as necessary to enable her to encourage others, for in suffering she found strength and solace in God's Word. Two of her best-known hymns—"Take My Life and Let It Be" and "I Gave My Life for Thee"—express truths known only to those who have traveled through shadows and darkness by the light of faith in Christ.

Havergal died at age forty-three. Her last utterance, "I *did* so want to glorify Him," seems to have been richly fulfilled.

> **FACT**
>
> Frances Ridley Havergal wrote: "I believe my King suggests a thought, and whispers me a musical line or two, and then I look up and thank Him delightedly and go on with it. That is how my hymns come."

Grace to all who love our Lord Jesus Christ with an undying love.
EPHESIANS 6:24

Commissioned to start a Dutch Reformed church in Garden Grove, California, Rev. Robert H. Schuller and his wife, Arvella, began Garden Grove Community Church in 1955. But it was a far cry from any other Dutch Reformed congregation in the country—as well as most other Protestant churches of that era. Today, the style would be described as "seeker sensitive." But when Schuller began, his goal was simply to find an innovative way to reach the unchurched.

For four years, Schuller preached from the roof of the concession stand at the Orange Drive-In Theater to a congregation seated in cars. More than fifty years later, Garden Grove Community Church has grown to a congregation of more than ten thousand members and hosts the world's most-watched television show, *The Hour of Power*, averaging more than thirty million viewers each week.

Though pastored by Schuller's son, Dr. Robert Anthony Schuller, since 2006, Garden Grove Community Church continues to attract both "seekers" and controversy. The church building, nicknamed the Crystal Cathedral, is covered with ten thousand panes of glass and rises to a height of twelve stories. Inside, an electric fountain and stream flow down the middle aisle. Though the building seats three thousand, glass doors slide open to allow worshippers to watch the service from their cars in the parking lot. Fifty years may have changed the appearance of Garden Grove Community Church, but its mission remains the same: "Find a need and fill it; find a hurt and heal it."

Important Sites

The Crystal Cathedral
Garden Grove, California

The word *cathedral* is usually reserved for a building that's the seat of a bishop—and there's no crystal used in the construction of Garden Grove Church. So how did the church get its nickname? Schuller's frequent use of alliteration in sermon and book titles made the term *Crystal Cathedral* a perfect fit.

FACT

Jesus said, "It is not the healthy who need a doctor, but the sick."
MATTHEW 9:12

The Medieval Inquisition, instituted by the Church of Rome in the early thirteenth century, was created for the express purpose of silencing heretics. It consisted of a tribunal in which suspects were accused, questioned, and commanded to recant. If defendants refused to recant (and sometimes even if they did recant), the court meted out severe penalties, including torture and death. Initially, the Inquisition was limited to certain regions in Europe where particular heresies found listening ears.

In 1478, however, King Ferdinand V and Queen Isabella I received papal approval to establish the Inquisition in Spain. Initially, the Spanish Inquisition focused its attention on Jewish and Muslim converts to Christianity. Converts were suspected of being Christians of convenience and thus susceptible to crimes against the state.

Soon, Christians themselves came under scrutiny. Anyone suspected of Protestant leanings came under fire. No Spaniard could rest secure. Even Ignatius of Loyola and Teresa of Avila, both later elevated to sainthood by the church, fell under the suspicious gaze of the Inquisition.

Groundbreaking Events

The Spanish Inquisition

When the Church in Rome handed authority for the proceedings of the Inquisition to secular authorities, it became an instrument of political control. The Inquisition in Spain under the grand inquisitor Tomás Torquemada surpassed similar tribunals in other parts of Europe in intensity and cruelty.

The late 1700s saw the excesses of the Spanish Inquisition losing to new ideas and enlightened thinking. While it targeted suspect witches to some extent, its days of being a feared and fearsome force were over. The Inquisition gradually weakened and was abolished in the early 1800s.

> **FACT**
> From the eighteenth century, Spain lagged behind the rest of Europe in economic development. Spanish liberals and Protestant historians have long pointed to the Inquisition's suppression of human rights as the reason. Not until the fall of the repressive Franco regime in 1975 have Spaniards been able to freely pursue studies of the Inquisition.

Our pursuers were swifter than eagles in the sky;
they chased us over the mountains and lay in wait for us in the desert.
Lamentations 4:19

Thomas Aquinas, a prolific writer, lent his considerable scholarship and spiritual experience to the composition of a manual for beginners in religion.

The great doctor of the church begins his most famous work, *Summa Theologica*, by acknowledging the difficulties faced by the students of religion of his day—conflicting arguments, useless debates, and the lack of an orderly course of study—"which beget disgust and confusion in the minds of learners."

Aquinas skillfully organized massive amounts of information under topics, in turn followed by questions and answers, then summarized in a conclusion. The *Summa Theologica* contains 38 topics and 612 questions subdivided into 3,120 articles, including 10,000 objections and their answers, all following a consistent and logical pattern. He tackles thorny issues of doctrine, most especially the roles of mind and intellect in a Christian's comprehension of God. To this day, some Christians promote an intellectual knowledge of God, using reason to assess what is true or false about Him; other Christians claim that only intuitively and spiritually can one gain knowledge or experience of God. Aquinas asserts that both mind and intellect are necessary for a comprehension of the supernatural, affirming that only God comprehends all things.

Notable Books

Summa Theologica
By Thomas Aquinas (1273)

Aquinas succeeded in setting the doctrines of the Christian religion into an organized "scientific" framework. Aquinas's sound judgment, lack of jargon, and fairness in dealing with heresies, along with the humble voice of his own piety, combine in *Summa*. His thinking on the nature of human capacity to know God has influenced the development of Christianity through the centuries.

Aquinas worked on the composition of *Summa Theologica* from 1266 through 1273. Before he completed *Summa Theologica*, he underwent an intense religious experience that convinced him everything he had written in his life amounted to no more than straw. He wrote no more after that event, and died three months later.

FACT

My mouth will speak words of wisdom;
the utterance from my heart will give understanding.
PSALM 49:3

This thunderous, weighty hymn just seems to demand respect. A paraphrase of Psalm 46:1, it is the most well-known of Luther's hymns and the best loved of the Lutheran and Protestant traditions. It has even been called "The Battle Hymn of the Reformation."

In actuality the original melody for this hymn differs dramatically from what congregations sing in most Protestant churches. Described as extremely rhythmic, it bends to all the nuances of the text. Around the time the hymn was translated into English, some disputed Luther's authorship. Since then, however, it has been clearly established that Luther did compose the tune to go with the lyrics he had written earlier.

Tradition has it that Luther and his companions sang this hymn as they marched into the city of Worms in 1521 for the Diet of Worms, an assembly best known for addressing Luther's *Ninety-Five Theses* and the Protestant Reformation.

Songs of the Faith

"A Mighty Fortress Is Our God"

Words and Music
by Martin Luther (1529)
Translated into English
by Frederic H. Hedge (1853)

A mighty fortress is our God, a bulwark never failing;
Our helper He, amid the flood of mortal ills prevailing:
For still our ancient foe doth seek to work us woe;
His craft and power are great, and, armed with cruel hate,
On earth is not his equal.

That word above all earthly powers, no thanks to them, abideth;
The Spirit and the gifts are ours through Him Who with us sideth:
Let goods and kindred go, this mortal life also;
The body they may kill: God's truth abideth still,
His kingdom is forever.

FACT

This song has been called "the greatest hymn of the greatest man of the greatest period of German history."

God is our refuge and strength, an ever-present help in trouble.
PSALM 46:1

T he Pilgrims lost no time in getting the kids enrolled in college. In 1636, a mere sixteen years after landing on the shores of the New World, the Massachusetts Bay colonists established Harvard, now the oldest institution of higher learning in the United States. While the college was not associated with a Christian denomination, its course of study reflected the Puritan philosophy of its founders. Indeed, many early scholars went on to become ministers in Puritan congregations.

Miscellany

In 1693, the College of William and Mary opened in Virginia. This second oldest institution of higher learning was established by a group

The Protestant Beginnings of American Universities

of Anglican leaders to train men for the ministry. Yale, the third oldest such institution, opened in 1701 in Connecticut for the training of Congregationalist men for religious and secular leadership positions. New Jersey's Princeton opened in 1746 in affiliation with the Presbyterian Church to educate Christian men, "different sentiments in religion not withstanding."

The religious roots of the nation's leading universities began to weaken after the Civil War. Increasing tension between scientific research and biblical truths divided administration, faculty, and student populations. Curriculum broadened to embrace empirical research over and above biblical studies and moral philosophy. Also, as colleges extended their admissions policies to accept applicants of other faiths, they increasingly downplayed Christianity's role in their early history.

While Harvard, Yale, and Princeton remain private universities, William and Mary became a state-supported institution in 1906. The presence of a cross in its historic Wren Chapel recently gave rise to charges of a church-state conflict, though the cross continues to be displayed in recognition of the College's Anglican heritage.

Matthew Arnold said, "Culture is acquainting ourselves with the best that has been known and said in the world, and thus with the history of the human spirit." When colonists and early Americans established schools and colleges, "the best" meant a liberal arts education focused on the Hebrew and Greek texts of the Bible and other significant works.

---

*Jesus said, "If you hold to my teaching, you are really my disciples.
Then you will know the truth, and the truth will set you free."*
JOHN 8:31–32

In 1538, when John Foxe was twenty-one years old, he witnessed the burning of William Cowbridge. The event foreshadowed what would become his legacy, *The Book of Martyrs*, a record of those who had died for their faith. A studious and devout young man, Foxe had a growing displeasure with the Church of England and King Henry VIII. In 1545, he became a Protestant, thereby positioning himself in conflict with the tenants of the Church of England. Foxe resigned from a fellowship at Magdelene College and looked to other evangelicals for support and guidance as he stood against the injustices he witnessed in the religious climate of England.

While Foxe wrote and gave pro-reform Protestant sermons and speeches, he became increasingly enraged by the quick use of the death penalty for minor infractions practiced by the contemporary religious elite. Feeling personally threatened by Bishop Stephen Gardiner, Foxe fled to Germany for refuge. There he published a Latin history of the Christian persecutions, a precursor to his famous literary work.

Men of the Faith

John Foxe (1517–1587)

Author of *Foxe's Book of Martyrs*

On March 20, 1563, Foxe published the first English edition of *The Book of Martyrs* from the press of John Day. Foxe's honor and advocacy of religious tolerance was far ahead of his day. John Foxe and his *Book of Martyrs* (now known as *Foxe's Book of Martyrs*) were reportedly instrumental in influencing Queen Elizabeth to end the cruel practice of putting to death those of opposing religious convictions.

FACT

John Foxe wrote, "Princes, kings and other rulers of the world have used all their strength and cunning against the Church, yet it continues to endure and hold its own."

I saw under the altar the souls of those who had been slain because of the word of God and the testimony they had maintained.
REVELATION 6:9

Flouting mid-nineteenth-century Southern sensibilities, sisters Angelina and Sarah Grimke argued for the abolition of slavery. As the daughters of a South Carolina judge and plantation owner, they had seen slaves suffer under the crack of the whip and witnessed the injustices and degradation slavery produces. The sisters' outspokenness made them unwelcome among their slave-holding neighbors, and they moved North, where they joined the Religious Society of Friends—the Quakers.

Sarah and Angelina were among the first women in the United States to lecture publicly against the institution of slavery in the South and racial discrimination in the North. Both wrote antislavery pamphlets that were burned in the South. Both received official warnings of arrest should they ever return home. Meanwhile, a number of religious leaders gasped at the spectacle of women voicing their opinion on political issues.

Women of the Faith

Angelina Grimke
(1805–1879)
Sarah Grimke
(1792–1873)
Abolitionists and feminists

Noting that their negative comments on slavery highlighted the blatant sexism in American society, the sisters added to their campaign the issue of women's equality. While some abolitionists fought to keep the movement strictly focused on the plight of slaves, others, like the Grimkes, insisted on equality for both blacks and women.

Angelina married fellow abolitionist and feminist Theodore Weld and settled with him in New Jersey. With Sarah, she opened a school, followed by another in New York. During the years of the Civil War, Angelina actively supported Abraham Lincoln in her writings and lectures. She continued to work to end racial discrimination and for women's suffrage until her death in 1879.

Sarah Grimke's powerful writing formed the foundation of the modern feminist movement. Comparing the status of women to that of slaves, she demanded: "All I ask of our brethren is that they will take their feet from off our necks."

FACT

We were all baptized by one Spirit into one body—whether Jews or Greeks, slave or free—and we were all given the one Spirit to drink.
1 CORINTHIANS 12:13

Beneath mounds of sand and dirt in modern Syria, for 1,700 years lay the remnants of the oldest known Christian house-church in existence. And in that church, excavated in the 1920s, were some of the earliest examples of Christian art. The walls of the house, converted to use as a church, depicted central themes of the Christian faith. Frescoes include the miracles of Jesus, the Good Shepherd, Adam and Eve, David and Goliath, Peter walking on water, and the women at the tomb on the morning when God's power raised Jesus from the dead.

The home itself was built in a typical Roman style with a central pool and a raised room with a large table near the entrance. Christians would have used the pool for baptisms and the raised room for celebrating the Lord's Supper. The paintings on the walls would have edified all who worshipped there, but most likely they were intended primarily for instruction of converts preparing for baptism.

The first followers of the risen Christ were also practicing Jews. Like other pious Jews, they prayed and worshipped at the temple in Jerusalem or at their local synagogues. The Christian community grew and included temple leaders and priests. Soon, opposing Jewish groups objected to large crowds of worshippers listening to Jesus' apostles and undertook to disperse the Christians. Private homes increasingly became the meeting place of choice, particularly as Gentile converts joined the congregations.

Important Sites

Dura-Europos
Syria

The house-church in Dura dates to a time barely a hundred years after the writing of the New Testament. The themes depicted on its walls tied these believers to other Christian communities around the Roman Empire and fellow believers who shared their faith in Jesus.

FACT

In 1930, the house-church of Dura-Europos was totally dismantled and reconstructed at Yale University in New Haven, Connecticut. This is where it remains today. However, this sacred site of the Christian faith is not open to visitors.

[The believers] broke bread in their homes
and ate together with glad and sincere hearts.
ACTS 2:46

An accomplished sculptor, Michelangelo had not lifted a paintbrush beyond his student days. That is, until Pope Julius II requested his services to paint the vaulted ceiling of the restored Sistine Chapel. A pope's personal invitation is not something lightly dismissed.

The work took more than four years to complete. The ceiling, about 131 feet long by 43 feet wide, required more than 4,000 square feet of frescoes (paint applied to damp plaster). Nine scenes from the book of Genesis, from the Creation of the world to the Flood, form a center column that runs the length of the ceiling. On the sides are portraits of the Old Testament prophets who foretold the coming of the Christ. Portraits and scenes along the upper part of the walls depict the history of ancient Israel. Decorative cherubs and sibyls float throughout. Overall, more than three hundred painted figures grace the ceiling.

Groundbreaking Events

Michelangelo Paints the Sistine Chapel
Vatican City

Although Michelangelo designed and sketched the cartoons and painted almost every inch of the frescoes, numerous assistants took part in the project. They prepared the plaster, mixed paints, and delivered tools and material to the artist perched atop the scaffolding. Occasionally, a senior assistant painted an inconsequential figure or minute patch of scenery. Michelangelo is known to have fired assistants at a moment's notice, however, not allowing any one painter cause to credit himself with even a small part of the magnificent work.

Michelangelo completed his masterpiece in October of 1512, and Pope Julius marked the occasion with a solemn mass on November 1, the Feast of All Saints.

Despite scenes from the movies and popular perception, Michelangelo probably didn't paint the ceiling while lying on his back. His scaffolding system followed the curvature of the ceiling's vault. He may have needed to bend backward at times, but not lie down, to reach the surface of the ceiling.

FACT

I love the house where you live, O LORD,
the place where your glory dwells.
PSALM 26:8

The tell-all exposé dates back not to the first sizzling disclosure heard on tabloid television, but to St. Augustine's *Confessions*, written in 397.

In his autobiography, Augustine grapples with some of the most intimate questions of spiritual life. He writes passionately and piercingly about his battle with temptations of the flesh as he struggled to live a holy life. *Confessions* covers Augustine's first thirty-five years, describing in detail his myriad sins and shortcomings, his youthful rebellion against God, and his ultimate acceptance of Christ.

Unlike a typical self-portrait, Augustine's *Confessions* hardly mentions—even omits—significant life events not connected to his spiritual growth, yet explores in detail minor events that pertain to his commitment to Christianity. With keen insight, he unflinchingly delves into the psychology of the human spirit. The authenticity of Augustine's voice and his willingness to bare his soul for the sake of guiding fellow spiritual travelers has endeared *Confessions* to generations of Christians.

Notable Books

Confessions and City of God
By Augustine of Hippo (397, 410)

Another of the prolific writer's classics is *City of God*, a history from a distinctly Christian perspective. Written after the Goths sacked Rome in 410, *City of God* defends Christians against the charge they were responsible for the disaster. Critics maintained that Christians, in worshipping the God of the Bible, had offended traditional Roman gods. Augustine points to the many and various calamities woven throughout Rome's long history. He then proceeds to explain these and contemporary events in light of the struggle between two societies, symbolized by Jerusalem, the City of God, and Babylon, the city of those in rebellion against God.

FACT

St. Augustine wrote, "My inner self was a house divided against itself. Why does this strange phenomenon occur? The mind gives an order to the body and is at once obeyed, but when it gives an order to itself, it is resisted. What causes it?"

I do not understand what I do.
For what I want to do I do not do,
but what I hate I do.
ROMANS 7:15

It was called "the escarpment," an ancient upthrust ledge near the city of Lockport, New York. Pastor Maltbie Babcock hiked up to the area almost every day. Before leaving the house he would often say, "I am going out to see my Father's world." It's easy to understand how sitting atop the escarpment day after day would have inspired him to write the poem he called, "This Is My Father's World." It must have been wonderful looking down on God's creation—the green of farms and orchards giving way to the blue of Lake Ontario.

Unfortunately, Babcock

Songs of the Faith

"This Is My Father's House"

Words by Maltbie D. Babcock (1901)
Music by Franklin L. Sheppard (1915)

met an untimely death in 1901. His grieving wife, Catherine, gathered and published many of the pieces he had written, among them this beautiful poem. It was set to a traditional English melody known as *"Terra Beata,"* meaning "blessed earth," by Franklin L. Sheppard—a friend—after Babcock's death. Shepard was editing a Presbyterian songbook for children at the time and included the hymn.

This is my Father's world, and to my list'ning ears,
All nature sings, and round me rings the music of the spheres.
This is my Father's world, I rest me in the thought
Of rocks and trees, of skies and seas;
His hand the wonders wrought.

This is my Father's world, O let me ne'er forget
That though the wrong seems oft so strong, God is the Ruler yet.
This is my Father's world, the battle is not done;
Jesus who died shall be satisfied,
And earth and heaven be one.

Maltbie D. Babcock wrote, "To face every opportunity of life thoughtfully and ask its meaning bravely and earnestly, is the only way to meet the supreme opportunities when they come, whether open-faced or disguised."

FACT

The heavens are Yours, the earth also is Yours;
the world and all its fullness,
You have founded them.
PSALM 89:11 NKJV

Drivers of a certain age may still shudder to see a swarm of motorcyclists pull up beside them at a stoplight. In the 1950s, you would have prayed for a fast getaway, your head reeling with lurid newspaper stories of biker mayhem. Now you're likely to glance over and see riders you recognize—from your church.

Local motorcycling organizations formed in the early years of the twentieth century. In 1924, the American Motorcyclist Association (AMA) was founded by motorcycle manufacturers to promote riding among the general public. The AMA supported rider clubs with national fellowship events, rider education programs, and public relations.

Christian biker clubs got on the road in the 1970s as motorcycling went mainstream. Clubs formed among local Christian riders (many of whom were ministers) to promote fellowship, hone riding skills, and spread the gospel in the biking community. Groups identified themselves by wearing T-shirts or jacket patches sporting a Bible verse, cross, or praying hands. Many clubs sponsored community food and clothing drives and took their ministry to shelters, jails, and even among "hard-core" bikers—those you *don't* want to see in the rearview mirror.

Miscellany

Bikers for Christ

Christian motorcycle clubs

The Christian Motorcyclists Association (CMA), in existence since the 1970s, now claims more than one hundred thousand members nationally and internationally. Soldiers for Jesus and Bikers for Christ are also large international ministries that organize Christian bikers around a wide range of community and charitable activities. The Christian club associations routinely screen applicants, often requiring references and a waiting period before granting membership. Their consistently positive press has earned Christian bikers widespread respect and admiration.

FACT

The Wild One, a 1953 movie based on a biker gathering gone awry in Hollister, California, reinforced the public's negative (and fearful) view of motorcyclists. In response to the movie, the AMA wrote in defense of the 99 percent of cyclists who were law-abiding citizens and condemned the 1 percent who belong to "outlaw" clubs.

In your majesty ride forth victoriously in behalf of truth, humility and righteousness.
PSALM 45:4

Though he was raised by a churchgoing family in the Church of Ireland, C. S. Lewis—or Jack, as he liked to be called—was a confirmed atheist by the age of thirteen. Three years earlier, at the age of ten, Jack's mother had died of bone cancer, and Jack was forever altered by the loss. Young Lewis separated himself from Christianity when he began to see it as a chore and a duty. Instead, Jack began to fancy the occult and Norse Mythology. Those ideologies gave him a sense of "Northerness," or joy as he would later describe it.

Jack also liked the works of George MacDonald, a Scottish minister and author of fairy and fantasy tales. One day, while Jack was waiting for a train, he read MacDonald's book *Phantastes*, which had a profound effect on him. Jack said, "A few hours after reading it, I knew I had crossed a great frontier." Later he was influenced by his colleague and friend, fellow Oxford scholar and Christian J. R. R. Tolkien. Jack wrote in his book *Surprised by Joy*, "I came into Christianity kicking and screaming." Jack finally converted to Christianity in 1931.

Men of the Faith

In addition to *The Chronicles of Narnia* and his autobiography *Surprised by Joy*, Lewis wrote many other books that have become Christian classics: *Mere Christianity* (originally short radio essays), *The Screwtape Letters*, *The Four Loves*, and the science-fiction trilogy, *Perelandra*, *Out of the Silent Planet*, and *That Hideous Strength*. C. S. Lewis would become a lifelong scholar, great thinker, teacher, and in the eyes of many, the greatest writer the Christian world has seen in the twentieth century.

C. S. Lewis (1898–1963)
British author and scholar

As a young boy, Jack and his brother, Warnie, often wrote and illustrated their own animal stories, together creating the world of Boxen, inhabited and run by animals.

FACT

Incline your ear, and come unto me: hear, and your soul shall live;
and I will make an everlasting covenant with you,
even the sure mercies of David.
ISAIAH 55:3 KJV

Through CDs, videos, and concerts, Gloria Gaither and her husband, Bill, have been bringing the joy and exuberance of Southern Gospel music to audiences across the country for more than forty years.

Gloria's Christian parents brought up their daughter to live life as a God-sent adventure. They taught her to savor and enjoy the day, and strive for excellence in all things. Early on, the beauty and power of words captivated Gloria, and she went on to earn an advanced degree in English literature. After her graduation, she and Bill taught high school until their burgeoning music ministry edged out their day jobs.

Women of the Faith

Gloria Gaither (b. 1942)

Author, speaker, singer,

and songwriter

Gloria is now a sought-after speaker and prolific author of books and musicals, in addition to teaching songwriting at Anderson University in Indiana. She also performs with her husband in concerts and television specials.

Commitment to her family, however, is at the heart of all Gloria's endeavors. Many of her songs give voice to family and social issues. She has written devotionals to inspire and encourage women, and is an outspoken advocate for the preservation of the family. The safeguarding of things that are "priceless" motivates her involvement in social issues.

"Because He Lives," one of Gloria's most popular songs, was inspired by the birth of their son, Benjamin, in July 1970. At a low point in their lives, Gloria and Bill began to fear for the well-being of children in a world seemingly on a downward spiral. Benjamin's birth restored their hope, affirming God's continued love and care, despite an uncertain future.

FACT

Gloria is the principal lyricist for more than six hundred of the Gaithers' songs.

[Jesus said,] "Do not be afraid, little flock,
for your Father has been pleased to give you the kingdom."
LUKE 12:32

In the early 1800s, African-Americans were not prohibited from attending local churches, but their rights within those churches were limited. They were not allowed to vote on church matters or join committees. They were often relegated to sit in balcony pews. But in 1805, pastor Thomas Paul and twenty-three other African-Americans (fifteen of them women) established the African Meeting House in Boston. Today this redbrick building is considered the oldest African-American church edifice in the United States.

Important Sites

The African Meeting House
Boston

The African Meeting House, which later became known as the African-American First Baptist Church of Boston, is remembered not only as the first black church north of the Mason-Dixon line, but as a powerful force in the fight against slavery. Nicknamed "the Abolitionist Church," the African Meeting House was a popular stop for "self-emancipated" individuals assisted by the Underground Railroad. The church housed abolitionist meetings, fundraisers, and political rallies, and also hosted well-known speakers such as Frederick Douglass. When the Civil War began, the African Meeting House held recruitment meetings for black soldiers.

In 1898, the church moved from Beacon Hill to its present building in the Roxbury community where it became known as the People's Baptist Church. Today the African-American Meeting House, fittingly located on Joy Street, houses the Afro-American History Museum. It's listed as a National Historic Landmark and is part of the Black Heritage Trail, a walking tour highlighting the history of nineteenth-century Boston's African-American community.

In what seems like a step backward, at the public dedication of the African Meeting House in 1806, the first floor pews were reserved for those "benevolently disposed to the Africans" while the church's African-American members sat where they had previously been forced to sit—in the balcony.

FACT

You are all children of God through faith in Christ Jesus.
GALATIANS 3:26 NLT

On the eve of All Saints' Day in 1517, the city of Wittenberg, Germany, is in a celebratory mood. Townspeople, students, professors, and pilgrims gather in the marketplace and mill around the church in anticipation of festivities ahead. Then through the crowds strides popular university lecturer and priest Martin Luther. As he approaches the church, he pulls out a document and nails it to the community bulletin board—the Castle Church door.

Groundbreaking Events

Luther Posts the
Ninety-Five Theses
Wittenberg, Germany

Written in Latin for the attention of clergy and academics, Luther's document galvanized the increasingly vocal reform movement within the Roman Catholic Church. Within two weeks, his points of debate were being discussed throughout Germany by clergy and laymen alike. Within a month, all Christendom had heard of the Augustinian monk of Wittenberg.

Years before, Luther and others had begun to question abuses in the sale of indulgences. One John Tetzel, a charismatic monk and persuasive salesman, frequently worked the Wittenberg circuit. In a setting much akin to a circus, Tetzel equated his letters of indulgence to a passport to heaven, no repentance required (only money). In university lectures and from the pulpit, Luther preached against Tetzel's excessive claims, reiterating the primacy of sincere confession and repentance followed by absolution from the mouth of a priest.

The *Ninety-Five Theses* addressed the use of indulgences and other current practices that Luther found contrary to scripture. Far from the academic discussion Luther envisioned, debate spread like wildfire across Western Europe. Luther's posting on October 31, 1517, ignited the Protestant Reformation.

FACT

In the opening lines of his *Ninety-Five Theses*, Luther wrote: "Out of love and zeal for the elucidation of truth, the following theses will be debated at Wittenberg, the Reverend Father Martin Luther, Master of Arts and Sacred Theology, presiding. He begs that those who cannot be present at the oral discussion will communicate their views in writing. In the name of our Lord Jesus Christ. Amen."

Therefore, since we have been justified through faith, we have peace with God through our Lord Jesus Christ, through whom we have gained access by faith into this grace in which we now stand.
ROMANS 5:1–2

The Bishop of Carthage, Cyprian, penned a number of significant treatises, the most famous being *De Unitate Catholicae Ecclesiae* (*The Unity of the Catholic Church*).

De Unitate, a pamphlet written in the year 251, responded to a threatened schism in the church. The dispute centered around the treatment of Catholics who had renounced their faith under the persecution of the Roman emperor Decius. While some bishops received lapsed church members back with little fanfare, others withheld forgiveness, thus making reentry into the church (and consequently salvation) unattainable. Cyprian supported the position of Pope Cornelius, who called for sincere repentance on the part of returning Catholics as a condition for forgiveness, the ultimate full admission into the church. In *De Unitate*, Cyprian argues for close agreement among the bishops in this matter to ensure and enforce church unity.

Cyprian presented *De Unitate* to a council of bishops in 251, hoping to get the backing of the majority of churchmen in attendance. *De Unitate* maintained that any bishop out of agreement with his brother bishops cuts himself off from the unity of the church, and hence unity with Christ. In his document, Cyprian cited

Notable Books

De Unitate Catholicae Ecclesiae
By Cyprian (251)

the headship of St. Peter, the first bishop, as a symbol of this unity, though not necessarily allowing the successor to Peter—the pope in Rome—authority over all other bishops.

Protestants in later centuries picked up on Cyprian's distinction. Protestant churches teach to this day that Christ pointed to Peter's strong assertion of faith as what bound the church together, and not Peter himself.

Cyprian wrote, "There is one God and one Christ, and one Church, and one Chair founded on Peter by the word of the Lord. It is not possible to set up another altar or for there to be another priesthood besides that one altar and that one priesthood. Whoever has gathered elsewhere is scattering."

FACT

There is one body and one Spirit—just as you were called to one hope when you were called—one Lord, one faith, one baptism; one God and Father of all, who is over all and through all and in all.
EPHESIANS 4:4–6

The beautiful carol "Silent Night" was much more than a casual inspiration; it was the miraculous answer to prayer.

A young priest named Joseph Mohr was preparing for a special Christmas Eve service one unusually cold night when he noticed that the church organ was not working. He did his best to get the old instrument operating again, but to no avail. Uncertain what to do, he paused to pray. It was then that he remembered a Christmas poem he had written several years earlier.

Songs of the Faith

"Silent Night" ("*Stille Nacht*")

Words by Joseph Mohr (1818)
English translation: John F. Young (1863)
Music by Franz Grüber (1820)

He had played with a few melodies, shared it with a few friends, but never sought to have it published.

Mohr pulled the poem from a desk drawer, bundled up, and hurried out into the cold. Just a few hours before the service was to begin, he sought help from his friend, schoolteacher and composer Franz Grüber. Mohr asked the surprised man if he could write music for his poem in the hours left before the Christmas Eve service

Not only did Grüber accomplish the task, but with time to teach it to the choir. Accompanied by Mohr on the guitar, the simple melody filled the church.

The story of how the song was written traveled quickly, and its popularity skyrocketed. An Austrian singing group carried the melody to New York, where it was well received. "Silent Night" has now been recorded more than any other song in history.

> *Silent night, holy night!*
> *All is calm, all is bright.*
> *Round yon Virgin, Mother and Child.*
> *Holy infant so tender and mild,*
> *Sleep in heavenly peace,*
> *Sleep in heavenly peace.*

FACT

A manuscript has been found that seems to indicate that the music for "Silent Night" was written by Grüber, but two to four years later. This much-told story could be simply folklore.

[The angel said,] "This will be the sign to you:
You will find a Babe wrapped in swaddling cloths, lying in a manger."
LUKE 2:12 NKJV

Comedian Jay Leno exposed an unfunny fact: Many in his audience could not recite even one of the Ten Commandments. No one could name even one of Jesus' disciples. Gallup surveys received similar responses among the general population. High school and college educators have said for decades: Most students today do not know enough about the Bible to understand basic biblical references and allusions in history, art, and literature.

The 2006 National Bible Week campaign aimed to reverse the trend. They erected five thousand billboards with a message printed in large letters: AN EDUCATED PERSON KNOWS THE BIBLE. Sponsored by the Bible Literacy Project and the National Bible Association, the campaign urged public schools to teach the Bible, not to proselytize but to promote cultural literacy.

Miscellany

Campaign for Bible Literacy

The academic establishment—religious and secular—said "amen" to the message. High school teachers and university professors surveyed named books commonly read in literature and history classes that require Bible background to understand. They reported that artwork depicting religious themes confuses students unfamiliar with Bible stories. Without a working knowledge of the Bible, students are hard-pressed to understand how it affected and often directed the formation of American culture.

When public high schools and colleges offer elective courses in Bible literacy, however, opponents of "religious" classes on taxpayer turf inevitably turn hot. As yet, however, the fiery furnace of controversy has allowed most school districts to emerge unscathed. The majority of states have successfully implemented a program of scholarly, academic-related Bible instruction in the classroom.

The Bible Literacy Project's textbook, *The Bible and Its Influence,* is widely used in public high school English and Social Studies courses. Meant to be read alongside the Bible, the textbook aims to introduce students to the significant narratives, characters, and symbols of the Bible found throughout English and European art and literature.

FACT

"Great is the LORD's anger that burns against us because our fathers have not obeyed the words of this book."
2 KINGS 22:13

From his humble upbringing on a North Carolina dairy farm, William Franklin Graham Jr., better known as Billy Graham, has become one of the most recognizable figures in modern Christianity and an advisor to every sitting president since Harry Truman.

Born days before the end of World War I, Graham graduated from Wheaton College in Illinois during World War II. Soon he was preaching evangelistic messages with the Youth for Christ organization, and his 1949 Los Angeles "crusade" (a term he popularized) brought him international attention.

Since founding the Billy Graham Evangelistic Association in 1950, Graham has used crusades, radio, television, movies, books, magazines, and newspaper columns to help people find a personal relationship with God, which he believes comes through knowing Christ.

Graham, a man of deep personal conviction, was an outspoken opponent of segregation during the 1960s civil rights movement. He refused to speak to segregated crowds and once tore down the ropes put up by organizers. He said, "There is no scriptural basis for segregation. . . . The ground at the foot of the cross is level."

Men of the Faith

Billy Graham (b. 1918)

American evangelist

It is estimated that more than two hundred million people have heard his live gospel presentations in some 180 countries and territories—while countless others watched on television. Graham's bestselling autobiography, *Just As I Am*, was published in 1997.

Time magazine featured Billy Graham among its 100 most important people of the twentieth century. Other names on the list included Ronald Reagan, Winston Churchill, Adolf Hitler, Martin Luther King Jr., Henry Ford, and Albert Einstein.

FACT

In an opinion survey on achievements in religion, Graham was ranked second—after God.

"Therefore go and make disciples of all nations, baptizing them in the name of the Father and of the Son and of the Holy Spirit, and teaching them to obey everything I have commanded you. And surely I am with you always, to the very end of the age."
Matthew 28:19–20

Queen Victoria considered Elizabeth Fry a "very superior person." It's probable the queen so admired the older woman that she took her as a role model on how to effectively manage motherhood along with public responsibilities.

Elizabeth Fry was born in Norwich, England, to a devout Quaker family. As a young woman, she visited the sick, collected clothing for the poor, and opened in her house a Sunday school for local children. When she heard chilling stories about the treatment of women at Newgate Prison, Fry went to see for herself.

Conditions appalled her. She found three hundred women and children crammed together with no beds, nightclothes, or protection. Hardened criminals mixed with those accused of minor offenses and those awaiting trial. Fry began to visit regularly, supplying inmates with clothing and establishing a school and a chapel in the prison. Along with eleven other Quakers, she founded the Association for the Improvement of the Female Prisoners in Newgate.

Women of the Faith

Elizabeth Fry (1780–1845)

Prison reformer

Her efforts received notice, and she spoke on prison reform before the House of Commons. While the members of parliament gave favorable reviews to her work, they resisted her contention that "capital punishment was evil and produced evil results." Opinion favored the death sentence as a way to keep "the dread of punishment in the criminal classes," and some members of parliament considered Fry's views threatening to social order. Eventually, however, Fry and others moved the government to legislate improvements to the prison system.

At her death in 1845, more than a thousand people came to pay their respects to a fearless, compassionate, and quintessentially modern woman.

In an 1813 letter to her children, Elizabeth Fry wrote, "I have lately been twice to Newgate to see after the poor prisoners who had poor little infants without clothing, or with very little and I think if you saw how small a piece of bread they are each allowed a day you would be very sorry."

FACT

"The LORD looked down from his sanctuary on high, from heaven he viewed the earth, to hear the groans of the prisoners and release those condemned to death."

PSALM 102:19–20

One of the greatest manuscript discoveries of modern times might never have happened if it weren't for a stray goat. In 1947, two Bedouin cousins were throwing rocks onto the cave-riddled hillsides of Israel's Judean wilderness, trying to startle a wayward goat out of hiding. But instead of hearing a goat's bleat, the boys heard pottery shatter. Muhammed ehd-Dhib, nicknamed "the Wolf," climbed up into a small cave to investigate. There he found lidded jars containing ancient scrolls.

After Wolf's discovery, both archaeologists and thieves began scouring the surrounding hills. By 1956, eleven caves had been found, containing about 850 scrolls. From tens of thousands of fragments, two hundred separate books written in Hebrew, Aramaic, and Greek as early as 250 BC were recovered from the Qumran Caves. The manuscripts include hymnals, sermons, rules of warfare, and commentaries on Hebrew scripture. But the most significant find is 122 handwritten copies of books of the Old Testament. Every book is represented except Esther. Aside from a few spelling and verb tense errors, the scripture written on the scrolls is in substantial agreement with modern-day translations of the Bible.

Important Sites

The Qumran Caves

Israel

The Isaiah Scroll (one of twenty-four copies of Isaiah found in the Qumran Caves) is considered one of the most important manuscript finds in history. Found virtually intact, this manuscript is more than a thousand years older than any previously known copy of Isaiah. The manuscript is currently housed in the Shrine of the Book Museum in Jerusalem.

FACT

All of the Dead Sea Scrolls are written on animal skins or papyrus, except for one. It's incised on a thin sheet of copper. This scroll lists sixty-three treasures hidden in the Judean wilderness. In 1960 the total treasure was estimated to be worth more than one million dollars, but none of the treasure has been recovered.

He will be the sure foundation for your times, a rich store of salvation and wisdom and knowledge; the fear of the LORD is the key to this treasure.
ISAIAH 33:6

With his *Ninety-Five Theses*, Martin Luther clearly had opened a can of worms. Four years later, he was called to face an Imperial assembly to eat not worms, but words.

The Diet of Worms took place in an atmosphere of intrigue and political maneuvering. Though Pope Leo X had issued a letter of excommunication against Luther, the young Emperor Charles V was reluctant to enforce it. To do so would have alienated the powerful Frederick the Wise of Saxony and the restless German princes. Charles, therefore, convened a hearing in the German city of Worms, at which Luther would appear and speak for himself.

The dignitaries in attendance included Emperor Charles V, the Electors of Germany, archbishops, bishops and other high-ranking churchmen of the Empire, in addition to noblemen, knights, and distinguished townsmen. On April 17, 1521, Luther appeared before the assembly. Pointing to a stack of books, the presiding officer asked Luther if he would acknowledge authorship of the books and revoke the heresies they contained. Luther claimed authorship, but requested time to consider the rest of his answer, as it touched on matters of faith and salvation.

Groundbreaking Events

The Diet of Worms

Worms, Germany

The next day, Luther's answer rang boldly and clearly. After summarizing his reasons, Luther declared: "I am neither able nor willing to recant, since it is neither safe nor right to act against conscience. On this I take my stand. I can do no other. God help me." Luther's speech in defense of the individual conscience grounded in God's Word against unbiblical regulations of church and state reverberate in Western society to this day.

After Luther made his world-famous statement, cheers and boos disrupted the proceedings. The Emperor adjourned the court, and Luther went into hiding for his own safety. Later, the Diet issued the Edict of Worms, which declared Luther an outlaw and banned his writings.

FACT

God is our refuge and strength, an ever-present help in trouble.
Therefore we will not fear, though the earth give way
and the mountains fall into the heart of the sea.
PSALM 46:1–2

Josephus's two historical works, *The Jewish War* and *Jewish Antiquities*, together shed more light on New Testament times than any other document outside the Bible. His books are essential reading for anyone who hopes to grasp the political, social, and religious environment Jesus, His disciples, and the new Christians inhabited.

The Jewish War, Josephus's seven-volume work published in AD 77–78, traces Jewish history from Maccabean times in the second century BC to the Jewish revolt and Roman victory, events Josephus personally witnessed and, to an extent, participated in. His account lauds Jewish culture and asserts the superiority of the Jewish faith over and above the religion of the pagan Romans. Written under the patronage of the Roman emperor, however, *The Jewish War* may well have been intended and used as a cautionary tale to any would-be insurrectionist currently seething under Roman rule.

Jewish Antiquities, a twenty-volume work published AD 93–94, is an even more ambitious project. Josephus opened with the Creation of the world and ended with current events. He consulted ancient texts as well as contemporary sources, including eyewitness accounts and personal experience. Of special interest to Christians, *Jewish Antiquities* cites a number of biblical figures,

Notable Books

The Jewish War and Jewish Antiquities

By Flavius Josephus (circa 78)

including Jesus, his half-brother James, and John the Baptist. The author, though not a Christian, probably read early Christian documents available to him. He briefly outlines Jesus' ministry, crucifixion, death, and the various reports of His resurrection. Josephus notes that "the tribe of the Christians, so named after him, has not disappeared to this day."

FACT

Some translations of *Jewish Antiquities* suggest that Josephus recorded Jesus' resurrection as fact, as opposed to the reports of other people. If he stated the event as fact, the reference may indicate that he embraced Christianity.

After the people saw the miraculous sign that Jesus did, they began to say, "Surely this is the Prophet who is to come into the world."
JOHN 6:14

DAY
III

Exhausted and spiritually depleted by the bloody horrors of the Civil War, Philadelphia rector Phillips Brooks knew he was in serious need of rest and renewal. Earlier in the year, he had given the funeral message for President Abraham Lincoln, a most sobering experience.

Brooks felt it would help his state of mind to spend Christmas in the Holy Land in the winter of 1865. The streets of Jerusalem were clammering with tourists, and Brooks wanted some quiet time. Then an idea seized him. On a borrowed horse, he set out alone across the desolate countryside. Locals had warned him that he might encounter thieves, but he was undeterred.

Just as evening was upon him, with a clear sky full of stars above, Brooks entered the little village of Bethlehem. As he rode through the streets, he felt overwhelmed with awe, realizing that he was in the place where Jesus had been born.

Back at home, he had difficulty putting his experience into words for his congregation. But three years

Songs of the Faith

"O Little Town of Bethlehem"

Words by Phillips Brooks (1867)
Music by Lewis H. Redner (1868)

later, while preparing for the Christmas Eve service of 1868, the words of "O Little Town of Bethlehem" came to him—he says almost effortlessly. He shared the poem with his church organist, Lewis Redner, who wrote the melody for the Sunday school children's choir.

> *O little town of Bethlehem*
> *How still we see thee lie*
> *Above thy deep and dreamless sleep*
> *The silent stars go by*
> *Yet in thy dark streets shineth*
> *The everlasting Light*
> *The hopes and fears of all the years*
> *Are met in thee tonight.*

Phillips Brooks is now recognized as the greatest American preacher of the nineteenth century. The first volume of his collected sermons sold more than two hundred thousand copies in 1878 and is still read and studied today.

FACT

The Lord says, "Bethlehem, you might not be an important town in the nation of Judah. But out of you will come a ruler over Israel for me."
MICAH 5:2 NIRV

Two boys, known troublemakers, were being particularly obnoxious in church one Sunday. Their pastor grabbed them and said, 'Where is God?' The stunned boys didn't know how to answer. The pastor told them, 'Go home and don't come back until you can tell me where God is.' Outside, the boys looked at each other. 'We're in big trouble now,' they agreed. 'They've lost God, and they're trying to blame that on us, too.'"

Christian stand-up comedy emerged in the 1970s. At first, Christian speakers used humor to enliven otherwise serious lectures. Then humorists like the Reverend Grady Nutt (an ordained Baptist minister) started focusing on Christian-themed jokes and routines alone. Nutt's frequent television appearances lifted Christian comedy from church basements into mainstream consciousness.

By 2002, the number of comedians performing Christian stand-up comedy had grown sufficiently to support the formation of the Christian Comedy Association (CCA). Begun with thirty-five members, the CCA now claims more than three hundred comedians in four countries. The group works to provide support and fellowship for Christian comedians, especially solo performers who spend a lot of time on the road. The CCA also serves as a development resource for Christian comedians who want to hone their craft.

Miscellany

Christian Comedians

Today, Christian comedians provide audiences with an alternative to secular performers who litter their routines with foul language and offensive jokes. Performing in diverse venues, Christian comedians view their work as a ministry and laughter as a gift from God. It can be said that they spread the gospel one smile at a time.

FACT

A minister told his congregation, "Next week I will preach about the sin of lying. In the meantime, please read Mark 17." The following Sunday, he asked who had read Mark 17. Every hand shot up. The minister smiled and said, "Mark has only sixteen chapters. I will now proceed with my sermon on the sin of lying."

Each one should use whatever gift he has received to serve others,
faithfully administering God's grace in its various forms.
1 PETER 4:10

As a child in Germany, Martin Luther believed he was watched by a great and just God, powerful enough to make lightning strike a boy for any small sin. Martin also believed that no matter how well he lived, in the eyes of God he was always sinful. He thought only the Virgin Mary and the saints could pardon his sins.

Years later, this burden still waged against his soul. Martin tried desperately to gain God's favor at the monastery where he studied. He wanted to be accepted and loved by God, so he fasted, performed good works, flagellated himself, said prayers, and even went on a pilgrimage. He became gaunt and depressed. The more he tried to please God, the more he became aware of his own sinfulness.

There, finally at the monastery, Martin received his own Bible, bound in red leather. Nothing he had ever received in his life meant so much to him. As he studied and researched the Bible, he began to understand its central truth: justification by faith alone. Luther wrote and taught on this principle, angering the pope. The church said he risked excommunication unless he recanted his words. Luther would not recant, and in so doing, initiated the Protestant Reformation.

Men of the Faith

Martin Luther (1483–1546)

Founder of the Protestant Reformation

Through his life and work, Luther emphasized that a person is saved by God's merciful kindness through the work of Christ, not by any human effort. A Bible translator, he encouraged the common people to read the scriptures and discover for themselves the message of life-affirming faith within its pages. Today, nearly seventy million Christians claim to belong to Lutheran churches worldwide, and another 320 million Protestants trace their history back to Luther's reforming work.

Frederick II, Elector of Saxony, didn't want Martin Luther punished as a heretic, so he had him escorted to the security of Wartburg Castle at Eisenach, where Luther grew a beard and lived incognito for nearly eleven months, pretending to be a knight called *Junker Jörg*.

FACT

Because of his great love for us, God, who is rich in mercy, made us alive with Christ even when we were dead in transgressions—it is by grace you have been saved.
EPHESIANS 2:4–5

The daughter of King Andrew II of Hungary had her future cut out for her. The king sent four-year-old Elizabeth to live in Thuringia, a region of central Germany, to grow up with the family of her future husband. Elizabeth, an unusually devout child, retained her piety despite the sumptuous and secular airs of the Thuringian court.

Ludwig IV, Elizabeth's betrothed, succeeded to the throne in 1221 upon the death of his father, and he and Elizabeth married the same year. The union proved a happy one, Ludwig encouraging and supporting his wife's religious observances and works of charity. Germans call him St. Ludwig in recognition of his capabilities as a ruler and goodness as a person.

In 1226, floods, famine, and an insect infestation brought ruin to Thuringia. Ludwig being away at the time, Elizabeth headed relief efforts. She distributed food and clothes to the poor. She personally saw to the installation of a hospital ward below the Wartburg castle, and she visited patients daily.

Women of the Faith

Elizabeth of Hungary (1207–1231)

Philanthropist and friend of the poor and sick

The following year, shortly after she had given birth to their third child, Elizabeth learned her husband had died while on a crusade to Palestine. The acting regent for their young son opposed her generosity with the revenues of her estates and expelled her from Thuringia, though by some accounts she left of her own accord. Nonetheless, Elizabeth relinquished her power as regent when it was restored to her and joined the third order of St. Francis. She died at age twenty-four, having spent her last years in tireless service to the poor and needy.

FACT

Elizabeth's spiritual advisor, a Franciscan monk, opened to her the ideals of St. Francis. He instructed her to cultivate the virtues of chastity, humility, patience, prayer, and charity, though she could not, because of her state in life, take the Franciscan's vow of poverty, a point Elizabeth regretted.

I will fulfill my vows to the LORD in the presence of all his people.
PSALM 116:14

King Solomon built Israel's first permanent temple around 960 BC. The Babylonians razed the temple in 586 BC, but a second temple was built about 515 when Persia, which had conquered Babylon, allowed Jews to return to Jerusalem. Centuries later, Herod the Great built a third temple on the same site as the earlier two. But in AD 70, the Roman Empire destroyed the temple once more, leaving just the western wall standing. The Romans wanted the wall to be a bittersweet reminder to the Jews, a symbol that Rome was the ultimate conqueror. However, the Jewish people did not see the wall as a monument to Rome's victory, but to God's faithfulness. His temple stood fast, just like His unbroken bond with His people.

Today, the Wailing Wall (so nicknamed because of all those who've mourned the destruction of the temple at this site) continues to be a place of both battles and prayer. The area is considered sacred to Jews, Christians, and Muslims. In 1929, the League of Nations declared that the wall and surrounding area was owned by the Muslims, but that Jews should have free access to worship there at all times.

Important Sites

The Wailing Wall
Jerusalem

Today, visitors of all religions are invited to approach the wall in silent prayer. In keeping with Jewish tradition, there is a divider separating men and women while they pray. Many visitors write their prayers on pieces of paper, which they then place in crevices on the wall. This practice has been around for hundreds of years, since Jewish tradition says the gate of heaven itself lies directly above the Western Wall.

The largest stone built into the Western Wall is 44 feet long, 10 feet high and 12–16 feet deep. It weighs approximately 570 tons. In contrast, the largest stone in the Great Pyramid of Egypt weighs only 11 tons.

FACT

We are the temple of the living God.
2 CORINTHIANS 6:16

Wild living. Public adultery. Gambling. Drinking. Corruption. Tabloid-worthy words describe abuses of the early sixteenth-century church. Priests, either hobnobbing with the rich and famous or bending an elbow at the local tavern, left their congregations under the care of unschooled vicars. Monasteries and convents had fallen into disarray. In the cantons of Switzerland as in the rest of Western Europe, such practices paved the way for reform.

The Swiss Reformation movement began in 1519 with Ulrich Zwingli's lectures on the New Testament. Zwingli questioned the authority of the church fathers and ecclesiastical hierarchy. Like Luther in Germany, Zwingli proclaimed the sole authority of the Bible in matters of faith and salvation. In 1523, he was summoned to appear before the general council and a papal representative. Zwingli brought with him sixty-seven statements, similar to Luther's *Ninety-Five Theses*, for discussion and debate. After hearing Zwingli's arguments, the council sided with the reformer and ordered all priests in the canton to change their wicked ways.

Groundbreaking Events

The Swiss Reformation

Reform took a more radical and extreme turn in Switzerland than it did in Germany. Along with the elimination of obvious abuses in the church came the destruction of organs, altars, artwork, stained-glass windows, and statues. Monasticism was abolished and priests and nuns encouraged to marry. Celebration of the Roman Catholic Mass and the Sacrament of Holy Communion were prohibited, replaced by a simplified worship service with a commemorative feast. The latter—the doctrine of the Lord's Supper—divides Christian denominations to this day.

FACT

In 1531, Zwingli, acting as chaplain and standard-bearer for the Protestant forces, was wounded at Kappel am Albis and later put to death by the victorious troops of the Forest Cantons. After Zwingli's death the Reformation made no further headway in Switzerland.

Certain men whose condemnation was written about long ago have secretly slipped in among you. They are godless men, who change the grace of our God into a license for immorality and deny Jesus Christ our only Sovereign and Lord.
JUDE 4

M y Dear Wormwood"—so begins thirty-one letters from Screwtape, a worldly-wise devil, to his apprentice-devil nephew, Wormwood. C. S. Lewis's *The Screwtape Letters*, a masterpiece of satire, continues to inspire and enlighten Christians decades after its first publication in 1942.

Full of helpful advice on how to lure a young convert to damnation, each letter proposes a perverse plan of action to confuse, obstruct, or negate the gospel message planted in the heart of the new believer. Screwtape knows better than to dangle obvious sins in front of the Christian, because he will immediately recoil from the idea. Instead, the savvy devil endorses stealthier methods—worldly, carefree friends; unwholesome imaginings; small indulgences; shallow thinking; and other seemingly "petty" shortcomings—to overcome the faith of Wormwood's subject. Screwtape has had success by using intellectual fads, transitory pleasures, disillusionment with other Christians, works of righteousness, and easy discipleship, and he urges his nephew to try these things to get his assigned subject safely on the road to hell. Along with Wormwood, readers examine honesty, goodness, and holiness—not how to attain these virtues, but how to avoid them!

Notable Books

The Screwtape Letters

By C. S. Lewis (1942)

The classic book's wry, witty perspective entertains at the same time it instructs. Readers come to realize that the battle of good versus evil is fought not in a fantasy tale of bigger-than-life characters somewhere in the universe, but in the private thoughts and daily actions of those who call Jesus Christ their Lord and Savior.

Randall Wallace, the writer of screenplays for *Pearl Harbor*, *Braveheart*, and other major films, wrote a screenplay for a movie based on *The Screwtape Letters*.

FACT

The Spirit clearly says that in later times some will abandon the faith and follow deceiving spirits and things taught by demons.
1 TIMOTHY 4:1

Philip Bliss is definitely a contender for the most famous Christian songwriter in history. He might have easily won the title had it not been for a tragic train derailment that took his life at the age of thirty-eight.

Bliss was born in a log cabin in the Pennsylvania mountains and introduced to faith early by participating in his family's daily prayers. As an awkward, barefoot, ten-year-old boy, he went into town one day to sell vegetables and heard music coming from a nearby home. Fascinated, he stumbled into the parlor where a young girl was playing the piano. She shooed him out, but the tones of the piano would be with him forever.

Songs of the Faith

"Hallelujah! What a Savior!"

Words and Music by Philip P. Bliss (1875)

At eleven years of age, Bliss left home to work in a lumber camp and made his first public profession of faith at the age of twelve. In time, he received his teaching credentials and began to teach music. A chance meeting with hymnwriter William B. Bradbury convinced him to focus on writing songs and hymns.

Bliss wrote the hymn, "Hallelujah! What a Savior!" shortly before he died. He sang it to great effect one night at the state prison in Jackson, Michigan, after preaching a sermon on the Man of Sorrows.

> *Man of Sorrows! what a name*
> *For the Son of God, who came*
> *Ruined sinners to reclaim.*
> *Hallelujah! What a Savior!*
>
> *When He comes, our glorious King,*
> *All His ransomed home to bring,*
> *Then anew His song we'll sing:*
> *Hallelujah! What a Savior!*

FACT

Bliss would often sing this hymn as a solo, asking the congregants to join him by shouting out the words when he reached the single phrase "Hallelujah! What a Savior!"

He was despised and rejected by men, a man of sorrows, and familiar with suffering.
ISAIAH 53:3

*B*lue laws, regulations dating back to early seventeenth-century Puritan colonies of New England, forbade the breaking of the Sabbath. Forbidden actions included missing church, drinking alcohol, quarreling, having sex, and flaunting flamboyant attire.

After the American Revolution, church-governed communities dissolved, and blue laws, while often still on the books, were rarely enforced. The emergence of the prohibition movement in the latter years of the nineteenth century, however, revived Sunday regulations similar to some of the blue laws. Restrictions varied by state, and sometimes by municipality, but they mainly targeted the Sunday sale

Miscellany

America's Blue Laws

of liquor and tobacco. The statutes also curtailed Sunday shopping and censored entertainment, such as plays, music, and films.

These "new blue laws" repeatedly escaped charges of the church dictating to the state because the laws did not imply the establishment of a national or state religion. Nonetheless, challengers continued to argue their case, most particularly concerning Sunday closure laws—state or district laws forbidding, or severely restricting, Sunday retail store hours.

Many conservative Christians believe the repeal of blue laws—especially Sunday shopping and alcohol sales—accounts for the: decline of church attendance; decrease in offerings; increased alcohol consumption, especially among the young; and upsurge in drug use. Irrefutable is the lack of a day of rest and reflection available to most Americans, a time free of the lures of the marketplace and the opportunity to earn (or spend) more money. The pace never stops. Not even on Sunday.

Tradition has it that blue laws were originally written on blue paper, hence the name. Lack of physical evidence, however, has raised the suspicions of historians, many of whom believe the term *blue* simply referred to the moral rigidity of adherents, as in *bluenose*, a prude.

FACT

[Jesus said,] "The Sabbath was made for man, not man for the Sabbath."
MARK 2:27

In late 1735, on board a ship bound for America, the young Anglican minister John Wesley and his fellow passengers encountered a fierce storm. Though he was chaplain of the vessel, Wesley feared for the lives of the passengers. As the ship tossed about on the ferocious waves, he noticed a group of German Moravians quietly singing hymns below deck. Impressed, Wesley asked the leader of the group about the nature of his calm serenity. The German replied, "Do you have faith in Christ?" Though Wesley replied that he did, he wondered if his words were spoken in vain.

This event served to strengthen Wesley as he believed the grace of Christ was issued on the practices (or disciplines) of prayer, scripture reading, meditation, Holy Communion, and charitable acts such as prison visitation, etc. These methods of "Christian Perfection" became known as Methodism and were the means by which the Christian believer became transformed.

Men of the Faith

John Wesley
(1703–1791)
Early Methodist leader

As Methodism continued to organize, Wesley remained in the Anglican church, and rallied his followers with these words: "Do all the good you can, by all the means you can, in all the ways you can, in all the places you can, at all the times you can, to all the people you can, as long as ever you can." Wesley joined George Whitefield, and together the two took Methodism to greater organization and prominence.

John Wesley's teachings also influenced the Holiness movement, from which came Pentecostalism and the Charismatic movement.

FACT John Wesley wrote, "The world is my parish."

Trust in the LORD, and do good; so shalt thou dwell in the land, and verily thou shalt be fed.
PSALM 37:3 KJV

Dorothy Day learned about poverty the hard way—she lived it. The Day family occupied a tenement flat in Chicago's notorious South Side for a time before John Day found work and the family relocated to more comfortable quarters. While most people gladly leave slums behind, Dorothy Day did not. She returned frequently.

As a young woman, Day moved to New York, where she worked as a reporter for a socialist newspaper and magazine. She periodically visited a Catholic church, attracted by its spiritual traditions and open door to the city's poor and dispossessed. Over the years, her interest—and her faith—grew. Despite the conflict between her leftist ideology and the Catholic faith, Day eventually joined the church.

Women of the Faith

Dorothy Day (1897–1980)
Founder of the Catholic Worker Movement

Meeting Peter Maurin, a Catholic who embraced a lifestyle of prayer, poverty, and service, proved a turning point in Day's life. He encouraged her to start a newspaper to promote social values for the transformation of society. Day did so, and the first issue of the *Catholic Worker* hit the streets on May 1, 1933. At once radical and religious, it fearlessly exposed social wrongs and called on readers to make things right.

Practicing what they were preaching, Maurin and Day sheltered homeless people in their apartments. Their efforts led to a series of rented houses for destitute men and women and a volunteer staff. By the mid-1930s, Catholic Worker houses had spread throughout the country.

Dorothy Day spent the rest of her life promoting social change, pacifism, and the cause of the poor and helpless.

Dorothy Day, accused of aiding bums and drunkards, wrote: "They live with us, they die with us, and we give them a Christian burial. We pray for them after they are dead. Once they are taken in, they become members of the family. Or rather they always were members of the family. They are our brothers and sisters in Christ."

FACT

[Jesus said,] "I was hungry and you gave me something to eat, I was thirsty and you gave me something to drink, I was a stranger and you invited me in."
MATTHEW 25:35

Megiddo is one of the most famous battlegrounds in the world, known both for its past battles and for its part in the decisive future battle between good and evil, as described in Revelation. *Armageddon* is a Greek derivation of the word *Har Megiddo*, which means Mount Megiddo.

War is nothing new to the city of Megiddo. Historians believe that more decisive battles have been fought at this international crossroad than anywhere else in the world. Assyrians, Canaanites, Egyptians, Greeks, Israelites, Persians, Philistines, and Romans all fought on this land, which has been continuously occupied for almost six thousand years. It was even the site of a critical World War I battle in 1918.

Between twenty-three and thirty different cities have been built, one on top of the other, on what has been referred to as the "cradle of archaeology of Israel." For more than a century, archaeological excavations have continued on this fifteen-acre plot of land. Archaeologists have uncovered massive palaces and temples, sophisticated water systems, and even a stable that could accommodate 450 horses.

Important Sites

Megiddo
Israel

In 2002, a monumental discovery was made not by an archaeologist, but by a convict. Ramil Razilo was removing rubble to build a new ward for the neighboring military prison when he uncovered an elaborate mosaic floor. A Greek inscription on the floor stated the site was consecrated to THE GOD JESUS CHRIST. This new discovery in Megiddo is believed to be a third-century Christian church, the oldest in the Holy Land.

FACT

A 229-foot-long tunnel dating back to the ninth century BC was found in Megiddo. It was cut out of rock below the city and led to a hidden spring outside the city walls. This allowed residents to get fresh water without leaving the safety of the city.

Then they gathered the kings together to the place that in Hebrew is called Armageddon.
REVELATION 16:16

In 1525 in Zurich, a small group gathered for a service of baptism. This ceremonial rite was not being performed for infants, but for men and women. Thus was born the Anabaptist movement. The term *Anabaptist*, originally a derogatory label, referred to the practice of "rebaptizing" those already baptized as infants. Baptism, they argued, should be available only to believing and consenting adults.

Inspired by reforms taking place within the church, the Anabaptists, also known as Radical Reformers, aimed to reform the reformers. They believed the Protestant reformers, even revolutionaries like Zwingli and Calvin, were not going far enough in their efforts to rehabilitate the church.

Along with the practice of infant baptism, the Anabaptists challenged other long-held Christian beliefs and traditions. Unlike the more moderate reform movements, Anabaptists discouraged the attainment of academic degrees and considered higher education a waste of time. They deemed any layman qualified to interpret scripture, and they established no church hierarchy. They refused to bear arms or swear an oath in court. Holding to a literal reading of the Bible, Anabaptists sought to recreate for themselves the simple social and economic systems they believed existed in apostolic times.

Groundbreaking Events

The Anabaptist Movement

Luther and other reformers dismissed the Anabaptists as unworthy of notice and made no attempt to include the group under the umbrella of the reform movement. They were marginalized, and in many instances, came under persecution from both Roman Catholic and Protestant authorities. As a result, many Anabaptist groups migrated to the Balkans, the Rhineland, and the Netherlands.

Today's Amish trace their religious ancestry directly to the Swiss Anabaptists of the sixteenth century. The Amish take their name from Jacob Amman, a Swiss-born Anabaptist who moved to Alsace, later becoming an elder and spokesman in the Swiss Mennonite Anabaptist community. Amman and his followers broke from the Mennonites to initiate reforms unacceptable to Mennonite leaders.

FACT

You were washed, you were sanctified, you were justified in the name of the Lord Jesus Christ and by the Spirit of our God.
1 CORINTHIANS 6:11

Brother Lawrence, a seventeenth-century Carmelite monk, yearned to live every moment of his day in the presence of God. He aspired to a habitual state of holy communion that would draw no distinction between times of work and times of prayer, times for chores and times for worship. During his lifetime, his reputation as a gifted mystic and spiritual counselor drew devoted students and followers. After the monk's death in 1691, one of his disciples collected his letters and transcriptions of conversations into the spiritual classic *The Practice of the Presence of God*.

The key to communion with God, Brother Lawrence proposed, rests in the faithful practice of spiritual discipline. In *The Practice of the Presence of God*, he describes three degrees of union of the soul with God (general, virtual, and actual) and outlines techniques to reach each level, including unceasing worship, setting one's mind on God at all times, and acceptance of whatever conditions and circumstances life brings.

Notable Books

The Practice of the Presence of God
By Brother Lawrence (c. 1691)

He spent his lifetime in a continual effort to get closer to God by attaining ever higher levels of perfection in thought and action. His stellar conduct, focused mind, and deepening knowledge of the divine, he believed, would assure him the communion he sought so earnestly. Despite the human effort required, Brother Lawrence humbly attributed to God any degree of progress he achieved.

Today, committed Christians recognize, as Brother Lawrence did, the link between religion of the heart and religion as it is lived out in the mundane activities of daily life. Christianity not practiced in the real world is, in essence, Christianity not practiced at all.

FACT

In his role as cook for his monastery, Brother Lawrence referred to himself as "the lord of pots and pans." His legacy of deep spiritual insight was acquired not from years of theological study, but from his willingness to practice the presence of God wherever he happened to be. And he happened to be in the kitchen.

So whether you eat or drink or whatever you do, do it all for the glory of God.
1 CORINTHIANS 10:31

J ohn Newton's devoutly religious mother died just before he turned seven years old. By age eleven, he'd joined his father's ship in hopes of becoming a seaman. He later served on other ships and bore the reputation of being quite rebellious and immoral. When he worked on the islands and mainland of West Africa, he witnessed the cruelty of slavery firsthand, and became the captain of his own slave ship, transporting slaves to America.

On March 10, 1748, after a close brush with death during a particularly stormy voyage back to England, John began reading a book by a Dutch monk, Thomas à Kempis, called *Imitation of Christ*. The book and his experience greatly influenced his eventual conversion to Christianity.

Songs of the Faith

"Amazing Grace"
Words by John Newton (1779)

Music by James P. Carrel and David S. Clayton (1831)

John studied for ministry and was ordained by the Anglican Church. He served as pastor near Cambridge, England, and held additional services in larger venues where people enthusiastically gathered to hear the story of his conversion.

John began writing hymns when he couldn't find enough simple and heartfelt congregational songs as opposed to the staid and more formal hymns of the Anglican Church. Through his hymn "Amazing Grace," he continues to share his testimony of God's grace in his life. Today, it is arguably the most popular hymn in the English language.

Amazing grace, how sweet the sound,
That saved a wretch like me!
I once was lost, but now am found,
Was blind but now I see.

The last stanza, which begins "When we've been there ten thousand years" was added by an unknown author and appeared as early as 1829.

FACT

"I was blind but now I see!"
JOHN 9:25

The history of Christianity teems with cults and sects obsessed with end-time events. In the 1930s, Seventh-Day Adventist Benjamin Boden gathered a group of followers and formed the Branch. They settled in Waco, Texas, living in a compound they named Mount Carmel. After Boden died, his wife, Lois, took over leadership. Among her flock was Vernon J. Howell, a handsome, charismatic young man who had joined the community in 1983.

Howell struggled for control of the group, which he eventually gained. He considered himself God's "seventh messenger" who would be instrumental in bringing on the Apocalypse. In 1990, he changed his name to David Koresh to highlight his place as heir to the throne of King David. His ability to preach for hours afforded him an aura of intelligence and inspiration. Koresh put his followers under strict rules of behavior that changed at his say-so (and didn't apply to him). He renamed the group the Branch Davidians and the compound Ranch Apocalypse.

Miscellany

David Koresh and the Branch Davidians

Over the years, charges involving possession of illegal weapons and rumors of polygamy and child abuse accumulated. On April 19, 1993, a standoff between the Davidians and federal agents climaxed in a horrific shoot-out and a spectacular fire that destroyed the compound. Four agents were killed, along with about eighty cult members, including Koresh.

Debate continues as to who started the fatal fire and how the entire tragedy could have been avoided. The incident brought to light the crucial role religious beliefs can play in understanding human motivation and behavior.

FACT

In an act of retribution for the government's actions at Waco, Timothy McVeigh detonated a truck of explosives outside the Alfred P. Murrah Federal Building in Oklahoma City, Oklahoma, on April 19, 1995. The blast killed or injured hundreds of workers, including children enrolled in an on-site daycare center.

[Jesus said,] "Watch out for false prophets. They come to you in sheep's clothing, but inwardly they are ferocious wolves."
MATTHEW 7:15

Charles Grandison Finney was born in New England into a nonreligious family, but began to attend a Presbyterian church and study scriptures as a young man. Upon experiencing a manifestation of the Holy Spirit in 1821, the former nonbeliever committed his life to Christ.

Finney, however, remained skeptical of some aspects of Calvinist doctrine, most particularly *passive salvation*, that is, salvation open only to those predestined to receive it. He believed God's love for all made salvation available to all. Therefore, Finney reasoned, each person chooses to accept or reject God's grace. Despite his non-Calvinist leanings, the Presbyterian Church ordained him.

As a preacher, Finney broke with church tradition. He enabled women to pray publicly with men. He held a series of church services on consecutive days, and employed colloquial idioms in his sermons. He prayed aloud for individuals by name, and he granted immediate church membership to new converts. Unheard of!

Men of the Faith

Charles G. Finney
(1792–1875)
Evangelist and author

Finney and his followers, dubbed New School Calvinists, faced a motion among conservative clergy to officially restrict or ban their activities. When the conservatives' efforts failed, Finney took revival meetings to major cities in America and Great Britain. The meetings, noted for their spiritual outpourings and mass conversions, drew huge audiences.

In 1835, Finney began his association with Ohio's Oberlin College and Theological Seminary, where he served as president from 1851–1866. He wrote several influential and widely read books, including *Autobiography of Charles G. Finney*; *Lectures on Revivals*; *Lectures of Professing Christians*; and *Systematic Theology*.

Charles G. Finney wrote, "Faith, from its very nature, purifies the heart."

FACT

Let us fix our eyes on Jesus, the author and perfecter of our faith.
HEBREWS 12:2

THE EMIGRANT'S FRIEND, reads the inscription on the headstone of Caroline Chisholm's grave in Northampton, England. The simple epitaph encapsulates a life rich in selfless service on behalf of aliens and strangers.

From an early age, Caroline participated in her evangelical parents' charitable activities. Her acceptance of Captain Archibald Chisholm's marriage proposal hinged on his support of her philanthropic work. Captain Chisholm, of the East India Company and a Roman Catholic, no doubt influenced his wife's subsequent conversion to Catholicism.

The Chisholms were posted to Madras (now Chennai), India, where Caroline Chisholm established a school for the daughters of European soldiers. During an extended leave, the couple sailed for Australia and settled in Windsor, New South Wales, where Caroline and their three sons remained after the Captain was recalled to service. Caroline found the government woefully negligent in helping immigrants find work in their new country.

Women of the Faith

Caroline Chisholm (1807–1877)

Reformer and philanthropist

Caroline matched newcomers with employers and provided unaccompanied girls with safe shelter. The governor initially rebuffed her proposal for a girls' home, but finally granted her permission to open a place where female immigrants could stay.

After Captain Chisholm's retirement, he worked alongside his wife to advance the cause of immigrants in Australia. Back in England, Caroline testified before two House of Lords committees in London on social reform initiatives. She wrote a number of influential reports and pamphlets and, along with her husband, handled an average of 140 letters a day concerning Australian affairs.

FACT

The Chisholms disdained financial reward and shunned public recognition for their charitable work, leading to their relative obscurity in both Australia and England. In their last years, they occupied humble lodgings in London. Both Caroline and her husband died in 1877 and were buried in the same grave at Northampton.

You are no longer foreigners and aliens, but fellow citizens with God's people and members of God's household.
EPHESIANS 2:19

On August 9, 1945, an atomic bomb forever linked the city of Nagasaki, Japan, with an image of death. Today, the city stands as a living memorial to the seventy-five thousand people who perished that day. But more than four hundred years earlier, death made a different kind of impact on the people of Nagasaki as twenty-six Christians bravely faced martyrdom for their faith.

In 1587, a ban was decreed on the Christian faith in Japan. As a warning to those who continued to preach the gospel, twenty-six Christian leaders were forced to take a thousand-mile journey from the towns of Kyoto, Osaka, and Sakai to Nagasaki. The men and boys (one as young as twelve) walked much of the distance barefoot through the snow. Twenty-six crosses awaited them on Nishizaka Hill. The martyrs continued to sing and preach God's Word as they were hung on the crosses with iron clasps and then executed with a lance.

Important Sites

Twenty-Six Martyrs Monument
Nagasaki, Japan

The martyrs' deaths had quite a different effect on Nagasaki's large Christian population than the Japanese rulers had hoped for. Christians began to turn more boldly toward Christ, instead of away from Him. In 1598, Christians began making pilgrimages to Nishizaka Hill.

In 1962, a wall of twenty-six life-sized bronze figures was built to commemorate the spot where the martyrs died. An adjacent museum gives visitors a visual history of Christianity in Japan, from its earliest roots through the executions of the twenty-six martyrs and the perseverance of the Christian underground through three hundred years of heavy persecution.

Every year from 1629 through 1857, residents of Nagasaki were forced to walk on *fumie*, bronze images of Christ, to prove that they were not Christians.

FACT

Precious in the sight of the LORD is the death of his saints.
PSALM 116:15

In 1525, reformer William Tyndale published the first-ever English language New Testament. Before he could make much headway on the Old Testament, however, he was imprisoned and martyred for his heretical activities. Tyndale's friend and follower, Miles Coverdale (also noted as "Cloverdale" in some references), took up the task of completing the monumental project.

Coverdale, less proficient in Hebrew than Tyndale, translated the Old Testament from the Latin Vulgate and Luther's German translation. He interspersed his work with parts of the Old Testament already completed by Tyndale, and, together with Tyndale's existing New Testament, Coverdale produced the first complete English language Bible. It was published in Zurich, Switzerland, on or around October 4, 1535.

Known as the Coverdale Bible, the translation never won popular acclaim at the time. Coverdale's often tender and melodious phrasing, however, has added a number of enduring poetic expressions to the English language. Many parts of the liturgy in church services today have been taken from Coverdale's translation. Coverdale's Psalms, particularly pleasing in tone, were incorporated into the Great Bible and are found in *The Book of Common Prayer*. Choral arrangements of the Psalms often use Coverdale's text.

Groundbreaking Events

The First Complete Bible Printed in English

Zurich, Switzerland

Parts of the Coverdale Bible were included in the next English translation, the Matthew-Tyndale Bible of 1537. Coverdale, along with others, worked on the Great Bible of 1539 and edited a revision of it in 1540. He contributed to the Geneva Bible of 1560 and published an English New Testament of his own. By some estimates, Coverdale contributed to, or took part in the production of, more editions of the Bible than anyone else in history.

FACT

The preface to the Coverdale Bible reads, "Go to now (most dear reader) and sit down at the Lord's feet and read his words, and, as Moses teaches the Jews, take them into your heart, and let your talking and communication be of them. . . . And above all things fashion your life and conversation according to the doctrine of the Holy Ghost therein."

The unfolding of your words gives light; it gives understanding to the simple.
PSALM 119:130

What does it mean to follow Christ? For Lutheran pastor Dietrich Bonhoeffer, it meant facing a firing squad rather than capitulating to the demands of Nazi Germany. His book, *The Cost of Discipleship*, poses the question to Christians who claim they want to commit themselves to discipleship.

First published in German in 1937 and in English in 1949, *The Cost of Discipleship* centers on Jesus' Sermon on the Mount (Matthew 5–7). Dietrich, a gifted theologian and Lutheran pastor, examines how Jesus' words translate into the everyday lives of ordinary people. He ponders what Jesus would tell present-day believers and what His will would be for modern Christians in their various walks in life.

Notable Books

The Cost of Discipleship
By Dietrich Bonhoeffer (1937)

Bonhoeffer draws a clear distinction between what he calls "cheap grace" and "costly grace." While the Bible clearly teaches that God's grace is free to everyone, it is not cheap. Cheap grace, says Bonhoeffer, comes from a shallow and sentimental understanding of Christianity. It requires nothing more than a willingness to bypass the dark facts of the human condition and bask in the sunshine of God's love. It is "grace without discipleship."

Costly grace, however, requires serious inquiry into the gospel message and a Christian's commitment to live it daily on an individual basis and within one's personal circumstances. It may cost one disciple the selfless gift of his time, another her effort, and another his money. It cost Bonhoeffer his physical life. Discipleship "is costly because it costs a man his life," Bonhoeffer wrote, "and it is grace because it gives a man the only true life."

In 2000, the film, *Bonhoeffer: An Agent of Grace* was released. Justus von Dohnanyi, who plays Eberhard Bethge, is a great-nephew of the real Dietrich Bonhoeffer, as well as the grandson of Hans von Dohnanyi (portrayed by Ulrich Noethen).

FACT

---

*[Jesus said,] "Anyone who does not carry his cross
and follow me cannot be my disciple."*
LUKE 14:27

Though blinded at six weeks of age through improper medical treatment, Fanny Crosby was never bitter about her condition. In 1844, at eight years of age, she wrote her first book of poetry entitled, *A Blind Girl and Other Poems.*

Before her death at age ninety-five, Crosby wrote more than eight thousand gospel songs. The words to one of her most beloved hymns, "Blessed Assurance," has been used in evangelical worship for the past century and is also inscribed on her headstone.

Crosby told the story about a gentleman she met while at a meeting in Exeter Hall, London, in 1890. He described a scene he witnessed during the recent war with Transvaal. When the soldiers going to the front would pass another group of soldiers they recognized, they would greet them with the statement, "Four-nine-four, boys; four-nine-four." The other group of soldiers would answer with the phrase, "Six further on, boys; six further on." It happened that small editions of the book *Sacred Songs and Solos* had been given to the troops. Number 494 was the hymn "God Be with You Till We Meet Again," and number 500 (six further on in the hymnal) was "Blessed Assurance."

Songs of the Faith

"Blessed Assurance"
Words by Fanny J. Crosby (1873)
Music by Phoebe P. Knapp (1873)

Blessed assurance, Jesus is mine;
Oh what a foretaste of glory divine!
Heir of salvation, purchased of God,
Born of His Spirit, washed in His blood,

Refrain:
This is my story, this is my song,
Praising my Savior, all the day long;
This is my story, this is my song,
Praising my Savior, all the day long.

FACT

"Blessed Assurance" was sung in the Academy Award–winning movies *Places in the Heart* (1984) and *Trip to Bountiful* (1985).

Let us draw near with a true heart in full assurance of faith, having our hearts sprinkled from an evil conscience, and our bodies washed with pure water.
HEBREWS 10:22 KJV

W hy don't more Americans attend church? Theories abound, not a few of them laying the blame right on the church doorstep. Outdated language, irrelevant liturgies, accusatory sermons, and dreary music conspire to keep people out of the pews on Sunday mornings.

The Willow Creek Community Church in suburban Chicago is recognized as the earliest of the seeker churches. Beginning with innovative worship events for teenagers in the mid-1970s, Willow Creek pursued the idea of offering creative, relevant, and engaging worship services for adults, all the while keeping the fundamental elements of a Bible-believing church.

Miscellany

Seeker Churches

Willow Creek's experiment caught on with progressive ministers and church leaders. More churches opened their doors to popular culture by incorporating contemporary music, multimedia presentations, humor, and nontraditional preaching styles into their worship services. The theory is that a relaxed, user-friendly, affirming experience will entice nonchurchgoers and the unchurched to file down the aisle and take a seat. In-depth Bible study can follow later.

Critics warn that the seekers' emphasis on satisfying human preference and felt needs overshadows the gospel and places the individual, rather than God, at the center of the service. But no one can deny that through the doors of these churches come individuals who would probably never hear the gospel otherwise.

Evangelist and author Rick Warren founded Saddleback Valley Community Church in Southern California, another early seeker church. Because he believed the needs of churchgoers were being met, he devoted his ministry to reaching the unchurched. Saddleback's first public service in 1980 drew 205 people, most of whom had never been to church.

FACT

"I love those who love me, and those who seek me find me."
PROVERBS 8:17

A well-intentioned relative advised the morose young man to get married. Another suggested he enlist in the army, and yet another thought a pinch of tobacco would do the trick.

Upon seeking pastoral guidance, George Fox inadvertently put his foot in his minister's flower bed and received a shower of verbal fire and brimstone. Fox looked to the Lord as a last resort.

Born in Leicestershire, England, to religious parents, Fox was disgusted by what he saw as the hypocrisy of clergymen who lived lives of luxury and overindulgence. He pursued the simple life of a shoemaker and had little formal education, yet he engaged educated men in religious discussions.

After personal Bible study convinced him of the Protestant church's dead ritualism, Fox took to the road as an itinerant preacher. His zealous spirit, powerful

Men of the Faith

George Fox
(1624–1691)
Reformer

oratory, and stark message of repentance struck fear and awe in his listeners. Many of them trembled, and scoffers labeled his growing band of followers Quakers. Quakers shunned clergy and ritual, believing every soul answered directly to God. They embraced the concepts of religious tolerance and the equality of all individuals before the law, and in doing so they became outlaws themselves.

Fox was jailed repeatedly for his iconoclastic views, and Quakers endured persecution until the Toleration Act of 1689 granted them some measure of freedom to practice their religion. When Fox died, however, his body was denied interment in consecrated ground. Instead, he lies in Bunhill Fields Burial Ground in London, a plot reserved for Dissenters and Quakers. His best-known book, *Fox's Journal*, was published three years after his death.

> **FACT**
>
> A man known for his sharp discernment of character, Fox compared human qualities to those attributed to animals. He believed he could read a person's temperament upon meeting, and would remark, "I see the spirit of a cunning fox in you," or, "Thou art as vicious as a tiger."

Speak to one another with psalms, hymns and spiritual songs.
Sing and make music in your heart to the Lord.
EPHESIANS 5:19

As a six-year-old, she announced she could see guardian angels hovering over people walking down the street. Young Catherine's spiritual visions, self-imposed austerities, and devotion to Christ led her to join the Dominican Tertiaries as a teenager. As a third-order Dominican, she lived at home and occupied a small room where she spent long hours in prayer and in conversations with Christ.

Catherine devoted herself to the care of the sick and worked tirelessly for the conversion of sinners. She became known for her radiant happiness despite her own ill health. Townspeople sought her out for her spiritual insight, as well as for her practical skills. Catherine attracted a diverse following—nobles, commoners, religious, secular, men, women—which she called her "family," or the *Caterinati*.

Ongoing violence between regions of Italy burdened her heart. In 1375, she sent letters to Pope Gregory XI, begging him to leave Avignon and return to Rome for the sake of protecting and unifying Christendom against the infidels, and to bring peace to Italy. Gregory returned to Rome, but died shortly thereafter. Successor Urban VI's claim was hotly contested by a rival pope. Urban requested Catherine's presence in Rome, where she enthusiastically sent out volumes of letters to churchmen and civil leaders on behalf of Urban.

Women of the Faith

Catherine of Siena (1347–1380)

Christian mystic and doctor of the church

Catherine's health deteriorated further under the pressure of her work with the afflicted and destitute of Rome and her vigorous efforts to bring peace and reform to the church. After a three-month period of suffering from an agonizing but unnamed illness, Catherine died in Rome in 1380.

> The letters and essays of Catherine of Siena are considered classics of the Italian language. She wrote in the Tuscan vernacular of her time. Her *Dialogue*, or *Treatise on Divine Providence*, consists of mystical conversations between the Eternal Father and the human soul. In addition, she authored a series of prayers and a collection of nearly four hundred letters.

FACT

"Blessed are the peacemakers, for they will be called sons of God."
MATTHEW 5:9

It's just a large hunk of rock. But for Christians, Jews, Muslims, and even ancient Semites, this stone on the peak of Mount Moriah marks a place of great importance. For Muslims, it marks where their prophet, Muhammad, supposedly pushed off of Earth and headed toward heaven. For Christians and Jews, it's revered as the place where Abraham raised his knife to sacrifice his son, where Jacob dreamed of angels ascending a golden ladder, and where Solomon built the temple of Jerusalem in the tenth century BC.

However, since the destruction of Solomon's temple in 586 BC, this rock has truly been a stone of contention. After the temple was rebuilt and destroyed once more, the site has been home to a temple for a Roman god, a Christian shrine constructed by Constantine, and then a garbage dump. When Jerusalem came under Persian rule in 638, a domed Muslim shrine gilded in gold was built on the "temple mount." During the Crusades, the dome was converted into the Temple of Our Lord, replacing the crowning Muslim crescent with a gold cross.

Important Sites

The Temple Mount
Jerusalem

In 1187, the area once again came under Muslim control. The Dome of the Rock was refurbished to rival the glory of the nearby Church of the Holy Sepulchre. Until the mid-nineteenth century, non-Muslims were barred from entering the shrine. But today, the "temple mount" is open to everyone. The 56- x 42-foot rock lies unobstructed beneath the dome, surrounded by arches built from the ruins of Jerusalem churches destroyed by the early Persians.

FACT

Ancient Semites believed this rock was where the underworld intersected with the world of the living. Beneath the stone lies the cave-like Well of Souls, where according to folklore, one could hear the whispers of the dead.

[Solomon said,] "But will God really dwell on earth? The heavens,
even the highest heaven, cannot contain you.
How much less this temple I have built!"
1 Kings 8:27

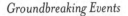

W hat makes it great? In this case, its size. While the Great Bible measured around fourteen inches tall by eleven inches wide—not extraordinary to anyone accustomed to glossy coffee-table books—its bulk was singular at the time and begged its descriptive name.

King Henry VIII, upon breaking with the Roman Catholic Church over his divorce and remarriage, proclaimed himself head of the Church of England. Not wanting to adopt any of the existing translations, he had a new version made to order in 1539. The Archbishop of Canterbury, Thomas Cranmer, hired translator Miles Coverdale to oversee the effort. The complete work—printed on fine parchment and beautifully illustrated throughout—became known as the Great Bible and was the first English Bible authorized for public use. A copy was distributed to every parish church and chained to the pulpit to prevent any chance of the Good Book sprouting legs and disappearing. Over the years, however, many disappeared, because only two copies are known to exist today.

Groundbreaking Events

The Printing of the Great Bible
England

By royal decree, each congregation appointed a reader so that illiterate Englishmen could hear the Bible in their spoken tongue. By all accounts, the Great Bible was well received by the clergy and warmly welcomed by a populace eager to hear and discuss the Word for itself. The Great Bible, a competent translation and adequate for teaching, marked a pause in the flurry of new and improved Bible translations.

Less than a decade later, Henry turned against Protestantism. He issued a proclamation banning the often impolite notes and commentaries of earlier versions. His death in 1547 halted further prohibitions, and his successor, Edward VI, lifted the ban. New editions of previous Bibles flourished once again in England.

The richly illustrated title page of the Great Bible shows Henry VIII handing out Bibles to clerics and laymen alike. The picture's message: The Pope in Rome had no authority over the church in England. The king now reigned supreme over matters of church and state and was solely in charge of distributing the Word of God.

FACT

Like newborn babies, crave pure spiritual milk,
so that by it you may grow up in your salvation,
now that you have tasted that the Lord is good.
1 PETER 2:2–3

Decades ago, most people filling the pews of mainline Christian churches knew little about cults. But when their sons, daughters, and friends started drifting away from the faith of their childhood to follow mysterious spiritual paths, interest perked up. Parents and pastors alike, alarmed at the rapid growth of cults in the United States and worldwide, started asking why and looking for answers.

Theologian Walter Martin published *The Kingdom of the Cults* in 1965, and the book has been reprinted and updated many times since. Now a classic of Christian apologetics, *The Kingdom of the Cults* explores the beliefs of active, proselytizing cults. Martin reviews, in unbiased statements of fact, the teachings of various cults based on their published creeds and documents. He then compares and contrasts their claims with what the Bible teaches. His well-researched and readable book describes the differences between contemporary cults (including those that describe themselves as Christian). Martin offers readers a method for determining whether or not a particular group should be regarded as a cult according to the Bible's teachings and Christian orthodoxy. In addition, he includes sections on related topics, such as mind control, end-times theology, psychological manipulation, and the lure of Eastern philosophies.

Notable Books

The Kingdom of the Cults
By Walter Martin (1965)

The Kingdom of the Cults provides concerned Christians with information and background they need to reach out to those who are embroiled in cult culture. As a tool for anyone curious about cults or wondering how his or her own beliefs compare to the clear teachings of the Bible, this book remains an invaluable resource.

FACT

As might be expected, the book's conclusions have riled some groups described as cults, and have startled some members of cults who were unaware of their group's deviation from Christian doctrine. Later editions of *The Kingdom of the Cults* include refutations, though none fault the accuracy of Martin's reporting.

I tell you this so that no one may deceive you by fine-sounding arguments.
COLOSSIANS 2:4

Preacher, poet, hymnist, scholar—Reginald Heber wore a variety of hats, and wore each one well. Born to a wealthy family in Cheshire, England, he distinguished himself as a gifted student. After completing his academic education and receiving his ordination, Heber was appointed rector at an Anglican parish in Shropshire, where he was admired and respected for his service, compassion, and generosity. Later, he lectured at Oxford, then served as Missionary Bishop of Calcutta (now Kolkata), India.

Heber regularly wrote poems, sermons, and hymns. The hymns often pertained to a specific time of year in the liturgical calendar. "Holy, Holy, Holy," for example, was written for Trinity Sunday. He attempted to secure official authorization to use his hymns in the church, but the Bishop of London withheld permission. Heber saw a few hymns printed in the *Christian Observer*, but most of his work was published after his death under the title *Hymns Written and Adapted to the Weekly Church Service of the Year* (1827). His hymns became Christian favorites, including "From Greenland's Icy Mountains," "Brightest and Best of the Sons of the Morning," and "The Son of God Goes Forth to War."

Songs of the Faith

"Holy, Holy, Holy"
Words by Reginald Heber (1826)
Music by John B. Dykes (1861)

In 1861, John B. Dykes, a musician and composer, wrote the tune "Nicaea" for Heber's "Holy, Holy, Holy." Dykes chose the tune's name because Heber's text so clearly proclaims the Trinity, a doctrine articulated at the Council of Nicaea in 325.

Holy, holy, holy, Lord God Almighty!
Early in the morning our song shall rise to Thee;
Holy, holy, holy! merciful and mighty!
God in three Persons, blessed Trinity!

"Holy, holy, holy is the Lord God Almighty,
who was, and is, and is to come."
REVELATION 4:8

Francis of Assisi, the robed figure you see standing in your neighbor's garden with a bird on his shoulder, enjoys nearly universal admiration. Catholics and non-Catholics alike embrace the beloved thirteenth-century monk-made-saint as a gentle spirit who cherished God's creatures great and small.

It's only appropriate that the Blessing of Pets would be held in conjunction with St. Francis's feast day. On or near October 4, priests and ministers of various denominations across the United States conduct the ceremonies. The Blessing of Pets begins with a procession of animals—Fido and Fluffy, of course, and also horses, hamsters, iguanas, and fish (the latter needing some assistance with the walking requirement). Then the celebrant leads a liturgy during which each pet's able companion brings the animal forward for a blessing. The ritual celebrates the special bond between humans and animals, and recognizes animals' service and usefulness to humans.

Miscellany

Holy Cow!

The blessing of animals, however, probably didn't originate with St. Francis. Olvera Street in Los Angeles, for example, honors the tradition of San Antonio de Abad (St. Anthony of the Desert), a third-century hermit said to have blessed animals. In past days, Catholics brought animals into church on St. Anthony's feast day for a blessing to ensure fertility. Olvera Street celebrates the Blessing of Pets on the Saturday before Easter, when a parade of animals passes a platform where a church dignitary stands. A cow leads the procession, an honor accorded her because of all she gives to humanity. Each creature receives a blessing as it goes by.

FACT

The following is the Franciscan Blessing of Pets: "*Blessed are you, Lord God, maker of all living creatures. You called forth fish in the sea, birds in the air and animals on the land. You inspired St. Francis to call all of them his brothers and sisters. We ask you to bless this pet. By the power of your love, enable it to live according to your plan. May we always praise you for all your beauty in creation. Blessed are you, Lord our God, in all your creatures! Amen.*"

Your righteousness is like the mighty mountains, your justice like the great deep. O LORD, you preserve both man and beast.
PSALM 36:6

Bound to the stake with wood and straw heaped around him, the condemned reformer John Hus cried out, "In 100 years, God will raise up a man whose calls for reform cannot be suppressed." One hundred and two years later, Martin Luther ushered in the Protestant Reformation when he nailed his *Ninety-Five Theses* to the church door at Wittenberg.

Born in Bohemia (now part of the Czech Republic), John Hus studied theology in Prague and was ordained to the priesthood in 1400. He embraced reformer John Wycliffe's teachings, and began preaching against abuses in the church. Hus challenged the practice of distributing only bread during communion. He believed the Bible should be available in the vernacular for all to read. Hus's criticism of church officials who meddled in state affairs earned him

Men of Faith

John Hus (Jan Huss) (1369–1415)

Reformer and martyr

the ire of the archbishop, who excommunicated him in 1412. He acquired more enemies when he railed against the sale of indulgences to finance a fight between two claimants to the papacy.

In 1414, Hus was brought before the Council of Constance and accused of teaching heresy. Hus denied ever teaching false doctrine (his criticisms pertained to church practice, not theology). Nonetheless, the council declared him guilty and sentenced him to burn at the stake. During the burning on July 6, 1415, his executioners used pages torn from Wycliffe Bibles to fan the flames.

Followers of John Hus later became known as Moravians. In the mid-eighteenth century, Moravians settled in Pennsylvania, New Jersey, and South Carolina. Today, the Moravian Church is active in sixteen U.S. states and in two provinces of Canada.

John Hus said, "*O God and Lord, now the council condemns even thine own act and thine own law as heresy, since thou thyself didst lay thy cause before thy Father as the just judge, as an example for us, whenever we are sorely oppressed.*"

FACT

[Jesus said,] "Blessed are you when people insult you, persecute you and falsely say all kinds of evil against you because of me. Rejoice and be glad, because great is your reward in heaven."
MATTHEW 5:11–12

Christian missionary Pothinus brought Christianity to Gaul (modern-day France) in the middle of the second century. He established churches in Lyons and nearby Viennes.

As Christianity took hold in the area, especially among immigrants from Asia Minor, fear and suspicion spread among the pagan populace. Citizens shunned and ridiculed their Christian neighbors. Officials arrested them at will. Upon refusal to denounce their faith, Christians were imprisoned and tortured.

In the summer of AD 177, persecutions intensified as rumors of obscene Christian practices, such as incest and cannibalism, ignited public rage. At the same time, the Roman governor, who was expected to throw a public party in honor of Emperor Marcus Aurelius, arrived in the city. Big shindigs can cost a bundle, then as now. The budget-conscious governor figured: Why pay good money to professional gladiators and wrestlers when you can bring on the Christians and torture them for free? So that's what he did.

Women of the Faith

Blandina (b. unknown—d. 177)

Slave and Christian martyr

Among the selected "entertainers" was Blandina, a young slave girl. Throughout horrific tortures, she would declare only, "I am a Christian, and we do nothing vile." For the grand finale, her captors tossed Blandina and a band of Christian cohorts into the city's amphitheater where wild beasts were posed to tear them apart. Blandina exhorted her fellow prisoners to remain faithful, astonishing even the pagan onlookers with her loyalty to Jesus Christ.

Blandina, the last to die, was gored and trampled by a bull. A marker in the ancient amphitheater commemorates Blandina's death and the deaths of the Christians martyred with her.

> FACT
>
> The bodies of all martyrs were left exposed and guarded by soldiers for six days, then burned to ashes and strewn in the Rhône River. By doing so, the pagans believed they blocked any chance of resurrection for the Christians.

God chose the foolish things of the world to shame the wise;
God chose the weak things of the world to shame the strong.
1 CORINTHIANS 1:27

In 1791, President George Washington commissioned Major Pierre L'Enfant to design an architectural plan for the new capital city of the United States. That original plan included a "national house of prayer." Almost two hundred years later, the Cathedral Church of St. Peter and St. Paul (more commonly known as the National Cathedral) was finally complete.

The National Cathedral was the longest-running construction project in the history of Washington, D.C. Eighty-three years to the day after the first foundation stone was laid, the final touches on the west towers were finished. The west towers are adorned with 288 angels—and Darth Vader. In keeping with the tradition of Gothic architecture, *grotesques* were included in the cathedral's design. Unlike gargoyles—of which the National Cathedral has 110—grotesques are not waterspouts, but are similar in design. The National Cathedral held a contest for children to design four grotesques, and one of the winning drawings was the villain from Star Wars. With the help of binoculars, Vader's visage can be seen high on the northwest tower.

Important Sites

The National Cathedral

Washington, D.C.

Though its impressive architecture makes the National Cathedral noteworthy, what makes it an important site is its unique place in history. It's where leaders gather to pray during times of national crisis, such as after 9/11; to celebrate national victories, such as the end of the Iranian hostage crisis; and to mourn the passing of great Americans, such as Martin Luther King Jr., whose funeral was held at the National Cathedral only five days after he preached his final sermon there.

The cornerstone for the National Cathedral came from an open field near Bethlehem. It was inset into a larger piece of American granite and inscribed with the words of John 1:14 (KJV): THE WORD WAS MADE FLESH, AND DWELT AMONG US.

FACT

If my people, who are called by my name, will humble themselves
and pray and seek my face and turn from their wicked ways,
then will I hear from heaven and will forgive their sin and will heal their land.
2 CHRONICLES 7:14

The Council of Trent was the Roman Catholic answer to the Protestant Reformation. Convened in Trent in northern Italy, multiple council sessions spanned eighteen years—1545 to 1563. It arose chiefly to precisely define and explain crucial doctrines of the Roman Catholic Church. Decisions and decrees promulgated by the council determined Roman Catholic belief and practice until the Second Vatican Council of the mid-twentieth century.

Persuasive claims of the Reformation made it imperative for bishops to enunciate Roman Catholic theology and answer the charges leveled against it by the reformers. Foremost among those charges concerned the authority of church tradition versus scripture. The council reaffirmed the authority of church tradition along with scripture, in sharp contrast to the reformers' insistence on scripture alone.

In addition, glaring abuses within the church needed attention. The council took disciplinary action against unfit clergy and closed some of the older religious orders that had fallen into corruption. To protect the beliefs and morals of people with access to newly printed books, tracts, and pamphlets penned by reformist authors, the council drafted an index of prohibited books. Its emphasis on correct doctrine and sound teaching gave momentum to the newly formed Jesuit order, whose principle mission lay in religious education.

Groundbreaking Events

The Council of Trent

While the council didn't succeed in halting the progress of the Protestant Reformation, it greatly strengthened the Roman Catholic Church. The council clearly defined the church's doctrine and practice and cleaned up flagrant abuses within, providing for an organization better equipped to lead, teach, and strengthen the faithful.

FACT

The council was convened under Paul III, but closed by his successor, Pius IV. The forward-thinking Pius overcame multiple political hurdles to reform the papal court, reverse the excesses of the Inquisition, and bring the disorganized council to a productive conclusion.

You, dear friends, build yourselves up in your most
holy faith and pray in the Holy Spirit.
JUDE 20

I f it's true for you, then it's true." The popular put-down may stun Christians who have heard Jesus' claim, "I am. . . the truth" (John 14:6).

Francis A. Schaeffer, celebrated author and founder of L'Abri Fellowship in Switzerland, examines the hold of subjective truth in *The God Who Is There*. In his book, Schaeffer describes how subjective thinking, prevalent throughout contemporary culture, makes the existence of absolute truth an impossibility. Therefore, the gospel of Jesus Christ, which claims to be the one and only truth, cannot be true.

When *The God Who Is There* was first published in 1968, few ordinary Christians were aware of the gradual chipping away of the concept of truth going on in Western intellectual circles. Today, most everyone has heard the term *postmodernism* and the voices of adherents who assert that "all truth is relative."

Notable Books

The God Who Is There
By Francis A. Schaeffer (1968)

The God Who Is There upholds the truth of the gospel message and equips readers with the knowledge needed to intelligently engage contemporary culture in a conversation about the gospel's claims. Prophetically, Schaeffer shows how public communicators and social leaders use words to hide, complicate, and manipulate reality to their own ends. In addition, he points to the dehumanization that results from the absence of a concept of universal truth, a result manifestly evident in society today. Destructive individuality and degradation of the dignity of life stem from a simple, smug thought: "I'll decide if it's true, thank you very much." Schaeffer calls for a return to the absolute truth of the God who is there.

Francis A. Schaeffer wrote, "We not only believe in the existence of truth, but we believe we have the truth."

FACT

Jesus answered, "I am the way and the truth and the life.
No one comes to the Father except through me."
JOHN 14:6

While staying in New York in the spring of 1905, Civilla Martin and her husband met and became good friends with a Christian couple, the Dolittles. Mr. Dolittle was crippled and used a wheelchair to get him to and from his business, and Mrs. Dolittle had been ill and bedridden for almost twenty years. During one of their visits with the couple, Civilla's husband commented on the couple's obvious optimism and happiness despite physical circumstances.

Mrs. Dolittle quickly responded, "His eye is on the sparrow, and I know He watches me." Her expression inspired Civilla Martin to verse the hymn that is still so popular today.

Songs of the Faith

"His Eye Is on the Sparrow"

Words by Civilla D. Martin (1905)
Music by Charles Gabriel (1905)

Many associate the song with the African-American blues singer and actress Ethel Waters, who so loved this song that she used its title for her autobiography. In 1957, she sang this song as a solo while attending a Billy Graham crusade in Madison Square Garden. She says the experience changed her life forever.

Why should I feel discouraged, why should the shadows come,
Why should my heart be lonely, and long for heaven and home
When Jesus is my portion? My constant friend is He:
His eye is on the sparrow, and I know He watches me;
His eye is on the sparrow, and I know He watches me.

Refrain:
I sing because I'm happy,
I sing because I'm free,
For His eye is on the sparrow,
And I know He watches me.

FACT

Ethel Waters sang "His Eye Is on the Sparrow" five more times during the final weeks of the 1957 Billy Graham crusade, and she returned each year to sing the song, making it one of the hallmarks of Billy Graham's crusades.

[Jesus said,] "Are not two sparrows sold for a penny? Yet not one of them will fall to the ground apart from the will of your Father. And even the very hairs of your head are all numbered. So don't be afraid; you are worth more than many sparrows."
MATTHEW 10:29–31

In the Loss of Your Beloved Companion," the greeting card reads. Though your significant other is still alive and kicking, your cherished pooch has gone to the great chow bowl in the sky. Your friends commiserate with you in your grief.

In the not-too-distant past, marking the loss of a pet with rituals reserved for human death was virtually unheard of. Now cards, memorial gardens, and even pet chaplains help humans mourn the loss of their furred and feathered companions.

Pet chaplains, most often working with veterinarians, recognize the spiritual aspect of bonds broken by the death of a beloved pet. In many households, a pet has been a companion for ten or twenty years—or longer. Such a pet is considered part of the family and is deeply mourned. Pet chaplains pray for and bless sick and dying animals, some even administering last rites and other rituals for the dying. The chaplains comfort the pet's human caregivers, even standing with them when surgery or euthanasia is performed. Upon the death of the pet, chaplains work with the bereaved by conducting a respectful and meaningful memorial service and burial.

Miscellany

Pet Chaplains

Do animals go to heaven? The Bible offers no definitive answer, yet many Bible interpreters find reason to say yes. They cite Isaiah 65:25, which refers to God's kingdom as a place where wolf, lamb, and lion live together in peace. Also, heaven's description as a place of great happiness certainly *must* include animals!

While the concept of pet ministry has arisen fairly recently, sacred texts from the world over acknowledge a relationship between humans and animals and the duty of humans to care for animals. Indeed, in the biblical story of creation, God gives Adam stewardship over all the creatures of land, sea, and sky, a responsibility of humankind to this day.

A righteous man cares for the needs of his animal.
PROVERBS 12:10

By the second century, Christianity had spread throughout Asia Minor and Europe. The thrill of expansion, however, was matched by the turmoil caused by conflicting customs, interests, and interpretation of scripture. Irenaeus, learned priest and prominent theologian, distinguished himself as a mediator in disputes between the Eastern and Western churches. He served as Bishop of Lyons after the martyrdom of St. Pothinus, and he devoted himself to his priestly duties and to writing. Today, Irenaeus is revered for his writings.

In a five-book treatise, *Detection and Overthrow of the False Knowledge*, Irenaeus argued against gnosticism, a popular heresy. Gnostics claimed they possessed secrets passed on by Jesus to a select few, namely themselves. Irenaeus pointed out that the current bishops of various cities had studied under people who had followed Jesus' disciples, and not one of whom ever boasted having received any "secret knowledge" from the Lord. In forming his argument, Irenaeus summarized the assertions of gnosticism and other heresies, leaving later researchers a wealth of information about doctrine and heresies in the early church.

Men of the Faith

Irenaeus (c. 130–c. 202)
Bishop, theologian, and writer

The depth of Irenaeus's faith and the scope of his learning are evident in his treatise, *Proof of the Apostolic Preaching*. In this work, he confirms Christian doctrine on the basis of Old Testament prophecies that illustrate the truth of the gospel. Irenaeus's other writings include letters and homilies.

The thoughtful and scholarly writings of Irenaeus have earned him his place as the first great theologian of the Church.

FACT

Irenaeus's writings, along with those of Clement of Alexandria and Tertullian of Carthage, reveal that all but one of the twenty-seven canonical books of the New Testament were known and read in the Christian church, the exception being the Second Letter of Peter.

I write these things to you who believe in the name of the Son of God so that you may know that you have eternal life.
1 JOHN 5:13

From humble beginnings in South Carolina, the daughter of former slaves rose to become a nationally recognized figure in the American civil rights movement.

A gifted student, Mary McLeod received a scholarship to attend Moody Bible Institute in Chicago with the intention of serving as a missionary in Africa. She applied, only to discover that there were "no openings for Negro Missionaries in Africa." After a year of study at Moody, she returned to the South and commenced her career as an educator. There she met and married Albertus Bethune.

Mary McLeod Bethune honed her teaching skills under the tutelage of gifted mentors. Her missionary spirit undaunted, she visited jails, sawmills, and clubs, bringing the gospel wherever young people gathered. She opened a small school for African American girls in Daytona Beach, Florida, in 1904. Her organizational skills and fund-raising ability enabled her to add a high school, then later a junior college. The institution Bethune established became the coeducational Bethune-Cookman College (now University).

Women of the Faith

Mary McLeod Bethune
(1875–1955)

Educator and civil rights leader

Bethune inspired African Americans across the country as she worked with the National Council of Negro Women and Franklin Roosevelt's National Youth Administration to end racial discrimination. She served as president of the National Association of Colored Women, representing the African-American community in conferences on education, child welfare, and home ownership. Several presidents summoned Bethune to serve as advisor on minority affairs. These and many other distinguished positions of national and international note fill an impressive résumé of lifelong achievement.

Mary McLeod Bethune is buried on the campus of Bethune-Cookman University.

The Mary McLeod Bethune Council House in Washington, D.C., is a registered historic site. Her last home in Washington, it served as headquarters of the National Council of Negro Women. Bethune and members of the council met there to plan and develop programs to increase opportunities available to African-American women.

FACT

Teach me your way, O LORD; lead me in a straight path because of my oppressors.
PSALM 27:11

A popular lunch spot in London is a designated public "open space" filled with beautiful gardens. It's half park and half fence-enclosed cemetery. Though first used as a graveyard in Saxon times, in the 1600s this area of London was set aside as a cemetery for victims of the plague, because there wasn't enough room for all of the bodies in church cemeteries.

For members of the Church of England, being buried in the "consecrated ground" of a churchyard was important. For those outside the Anglican Church, their final resting place was inconsequential. What mattered was they were heaven-bound. So, in the seventeenth century, Bunhill Fields was adopted as a burial place for anyone who practiced religion outside of the Church of England.

Referred to as Dissenters or Nonconformists, Protestants such as John Bunyan (author of *The Pilgrim's Progress*), Isaac Watts (author of more than seven

Important Sites

Bunhill Fields

London

hundred hymns), John Owens (minister and theologian), and Susannah Wesley (mother of nineteen children, including evangelists Charles and John Wesley), can be counted among the well-known Christians buried here. According to local legend, John Wesley's Chapel, which is across the street from Bunhill Fields, was built to align with Susannah Wesley's grave, so John could always see his mother.

Damaged during the air raids of World War II, Bunhill Fields underwent extensive reconstruction in 1960. Today, visitors can visit 2,333 monuments and 1,920 headstones spread out over the ten-acre site. But those memorials only bear witness to a few of the more than 120,000 people buried here.

FACT

Bunhill Fields was originally known as Bone Hill Fields. Cartloads of bones were deposited here to make more room in the cemetery surrounding St. Peter's Cathedral. A thin layer of soil was placed over the bones, creating a "hill."

[Jesus said,] "Don't be so surprised! Indeed,
the time is coming when all the dead in their graves
will hear the voice of God's Son, and they will rise again."
JOHN 5:28–29 NLT

Readers of the Good Book have Stephen Langton and Robert Estienne to thank for numbered chapters and verses. Langton, an early thirteenth-century Archbishop of Canterbury, devised the chapter divisions first used in the Wycliffe English Bible of 1382 and still in use today. Estienne, also known as Stephanus, divided chapters of New Testament books into verses in 1555. As for Old Testament books, Stephanus generally went along with the system devised in 1448 by a Jewish rabbi, Nathan. The Geneva Bible of 1560 became the first complete English language Bible to print numbered chapters and verses.

But why "Geneva"? When staunchly Roman Catholic Mary Tudor ascended the throne of England in 1553, the persecution of Protestants resumed. Hundreds of English clergymen and scholars settled in Geneva under the protection of Genevan civil authorities. These reformers used their time in exile to produce a Bible in English, free of either Church of England or Roman censure.

Groundbreaking Events

In addition to numbered chapters and verses, the Geneva Bible includes numerous marginal notes and commentaries. Penned by John Calvin, John Knox, and Miles Coverdale, among others, text notes fill

The Geneva Bible

almost a third of the book. The notes, intended to help general readers grasp biblical truths, ran afoul of the powers that be at the time. Some notes editorialized strongly against corrupt governments.

The Geneva Bible won instant acceptance among the populace. If a bestseller list had existed at the time, the Geneva Bible would have topped the list in England, Scotland, and Ireland for the next half century.

The Geneva Bible is known among book collectors as the "breeches Bible." The nickname comes from the words of Genesis 3:7, which state that Adam and Eve sewed fig leaves together and clothed themselves in "breeches."

FACT

The Lord announced the word,
and great was the company of those who proclaimed it.
PSALM 68:11

Apologetics—the defense of the Christian faith against the assertions of empirical reasoning and scientific claims— offers informed, fact-based analyses of the Christian religion and the essential teachings of the faith. C. S. Lewis, a brilliant academic and one-time atheist, was particularly qualified to articulately address issues of belief and unbelief, and he did so with power and authority in his seminal book, *Mere Christianity*.

Mere Christianity tackles questions and objections, many involving complex spiritual concepts, that unbelievers pose to the Christian faith. He explores common reasons why unbelievers object to Christian doctrine, controversies that divide Christians from one another, and some of the stumbling blocks to faith, such as the mysteries of Holy Communion and the Triune God. Lewis presents rational arguments for the reality of the God of the Bible, and from there examines Christian beliefs in a logical, clear, and accessible way. Rather than hammering his points home with dogmatic statements, Lewis offers his reasoning in a conversational manner that invites unbelievers to simply consider the idea that the tenets of the Christian faith could be true.

Notable Books

Mere Christianity
By C. S. Lewis (1952)

As Lewis completed the essays that eventually were collected in *Mere Christianity*, he sent them for review and comments to Roman Catholic, Presbyterian, Methodist, and Church of England theologians. The scholars agreed on Lewis's chief points and propositions about the Christian faith. *Mere Christianity* was enthusiastically received at its debut in 1952, and continues to this day to engage and influence Christians and non-Christians alike.

FACT

Mere Christianity is a compilation of essays Lewis read over the radio in 1943. His popular lectures addressed issues and questions around the Christian religion, most particularly those arising from scientific inquiry. Lewis first published the material in three books, which were subsequently combined into one book.

Always be prepared to give an answer to everyone who asks you to give the reason for the hope that you have. But do this with gentleness and respect.
1 PETER 3:15

On his deathbed, D. L. Moody said to friend Will Thompson, "I would rather have written 'Softly and tenderly, Jesus is calling' than anything I have been able to do in my whole life."

Thompson, called the Bard of Ohio, studied music in the United States and in Europe. When publishers rejected his compositions, he established Will L. Thompson & Company, where he happily accepted his own manuscripts. He was a prolific poet, lyricist, and composer known for numerous hymns, including "Jesus Is All the World to Me."

Songs of the Faith

"Softly and Tenderly (Jesus Is Calling)"
Words and Music
by Will L. Thompson (1880)

"Softly and Tenderly" was sung at the memorial service for Martin Luther King Jr. in 1968 and was included in Johnny Cash's *Precious Memories* album released in 1975. It was also sung in the Academy Award–winning movie *Trip to Bountiful* (1985). It appears in church hymnals today and remains for many an all-time favorite.

Softly and tenderly Jesus is calling,
Calling for you and for me;
See, on the portals He's waiting and watching,
Watching for you and for me.

Why should we tarry when Jesus is pleading,
Pleading for you and for me?
Why should we linger and heed not His mercies,
Mercies for you and for me?

Refrain:
Come home, come home,
You who are weary, come home;
Earnestly, tenderly, Jesus is calling,
Calling, O sinner, come home!

Will L. Thompson said, "No matter where I am, at home or hotel, at the store or traveling, if an idea or theme comes to me that I deem worthy of a song, I jot it down in verse. In this way I never lose it."

FACT

[Jesus said,] "Here I am! I stand at the door and knock. If anyone hears my voice and opens the door, I will come in and eat with him, and he with me."
REVELATION 3:20

Rural pastors may recall the days of tithes paid in eggs and sausage, and elderly parishioners might still prefer to drop cash instead of a check into the collection plate. Of course, that's changed over the years. Now, most churchgoers write a check, and a growing number don't write anything at all. An amount is automatically withdrawn from their bank accounts.

As people conduct more and more of their banking online and authorize automatic deductions from their account for bills, sometimes a check for church is the only one they write. So why not take care of that electronically, too? Large urban churches have been accepting credit and debit cards for several years, and some now encourage parishioners to sign up for weekly or monthly electronic funds transfer. The Web sites of a few churches allow for online giving, which proves particularly convenient for frequent travelers. A few others are experimenting with specially designed ATMs placed in the church lobby. In addition to helping congregants manage planned giving, the PIN-secured kiosks allow for cash gifts with printed receipts and recorded documentation for tax purposes.

Miscellany

Electronic Giving

Not all congregations, however, are ready to go with the cash flow. Church leaders warn against separating the worshipper from the physical act of dropping their gift into the plate each Sunday. Rather than a visible response of worship and gratitude to God, giving becomes a passive experience. Nonetheless, churches that offer giving options report an increase in contributions because the offering comes in every week, even if the parishioner doesn't.

FACT

Of those churches that offer electronic giving options, some shy away from credit cards. They note a conflict between warning parishioners about the dangers of indebtedness and then becoming part of the problem by accepting credit-card offerings. Also, should a parishioner fall into bankruptcy, the church would find itself in the unseemly position of a creditor.

Each man should give what he has decided in his heart to give,
not reluctantly or under compulsion, for God loves a cheerful giver.
2 CORINTHIANS 9:7

DAY
155

The Protestant reformer of Scotland began his adult life as a Roman Catholic priest. In the early 1540s, Father John Knox came under the influence of George Wishart, a zealous Protestant who preached throughout the Scottish lowlands.

Around 1545, Knox publicly professed himself a Protestant. He joined the parish church of St. Andrews, on Scotland's eastern coast, as a preacher. St. Andrews Castle, a refuge for persecuted Protestants, fell to Roman Catholic forces in 1547, and Knox was taken prisoner. He was put to work on a French vessel as a galley slave. After nineteen months of rowing, he won release, but he was left with lifelong health problems.

Rather than risk rearrest in Scotland, Knox served the Reformed Church in England and on the Continent, not returning to his home country until 1559. After the Reformed Protestant religion became legal (and Catholicism illegal) in Scotland in 1560, Knox was named minister of the Church of St. Giles in Edinburgh. At the same time, Knox began

Men of the Faith

John Knox
(c. 1513–1572)
Reformer

his most significant writing, *The History of the Reformation in Scotland*.

The History of the Reformation in Scotland, among other things, recounts Knox's conflict with Mary, now Queen of Scots and a Roman Catholic. She had returned from France in 1560 to rule a country no longer Catholic and a people who looked more to Knox than the monarchy for leadership. Mary tried to coax the fiery preacher into tolerating her private practice of Catholicism, but to no avail. Five years later, Mary was forced to abdicate the throne in favor of her infant son, James the IV of Scotland (James I of England).

> At the graveside of John Knox, the regent of Scotland commented, "Here lies a man who in his life never feared the face of man, who has been often threatened with dagger, but yet has ended his days in peace and honor."
>
> FACT

"You must go to everyone I send you to and say whatever I command you. Do not be afraid of them, for I am with you and will rescue you," declares the LORD.
JEREMIAH 1:7–8

She was a tiny woman—four feet three inches tall. But Lottie Moon was not short on ambition, courage, and determination. She could have enjoyed an easy life at Viewmont, her parents' fifteen-hundred acre, slave labor, tobacco plantation in Virginia, but spirited and outspoken, she wanted to make a difference.

Edward Harris Moon, Lottie's father, was killed in a riverboat accident when she was just thirteen. With the onset of the Civil War, Lottie knew she needed to stay and help her mother maintain the family estate. Afterward, she settled into a teaching career.

In 1872, Lottie's younger sister, Edmonia, accepted a call to go to North China as a missionary, and Lottie soon followed. She and Edmonia taught in a girls' school until Lottie discovered her real passion—direct evangelism.

At the age of forty-five, Moon moved into China's interior to evangelize full-time. Heartbroken by the shortage of workers, she waged a writing campaign, describing the great need. When the poorly funded missionary board could not provide additional missionaries, she urged Southern Baptist women to organize mission societies to raise the needed funds. The result was the Women's Missionary Union, which collected enough in its first Christmas offering to send three new missionaries to China. Since 1888, the annual Lottie Moon Christmas Offering for Missions has raised a total of $1.5 billion.

Women of the Faith

Lottie Moon
(1840–1912)

Pioneer of the Mission Fund

Lottie Moon died on Christmas Eve, 1912, at the age of seventy-two while en route home to the United States. She has come to personify the missionary spirit for millions of Christians.

FACT

Lottie Moon was unusually adept at foreign languages. She was fluent in French, Italian, Chinese, and Spanish. She could also read Latin, Greek, and Hebrew.

How, then, can they call on the one they have not believed in? And how can they believe in the one of whom they have not heard? And how can they hear without someone preaching to them? And how can they preach unless they are sent?
Romans 10:14–15

M artin Luther, Dietrich Bonhoeffer, and Johann Wolfgang von Goethe have all walked the aisles of St. Peter's Basilica in Vatican City. The basilica itself is world-renowned for its architecture, art, and religious significance for the Catholic Church. Here the Renaissance artist Michelangelo's multitalented genius is on display in the painting of the Sistine Chapel, the sculpture of his emotive Pietá, and the architectural design of the basilica's massive dome. But it's what lies beneath the floor of the dome that makes St. Peter's Basilica an important site.

Beneath the current city-state of Vatican City runs the former site of Caligula's Circus. During the time of Nero, the circus was a place of athletic games, chariot races, and the public executions of Christians. According to tradition, the apostle Peter was crucified, upside-down, at the circus. Peter's followers then buried the apostle's body outside the circus walls on Vatican Hill in a small, slope-roofed shrine. In the fourth century, Constantine built the original St. Peter's Basilica on top of this shrine. That structure was torn down in the sixteenth century and construction began on the basilica visitors see today.

Important Sites

St. Peter's Basilica
Vatican City

A little more than a century later, the second St. Peter's Basilica was completed. Over the years, people came to doubt the truth of the dome marking the spot where Peter's body was buried. However, in 1939, excavations began beneath the Sacred Grottoes under the floor of the basilica. Numerous pagan and Christian tombs were discovered, including one believed to belong to the apostle.

St. Peter's Basilica was the world's largest church until the Basilica of Our Lady of Peace was built in Cote d'Ivoire in 1989. Though the surface area of the African church is larger, it only holds eighteen thousand people. St. Peter's can hold sixty thousand.

FACT

---

*[Jesus said,] "I tell you that you are Peter, and on this rock
I will build my church, and the gates of Hades will not overcome it."*
MATTHEW 16:18

In sixteenth-century Scotland—as in many parts of the world then and now—religion played a significant role in everyday life. The church provided education for the young and dictated the mores and laws of the land. For the faithful, the church also held the keys of heaven. Whether to stay with the pope or side with the reformers was a weighty topic, for it meant the difference between heaven and hell. The decision to break away from the Roman Catholic Church never happened without struggle and, often, with bloodshed.

Years leading up to the Scottish Reformation found a formerly staunchly Roman Catholic populace influenced by Protestant ideas coming from the Continent via books and pamphlets. Although the papist monarchy banned such publications, a sufficient number fell into the hands of Scottish readers. Soon, a core of influential Scots was agitating for personal expression and individual freedom in thinking and in worship.

Groundbreaking Events

The Reformation in Scotland

Years of political wrangling and royal intrigue ensued. Meanwhile, John Knox returned from exile in 1559 to support the growing Protestant movement. With the death of the Roman Catholic queen mother in 1560, Scottish Protestant leaders quickly assembled an extraordinary parliament. They did away with the Catholic mass and then approved what came to be known as the Scots Confession of 1560, a document penned in large part by Knox. The same year, Knox and others composed the *First Book of Discipline*, a foundational document of the Scottish reformed church. On December 20, 1560, parliament adopted Presbyterian Calvinism as the official religion of Scotland.

FACT

Martin Luther commented: "If you think properly of the Gospel, please don't imagine that its cause can be advanced without tumult, offence and sedition....The word of God is a sword, it's war, ruin, offence, perdition, and poison. If I am immoderate, at least I am simple and open."

"They will ask the way to Zion and turn their faces toward it.
They will come and bind themselves to the LORD in an
everlasting covenant that will not be forgotten."
JEREMIAH 50:5

Wondering how to control your kids? James Dobson's child-raising classic, *Dare to Discipline*, throws cold water on permissive child-raising practices. Published in the early 1970s as the don't-trust-anyone-over-thirty generation found themselves parents dealing with the trauma of toddlers and tantrums, Dobson's readable, straightforward guide found a place on the bookshelves of numerous Christian homes.

Dare to Discipline promotes the exercise of unapologetic parental authority, consistently enforced rules, and values-driven childhood character development. He draws from biblical principles to equip parents with methods and techniques designed to reinforce good behavior, punish bad, and instill Judeo-Christian morals and ethical values in children. Dobson calls for strong, consistent leadership from parents, obedience and willing submission from children, and mutual respect within families. He connects a child's experience with authority in the home to his or her ability to accept and interact with authority in the classroom, workplace, and community.

Notable Books

Dare to Discipline

By Dr. James Dobson (1970)

To this day, *Dare to Discipline* causes flare-ups in discussions of how to raise children. Dobson's chapter on corporal punishment condones spanking of young children as an effective way to instill respect for the authority of the parents, and, by extension, respect for civil authority. Anti-spanking advocates decry his advice, linking spanking with violence, bullying, and child abuse.

Dare to Discipline's phenomenal sales and staying power, however, indicate that Christian parents today still value Dobson's practical, grounded advice. An updated and expanded version of the classic, *The New Dare to Discipline*, addresses family issues that emerged in the last decades of the twentieth century, such as substance abuse.

Dr. James Dobson wrote, "Children are not casual guests in our home. They have been loaned to us temporarily for the purpose of loving them and instilling a foundation of values on which their future lives will be built."

FACT

Train a child in the way he should go,
and when he is old he will not turn from it.
PROVERBS 22:6

Horatio and Anna Spafford were still grieving the death of a son when the great Chicago fire destroyed almost everything they owned. Two years later, in 1873, Horatio felt his family needed a vacation and arranged a voyage to Europe for himself and his family where they were looking forward to hearing Dwight L. Moody preach.

Delayed because of pending business, Horatio sent Anna and his four daughters ahead of him on the ship *Ville du Havre*. Halfway across the Atlantic, a sailing vessel rammed the ship during the night, cutting it in half. In the confusion, Mrs. Spafford watched in horror as her four daughters were swept to their deaths. In an odd twist of fate, a falling mast struck her unconscious—and a wave carried her body to a piece of floating wreckage, where she later regained consciousness.

Songs of the Faith

"It Is Well with My Soul"
Words by Horatio G. Spafford (1873)
Music by Philip P. Bliss (1876)

When she and other survivors reached Wales, she cabled two words to her husband: "Saved alone."

Filled with sorrow, Horatio set sail on the earliest ship to join his grieving wife. When the ship reached the spot where his daughters were lost at sea, he wrote with courage from the depths of his soul the words to one of the most beloved hymns of all time, "It Is Well with My Soul."

> *When peace, like a river, attendeth my way,*
> *When sorrows like sea billows roll;*
> *Whatever my lot, Thou has taught me to say,*
> *It is well, it is well, with my soul.*

> *Refrain:*
> *It is well, with my soul,*
> *It is well, with my soul,*
> *It is well, it is well, with my soul.*

FACT

The music, written by Philip Bliss, was named after the ship on which Spafford's daughters died, *Ville du Havre*.

Have mercy on me, O God, have mercy on me, for in you my soul takes refuge.
I will take refuge in the shadow of your wings until the disaster has passed.
PSALM 57:1

The mother of all megachurches resides not in America, but in Seoul, South Korea. Yoido Full Gospel Church claims a membership approaching one million people.

Though both Catholic and Protestant missionaries in Korea suffered persecution and even martyrdom prior to World War II, the postwar years saw a surge in Christian missionary activity. In 1953, the Korean Assemblies of God established a Bible school to train Korean preachers. One student, Paul Yonggi Cho, proved himself an intelligent and ambitious student. Cho, a convert, graduated from the Bible school in 1958 and planted a small tent church in a Seoul slum. Shortly thereafter, reports of a healing at the church drew attention, and the congregation grew rapidly. Cho opened a revival center to accommodate his expanding membership. In addition to his healing ministry, Cho preached a prosperity gospel, offering assurances of personal riches to his impoverished and often desperate listeners.

Miscellany

Yoido Full Gospel Church
Seoul, South Korea

In 1973, Cho built Yoido Church to accommodate his ever-swelling numbers of Sunday worshippers. Six years later, with a membership of one hundred thousand, Yoido had become the largest church in the world. Renamed Yoido Full Gospel Church, current membership exceeds eight hundred thousand and continues to grow.

The expansion of Christianity in South Korea remains phenomenal. From an insignificant minority less than fifty years ago, Christians now account for one-third of the population in South Korea. Some scholars note that Christianity, with its promise of hope and ethos of personal worth and empowerment, particularly appeals to Koreans, whose history is interwoven with foreign oppression and domination by other Asian powers.

Dr. Cho has written several books on the theology of personal prosperity through baptism in the Spirit and on strategies to achieve and manage church growth. In 1976, Cho founded an ecumenical organization to train pastors to spread the message, and in 1989 began a Christian newspaper, the widely distributed *Kook Min Daily News*.

FACT

Many who heard the message believed,
and the number of men grew to about five thousand.
ACTS 4:4

Sometimes it takes a few tries to settle on a career. George MacDonald attended Scotland's Aberdeen University, where he took prizes in chemistry and natural philosophy. After teaching in London for a few years, he studied for the Congregationalist ministry in Highbury. His gig as a pastor lasted no longer than his stint as a teacher. The members of his congregation took umbrage at some statements from the pulpit and showed MacDonald the church door.

Ill health plagued MacDonald, and he spent some recovery time in Algiers.

Men of the Faith

George MacDonald
(1824–1905)

Preacher, poet, and author

Upon returning to England, he decided to become a professional writer. At the same time, he joined the Church of England and preached occasionally. He had several poems published in the 1850s. Recognition and success came his way in the 1860s with a series of novels about life in rural Scotland. Further success came with the publication of his Christian allegories for adults and his charming children's novels. In 1872, he embarked on an American lecture tour and mixed with leading thinkers of the day, including Emerson.

George MacDonald's life's work included more than fifty volumes of adult fiction and nonfiction, children's stories, poetry, and sermons. He is best known, however, for his allegorical children's books.

MacDonald's income from writing, however, did not provide for the needs of his family. At the request of Queen Victoria, he began receiving a pension in 1877. For the sake of his health, the family spent much of the time in Italy, where the household enjoyed friends, music, and storytelling.

FACT

C. S. Lewis wrote of him, "I know hardly any other writer who seems to be closer, or more continually close, to the Spirit of Christ Himself."

Don't you know that you yourselves are God's temple
and that God's Spirit lives in you?
1 CORINTHIANS 3:16

T hough she was born a slave, one of thirteen children, Amanda Smith rose to international fame as a Methodist missionary evangelist. Her preaching ministry took her around the world.

Amanda was born in 1837 in Long Green, Maryland. Early in her life, her father was able to buy freedom for himself, his wife, and five of his children—the others were born free—by making brooms and husk mats after working all day in the field.

At the age of thirteen, Amanda went to Pennsylvania, where she took her first job as servant to a widow with five children. It was there that she attended a revival in the Methodist Episcopal Church and had her first personal encounter with the Lord. After receiving prayer, she resolved she would "be the Lord's and live for Him."

In her autobiography, Amanda describes the night when God touched her and took away her fear of people, freeing her to begin her evangelistic work.

Women of the Faith

Amanda Berry Smith (1837–1915)
First black woman evangelist

The following years were difficult, filled with diligent work and hardship, but she grew steadily in her relationship with the Lord and learned to trust Him with her needs. Her beautiful singing voice began to open opportunities for her to preach through the eastern states and as far south as Texas. Eventually, she was invited to preach in England, India, Liberia, and Africa.

Fourteen years later, she returned to establish the Amanda Smith Orphans' Home for Colored Children in Harvey, Illinois. She made the first payment on the building with money from sales of her autobiography.

Amanda Smith was lovingly referred to by a fellow minister as "God's image carved in ebony."

FACT

Now to him who is able to do immeasurably more than all we ask or imagine, according to his power that is at work within us, to him be glory in the church and in Christ Jesus throughout all generations for ever and ever!
EPHESIANS 3:20–21

"Our new room"—that's how John Wesley referred to the chapel he wanted to build in Bristol, England. But the oldest Methodist chapel in the world became more than just a meetinghouse for worship. It also served as a school and a medical dispensary for Bristol's poor.

Built in 1739, the New Room was expanded in 1748 to the size visitors see today. In the lower part of the building, Wesley's double-decker pulpit still stands. (Wesley preached his sermons from the upper level and used the lower level during the remainder of the service.) Above the chapel is a suite of bedrooms surrounding a common meeting area. This is where Wesley and other traveling preachers bedded down for the night and prepared their sermons. In the common room there's a small window that opens into the chapel below—supposedly so Wesley could keep an eye on the other preachers when they spoke. Wesley spent about fifteen hundred nights upstairs in the New Room, when he wasn't traveling the countryside, preaching in the open air, before eventually moving to London.

Important Sites

John Wesley Chapel(s)
Bristol, England

In 1776, Wesley built a chapel in London solely for preaching and communion. Also referred to as the "John Wesley Chapel," this location has earned the nickname the "Cathedral of World Methodism." Wesley spent the remainder of his life here. Today, this Wesley's Chapel is still used for "preaching and communion." A museum in the church crypt and Wesley's house next door are open to the public as museums.

FACT

Margaret Thatcher (the former British Prime Minister) is a devout Methodist and was married at the John Wesley Chapel in London in 1951.

They devoted themselves to the apostles' teaching and to the fellowship, to the breaking of bread and to prayer.
ACTS 2:42

They weren't called Baptists yet. Just a group of devout believers in England, reading the Bible, applying it to their lives—and finding the Church of England failing to meet their spiritual needs. The reformed church in England, they felt, had departed from the biblical message of love, faith, and simplicity and, in many instances, had not completely divorced itself from Roman Catholic custom and practice. Like other groups of dissatisfied Protestants, they drifted away from the church and formed independent congregations. This particular group's practice of baptizing only believing adults earned them the once-derogatory name "Baptists."

Instances of persecution, in addition to laws stipulating that all Englishmen must attend Church of England services, led Baptists and other nonconformists to relocate to the friendlier religious climate of Holland. In 1608, the first General Baptist Church, under the leadership of John Smyth, was established in Amsterdam. A former English clergyman, Smyth, along with colleague Thomas Helwys, formed

Groundbreaking Events

The First "Baptists" Baptized

a congregation around Bible study and personal confession of faith in Jesus Christ, followed by believer's baptism. Smyth set the example by baptizing himself, and then he baptized other professing Christian adults.

Affiliated groups and offshoots arose when some members of the Amsterdam congregation, headed by Helwys, returned to England to face their former persecutors. Other groups of members, attracted by the promise of religious freedom, crossed the Atlantic to settle in the New World. The seventeenth century saw Baptist congregations flourishing throughout the American colonies.

In Christian circles, Baptists are known for their practice of baptizing by immersion, a custom developed in the years following 1608. Prior to that time, baptisms were conducted the traditional way, by sprinkling or pouring water on the forehead of the recipient.

FACT

" 'What are you waiting for? Get up, be baptized and wash your sins away, calling on his name.' "
ACTS 22:16

C. S. Lewis's Christian fantasy delights children and enthralls adults. *The Chronicles of Narnia*, a collection of seven stories, relates the adventures of four children who find themselves wandering in a mysterious, magical forest. They meet various talking beasts, a wicked witch, and an all-powerful lion—the only one who can break the witch's deadly spell over the land. Through his characters, situations, and plot development, Lewis weaves a profound allegorical tale of good and evil, faith and despair, salvation and sin.

The Chronicles of Narnia introduces readers to Peter, Susan, Edmund, and Lucy. Staying in the home of an elderly professor, the children stumble into the world of Narnia through a secret door in an old wardrobe. Lewis is said to have started the stories to amuse four children staying at his country home during the London bombings of the Second World War. Intrigued by the children's love of make-believe, Lewis entertained them with the imaginative story that later developed into the timeless tale of Narnia.

Notable Books

The Chronicles of Narnia
By C. S. Lewis (1952–58)

Literary and biblical allusions dot the Narnia landscape, from the myth of Orpheus to the book of Revelation. Lewis's spiritual insights are revealed as the story's diverse characters interact with one another and solve their arguments, problems, and dilemmas. As generations of parents have found as they read the entertaining tales to their children, the stories provide natural conversation openers for subjects such as fear and anger, faith and hope.

The series in whole and in part has been adapted to stage, cinema, and television many times.

FACT

Lewis completed the stories during the 1950s, saying his initial ideas came to him from images of "a faun carrying an umbrella, a queen in a sledge, a magnificent lion." He added more characters, many of them based on people he knew, fairy tales, or the thoughts of his own imagination.

Thanks be to God! He gives us the victory through our Lord Jesus Christ.
1 CORINTHIANS 15:57

In her brief forty-three years, Sarah Flower Adams lived a vibrant and productive life. Born in Harlow, England, she became an actress and played the part of Lady Macbeth in London. Although her physical handicaps limited her ambitious spirit, she was widely known for her literary accomplishments, charm, and character.

Sarah's sister, Eliza, was an accomplished musician who often wrote music for Sarah's poems and hymns. When asked by their pastor, Reverend William Johnson Fox, to help him compile a hymnal for his congregation, the two sisters eagerly committed to the project and contributed thirteen texts and sixty-two new tunes. In the process of finalizing the hymnal, Fox expressed a need for a song that would help him conclude a sermon he was preparing about Jacob and Esau. Eliza felt Sarah could write an excellent

Songs of the Faith

"Nearer, My God, to Thee"

Words by Sarah F. Adams (1841)

Music by Lowell Mason (1856)

hymn for both sermon and hymnal about the biblical account of Jacob sleeping on a stone and dreaming of angels—words that would reflect the common yearning to experience God's nearness and presence in times of deep need.

Today, this hymn is found in nearly every published hymnal around the world in many translations. "Nearer, My God, to Thee" was one of the hymns included in that new hymnal published in 1841, entitled *Hymns and Anthems*. It was introduced in America in 1844, but gained popularity twelve years later when it was set to the music, "Bethany," by Lowell Mason.

Nearer, my God, to Thee, nearer to Thee!
E'en though it be a cross that raiseth me,
Still all my song shall be,
Nearer, my God, to Thee;
Nearer, my God, to Thee, nearer to Thee!

This hymn was President William McKinley's favorite. It was played and sung at memorial services throughout our land in 1901. There is also the well-known 1912 account of the ship's band playing strains of this hymn as the *Titanic* was sinking and fifteen hundred people slipped into eternity.

FACT

Draw nigh to God, and he will draw nigh to you.
JAMES 4:8 KJV

Oral traditions and ancient texts from around the world mention a time when water covered the earth. Many tell how eight people and hosts of animals entered an ark, surviving the flood in safety. Though many flood traditions exist, most modern-day explorations for the ark begin with the biblical account of the Great Flood found in Genesis 6:9–9:19. According to the Bible, "the ark came to rest on the mountains of Ararat" (8:4), an extensive mountainous region in the ancient kingdom of Urartu. Thus, Mount Ararat and the surrounding region in present-day eastern Turkey and western Iran have received the greatest amount of attention in the search for Noah's ark.

The volcanic Mount Ararat, which rises 16,945 feet, forbids all but the heartiest explorers. Though its steep heights provide adequate cover for possible remains of the ancient vessel, movements of the mountain's ice cap, would, over time, pulverize even petrified wood. Nonetheless, most alleged sightings of a boat-like structure visible through the ice have occurred on Mount Ararat, so the search continues there. The Bible's reference to "the mountains of Ararat," however, suggests an entire region in the kingdom of Urartu, which covers miles of mountainous terrain that is icy, remote, and inhospitable.

Miscellany

Noah's Ark

Mount Cudi, located about 250 miles southwest of Ararat, has its supporters, too. Still in the "mountains of Ararat," Mount Cudi, at just over seven thousand feet, offers a more promising place to land an ark and release animals. The exact location of Mount Cudi, though, remains the subject of scholarly debate.

Despite the flood of research devoted to the topic, no one has definitively located Noah's ark—at least not yet!

FACT

Noah's ark, with the capacity of 522 railroad cars, could hold 125,280 sheep-sized animals. If, for example, from two dogs came all species of dogs today, Noah would have needed only about sixteen thousand individual animals aboard to repopulate the earth.

---

*[God said,] "Never again will all life be cut off by the waters of a flood;
never again will there be a flood to destroy the earth."*
GENESIS 9:11

The foremost Christian apologist of the second century was born into a pagan family. Justin Martyr studied Stoic and Platonic philosophy at Ephesus (near modern-day Selcuk, Turkey). At around thirty years of age, he converted to Christianity and became its staunch defender.

Like many philosophers, Justin never met a dispute he didn't want to enter. One of his major writings, *Dialogue*, stemmed from a debate with Trypho, a Jew, on the assertions of the gospel. He proceeded to Rome and opened a Christian school. In Rome, he came up against opposition in the person of a fellow philosopher, Crescens. Crescens's vehement denunciation of Christianity spurred Justin to write another of his major works, *Apology*, a treatise on the moral values of the faith. Later, he wrote a shorter treatise, creatively titled *Second Apology*, addressed to the Roman Senate after the accession of Marcus Aurelius in the year 161. Many works by Justin Martyr

Men of the Faith

Justin Martyr
(c.100–c.165)
Philosopher and apologist

have been lost, and other treatises remain in fragmentary form, or are quoted or referred to in the works of other early writers.

Justin was publicly denounced as a Christian, an accusation he could hardly deny. Historical documents record the court proceedings in which Justin, along with six other defendants, were ordered to perform a sacrifice to the gods of Rome. Justin replied, "No right-minded man forsakes truth for falsehood." He spoke for the group when he said, "Do with us as you will. We are Christians, and we cannot sacrifice to idols." Seven heads rolled in response to his bold and courageous declaration of faith.

Justin Martyr attributed his conversion to a mysterious man he once met. The man pointed him to the Spirit-inspired prophets of the Old Testament who could lead Justin to truth.

[Jesus said,] "Because of this, God in his wisdom said, 'I will send them prophets and apostles, some of whom they will kill and others they will persecute.'"
LUKE 11:49

Catherine Mumford was born in Ashbourne, Derbyshire, in 1829. By the time she was twelve, she had read through the Bible eight times. Catherine first glimpsed her call to social justice when she stood up for a drunken man she felt had been mistreated by a local policeman.

In 1852 Catherine met William Booth, a Methodist minister. While they shared the same view on social reform, Catherine highly objected to William's nonfeminist views on women, especially a woman's role in the church and her right to preach. Despite their differences, Catherine and William married on June 16, 1855.

One morning in 1860 at Gateshead Bethseda Chapel, Catherine recalled, she suddenly felt compelled to stand up and speak. She found herself preaching her first sermon, and it so impressed her husband that he changed his mind about women preachers. Catherine soon gained a reputation as an extraordinary speaker and began preaching revivals at London's Christian Mission, which later became the Salvation Army.

Women of the Faith

Catherine Booth
(1829–1890)

Female preacher, activist, and cofounder of Salvation Army

When the Church of England called William Booth the anti-Christ for elevating women to a man's status, William answered his accusers, "The best men in my army are the women." In 1882, a London survey reported that on one weeknight, there were almost seventeen thousand worshipping with the Salvation Army compared to eleven thousand in mainline churches.

Catherine's tireless campaigns for social reform included organizing Food-for-the-Million Shops, where the poor could buy affordable meals; cooking Christmas Day dinners to feed the poor; waging war on match factories that presented health risks from unsafe chemicals; and fearlessly fighting for better wages for women.

FACT

Catherine Booth died of cancer in October 1890. Her husband carried out the campaigns she'd started. Catherine and William Booth had eight children, all of whom were active in the Salvation Army.

Dear children, let us not love with words or tongue but with actions and in truth.
1 JOHN 3:18

In a cave five miles outside of Jerusalem, a fourteen-point silver star marks the traditional birthplace of Christ. The humble surroundings Mary and Joseph may have taken refuge in during Christ's birth have undergone considerable transformation since that time. In AD 333, Helena, the mother of Constantine, built a basilica on this spot. Heavily damaged in 529 during civil unrest, it was rebuilt in 565 by the Emperor Justinian I.

Today, the Basilica of the Nativity, which is Greek Orthodox, shares this sacred site with the Roman Catholic Church of St. Catherine. Monastic communities for Greek Orthodox, Roman Catholic, and Armenian Apostolic are also located there. The three Christian sects have arranged how to share responsibilities and space within the basilicas. In the lower "Grotto of the Nativity" itself, the Orthodox church is in charge of six silver lamps around the "birthplace"; the Armenian church, five lamps; and the Catholic church, four. Add the fact that both Christians and Muslims consider this spot sacred, and the angel's proclamation of "peace on earth" seems to have been put to the test.

The Basilica of the Nativity is the only major church in the Holy Land that has survived intact from early Christian times and is one of the oldest continuously operating churches in the world. To enter it, visitors must walk through the Door of Humility, which is less than four feet tall. Some historians believe the door was lowered to prevent invaders from riding into the church on horseback.

Important Sites

The Basilica of the Nativity
Jerusalem

When Commander Shahrbaraz of Persia invaded the area in AD 614, it is said that he was so moved by the church's artistic depiction of the three magi wearing Persian clothing that he demanded the Basilica of the Nativity not be destroyed.

She [Mary] brought forth her firstborn Son, and wrapped Him in swaddling cloths, and laid Him in a manger, because there was no room for them in the inn.
LUKE 2:7 NKJV

King James I of England had reason to dislike the unauthorized but ever-popular Geneva Bible. Its decidedly Protestant leanings conflicted with the more moderate position of the Church of England. And certain marginal notes seemed to condone civil disobedience, a disturbing concept for any reigning monarch. For example, the account of Pharaoh's order that all newborn Hebrew males be killed and the midwives' refusal (Exodus 1:8–22) is accompanied by a note approving the midwives' stance. The king pronounced the commentaries of the Geneva Bible "partial, untrue, seditious, and savoring of dangerous and traitorous conceits."

In 1604, at the behest of Puritan scholar Dr. John Reynolds, the king happily authorized a new English-language Bible. Fifty-four top theologians, scholars, and experts in biblical languages assembled for the task. They divided into panels, each with particular books of the Bible to translate. Teams worked directly from Hebrew and Greek manuscripts. Completed translations were then presented to a committee of two (two translators from each panel) for review. Their purpose was to ensure that the translating panel had complied with strict rules of translation imposed on the project. In addition, the committee screened for any one translator's or team's prejudices or political leanings.

Groundbreaking Events

Publication of the King James Bible (1611)

The completed work was published in 1611.

While accuracy ranked foremost in the translators' minds, they also put considerable emphasis on how the words sounded when read aloud. Their attention to this detail and their extraordinary language skill give the King James Version, or Authorized Version, of the Bible its distinctive cadence and rhythm, a quality that, in the opinion of many, remains unmatched to this day.

> **FACT** Though commissioned by King James, the Authorized King James Version of the Bible was never formally accepted by the king, nor was it ever decreed the only Bible to be read in church. Not until 1661 did the Church of England's Prayer Book incorporate King James Version passages in its scripture citations.

The LORD is my shepherd; I shall not want. He maketh me to lie down in green pastures: he leadeth me beside the still waters.
PSALM 23:1–2 KJV

A bestseller among Christian apologetics, *More Than a Carpenter* started out as an attempt to discredit the claims of Christianity. As a student at Kellogg College in Michigan, Josh McDowell sought to disprove the resurrection of Jesus Christ with historical evidence to the contrary. In doing so, he found no such evidence, and instead discovered solid intellectual reasons for the reliability of scripture. From skeptic to convert, McDowell became a leading speaker, author, and evangelist devoted to telling an unbelieving world the truth about Christianity.

More Than a Carpenter, one of McDowell's several popular books, directly addresses the most common complaint against Christianity: How could anyone believe Jesus was the Son of God? Under compelling chapter titles such as "Lord, Liar, or Lunatic?" "Who Would Die for a Lie?" and "Isn't There Some Other Way?" McDowell critically examines the identity of the Jesus of the Bible. He shows how research and extrabiblical sources support Jesus' claims of divinity, and he points to actions of Jesus' disciples that make little sense unless they, in fact, had seen and interacted with Jesus after his resurrection from the dead. McDowell includes opinions of experts in various fields of biblical history to address the issue of Jesus' divinity and his claim on the lives of his followers.

Notable Books

More Than a Carpenter
By Josh McDowell (1977)

McDowell concludes his study with a personal testimony about his conversion. In the chapter titled "How He Changed My Life," McDowell illuminates the real and powerful ways the living Jesus works in his life today.

McDowell's college research to discredit Christianity became the nucleus of his later seminary thesis. Written in twelve hours, it was later published as *More Than a Carpenter*, which has since been translated into more than fifty languages.

FACT

[Jesus said,] "I and the Father are one."
John 10:30

Sabine Baring-Gould says it took him only fifteen minutes to write the time-tested lyrics to "Onward Christian Soldiers." Baring-Gould, Squire and Parson of the parish of Lewtrenchard in West Devon, England, remembers searching for music to meet a specific need.

It was the night before Whit Monday (the holiday celebrated the day after Pentecost), and Reverend Baring-Gould was planning a school festival. Children from a neighboring village had been invited and the parson wanted the children to sing as they marched from one village to the other. Unfortunately, he could find no marching music appropriate for the occasion. Finally, he decided to write something himself. The result was this great hymn.

Songs of the Faith

"Onward Christian Soldiers"

Words by Sabine Baring-Gould (1864)

Music by Arthur S. Sullivan (1871)

Originally, he entitled the piece "Hymn for Procession with Cross and Banners," and set it to a melody from Joseph Haydn's Symphony in D, No. 15. The slow movement of the piece caused it to lag in popularity until composer Arthur Sullivan wrote a new tune for it. He entitled the melody "St. Gertrude," after the wife of a friend.

"Onward Christian Soldiers" has been sung in a number of films including *Mrs. Miniver*, *M*A*S*H*, *Taps*, *Flyboys*, and *A Canterbury Tale*. It was also played at the funeral of President Dwight Eisenhower.

> *Onward, Christian soldiers, marching as to war,*
> *With the cross of Jesus going on before.*
> *Christ, the royal Master, leads against the foe;*
> *Forward into battle see His banners go!*
>
> *Refrain:*
> *Onward, Christian soldiers, marching as to war,*
> *With the cross of Jesus going on before.*

FACT

In 1986, an attempt was made to strip "Onward Christian Soldiers" from the Methodist hymnal due to its militaristic theme. Outraged churchgoers forced the committee to back down.

Endure hardship with us like a good soldier of Christ Jesus.
2 TIMOTHY 2:3

W ho was Jesus? In an effort to define the historical Jesus, a group of Protestants, Catholics, Jews, independents, and atheists met together in 1985 to discuss the matter. The clergy, professors, authors, and Bible specialists set about their task by examining whether or not Jesus actually said and did what the Gospels report.

After debate on each saying and action attributed to Jesus, participants voted on its authenticity by dropping one of four colored beads in a box:

- Red bead—It's true. Jesus said or did it, or something pretty close.
- Pink bead—Maybe Jesus said or did something like it.
- Gray bead—Well, it's something He might have said or done.
- Black bead—A figment of His later followers' fertile imaginations.

To the consternation of the larger Christian community, the Jesus Seminar declared more than 80 percent of Jesus' words and actions recorded in the Gospels unlikely at best, or simply unbelievable.

The group's findings follow a modern-day trend of separating the "Jesus of History" from the "Christ of Faith." Liberal theologians agree a good teacher named Jesus lived, but say that legends grew up around Him, tales fueled by His ardent and zealous disciples. Those who promote the idea discount the Gospels' accuracy and promote an individual's discovery of timeless truths as the essence of faith. As might be expected, the conclusions

Miscellany

The Jesus Seminar

of the Jesus Seminar fly in the face of what Christians have been taught about the Gospels. While liberal scholars applaud the work, conservative Christianity dismisses it as contrary to a true and clear reading of God's Word.

> C. S. Lewis wrote:"I am perfectly convinced that whatever the gospels are, they are not legends. . . . Christ bent down and scribbled in the dust with His finger. Nothing comes of this. No one has based any doctrine on it. And the act of inventing little irrelevant details to make an imaginary scene more convincing is purely a modern art."
>
> FACT

We did not follow cleverly invented stories when we told you about the power and coming of our Lord Jesus Christ, but we were eyewitnesses of his majesty.
2 PETER 1:16

It could be said that Charles Wesley sang the gospel into thousands of hearts. The author of more than fifty-five hundred songs and hymns, Charles, less well-known than his brother John Wesley, came from a family of poets and songwriters.

Wesley had a clever way of writing his music on the run. Using a system of shorthand, he would jot down his initial versions of the songs on small cards he kept in his pocketbook specifically for that purpose. Often songs came to him immediately after attending prayer meetings and taking communion.

The Wesley family was unusually large, even for that time. Charles's mother, Susannah, gave birth to nineteen children, though only ten survived to adulthood. Charles, youngest of the three surviving brothers, was approached by a wealthy man who offered to adopt him and make him his heir. Charles declined and chose instead to pursue his education.

Men of the Faith

Charles Wesley (1707–1788)

English hymn writer, poet, and preacher

While in his third year at Oxford, Charles entered into what he called a serious and methodical way of life. Along with his brother John, he persuaded several other young men to join him and together they applied this perspective to every aspect of their lives, especially their studies. This group was the Holy Club, and the ideas John and Charles crystallized during that time gave birth to the Methodist denomination.

After his time at the university, Charles became a popular itinerant preacher. In 1756, however, ill health forced him to confine his labors to Bristol and London, where the majority of his family resided. Surprisingly, he lived until 1788, his eightieth year.

FACT

In 1995, the Gospel Music Association recognized Charles Wesley's musical contributions to gospel music by listing his name in the Gospel Music Hall of Fame.

Sing to the LORD a new song; sing to the LORD, all the earth. Sing to the LORD, praise his name; proclaim his salvation day after day.
PSALM 96:1–2

T hat man over there says that women need to be helped into carriages, and lifted over ditches, and to have the best place everywhere. Nobody ever helps me into carriages, or over mud puddles, or gives me any best place, and ain't I a woman?" In 1854, those words rang out from a remarkable woman.

Born a slave in upstate New York, Isabella Baumfree endured a succession of heartless owners in her early years. As a teenager, she bore a daughter by a fellow slave, but was forced to marry one her master chose. Promised her freedom in 1826, a year before state emancipation was to take effect, Isabella left the house when her master reneged on his promise.

Women of the Faith

Sojourner Truth (1797–1883)

Abolitionist and feminist

Isabella arrived at the home of a couple who bought her services from her master. During this time, she experienced "the greatness of the Divine presence." She began attending the Methodist church, eventually traveling as an itinerant preacher and at times joining groups of like-minded believers. On June 1, 1843, Isabella changed her name to Sojourner Truth and resolved to continue traveling, preaching, and depending on the hospitality of strangers for her food and shelter.

Later, the publication of her memoirs provided an income and opened speaking opportunities. A charismatic woman, Sojourner spoke eloquently on women's rights, pacifism, and the abolition of slavery. During the Civil War, she worked among freed slaves at a government refugee camp.

The Mars Pathfinder Sojourner Rover is named after a woman who spoke the earthly (and celestial) truth.

A twelve-foot statue of Sojourner Truth will grace Monument Park in Battle Creek, Michigan, where she lived for more than twenty years.

FACT

For he who was a slave when he was called by the Lord is the Lord's freedman; similarly, he who was a free man when he was called is Christ's slave.

1 CORINTHIANS 7:22

At the age of twenty-five, Roger Schutz felt God calling him to found a Christian community where people of various denominations could meet on common ground. In 1940, while living in Taizé, near the demarcation line that split France during World War II, Roger and his sister offered hospitality to refugees of war—and later to Jews seeking refuge. In 1942, both brother and sister fled after a warning that their work had been reported to the authorities.

In 1944, Roger returned to Taizé to begin a monastic-based community open to both Catholics and Protestants, as well as anyone else seeking a deeper relationship with God. What began as an ecumenical community of about a hundred men now annually welcomes more than five thousand men and women from more than seventy-five countries. Participants, who reside in dorms or pitch a tent on the grounds, are encouraged to stay for a week and then return to their own local churches, putting into practice what they've learned.

Important Sites

Taizé

France

A typical day at the Taizé Community includes Bible study, group discussion, prayer, themed workshops, and three worship services. The unique music of the Taizé Community has influenced the worship styles of many churches worldwide. Meditative in tone, the songs repeat simple phrases from scripture, particularly the book of Psalms. Over New Year holiday, the community sponsors an annual event in a major European city, bringing tens of thousands of people from around the world together to worship, pray, and grow closer to God and each other.

FACT

During a worship service in 2005, a schizophrenic woman killed Brother Roger in front of twenty-five hundred worshippers in the Church of Reconciliation in Taizé. He was ninety years old.

All things are of God, who has reconciled us to Himself through Jesus Christ, and has given us the ministry of reconciliation.
2 CORINTHIANS 5:18 NKJV

English separatists—those groups of believers who had broken from the Church of England—either lived in England under persecution or moved elsewhere. One group of Puritans (so called because they endeavored to purify the church), labeled the Pilgrims, boarded a ship and set off for the New World.

Pilgrims aboard the *Mayflower* arrived off the coast of Massachusetts in November of 1620. They came with the vision of establishing a community in which they would be free to live lives set apart for God and in full accordance with biblical commands and doctrine. Their "city on a hill" would stand as a beacon of light for the rest of the world to see and emulate. They realized, however, that without complete agreement on how the community would govern itself, their "city" would soon collapse into anarchy.

Before disembarking, the Pilgrims drew up a social contract or covenant. Like the larger body of Puritans, Pilgrims believed in a sacred covenant instituted by God with humankind; and they also believed that such a covenant existed between individuals in any given community. With the Mayflower Compact (or covenant), the Pilgrims agreed to form a government and bind themselves to its rules. While not everyone aboard the *Mayflower* belonged to the Pilgrim's congregation, the leaders demanded that each male adult sign the Compact and pledge to live under the rules of the majority. The Mayflower Compact remained in force until the Plymouth Colony became part of the Massachusetts colony in 1691.

Groundbreaking Events

Pilgrims Sign the Mayflower Compact

The Mayflower Compact states, "[We,] Having undertaken, for the Glory of God and advancement of the Christian Faith and Honour of our King and Country. . .do by these presents solemnly and mutually in the presence of God and one of another, Covenant and Combine ourselves together into a Civil Body Politic, for our better ordering and preservation and furtherance of the ends aforesaid."

FACT

Everyone must submit himself to the governing authorities,
for there is no authority except that which God has established.
ROMANS 13:1

Quality-of-life topics exploded into public debate following the U.S. Supreme Court's 1973 Roe v. Wade decision. The legalization of abortion opened a question at the core of human identity: Is human life itself sacred and therefore inviolable, or is it subject to "quality of life" and other considerations? How each person answers that question affects laws and practices touching not only abortion, but infanticide, euthanasia, and the treatment of the physically and mentally disabled.

Influential Christian thinker Francis A. Schaeffer and former U.S. Surgeon General C. Everett Koop coauthored *Whatever Happened to the Human Race?* a study of hotly debated quality-of-life issues. Firmly on the side of the dignity of all human life, Schaeffer and Koop examine trends toward the cheapening of human life and future implications of decisions being made in response to medical and social progress. They blame the courts and medical profession for taking the lead in undermining basic human rights by broadening the conditions in which human life may be destroyed. Koop and Schaeffer also lay blame at the doorstep of Christians who remain silent while Judeo-Christian values are being discarded.

Notable Books

Whatever Happened to the Human Race?

By C. Everett Koop and
Francis A. Schaeffer (1979)

Together, Koop and Schaeffer energized evangelical voters and pro-life political movements in the last decades of the twentieth century. Believing the culture was skidding dangerously out of control, the two called for Christians to become involved in fighting the forces of humanism by getting the attention of legislatures and decision makers. The impact of the evangelical vote moved right-to-life issues to the forefront of political debate, where they remain to this day.

FACT

C. Everett Koop and Francis A. Schaeffer wrote, "We want to try to help tip the scales on the side of those who believe that individuals are unique and special and have great dignity."

*"Before I formed you in the womb I knew you,
before you were born I set you apart."*
JEREMIAH 1:5

Augustus Toplady experienced his conversion to Christ at age sixteen while visiting Ireland. At a small gathering in a barn, Augustus felt it strange that he would make things right with God in such an obscure place, far away from his home in England. Oddly enough, he penned this deeply moving hymn, "Rock of Ages," during a time of great religious controversy—the theological debate between Armenianism (espoused by John and Charles Wesley) and Calvinism (espoused by John Calvin).

In an attempt to make a spiritual analogy about England not being able to pay her national debt, and man not being able to satisfy a holy God, Toplady used the words of this hymn at the end of an article he wrote in 1776 for the *Gospel Magazine*. At that time, the hymn was entitled "A Living and Dying Prayer for the Holiest Believer in the World." Some have said the text bears obvious satirical statements against the Armenian concept of sanctification and the belief

Songs of the Faith

"Rock of Ages"

Words by Augustus M. Toplady (1763)

Music by Thomas Hastings (1830)

that it is possible to live without consciously sinning. Despite his controversial viewpoints, August Toplady was a deeply spiritual, evangelical teacher.

"Rock of Ages" is ranked as one of the best-known and most popular hymns ever written in the English language. Throughout history, it has ministered to people of all walks of life and faith.

> *Rock of Ages, cleft for me,*
> *Let me hide myself in Thee;*
> *Let the water and the blood,*
> *From Thy wounded side which flowed,*
> *Be of sin the double cure;*
> *Save from wrath and make me pure.*

Augustus Toplady wrote: "My heart beats every day stronger and stronger for glory. Sickness is no affliction, pain no cause, death itself no dissolution. . . . My prayers are now all converted into praise."

FACT

> *Moreover, brethren, I would not that ye should be ignorant,*
> *how that all our fathers. . .did all drink the same spiritual drink:*
> *for they drank of that spiritual Rock that followed them: and that Rock was Christ.*
> 1 Corinthians 10:1, 4 KJV

In the midst of a world of violence and suffering, how can we believe in an almighty and all-loving God? From the national shock of 9/11 to the private sorrow of a beloved child's seemingly senseless death, people ask *why*. To paraphrase the title of a long-popular book, why *do* bad things happen to good people?

The Craigville Colloquy, established in 1984, meets on a yearly basis to discuss the subject. For five days, about eighty Christian clergy, theologians, and laypeople gather in Craigville, Massachusetts, to wrestle with the thorny problem of human suffering and how to effectively console and counsel grieving parents, relatives, and friends. Participants challenge clichés and platitudes about angels and heaven so often echoed in scenes of intense grief. Theological concepts about suffering—inaccessible for those without a degree in theology—are pitted against the here-and-now needs of mourners at the graveside.

Miscellany

Craigville Colloquy

The purpose of the Craigville Colloquy is to prepare ministers and congregational leaders to be ready ahead of time for the unexpected, the unthinkable, the unspeakable. When it happens, what do you say? Insufficient and unsatisfactory answers, say some ministers, account for people leaving the church to find their solace elsewhere.

Unlike past generations, many young Christians today reject suffering as a means of discipline and spiritual growth. Perhaps the most difficult job for any pastor or loving friend is to accompany a bereaved person as he or she first shares in the sacred mystery of human suffering, pain, and grief.

FACT

In *Gospel of Sufferings*, Søren Kierkegaard wrote: "If God is love, then he is also love in everything, love in what you can understand and love in what you cannot understand, love in the dark riddle that lasts a day or in the riddle that lasts seventy years.... Right here is faith's struggle: to believe without being able to understand."

We also rejoice in our sufferings,
because we know that suffering produces perseverance;
perseverance, character; and character, hope.
ROMANS 5:3–4

Warfare between two Liberian villages left Prince Kaboo, the eldest child of a tribal chieftain, a prisoner. The victorious chief demanded an ever-increasing ransom for the boy, meanwhile subjecting him to brutal tortures. During a whipping, Kaboo saw an intense light and heard a voice telling him to run. Ropes holding him loosened, and he ran.

Kaboo escaped to Monrovia and worked at a plantation where missionaries invited him to church. When he heard a sermon about the apostle Paul's conversion, Kaboo recognized his own experience. He accepted Christ as his Savior, was baptized, and given the name Samuel Morris.

Missionaries, impressed with Morris's zeal, encouraged him to travel to America to receive an education. He did so, and Thaddeus Reade, president of Taylor University, enrolled him in the Indiana school. Morris's exotic background and simple faith touched his fellow students. He often asked other students to read aloud from the Bible. When one student told him he didn't believe in the Bible,

Men of the Faith

Samuel Kaboo Morris
(c. 1873–1893)
Convert

Morris is said to have replied, "My dear brother, your Father speaks to you, and you do not believe him? Your brother speaks, and you do not believe him? The sun shines and you do not believe it? God is your father, Christ your brother, the Holy Ghost your sun."

Morris planned to return to Liberia as a missionary to his people, but his life was cut short. He died of pneumonia on May 12, 1893. His life inspired many of his fellow students to serve as missionaries in Africa.

Samuel Kaboo Morris said, "I met a young boy who had been a slave of the enemy chief at the time I was a hostage. He said, 'We did not know what had happened to you. We saw the bright light flash over you. We heard someone call your name, and then you were gone.' After I told him about the miracle, he became a Christian, too."

FACT

As he neared Damascus on his journey,
suddenly a light from heaven flashed around him.
He fell to the ground and heard a voice say to him,
"Saul, Saul, why do you persecute me?"
Acts 9:3–4

Young Teresa had two options open to her: marriage or holy orders. Her chances of marrying into a good Spanish family, however, were diminished by her suspected Jewish ancestry and a rumored love affair. Teresa chose the convent.

The Convent of the Incarnation at Avila, a Carmelite order, was not exactly a house of holiness. Rather, it resembled a home for unmarried ladies of means. Nuns lived in private suites, wore jewelry, and entertained friends and relatives, including *devotos*—gentlemen who visited the sisters for "spiritual guidance."

Around forty years old and after recovering from malaria, Teresa's attention turned to the passion of Christ. She experienced visions, seen "not with the eyes of the body but the eyes of the soul." She initiated reforms of convent life, inspired by the primitive tradition of Carmel, a hermitical sect. Teresa and a small group of like-minded sisters opened their own small convent in Avila, which eventually led to the formation of the Discalced (barefoot) Carmelites, an austere and contemplative order.

Women of the Faith

Teresa of Avila (Teresa de Jesus) (1515–1582)

Reformer, author, and doctor of the church

Years of conflict between Calced and Discalced supporters ensued. During this time of turmoil, Teresa wrote a number of guidebooks to spiritual peace, including *The Interior Castle*, a classic of Christian literature. *The Interior Castle* and her other writings are noted for their simple style, practical advice, and lively humor. Her books, along with those of her friend, St. John of the Cross, remain essential resources for anyone who desires to become proficient in contemplation and prayer.

FACT

St. Teresa died just as the switch was being made from the Julian to the Gregorian calendar, which required the removal of eleven days. The date of her death in October of 1582 did not technically exist.

Be joyful in hope, patient in affliction, faithful in prayer.
ROMANS 12:12

Asermon in stone, Barcelona's La Sagrada Família, tells God's story with every element of its architecture. But it didn't start out that way. Begun in 1882 by architect Francisco Villar, the Temple *Expiatori de la Sagrada Família* (the Church of the Holy Family) was simply slated as a church for the city's poor. But when premier Spanish architect, Antoni Gaudí, took over the project a year later, he envisioned the church as the "last great sanctuary of Christendom."

Gaudí was a master of the surrealistic *Modernisme* style of architecture, incorporating both the whimsical and the arguably weird into his fairy-tale-like designs. His plans for La Sagrada Família included three different façades: the Nativity Façade, depicting the story of Christ's birth and childhood; the Passion Façade, depicting Christ's crucifixion; and the Glory Façade, depicting Judgment Day. Gaudí died in 1926. The Glory Façade and other important elements of the church are still far from finished. Working from Gaudí's models and plans (and funded entirely by private donation), it's estimated the middle of the twenty-first century will come before the final stone in La Sagrada Família is set in place.

Important Sites

La Sagrada Família
Barcelona, Spain

Though La Sagrada Família truly is Gaudí's masterpiece, it also became his obsession. After exhausting his own personal accounts to pay for ongoing construction, Gaudí spent the last fourteen years of his life living as a hermit on the construction site and begging for funds door-to-door. Gaudí's crypt can be found on the lower level of the church.

When complete, La Sagrada Família's tallest tower will be one meter less in height than the hill of Montjuïc, Barcelona's tallest point. Gaudí felt that his handiwork should not surpass God's.

FACT

And you are living stones that God is building into his spiritual temple.
1 PETER 2:5 NLT

So, what do you believe?" From its earliest days, the Christian church has been called upon by critics, converts, and the merely curious to define its doctrine. Succinct statements of faith emerged, sometimes causing division within churches, but more often than not pulling various congregations together under one umbrella of faith and profession.

The Westminster Assembly convened in 1643 in London for the express purpose of reforming the Church of England. The assembly wrote rules for church government and a guide for public worship services. It formulated statements of central doctrines and communicated with churches on the Continent. The assembly wrote a larger and a shorter catechism, and a new confession, which came to be known as the Westminster Confession of Faith.

Reaching consensus on common points of doctrine did not go smoothly. One of the Assembly's ministers, a fervent proponent of creating the Confession, Edmund Calamy, declared the process "sin and misery." Despite his despair, the Assembly completed the document in 1646. The Confession upholds the clear teachings of scriptures and names the sixty-six books of the biblical canon in which God reveals Himself to the human heart. It affirms God's continued preservation, protection, and presence, and defines His plan of salvation and His promise of eternal life to all who believe in Him.

Groundbreaking Events

The Westminster Confession of Faith

The Westminster Confession of Faith has stood the test of time as a reliable summary of Christian doctrine and faith. With some later revisions, the Confession remains a central document in Reformed and evangelical churches to this day.

FACT

One of the signs of a cult is the secretive and mysterious nature of the group's beliefs. Their public statements evade central issues, reserving such knowledge for "initiated" members. Legitimate church bodies provide clear statements of central beliefs and teachings in their creeds and confessions for anyone to examine.

[Jesus said,] "Whoever acknowledges me before men,
I will also acknowledge him before my Father in heaven."
MATTHEW 10:32

W hat do you want more than anything else in the world? That's the question pastor and author A. W. Tozer invites readers to consider in *The Pursuit of God*.

Tozer, an eloquent speaker and writer of the twentieth century, experienced deep personal intimacy with God. Among his colleagues and parishioners, he was highly regarded and widely recognized as a spiritual mentor and counselor. In *The Pursuit of God*, Tozer demonstrates how easy it is for Christians, surrounded by material things, to find themselves ensnared by passions, possessions, and attachments—suddenly trapped by the "tyranny of things." Consequently, personal priorities shift and God drifts from the number one spot in an individual's life, and the believer no longer says "no" to those things that hinder the pursuit of God. Tozer shows how true peace with God and a thriving relationship with God can happen only when the believer freely surrenders to God all private ambitions, desire for money, comfort, fame, and any other personal passion. In other words, to give up one's life not for self-inflicted privation, but so God can give it back again.

Notable Books

The Pursuit of God
By A. W. Tozer (1957)

Tozer leads the reader to not only relinquish anything standing between God and the soul, but to realize the cost of doing so. Suffering accompanies denying oneself the selfish pursuits of the flesh, the world's approval, and the thrill of instant gratification. For some Christians, the cost is steeper—persecution, even physical death. Yet *not* following Christ sacrificially and wholeheartedly costs the peace and blessedness found in Him alone.

A. W. Tozer wrote, "I am Thy servant to do Thy will, and that will is sweeter to me than position or riches or fame and I choose it above all things on earth or in heaven."

FACT

[Jesus said,] "No servant can serve two masters.
Either he will hate the one and love the other,
or he will be devoted to the one and despise the other.
You cannot serve both God and Money."
LUKE 16:13

Author and composer Russell Kelso Carter was born on November 18, 1849, in Baltimore, Maryland. Throughout his lifetime of seventy-nine years, he was a versatile and gifted man. His varied professions show his wide range of interests. They include: Methodist minister, sheep rancher, leader in the Holiness movement, textbook publisher, prolific writer of novels and hymns, and professor of science, chemistry, and mathematics. In his later years, he became a practicing physician.

Russell Carter penned the words to "Standing on the Promises" in 1866 while he served as professor of the Pennsylvania Military Academy, a school from which he had graduated in 1867. In his book *Music in Evangelism*, author Phil Kerr suggests that the hymn's music is one of rhythmic martial tone from Mr. Carter's military academy experience.

The words to this hymn clearly portray Carter's claim of daily dependence on God's promises for himself. Mr. Carter loved reading the stories of the Bible, especially scriptures about God's promises and reliance on His Word. The hymn was first published the same year it was written in a hymnal compiled by Russell Carter and John Sweeney, entitled *Songs of Perfect Love*. The straightforward and yet encouraging words of Carter's hymn have made this beloved hymn a favorite for the past century.

Songs of the Faith

"Standing on the Promises" (1886)

Words and music
by Russell Kelso Carter

Standing on the promises of Christ my King,
Through eternal ages let His praises ring;
Glory in the highest, I will shout and sing,
Standing on the promises of God.

Refrain:
Standing, standing,
Standing on the promises of Christ my Savior;
Standing, standing, I'm standing on the promises of God.

FACT

In addition to "Standing on the Promises," Carter wrote numerous other hymn texts and music, and in 1891 helped compile *Hymns for the Christian Life* for the Christian and Missionary Alliance denomination.

For no matter how many promises God has made, they are "Yes" in Christ.
2 CORINTHIANS 1:20

Opened in 1978, Heritage USA soon became one of the top theme parks in the nation. By the mid-eighties, the 2,400-acre "Christian Disneyland" attracted nearly six million visitors annually and employed more than two thousand people throughout the park, resort, shopping mall, amphitheater, television studios, and entertainment complex in Fort Mill, South Carolina. But the extraordinarily successful venture began to collapse barely ten years after its opening with the downfall of its visionary leader, Jim Bakker.

Jim and his wife, Tammy Faye, were two of televangelism's superstars during the 1970s and 1980s. They hosted the Pentecostal-oriented television program, *The PTL Club* ("Praise the Lord" and "People That Love"), and soon won the devotion of fervent followers with their mix of talk, entertainment, testimonies, and pleas for donations. Generous donations poured in, soon establishing the Bakkers not only as famous, but also rich—very rich. When the tax-exempt status of Heritage USA came under IRS scrutiny, the Bakkers lost few disciples to charges of fraud and tax evasion.

Miscellany

Jim and Tammy Faye Bakker

Publicity surrounding Jim's sexual liaison with his secretary, however, proved too much for the market to bear. He resigned in 1987, the multibillion dollar empire unraveled, and attendance at the theme park plummeted.

Heritage USA ultimately closed and fell into disrepair after several attempts by various developers to turn a profit on the property. But recently, portions of the Heritage USA property are being redeveloped and some of the original buildings renovated. The former Grand Hotel now hosts retreats and conferences and other religious gatherings.

> The former park's landmark twenty-one-story Grand Tower, unfinished and fallen into ruin, is slated for implosion. Plans to turn it into a retirement complex have been proposed, and its fate remains uncertain.
>
> FACT

Be very careful, then, how you live—not as unwise but as wise.
Ephesians 5:15

Who would die for a lie? Nearly all Jesus' disciples, who had witnessed his life, death, and resurrection, suffered martyrdom rather than change their testimony. Untold numbers of first- and second-generation Christians bore torturous deaths rather than deny Jesus as Lord.

Polycarp, bishop of Smyrna (now Izmir, seaport in Turkey), knew the apostle John and other eyewitnesses to the Lord's earthly ministry. He was a prolific writer of letters to the churches of western Asia, urging Christians to avoid materialism, dishonesty, and disunity. A Christian apologist, he countered the teachings of Marcion, an influential heretic who rejected Old Testament prophecies, and the preachers of gnostic heresies who claimed to possess Jesus' deep secrets. To the powers-that-be, however, Polycarp was a leading figure in a politically threatening cult.

Men of the Faith

Polycarp (69–155)
Bishop and martyr

When the authorities started closing in on Polycarp, he hid in a farmhouse and prayed. He fell into a trance and saw his pillow burning with fire. He awoke, reconciled to his impending execution, and made no further effort to escape his fate. He met those who had come to arrest him, provided them with food, and chatted affably with them before they led him away.

Standing trial in a stadium filled with a rambunctious crowd assembled for games, Polycarp was invited to curse Christ. He replied for all to hear, "I have served him for eighty-six years and he has done me no wrong. How can I blaspheme my king and Savior?" The crowd cried for blood, and they got it. Polycarp was burned at the stake.

FACT

Polycarp's martyrdom is among the most well-documented events of antiquity. In a letter from the Church of Smyrna to "all the brotherhoods of the holy and universal Church," the writer offers a full account of Polycarp's arrest, trial, and execution.

While they were stoning him, Stephen prayed, "Lord Jesus, receive my spirit."
ACTS 7:59

Listeners to BBC's broadcasts know the name Dr. Elaine Storkey. She is widely recognized as an authoritative Christian voice in contemporary culture.

Storkey's academic background includes studies in philosophy, sociology, and theology. She has taught in the United Kingdom and abroad and has served as executive director of the London Institute for Contemporary Christianity. She is a lecturer at Oxford University and a senior research fellow at Wycliffe Hall. As UK president of Tearfund, a relief organization, she mobilizes Christians to meet both the spiritual and physical needs of people who suffer under social injustices and the hardships of hunger and poverty. She has traveled throughout Africa and elsewhere in the world on behalf of the Christian charity.

Storkey has also helped bring media attention to often overlooked or underreported events, such as the 2005 elections in the Democratic Republic of the Congo and how churches have worked together to help heal the war-torn country's years of terror.

Women of the Faith

Elaine Storkey (b. 1943)
Author, academic, and speaker

In numerous books and articles, Storkey has grappled with the principles of Christianity and the challenges of twenty-first-century life. Subjects range from Christian feminism and marriage to the application of Christian ethics in the modern workplace. She urges Christians to find creative and innovative ways to build bridges between the truths of the gospel and the human needs in today's world. Rather than shunning contemporary culture, she asserts, Christians need to listen to it and understand it before they can effectively witness to it.

Elaine Storkey writes, "The question is whether we're prepared to consider a biblical ethics which invites us to seek justice and walk humbly with God, or whether we carry on putting ourselves first."

FACT

Do not conform any longer to the pattern of this world,
but be transformed by the renewing of your mind.
ROMANS 12:2

Twice a day, Lindisfarne becomes an island off the Northumberland coast of England. And twice a day, when the ocean tides recede, it rejoins the mainland. For more than thirteen hundred years, Christian pilgrims have braved the three-mile journey across the mudflats to reach the Holy Island, as it's been known since the eleventh century. Early pilgrims were guided by rock cairns. Today's visitors can walk the same path, following a series of fourteen-foot wooden guideposts, or drive across a paved causeway. However, when the tides begin to rise, both routes quickly disappear.

Though Lindisfarne is known for its natural beauty, the significance the island holds in the history of the Christian church has earned its renown. Nothing remains here of the first Celtic church but its legacy. King Oswald, the Christian king of Great Britain, asked the monks on the Scottish isle of Iona to bring Christianity to England. Aidan arrived in 635. He not only spread the gospel but bartered peace between warring tribes.

Important Sites

Lindisfarne
England

Although Aidan, and later a bishop named Cuthbert, was elemental in the spiritual growth of northern England, it's the *Lindisfarne Gospels* that helped make this "sometimes" island famous. Like the *Book of Kells*, the *Lindisfarne Gospels* are beautifully illuminated copies of the Gospels in Latin. In the late tenth century, a monk added Old English to the Latin text, making this the oldest surviving English Gospel. Today, the *Lindisfarne Gospels* are in the British Library in London.

FACT

On the first page of Luke in the *Lindisfarne Gospels*, there is an intricate design of over ten thousand red dots and a cat lounging in the right-hand margin, eyeing the birds that decorate the bottom of the page.

Everything that was written in the past was written to teach us, so that through endurance and the encouragement of the Scriptures we might have hope.
ROMANS 15:4

Before the 1960s, race sharply divided American towns and cities. Certain neighborhoods, schools, businesses, and churches were "white" and others "black." White home buyers in the fifties might remember a clause in their deeds that forbade the sale of their home to blacks.

Things began to change when Dr. Martin Luther King Jr. emerged on the public scene. The son of a minister and a minister himself, King challenged racial segregation and the oppression of blacks. In 1957, he was one of the founding members of the Southern Christian Leadership Conference (SCLC) and the organization's most prominent speaker and fund-raiser. Strongly influenced by Indian leader Mohandas Gandhi, King espoused nonviolent protest and persuasion to change the entrenched injustice of American racism.

On August 28, 1963, King, along with other black leaders, led a demonstration in Washington, D.C., for jobs and civil rights. King roused the crowd of two hundred fifty thousand with an eloquent address, his "I have a dream" speech. In his signature soaring oratorical style, King encapsulated the hopes of all oppressed Americans: "I have a dream that one day this nation will rise up and live out the true meaning of its creed: *We hold these truths to be self-evident, that all men are created equal.* . . . I have a dream that my four little children will one day live in a nation where they will not be judged by the color of their skin, but by the content of their character."

Groundbreaking Events

The Civil Rights March on Washington, D.C.

The Civil Rights Act, prohibiting segregation in public places and discrimination in education and employment, was passed in 1964. King was awarded the 1964 Nobel Prize for peace.

One of Dr. King's early demonstrations landed him in jail. Chastised by ministers who blamed him for causing disorder in the city, he wrote his widely distributed "Letter from Birmingham Jail." In it, King argued for the moral right of citizens to disobey unjust laws. The letter further elevated King as an influential moral leader.

FACT

This is what the LORD says: "Maintain justice and do what is right,
for my salvation is close at hand and my righteousness will soon be revealed."
ISAIAH 56:1

Genesis or geology? In the mid-nineteenth century, discoveries in geology gave rise to questions about the biblical account of the Great Flood. Bible-believing researchers credited the earth's present geological features to the effects of the Flood. Skeptical geologists claimed to have found little evidence supporting a global flood of epic proportions.

Theology professor John C. Whitcomb and professor of engineering Henry M. Morris collaborated on *The Genesis Flood*, a book designed to assert the facts of the Great Flood with evidence left in rock formations, ancient fossils, and past climatic events. While many Bible-believing researchers attempt to interpret the Bible in light of scientific data, often accepting part but not all of scriptural history, Whitcomb and Morris placed the Bible first, then provided scientific evidence as proof.

The Genesis Flood drew its share of critics who faulted the accuracy of the authors' research and questioned their conclusions. Whitcomb and Morris's literal interpretation of the Genesis events riled liberal Christians, too. Nonetheless, the book opened the door to the harmonization of biblical revelation and geological discovery. It brought Bible-believing Christians into the conversation and challenged the prevailing theories of evolutionists and "old earth" proponents who dismiss scripture as a reliable source of historical knowledge.

Notable Books

The Genesis Flood

By John C. Whitcomb and
Henry M. Morris (1961)

Morris later said, "God has apparently used our book to help thousands of people around the world take the Bible more seriously. It does not require great skills in biblical theology and hermeneutics and exegesis to understand God's message concerning the depth, extent, and significance of the Flood."

FACT

After Creation, the Great Flood (Genesis 6:9–9:19) is the greatest physical event in the history of the earth. The Old Testament writers cited the Flood repeatedly, and Jesus referred to the Flood as an actual event, as did the apostle Peter and the writer of Hebrews.

They deliberately forget that long ago by God's word the heavens existed and the earth was formed out of water and by water. By these waters also the world of that time was deluged and destroyed.
2 PETER 3:5–6

Charlotte Elliott was born in Clapham, England, in 1789. When she was a young adult, she was a popular portrait artist and writer of humor. By age thirty, her health had declined, leaving her bedridden and despondent.

A turning point came in Charlotte's life in 1822 when Dr. Ceasar Malan, a Swiss evangelist, visited the Elliott home and spoke these words to her, "You must come just as you are, a sinner, to the Lamb of God that taketh away the sins of the world." Dr. Malan's wise counsel concerning her spiritual and emotional state became her mission statement for life. Every year afterward, Miss Elliott celebrated that day as her spiritual birthday.

Songs of the Faith

"Just As I Am"
Words by Charlotte Elliott (1835)
Music by William B. Bradbury (1849)

Charlotte Elliott wrote "Just As I Am" in 1836—fourteen years after her life-changing experience. It was published that same year as only one of Miss Elliott's 115 hymns included in the second edition of *The Invalid's Hymn Book*. By writing the hymn from the voice of her own life's experience, she hoped to help raise funds for building a school for poor clergymen's children. That one hymn brought in more funds than all the other projects and bazaars combined.

Just as I am, without one plea,
But that Thy blood was shed for me,
And that Thou bidst me come to Thee,
O Lamb of God, I come, I come.

Just as I am, Thou wilt receive,
Wilt welcome pardon, cleanse, relieve;
Because the promise I believe,
O Lamb of God, I come, I come.

Charlotte Elliott wrote: "God sees, God guides, God guards me. His grace surrounds me, and His voice continually bids me to be happy and holy in His service just where I am."

FACT

Then Jesus declared, "I am the bread of life. He who comes to me will never go hungry, and he who believes in me will never be thirsty. . . . All that the Father gives me will come to me, and whoever comes to me I will never drive away."
JOHN 6:35, 37

"You will never know what you can accomplish until you say a great big yes to the Lord." So declared American Robert Gilmour LeTourneau (1888–1969), who said yes to the Lord at age sixteen. At age thirty, he dedicated his life to God as a businessman.

LeTourneau's first employment—leveling out farmland—got him thinking about a more efficient way to do the job. His thoughts took shape in a patent for the first all-welded scraper, a machine far superior and less expensive to produce than existing equipment. The scraper succeeded in the marketplace, and LeTourneau continued designing and building earthmoving machinery. He revolutionized the earthmoving and materials handling by introducing the rubber tire to the industry; he introduced new welding techniques that were adopted industry-wide; and he produced mobile drilling platforms put to use in seas around the world. With a career total of 299 patents, he ranks as one of the most productive inventors of all time.

Extraordinary financial success and worldwide recognition didn't lure LeTourneau away from his initial commitment to the Lord. As God's businessman, he used his money to establish missions in Africa and South America. He traveled extensively across the United States and abroad to personally share the gospel of Jesus Christ. As money just kept pouring in, he kept pouring it out in support of Christian causes. LeTourneau tithed, but he turned the time-honored concept upside down. He donated 90 percent of his income to God's work and retained only 10 percent for himself!

Miscellany

The Upside-Down Tithe
R. G. LeTourneau

With his wife, Evelyn, he founded LeTourneau University, an evangelical, interdenominational Christian university located in Longview, Texas.

> FACT
>
> LeTourneau took his witness to the workplace. He hired full-time chaplains in his manufacturing plants and established regular chapel services for employees to attend. He influenced millions with his best-selling autobiography, *Mover of Men and Mountains*.

*"Seek first his kingdom and his righteousness,
and all these things will be given to you as well."*
MATTHEW 6:33

T hree days after burning a Bible, Sundar Singh saw the radiant figure of Jesus Christ. From that day forward, Singh, steeped in the traditions of Hindu Sikhs, worshipped the Christian God.

Singh, born to a wealthy family in northern India, immersed himself in the Hindu religion of his beloved mother. He planned to become a *sadhu*, one who forsakes worldly wealth to follow a life of the spirit. At age fourteen, Singh's mother died, leaving the boy distraught and angry. He lashed out at Christians, declaring Jesus wrong—dead wrong, at that—and incinerated a Bible to emphasize his point.

On the verge of suicide, he prayed for god—any god—to reveal himself. He became aware of an unusual light, and in this light he saw Jesus radiating the love and peace he so desperately longed for. He realized that Jesus, alive and not dead, was indeed the true God. Singh fell on his knees in adoration. Against his family's wishes, Singh was baptized, donned a yellow robe, and became a sadhu for Christ, going from village to village and preaching the gospel to his people.

Men of the Faith

Sadhu Sundar Singh (1889–1929)
Evangelist

Following the example of Jesus, Singh used parables like this one to teach the people: "[Chased by an eagle,] the sparrow flew into my lap. By choice, it would not normally do that. However, the little bird was seeking for a refuge from a great danger. Likewise, the violent winds of suffering and trouble blow us into the Lord's protective hands."

Singh's missionary travels took him to Tibet, India, Ceylon (now Sri Lanka), Malaysia, Japan, China, Australia, and Western Europe.

In 1919, while spending time in the foothills of Tibet, Sadhu Sundar Singh disappeared. The exact whereabouts of his body and cause of his death remain unknown.

FACT

"'Who are you, Lord?'" I asked.
"'I am Jesus of Nazareth, whom you are persecuting,' he replied."
Acts 22:8–9

DAY 198

When Ida Sophia Scudder was old enough, she decided to break with the family tradition of becoming a missionary in India. Living there as a child, she'd witnessed too much famine, poverty, and disease. She hoped instead to marry and settle down in the United States.

In 1890 her plans changed when her mother became ill. Ida left immediately for India to help her father with his work. Unfortunately, he died just months after she arrived. In the midst of her grief, she stayed for some time, doing her best to tend to the needs of the people.

During that visit, Ida witnessed deplorable medical conditions, especially for women, due primarily to religious taboos. The experience ignited a great compassion and convinced her she should become a doctor and return to help the Indian people. She earned a medical degree in the United States and then returned to India.

Women of the Faith

Ida Scudder (1870–1960)

Medical missionary

On the first day of January, 1900, Dr. Scudder converted her modest house in Madras Province into a one-bed clinic. She couldn't have imagined that this humble beginning would become Christian Medical College (CMC)—the largest hospital in the world with two thousand beds. CMC is run by the Vellore Christian Medical College Association, a registered charitable society with the involvement of more than fifty Indian Protestant churches and other Christian organizations.

Known in India simply as Dr. Ida, she received thousands of congratulatory letters in 1952 after winning the Elizabether Glackwel Citation of the New York Infirmary, as one of five top women doctors. Ida Scudder died in 1960 at the age of ninety.

FACT

Ida Scudder graduated from Cornell Medical College in New York City in 1899. She was part of the first class at that school to accept women as medical students.

He who follows righteousness and mercy finds life, righteousness, and honor.
PROVERBS 21:21 NKJV

When the Roman Empire conquered the islands of the Aegean, the tiny isle of Patmos was designated as a place of exile for convicts. Its sparse vegetation, rugged terrain, and isolated location served as a natural prison. But those earthly boundaries couldn't keep the apostle John from journeying to heavenly realms. It was in Patmos, nicknamed the Jerusalem of the Aegean, that John wrote the book of Revelation and, some theologians believe, the fourth Gospel.

Today, the Grotto of the Revelation can be found on the lowest level of the whitewashed Monastery of the Apocalypse. Both tradition and historical records support this spot as the location where John lived during his exile, from AD 84 to 96. Visitors making their way down to the grotto pass several chapels along the way, as well as a small church dedicated to "John the Theologian." The chapels were constructed in 1088, while the surrounding monastery wasn't built until the seventeenth century.

Important Sites

Patmos
Aegean Sea

A monk is stationed at the opening of the grotto, guiding visitors down another thirteen feet into a rock grotto. Here visitors are shown the rock John used as a pillow and a cross carved into the wall, allegedly by the apostle himself. In the roof of the grotto a fissure is split into three parts, symbolic to many visitors of the Trinity. Tradition holds that this fissure is where the voice of an angel broke through the rock to tell John to write down his prophetic vision.

The Patmian School, which opened in 1713 on the grounds of the monastery, was the first school to officially teach Greek letters. It is now a theological seminary.

FACT

Blessed is the one who reads the words of this prophecy,
and blessed are those who hear it
and take to heart what is written in it,
because the time is near.
REVELATION 1:3

Quakers trace their beginnings back to the Protestant reforms of the sixteenth century. Unhappy with what they regarded as papist rituals and illegitimate authoritarianism of the Church of England, some English Protestants yearned to experience a personal, authentic relationship with God. George Fox is generally regarded as the founder of the Religious Society of Friends, their formal name.

These men and women sat in silence in meetings until one of their members, prompted by the Holy Spirit, spoke the word of God. Often, while experiencing the presence of the Spirit, members shivered or trembled, thus they became popularly known (often derisively) as Quakers.

Quakers espoused simple manners, dress, and lifestyle. For scriptural reasons, many refused to engage in combat, even in self-defense. Quakers championed a clear division between religious and secular authority and were willing to defy the state when necessary. Persecuted for their dissenting ways, many immigrated to the American colonies, buying land in New Jersey and Pennsylvania. The early 1700s found Quaker enclaves established and thriving throughout most of the colonies. Unlike the majority of settlers, Quakers aided Native Americans, protested slavery, and supported women's rights. Quakers became a potent force in the social conscience of the colonies.

Groundbreaking Events

The Religious Society of Friends Founded

FACT

As in the past, Quaker meetings today may be held without a named leader or specially trained minister. Other meetings take place under an ordained pastor who facilitates worship with some measure of programmed activities, depending on the tradition and desires of the congregation.

The fruit of the Spirit is love, joy, peace, patience, kindness, goodness, faithfulness, gentleness and self-control. Against such things there is no law.
GALATIANS 5:22–23

If a man is lost on the road of life, will he ask directions? The old jab at male reluctance to seek help holds no truth for the hundreds of thousands of men who have read *The Man in the Mirror: Solving the 24 Problems Men Face* by Patrick Morley. Morley, a former real estate developer, speaks as one who has "been there"—that is, lost. The born-again Christian wrote *The Man in the Mirror* based on his personal search for life's purpose and a deeper relationship with God.

The book explores what it means to be a man in late-twentieth-century America, as well as significant questions about life's ultimate meaning and how an ordinary man can make his life count. Morley's words resonate with achieving businessmen who find themselves working ever longer hours to attain an exalted title that confers no lasting satisfaction and a handsome salary that buys no real happiness. In the wake of their corporate glory, they often find their family lives disintegrating or nonexistent.

Notable Books

The Man in the Mirror: Solving the 24 Problems Men Face
By Patrick Morley (1989)

Morley addresses the problems of out-of-control ambition, broken relationships, faulty decision-making, and destructive emotions, all of which threaten body and spirit. Straightforward talk about the challenges men face in the "real world" is followed by practical ways men can effect lasting change in their lives and relationships based on sound biblical teaching.

In 1991, Morley founded Man in the Mirror, a ministry devoted to working with pastors and male congregational leaders to help men make positive life changes.

Text found on the Man in the Mirror Web site reads, "If you take virtually every problem in America today, at the root of it you will find the failure of a man (e.g., 93 percent of prisoners are male and 85 percent of these come from fatherless homes)."

FACT

You were running a good race.
Who cut in on you and kept you from obeying the truth?
GALATIANS 5:7

Henry van Dyke is recognized as one of the most prominent preachers in U.S. history. He was also an accomplished
author of bestselling books, devotionals, and lyrics.

In writing the hymn, "Joyful, Joyful, We Adore Thee," he wished
to express trust, hope, and a joyful interaction between God and all of His
creation. The second verse of the hymn focuses on God's glory and directing man's worship to the Creator. The fourth verse is an invitation for God's children to join with all of creation in a chorus of joy, praise, and encouragement for every circumstance in life. Hymnologists have stated that this particular hymn has some of the most joyous lyrics in the English language.

Songs of the Faith

"Joyful, Joyful, We Adore Thee"

Words by Henry van Dyke (1911)

Music: Beethoven's Ninth Symphony (1824)

Inspiration for the words came while van Dyke was a guest preacher at
Williams College in Williamstown, Massachusetts. When he presented the lyrics to
the college president, he explained that the Berkshire Mountains had inspired him
to write the hymn and that it should be sung to the music of Beethoven's "Hymn of
Joy." The text was first published in the third edition of van Dyke's *Book of Poems* in
1911. The tune for the hymn comes from the final movement of Beethoven's *Ninth
Symphony*, composed during 1817–1823 and published in 1826.

> *Joyful, joyful, we adore Thee, God of glory, Lord of love;*
> *Hearts unfold like flowers before Thee, opening to the sun above.*
> *Melt the clouds of sin and sadness; drive the dark of doubt away;*
> *Giver of immortal gladness, fill us with the light of day!*

FACT

Beethoven's *Ninth Symphony* was inspired by a poem entitled "Ode to
Joy," written by his German friend, Friedrich Schiller.

You will fill me with joy in your presence,
with eternal pleasures at your right hand.
PSALM 16:11

What would it be like to wake up one morning and find that millions of people—every single one of them Christian—have suddenly disappeared? Such is the setting for the first Rapture movie, *A Thief in the Night*. Issued in 1972, the widely acclaimed suspense saga and its three sequels (*A Distant Thunder*, *Image of the Beast*, and *Prodigal Planet*) depict events as they unfold in the years prior to Christ's Second Coming. They draw on the language and symbols of biblical prophecies, especially those found in the book of Revelation.

Miscellany

A Thief in the Night—the Movie

For two millennia, mysterious passages of perhaps the Bible's most mysterious book have set imaginations working overtime to construct an end-times scenario. Speculations include a one-thousand-year earthly reign of Jesus Christ, marked by perfect peace and prosperity on earth. Another theory depicts a "rapture"—the taking up of Christians into heaven—followed by great suffering on earth initiated by a malevolent figure, the Antichrist. Then Christ's one-thousand-year reign begins, after which the devil roams once more until the Battle of Armageddon and final judgment. Some—or a combination—of these events embraced by many conservative Christians served as the starting point for *A Thief in the Night* and subsequent end-times movies and books.

Apocalyptic speculation reached its peak in the years leading up to the dawn of the third millennium. "Prophets" predicted everything from the release of virulent computer worms to the coming of Jesus Christ at one minute past midnight on December 31, 1999. The moment passed without incident. There are some things that must remain a mystery until—the end-times.

In an interview, actress Patty Dunning revealed that during filming she was walking across a railroad trestle when she slipped and almost fell through the cracks. Perhaps the fact that she was a professional gymnast explains how she was able to avoid a sixty-foot fall.

FACT

"If the owner of the house had known at what time of night the thief was coming,
he would have kept watch and would not have let his house be broken into.
So you also must be ready, because the Son of Man will come
at an hour when you do not expect him."
MATTHEW 24:43–44

"It's just not in me to do right," Dawson Trotman wrote in his journal. "I'm a loser." Though handsome, popular, and academically gifted, the young man's assessment was well founded. His lifestyle had not changed, despite two sincerely uttered "decisions for Christ." He remained a liar, gambler, thief, and drunkard. In despair over his inability to carry out his good resolutions, Trotman begged God to enter his life.

God indeed entered Trotman's life, and he at last left his profligate ways behind. Working as a truck driver, he routinely picked up hitchhikers and told them about the life he had found in Jesus Christ. A sailor, Les Spencer, was impressed by Trotman's turnaround and asked him his secret. Trotman's teaching convinced Spencer, who then brought another sailor to Trotman for guidance. But why hadn't Spencer witnessed to the man himself? That question led to the founding in 1933 of the Navigators, an organization devoted to Christian development and training.

Men of the Faith

Dawson Trotman
(1906–1956)
Evangelist

From personal experience, Trotman knew that a decision for Christ means little without a practical follow-up plan. He grasped from his experience with Spencer that disciples need to learn how to share the gospel with others. Navigators helps Christians develop a disciplined approach to Bible study, a sound prayer life, and the ability to witness effectively. The interdenominational organization publishes *Discipleship Journal*, along with Bible-study guides, devotionals, and prayer books, and facilitates conferences on Christian growth and outreach.

Evangelist Billy Graham and his team adopted Trotman's program of Bible instruction and verse memorization—called B Rations—to keep converts true to their conviction.

FACT

Dawson Trotman died in a boating accident while rescuing a girl from drowning. Fellow evangelist Billy Graham preached at his funeral service.

"The righteous will hold to their ways,
and those with clean hands will grow stronger."
JOB 17:9

A human skull dangling from a pole greeted missionary Mary Slessor as she approached her new post. Old Town, a remote station in Calabara (now Nigeria), was not a hospitable place. The natives' reputation for cruelty and cannibalism kept most missionaries at a distance, but not Slessor. She went to teach the gospel of Jesus Christ.

Born in Scotland, Mary came from a working-class family. In her late twenties, she trained for mission work with the Presbyterian mission society and sailed for Calabar in West Africa. Once described as "a timid child," the now-intrepid woman entered a jungle of ferocious animals, poisonous insects, deadly diseases, and fearsome warriors. Her first assignment took her to Duke Town on the Calabar River.

Women of the Faith

Mary Slessor (1848–1915)
Missionary

Missionaries in Duke Town had established a chapel, school, and hospital. On any given Sunday, several hundred natives gathered at the mission station for services. Slessor taught at the mission school, learned the local languages, and traveled to neighboring villages. Despite the dangers, she ventured far inland, where tribes lived embroiled in terrifying superstitions and murderous customs. Slessor begged for permission to live among them. At last she received the coveted post: Old Town, deep in the jungle of Calabara.

Slessor's wisdom, love, and compassion for the people endeared her to the tribesmen, including the isolated and much-feared Okoyongs. Called "Ma" Slessor, she was deeply respected among natives, traders, and missionaries alike. Recognized as an outstanding missionary, she was awarded the Silver Cross in Nigeria before her death in 1915.

Mary Slessor wrote, "I have always said that I have no idea how or why God has carried me over so many funny and hard places and made these hordes of people submit to me, or why the Government should have given me the privilege of a Magistrate among them, except in answer to prayer made at home for me."

FACT

[Jesus said,] "I have given you authority to trample on snakes and scorpions and to overcome all the power of the enemy; nothing will harm you."

LUKE 10:19

Nazareth was Jesus' childhood home. Today, it's home to numerous churches built to commemorate that fact. The two most famous churches are the Basilica of the Annunciation and the Church of St. Joseph. The two churches are linked by a Franciscan convent built on the original site of the town of Nazareth.

Archaeological ruins below the Church of St. Joseph date to the first century. They include a cave believed to be the original workshop of Joseph, which was also used as the family's home. Tooled niches in the rock walls were typical in homes during the Roman period to store food and water. One of these was converted during the Byzantine era into a mosaic-tiled baptismal pool. Several churches have been built and destroyed on this site. The current Church of St. Joseph was completed in 1914.

Important Sites

Nazareth

Israel

The Church of the Annunciation marks the traditionally held location of Mary's home and her visit from the angel, Gabriel. (However, the Greek Orthodox Church believes Mary spoke to Gabriel at a nearby well, which is marked by the Greek Orthodox Gabriel's Church.) The first shrine built on this spot was an altar constructed during the fourth century. Several churches were built after that, the fourth of which was destroyed in 1955 to construct the modern-day basilica. The largest Christian basilica in the Middle East, the church's interior is decorated with mosaics, banners, and a variety of art that has come from church communities worldwide.

FACT

The Basilica of the Annunciation has a Web site where visitors from around the world are encouraged to light a candle via the Internet. For ten dollars, people can order a "light and pray" service, then watch a video feed of their candle being lit and specified prayer being prayed live in Nazareth.

God sent the angel Gabriel to Nazareth, a town in Galilee,
to a virgin pledged to be married to a man named Joseph, a descendant of David.
LUKE 1:26–27

Y ou've gotta walk the walk." As German Lutheranism developed during the sixteenth and seventeenth centuries, some within the church sensed its growing irrelevance. Lutheran pastors, so focused on matters of theology, were failing to provide sermons applicable to the everyday lives of their flock. The Lutheran church, laypeople felt, was no longer walking the spiritual walk.

A Frankfort pastor, Philipp Jakob Spener, emerged as an influential voice of the burgeoning piety movement. In his sermons, Spener preached on practical application of biblical concepts and how they relate to daily life. In 1670, he established *assemblies of piety*, private gatherings in his house for Bible reading, religious study, group devotions, and encouragement in the Christian life. The egalitarian assemblies promoted the active participation of women as well as men.

Spener's writings addressed the problems he found in the Lutheran church. He called for a new emphasis on: Bible literacy; spiritual knowledge resulting in a forgiving heart and charitable actions; practical ways to live a devout life, with pastors setting the example; and the significance of the priesthood of all believers. Pietism has been described as a "religion of the heart," elevating personal religious experience and incorporating elements of mysticism present in both Roman Catholic and Protestant tradition.

Groundbreaking Events

The German Piety Movement

Pietism spread rapidly throughout the Continent, British Isles, and American colonies. As a movement, Pietism reached the height of its popularity in the mid-eighteenth century before declining in later years. Its influence, however, is discernible in the theology, mission activity, and worship of many evangelical Protestant denominations today.

Pietism and the Enlightenment of the eighteenth century both opposed religious authoritarianism and upheld the significance of the individual. The concurrent movements diverged, however, in their evaluation of scripture. Proponents of the Enlightenment undermined the significance of the Bible, whereas for Pietists the Bible remained the unchanging and unalterable Word of God.

FACT

You are a chosen people, a royal priesthood, a holy nation,
a people belonging to God, that you may declare the praises of him
who called you out of darkness into his wonderful light.
1 PETER 2:9

Author, speaker, and former law professor Phillip E. Johnson defends creationism against the theory of evolution in *Darwin on Trial*. Using reason, logic, and scientific evidence, Johnson takes on neo-Darwinist claims of a common ancestor for both animals and humans and the hypothesis that new species emerge in the process of natural selection. His well-researched book seriously challenges the tenets of evolutionary science, and it remains a classic in the creation-evolution controversy.

Johnson begins by itemizing well-known inconsistencies and questions surrounding the theory of evolution. He notes the lack of transitional fossils between species and convincing molecular evidence for common descent. Johnson then delves into the way evolutionary scientists attempt to ward off criticism by framing their arguments in seemingly unassailable language. Most pointedly, Johnson states the fact that scientists can no more observe and recreate the creation of the world than can creationists, so both propositions ultimately remain impossible to prove.

Notable Books

Darwin on Trial

By Phillip E. Johnson (1991)

Darwin on Trial ends with Johnson's summary of Darwinism's role in U.S. education and religion. He proposes that despite strong evidence that undermines the credibility of the theory of evolution, the scientific community promotes it as a way to counteract the forces of religious fundamentalism.

The subject goes much further than an ideological battle between evolutionists and creationists. If life is, as evolutionists claim, random and purposeless, then the verdict falls in favor of naturalistic philosophies and values, which in turn translate into laws and legislative decisions that affect the life of every individual. *Darwin on Trial* pulls the subject out of the courtroom and plops it right into your own living room.

FACT

As a leader of the intelligent design movement, Johnson promotes Christian principles as the antidote to current materialistic worldviews currently taught in secular schools and universities.

Through him all things were made;
without him nothing was made that has been made.
JOHN 1:3

Born in Whitmore, Staffordshire, England, in 1839, Samuel John Stone became most well known as the poor man's pastor. After graduating from Oxford, he spent most of his time ministering to the humble folks and poorest people in London's East End. He had a heart of mercy for needy people and created a beautiful place where they could worship. Stone was an outspoken man of spotless character and defended without compromise the conservative faith that many fought against in his day.

Stone wrote a collection of twelve hymns based on the Apostles' Creed entitled, *Lyra Fidelium* (*Lyra of the Faithful*), in hopes of addressing the attacks of modern scholarship and liberalism that he felt might divide and destroy the church. All of Stone's writings were skillfully interwoven with his personal inspiration from scripture, and what has been described as a manly faith, dogma, prayer, and praise.

Songs of the Faith

"The Church's One Foundation"

Words by Samuel J. Stone (1866)

Music by Samuel S. Wesley (1864)

This particular hymn, based on the ninth article of the Creed, reveals Samuel Stone's belief that the unity of the Church must rely completely on recognition of Christ's Lordship as its head and not on man-made viewpoints or interpretation.

Two years later, all of the Anglican bishops gathered for the great Lambeth theological conference in London and chose Stone's hymn as the processional theme song.

> *The Church's one foundation*
> *Is Jesus Christ her Lord,*
> *She is His new creation*
> *By water and the Word.*
> *From heaven He came and sought her*
> *To be His holy bride;*
> *With His own blood He bought her,*
> *And for her life He died.*

The composer of the music for this hymn, Samuel S. Wesley, was the grandson of Charles Wesley and was recognized as one of the leading church musicians of his day.

FACT

Christ is the head of the church, his body, of which he is the Savior.
EPHESIANS 5:23

Judas Iscariot, keeper of the purse shared by Jesus and His disciples, proved an unworthy financial manager. He regularly had his hand in the communal denarii. Hardly a Christian congregation since can say it has never had a "Judas" in its midst—a pastor, leader, or trusted lay member secretly skimming the offering plate.

In 1979, a group of Christian leaders banded together to establish the religious equivalent of the Better Business Bureau: the Evangelical Council for Financial Accountability (ECFA). Today, more than two thousand churches, ministries, and charities claim membership, committing themselves to the ECFA's seven Standards of Responsible Stewardship. These standards, among other things, require financial transparency, integrity in raising funds and accepting donations, and responsible handling of resources. On a yearly basis, the ECFA scrutinizes a participating agency's financial statements, salary levels, donor appeals, and more. It conducts investigative on-site reviews at about 15 percent of its membership each year. In addition, the ECFA handles complaints against member organizations and provides help and information to the donating public.

Miscellany

The Evangelical Council for Financial Accountability (ECFA)

Public acceptance came quickly, and the ECFA effectively earned donor trust. The assurance of a review by outside auditors and the ready availability of an agency's financial records give present and potential donors confidence that their money goes for the purpose intended. Also, with the knowledge they are being monitored, organizations receiving donations have a great deal of incentive to ensure that no "Judas" suns himself in the Bahamas, courtesy of a generous, unknowing public.

FACT

In the 1970s, increasing donor concern over publicized mismanagement of funds by certain charities threatened contribution levels and public trust. Fund-raising appeals, also, were shown to contain misleading, inflated claims. Before the formation of the ECFA, donors had little way of receiving an impartial opinion on the health and integrity of a Christian organization.

"Why wasn't this perfume sold and the money given to the poor? It was worth a year's wages." He [Judas] did not say this because he cared about the poor but because he was a thief; as keeper of the money bag, he used to help himself to what was put into it.
JOHN 12:5–6

Kenneth Taylor grew up in the parsonages of the Presbyterian churches his father pastored in Oregon and Washington. A devout student of the Bible, Taylor nonetheless grappled with the old-fashioned language of the King James Bible.

He attended Wheaton College in Illinois, where his spiritual development took a detour. Upon reading the story of William Borden, a promising missionary who died of spinal meningitis at age twenty-five, Taylor held God responsible and turned away from him. God had the last word, however, as Taylor repented and surrendered his life to Christ.

Taylor went on to the Dallas Theological Seminary, then accepted an offer to edit *HIS* magazine in Chicago. From *HIS*, he joined Good News Publishers as a translator of tracts for missions; then joined the editorial staff at Moody Bible Institute.

Men of the Faith

Kenneth N. Taylor (1917–2005)

Author, editor, publisher, and Bible translator

Taylor remembered the problems he encountered when, as a child, he tried to decipher the old-fashioned language of the King James Bible. He embarked on a big project: paraphrase the entire Bible in modern-day English. In 1962, he established Tyndale House Publishers in his dining room and published *Living Letters*, a paraphrase of the New Testament. Sales soared after Billy Graham began using the paraphrase in his ministry. *Living Letters*, along with Taylor's paraphrase of other Bible portions, became *The Living Bible*. Tyndale now ranks as a leading publisher of Christian books and Bible resources.

Taylor also founded Evangelical Literature Overseas, an agency organized to distribute Christian literature abroad; and the Christian Booksellers Association (CBA), a trade association of Christian stores and publishers.

Drawing from the entire Bible, Taylor wrote kid-friendly Bible stories to read to his children. Later, Moody published the stories under the bestselling title, *The Bible in Pictures for Little Eyes*.

FACT

[Jesus said,] "You diligently study the Scriptures because you think that by them you possess eternal life. These are the Scriptures that testify about me."

JOHN 5:39–40

Wealthy landowners and aristocrats, Florence Nightingale's parents could not have imagined their daughter ever pursuing a nursing profession—an occupation typically left to prostitutes, alcoholics, and socially challenged people. But from age six when Florence nursed her first patient—an injured collie—back to health, she knew a seed of destiny had been planted in her heart.

At age seventeen, she penned, "God called me to His service—nursing." On her thirtieth birthday, Florence journaled, "Now, Lord, let me think only of Thy will."

In 1851 she ignored her social status and began wearing the blue cotton dress and muslin cap worn by nurses in training. One morning in 1854 Florence cried as she read an account of the inhumane conditions of the Crimean War where British soldiers were left to die without basic care due to a lack of nurses and few doctors. Florence was soon chosen to lead a team of nurses to Turkey where she often worked twenty-four-hour shifts in extremely unsanitary conditions.

Women of the Faith

Florence Nightingale (1820–1910)

Mother of modern nursing

Because she walked and carried her lantern down four-mile rows of beds to check on wounded soldiers each midnight hour, Florence became known as the Lady with the Lamp.

When the war ended, the mortality rate had sharply declined due to the work of Florence and of the 125 nurses under her supervision. She became known worldwide as a heroine. In 1859, her book *Notes on Nursing* became an international bestseller.

As the standard-bearer, Florence Nightingale transformed nursing into a profession for single women of impeccable moral standards.

FACT

In 1855 Queen Victoria saluted Florence's "pure spirit of duty toward God and compassion for man," with the presentation of a brooch inscribed, BLESSED ARE THE MERCIFUL.

You, O LORD, keep my lamp burning; my God turns my darkness into light.
PSALM 18:28

At the height of its success, Heritage USA was one of the most popular vacation destinations in the United States. This 2,300-acre complex included a Christian theme park, a water park, a church, a theater, television studios, vacation condominiums, and a residential complex. The PTL Television Network, following in the footsteps of the Christian Broadcast Network and Trinity Broadcasting Network, helped open the door for the rise of Christian television and televangelists.

Heritage USA opened in 1978 and closed twelve years later in 1989. Cofounder Jim Bakker went to prison for fraud and tax evasion, and Heritage USA fell into disrepair.

Seven years after Heritage USA shut down, MorningStar Fellowship Church began meeting on the property with a new vision for ministry. Since then, they have renovated the former Heritage Grand Hotel into a retreat and conference center, renaming the complex H.I.M. (Heritage International Ministries). They've also opened a Christian school. The long-range plan includes a hospice and assisted living/retirement home.

Important Sites

Heritage USA
Fort Mill, South Carolina

The history of this site is far from perfect and is a reminder that even leaders are fallen people. However, the new ministry that has emerged from Heritage USA is a living reminder of the sure hope of redemption.

Sixty-five thousand people donated $1,000 for lifetime memberships to Heritage USA, entitling them to an annual three-day stay. However, these memberships outnumbered available hotel rooms. After a $3.7 million settlement, these people were each reimbursed $6.54. The lawyers were paid the remaining $2.5 million.

FACT

Unless the LORD builds the house, its builders labor in vain.
PSALM 127:1

Instead of spending the Lord's Day hanging out with your hooligan friends, go to Sunday school. Robert Raikes, newspaper publisher and social reformer, established the first Sunday schools in Gloucester, England, in 1780. Raikes set up classrooms where poor and orphaned children could get a rudimentary education, learn scripture and the catechism, receive moral instruction, and keep out of trouble. Classes, largely lay-led, met in teachers' homes and were free.

Not everyone applauded Raikes's good intentions. Conservative churchmen questioned the propriety of teaching on Sunday. The privileged class perceived a threat to social stability should the lower sorts start questioning their station in life. Nonetheless, Sunday schools, underwritten by progressive religious and philanthropic supporters, quickly multiplied, and the Sunday School Movement rapidly gained momentum. By the time of Raikes's death three decades later, nearly five hundred thousand children throughout Great Britain were enrolled in a Sunday school program.

Groundbreaking Events

The Sunday School Movement

In the 1790s, Sunday schools were being established in American cities. Notable among them was a school begun in Philadelphia in 1791 for the purpose of teaching any illiterate man, woman, or child to read and write. Similar Sunday schools opened throughout the States, though most closed by the 1830s. In their place arose Sunday schools organized by Protestant churches, specifically for the religious education of children. Sunday schools of this kind won rapid acceptance among parishioners and clergy alike, and remain a vital part of Christian education and mission activity to this day.

> FACT
>
> An impoverished child's Sunday school education often promoted the education of his or her parents. Some adults attended the schools with their children, and many illiterate parents encouraged their children to bring home books and share their lessons with the rest of the family.

"Listen to my instruction and be wise; do not ignore it."
PROVERBS 8:33

A modern spiritual classic, Richard J. Foster's *Celebration of Discipline* has guided untold numbers of Christians to a deeper exploration of their faith.

Celebration of Discipline describes what Christians need to do to advance in spiritual maturity. With clarity and humor, Foster describes the three areas of discipline he considers central to the experience of Christianity. He defines these topics under three headings: the Inward Disciplines (meditation, prayer, fasting, study); the Outward Disciplines (simplicity, solitude, submission, service); and the Corporate Disciplines (confession, worship, guidance, celebration). After explaining the importance of each of these disciplines, Foster offers practical ways today's believers can incorporate them into their everyday lives to achieve a higher and deeper level of Christian consciousness.

In *Celebration of Discipline,* Foster departs from popular "instant fix" programs to focus on disciplines that take time and practice, yet yield true and lasting results. He invites Christians to structure their lives around beneficial and faithfully practiced spiritual disciplines. He opens controversial topics, such as the discipline of *submission*, a biblical virtue reviled by progressive Christians and dismissed even by many conservative believers. Foster urges Christians to properly understand the term and personally cultivate the kind of submission compelling one to willingly give up selfish desires in favor of genuine love for and healthy submission to others—a practice that brings true fulfillment and joy.

Notable Books

Celebration of Discipline
By Richard J. Foster (1978)

Foster's spiritual insights explore timeless Christian disciplines so often left behind in modern Christianity—disciplines well worth the effort to acquire and practice for a balanced spiritual life.

Foster, a Quaker, is a leading writer and speaker on Christian spirituality. He is the founder of Renovaré, an interdenominational movement committed to Christian spiritual renewal.

FACT

[Jesus said,] "I have come that they may have life, and have it to the full."
JOHN 10:10

She is often referred to as "the consecration poet." That description of Frances Ridley Havergal, born in 1836, at Astley, Worcestershire, England, was given because of the beautifully consecrated life she demonstrated. She began writing verse by the time she was seven years old and had memorized most of the Bible. From an early age she had great compassion for anyone with spiritual and physical needs.

Her father, William, an Anglican minister devoted to composing English hymns, was a great influence on her education, writing, and composing. A natural musician and brilliant pianist, Frances also sang so beautifully she was much sought after as a concert soloist. In 1874, she wrote the motto of her heart in the hymn, "Take My Life and Let It Be."

At age forty-two, Miss Havergal's physician told her she did not have long to live. Miss Havergal replied, "If I am really going, it is too good to be true."

Songs of the Faith

"Take My Life and Let It Be"
Words by Frances R. Havergal (1874)
Music by Cesar Malan (1827)

Take my life, and let it be consecrated, Lord, to Thee.
Take my moments and my days; let them flow in ceaseless praise.
Take my hands, and let them move at the impulse of Thy love.
Take my feet, and let them be swift and beautiful for Thee.

Take my voice, and let me sing always, only, for my King.
Take my lips, and let them be filled with messages from Thee.
Take my silver and my gold; not a mite would I withhold.
Take my intellect, and use every power as Thou shalt choose.

FACT

Frances placed her favorite text (1 John 1:7 KJV) at the foot of her bed placed where she could easily read it: "The blood of Jesus Christ his Son cleanseth us from all sin."

"Gather to me my consecrated ones,
who made a covenant with me by sacrifice."
Psalm 50:5

I was getting ready for church that Sunday morning when. . ." the unthinkable happened. Shortly before 8:00 a.m. on December 7, 1941, the Japanese air force launched a surprise attack on American shores. Two waves of Japanese warplanes bombed American battleships and military installations at and around Pearl Harbor, Oahu, Hawaii. Less than two hours later, American forces were left with 21 ships sunk or damaged; 347 aircraft destroyed or damaged; 1,178 American military and civilians wounded; and 2,403 American deaths, including 54 civilians.

Japanese Commander Mitsuo Fuchida led the first wave of attacks and stayed behind to observe the second wave, even though U.S. fire had compromised his plane. Fuchida's voice relayed the message *"Tora! Tora! Tora!"* ("Tiger! Tiger! Tiger!") back to his aircraft carrier to report that the surprise attack had succeeded.

Miscellany

Then there was American POW Jacob DeShazer, captured by the Japanese in 1942 after a bombing raid near Tokyo. While in prison, DeShazer embraced Christianity. After being liberated, he wrote an essay, "I

Mitsuo Fuchida
Evangelist

Was a Prisoner of the Japanese," in which he described his capture, conversion, and decision to forgive his captors. DeShazer's widely read testimony fell into the hands of Fuchida. Influenced by DeShazer's story, he bought a Bible and he, too, embraced the gospel message.

In 1950, Fuchida met DeShazer, who had returned to Japan as a Christian missionary. DeShazer encouraged Fuchida in his Christian walk. While DeShazer continued to establish churches throughout Japan, Fuchida took on the work of an evangelist, spreading the gospel in Japan and Asian communities in the United States.

Fuchida, who died in 1976, desired to be remembered primarily for the change of heart he experienced upon his conversion to Christianity. He wrote: "After buying and reading the Bible, my mind was strongly impressed and captivated. I think I can say today without hesitation that God's grace has been set upon me."

FACT

---

*"If you forgive men when they sin against you,
your heavenly Father will also forgive you."*
MATTHEW 6:14

Personal holiness and intellectual pursuits came early to Jonathan Edwards, the son of a modest Puritan minister and tutor. At age fourteen, young Edwards was already a student at Yale and reading John Locke. By the time he was nineteen, he had earned a Master's degree from Yale. At twenty-six, he was the sole preacher of the Northampton, Massachusetts, parish.

Revivals often occurred when Edwards preached. Ironically, it wasn't due to beautiful speech or theatrics. In fact, many often accused Edwards of a monotone speaking style.

After he spoke on justification by faith, the first revival came. One·month that winter, he saw six conversions. By spring, thirty souls a week were coming to Christ. Soon, he was front and center in what is considered the Great Awakening. Revival spread throughout Northampton with a fervor that threatened to shut down businesses. During it all, Edwards recorded and published his observations in various discourses and essays.

Men of the Faith

Jonathan Edwards (1703–1758)

Colonial American theologian and revivalist

Orthodox leaders were not impressed and many criticized the swooning, outcries, and convulsions seen at these revival meetings. Edwards defended his appeals to emotion and advocated the threat of terror of those still caught in their sins.

During the Great Awakening, Edwards delivered what may be the most famous sermon in American history, "Sinners in the Hands of an Angry God." Still read by historians and theology students today, the work is a prime example of the fire-and-brimstone style of preaching exemplified by the period. Today, Edwards is still regarded as one of if not *the* most important and great American preachers of all time.

FACT

Before undertaking his ministry work in Northampton, Edwards wrote on natural history, including essays on "flying spiders," light, and optics.

He alone is my rock and my salvation; he is my fortress, I will never be shaken.
PSALM 62:2

Next time you pour a tall glass of cold milk, thank Mary Engle Pennington. At a time when the sciences were closed to women, Pennington earned a PhD in chemistry and became a leading expert in refrigeration and methods of transporting and storing perishable foods.

Pennington was born into a well-to-do Quaker family and remained a lifelong Quaker. Her parents encouraged her intellectual development, and at a young age she became interested in medical chemistry. Though told by the headmistress of her school that science was unsuitable for women, Pennington applied to the school of science at the University of Pennsylvania. The dean admitted her, and she studied chemistry, biology, and hygiene. Upon completing the requirements for a bachelor's degree, the university granted her only a certificate of proficiency, which made her ineligible for graduate studies. A supportive faculty found a way around the technicality, and Pennington went on to earn her doctorate.

Women of the Faith

Mary Engle Pennington
(1872–1952)
Chemist and bacteriologist

In the following years, she opened the Philadelphia Clinical Laboratory, and her work became widely recognized. She was invited to head the bacteriological laboratory for the Philadelphia Department of Health and Charities, where she examined the problem of spoiled milk. She focused on the field of refrigeration and its effect on milk, eggs, and poultry. As chief of the U.S. Department of Agriculture's Food Research Laboratory, Pennington developed standards for the transportation of dairy products from farm to consumer. Her scientific research and recommendations to the government and to the general public resulted in regulations and practices that have ensured food safety to generations of Americans.

Pennington's civil service exam, required for the position at the Food Research Lab, was (unknown to her) submitted under the name M. E. Pennington. Though given the job, the civil service rescinded the offer after discovering her gender. An influential colleague intervened on Pennington's behalf, and she was allowed to keep the position.

FACT

Commit to the LORD whatever you do, and your plans will succeed.
PROVERBS 16:3

In the summer of 2004, workmen in Jerusalem were searching for the cause of a sewer blockage. Instead, they found the Pool of Siloam. Archaeologists converged on the site where the workmen had uncovered a series of stone steps. Further excavations revealed a man-made pool 225 feet in length, surrounded by three tiers of stone steps. Pottery shards, and four ancient coins imbedded in the plastered steps, helped confirm that the pool was used in the first century.

In August of 2005, archaeologists officially announced that the Pool of Siloam had been found. Of course, the pool where Jesus healed the blind man (as recorded in John 9) had been "discovered" before. About 150 feet away lies a 53 x 18-foot man-made pool. It has been referred to as the Pool of Siloam for centuries. This pool lies at the mouth of Hezekiah's Tunnel. Dug during the eighth century BC, the 1,750-foot tunnel feeds water from Gihon Springs into Jerusalem. During the first century, this was the city's only permanent water source.

Important Sites

The Pool of Siloam

Jerusalem

The "real" Pool of Siloam sits in one of the lowest spots in Jerusalem. Rainstorms would easily have filled it with mud and debris. Apparently, by the end of the first century it fell into disuse and was soon hidden from sight. During the fifth century, a church was built above the smaller pool and Christians began making pilgrimages to that site. Today, Christian pilgrims are arriving once more—to visit both Pools of Siloam.

FACT

Since the water flows intermittently through the tunnel of Hezekiah and into the two pools, an ancient legend said that a dragon lived below the ground. When awake, he drank from the stream, interrupting its flow. When he slept, it flowed freely.

"Go," [Jesus] told him, "wash in the Pool of Siloam" (this word means Sent).
So the man went and washed, and came home seeing.
JOHN 9:7

Computer users of a certain age may remember their first PC. The monitor's bulbous backside protruded across the desk and its screen displayed black text on a gray background. Text only. Sorry, no movies. And no Internet, either. But for early adapters, it sure beat a typewriter.

Until the late eighties, the Internet was a U.S. government-funded program restricted to academic and military use. As restrictions were lifted and the World Wide Web simplified Internet use, the Internet grew rapidly in acceptance and popularity. It's estimated that more than one billion people worldwide use the Internet today.

The potential for reaching people with this emerging technology did not escape the Christian community. Progressive evangelists and mission organizations immediately took to the Internet to proclaim the gospel. The Net eventually lured mainline churches and now, even small independent congregations have Web pages. Today, Roman Catholic bishops, stereotypically entrenched in tradition, use the Net's media capabilities to distribute photos, videos, personal reflections, live chats, and classes, as well as broadcast sermons and complete church services.

Groundbreaking Events

The Gospel Disseminated over the Internet

The Internet has proven a widely available and effective means to spread the gospel to people where they are. The Christian message reaches those who wouldn't ordinarily go to church and provides an invaluable resource for Bible commentary and open discussion of social issues. Also, the Internet penetrates otherwise closed societies. In China, for example, the Internet (even though filtered by the government) has played a role in disseminating the gospel and exposing the plight of persecuted Chinese Christians.

In December, 1990, Pope John Paul II said, "The Areopagus represented the culture center of the learned people of Athens, and today it can be taken as a symbol of the new sectors in which the gospel must be proclaimed. The first Areopagus of the modern age is the world of communications, which is unifying humanity and turning it into what is known as a 'global village.' "

FACT

"The God who made the world and everything in it is the Lord of heaven and earth and does not live in temples built by hands."
ACTS 17:24

Do we live our lives unaware of a second, invisible reality always moving around us, influencing us for evil or for good? That's the platform for Frank Peretti's groundbreaking novel, *This Present Darkness*.

The novel's chief protagonist is a godly pastor by the name of Hank Busche, who discovers a sinister plot to turn Ashton's college into a bulwark of New Age philosophy. Falsely discredited and facing death threats, Hank and his wife, Mary, go to prayer and cause heavenly forces to be deployed on their behalf. As the plot flips back and forth from earthly realm to heavenly realm, Peretti gives the reader a bird's-eye view of the action.

For a great many Christians, *This Present Darkness* brought to life a concept that had heretofore been vague and undefined. Creatures from the spiritual world now had both face and persona. They could be acknowledged and addressed.

Notable Books

This Present Darkness
By Frank E. Peretti (1986)

Of course, the novel was not without its detractors. Some literary critics argued that the characters were simplistically typecast in roles of good and evil. Some theological critics argued that the biblical metaphor of spiritual warfare has everything to do with the struggle of the soul against sin and nothing to do with combat between angels and demons. Others simply remind readers that the book is fantasy rather than biblical scholarship; this is based on, among other things, the inclusion of female angels, baby angels, and pip-squeak demons, which have no basis in scripture.

Regardless of how some authorities view the book, there is no denying its success with readers. The book has sold more than 2.5 million copies worldwide.

FACT

The sequel to *This Present Darkness*, entitled *Piercing the Darkness*, was published in 1988.

Our struggle is not against flesh and blood, but against the rulers, against the authorities, against the powers of this dark world and against the spiritual forces of evil in the heavenly realms.
Ephesians 6:12

John H. Sammis became a young, successful, New York businessman at age twenty-three. When he moved to Logansport, Indiana, to pursue his career, he also became active as a Christian layman. Some time later, he gave up his business career, became the YMCA secretary, and answered a call to full-time ministry. He attended McCormick and Lane Theological seminaries, graduated from Lane in 1881, and was ordained as a Presbyterian minister. In the following years he served as pastor in churches in Iowa, Indiana, Michigan, and Minnesota.

In 1886, during a service in Brockton, Massachusetts, where he was leading music for D. L. Moody, Daniel B. Towner heard a young man's testimony and jotted down his words: "I am not quite sure—but I am going to trust, and I am going to obey." Mr. Towner sent the words he'd written down to Reverend Sammis, and the great hymn "Trust and Obey" was born. It first appeared in *Hymns Old and New*, published in 1887.

Songs of the Faith

"Trust and Obey"
Words by John H. Sammis (1887)
Music by Daniel B. Towner (1887)

This favorite gospel hymn ranks as an excellent example of balance in the life of a believer between faith in Christ and good works that should naturally occur if one takes to heart the words of trusting and obeying Christ in daily living.

When we walk with the Lord in the light of His Word,
What a glory He sheds on our way!
While we do His good will, He abides with us still,
And with all who will trust and obey.

Refrain:
Trust and obey, for there's no other way
To be happy in Jesus, but to trust and obey.

D. L. Moody said, "The blood alone makes us safe, the Word alone makes us sure, but obedience alone makes us happy."

FACT

Samuel replied: "Does the LORD delight in burnt offerings
and sacrifices as much as in obeying the voice of the LORD?
To obey is better than sacrifice, and to heed is better than the fat of rams."
1 SAMUEL 15:22

There's nothing like a story with a happy ending, and *Unshackled!* has been broadcasting happy endings for decades. *Unshackled!* heard on more than 1,550 radio stations, is the longest-running drama in the history of radio.

Begun in 1950 by Harry Saulnier, the dramas depict the stories of social outcasts who have turned their lives around by accepting salvation through Jesus Christ. Saulnier, as superintendent of Chicago's Pacific Garden Mission, saw firsthand the transformative power of gospel preaching, prayer, and personal testimony. He longed for a way to reach more people with these inspiring stories of renewal and restoration, and found a solution in

Miscellany

Heard on the Air—*Unshackled!*

radio. Saulnier began with a fifiteen-minute radio program, *Doorway to Heaven*, in 1945. He told about the men—homeless, alcoholic, unemployed, drug-addicted— who had found salvation at Pacific Garden Mission.

Five years later, Saulnier gathered a group of writers and actors to produce compelling radio dramas based on true stories of redeemed souls and transformed lives. They used music, sound effects, and dynamic readings, hallmarks of the Golden Age of radio drama, to create inspirational, often sentimental, programs. Today, the award-winning show is translated and redramatized in Spanish, Arabic, Russian, Romanian Polish, Korean, and Japanese for audiences worldwide.

Initially, *Unshackled!* dramatized testimonials from the mission. Soon, letters arrived from wherever the broadcast was heard telling of conversion experiences, life changes, and spiritual renewal. These real-life stories were added to the *Unshackled!* repertoire. Now listeners can submit their stories online. Their personal salvation experiences are considered for the themes of future programs.

FACT

Pacific Garden Mission, founded in 1877 to "keep crooked men straight," is the oldest surviving Chicago rescue mission. The mission's evangelical Christian message, combined with practical help for the destitute, has earned it the nickname, the Hobo Church. A neon cross announcing JESUS SAVES still beckons Chicago's poor and downtrodden to its open doors.

"The Son of Man came to seek and to save what was lost."
LUKE 19:10

Controversial, sold-out, talented, blunt, gospel singer Keith Green absolutely refused to accept the spiritual status quo. His sermons set to music plowed a new course for what Christian music could be.

As a teenager, Keith was restless. He was raised Jewish, but had read the New Testament. The odd combination left him spiritually seeking. At fifteen, he ran away from home, looking for spiritual fulfillment and musical adventure. He experimented with drugs, eastern mysticism, and free love. When he was nineteen, he met a girl named Melody. Together they started exploring matters of faith. At age twenty, Keith and Melody were married.

Men of the Faith

Keith Green (1953–1982)

Gospel singer, songwriter, and musician

By the end of 1972, they had explored everything but the Bible and Christian Science. Keith didn't like the organized machine of Christian Science and so decided to deal with Jesus directly. Through simple prayers, he opened himself up to Christ, and Christ revealed himself to Keith in a deep and profound way. Keith Green had found what he was looking for.

After his conversion, Keith and Melody began to open their home to drug addicts and rejects. Talk of Jesus flowed freely. His music took a radical turn, too, and he began to pen such Christian classics as *You Put This Love in My Heart; Oh Lord, You're Beautiful;* and *You Are the One.*

Although Keith Green's fame grew, his heart always remained for the lost. In 1982, his life (along with the lives of two of his children) was cut short by a tragic plane crash. His work, music, and ministry still continue on through the work of Last Days Ministries.

Keith Green said, "I repent of ever having recorded one single song, and ever having performed one concert, if my music, and more importantly, my life have not provoked you into godly jealousy or to sell out more completely to Jesus!"

FACT

Prepare your minds for action; be self-controlled; set your hope fully on the grace to be given you when Jesus Christ is revealed.
1 PETER 1:13

The large house that Agnes grew up in with her older brother and sister sat next door to her family's church in Macedonia. She often helped her mother, Drana Bernai, who was deeply devoted to distributing food and clothing to the poor, bandaging wounds, or simply listening to lonely souls needing to talk. Agnes took her mother's words to heart, "When you help people like this, it is just like helping Jesus."

By the time she was twelve, Agnes felt her life's work also would be helping the poor. She left home at age eighteen to pursue her calling. Agnes moved into the slums where the "poorest of the poor" lived. She held the hands of the dying, scrubbed dirty toilets, and taught by example how to administer love and dignity to people others might overlook or ignore.

Women of the Faith

Mother Teresa
(1910–1997)
Missionary to India

Known by her religious name, Mother Teresa of Calcutta founded Missionaries of Charity in 1950. She and her twelve coworkers established orphanages, special homes for abused women, and hospitals for mental patients, lepers, alcoholics, drug addicts, and AIDS patients. Her commitment was to provide food, clothing, and shelter to her fellow man as if caring for Christ—and to do so with joy and a smile.

Mother Teresa received the Nobel Peace Prize in 1979. She used the nineteen-thousand-dollar prize money to build another leper colony and homes for the poor. Humbly serving her way to greatness, this simple woman died September 5, 1997, at age eighty-seven. She was honored and mourned at her funeral by more than twelve thousand people and dignitaries from around the world.

FACT

Mother Teresa said, "In our action, we are instruments in God's hand and He writes beautifully."

[Jesus said,] "The King will reply, 'I tell you the truth,
whatever you did for one of the least of these brothers of mine, you did for me."
MATTHEW 25:40

Though the Metropolitan Tabernacle in London is a relatively new building, the heritage of the Tabernacle holds a memorable place in history. It began with the Tabernacle Fellowship, a community of Baptists who braved persecution when the British parliament banned Christian organizations from meeting together in 1650. For thirty years, the Fellowship secretly met in a widow's home. In 1688, shortly after the ban was lifted, the Tabernacle Fellowship built the New Park Street Church near London's Tower Bridge.

Important Sites

The Metropolitan Tabernacle
London

In the early 1800s, under the leadership of Dr. John Rippon, the New Park Street Church became the largest Baptist congregation in Great Britain. But it was twenty-year-old pastor Charles Haddon Spurgeon who really helped the church flourish. Within weeks of Spurgeon's arrival, the growing church needed a larger venue. Five years later, the Metropolitan Tabernacle was under construction. In the interim, the church met at the Royal Surrey Gardens Music Hall, which held up to ten thousand people.

Completed in 1861, the Metropolitan Tabernacle was the largest church building of its day, seating 6,500 congregants. Historians consider Spurgeon's Metropolitan Tabernacle the precursor to modern-day megachurches. But the church burned to the ground twice, once in 1891 and again during air raids in World War II. The impressive stone portico survived both fires. In 1957, the rest of the church was rebuilt within the perimeter of the original church building. Although few residents remained in central London after the war, by the 1970s the congregation of the Metropolitan Tabernacle began to flourish once more.

Spurgeon and his congregation chose the prominent central London location for the Metropolitan Tabernacle because it was believed to be the site where clergy and laymen, known as the Southwark Martyrs, were burned.

FACT

"Keep watch over yourselves and all the flock of which the Holy Spirit has made you overseers."
ACTS 20:28

When early immigrants landed on the shores of the New World, no mega-bookstores awaited them. Indeed, no printing press existed on this side of the Atlantic. If you wanted a Bible or any other book, you brought it with you. Then you focused on the task of building your house and getting some sort of crop to grow to feed your family. That explains why the first book printed in America, *The Massachusetts Bay Psalm Book*, wasn't published until 1640.

Not until 1782 was the first English-language Bible printed in America.

Groundbreaking Events

The "Robert Aitken Bible" Printed

Several reasons explain the late date. First, copyright issues accompanied the King James Version, as the translation legally belonged to the English Crown. Second, tariffs made it more cost-effective to import Bibles from England than print them in the colonies. The Revolutionary War, however, froze trade between England and the colonies, so the supply of English language Bibles dwindled. Also, American pride was at stake. Patriotic Christians clamored for an American Bible.

Enter Scottish-born immigrant Robert Aitken. In 1769, he settled in Philadelphia, Pennsylvania, and established a bookshop and printing operation. Throughout the 1770s, Aitken produced several editions of the New Testament in English. By 1776, he had become the official printer for the U.S. Congress, and he petitioned Congress to authorize and fund a printing of the complete Bible. Receiving permission (but not funding, as it would smack of state sponsorship of religion), he published the King James Version of the Bible in 1782, minus the introductory address to King James I—and in violation of British law.

FACT

Most Americans are surprised to discover that the first Bible printed in the colonies was not in English, but in the language of the Algonquin Indians. Translated by the Puritan pastor John Eliot and printed in Cambridge, Massachusetts, in 1661, the Bible was used as a tool for the evangelization and education of the Native Americans.

Man does not live on bread alone but on every word
that comes from the mouth of the LORD.
DEUTERONOMY 8:3

*T*he Book of Common Prayer is actually the common title of a number of prayer books used in Anglican worship. The first consolidated book, produced in English in 1549, just after the English Reformation, includes prayers for morning worship, evening worship, and Holy Communion. It also provides the order of service for baptisms, confirmations, marriage ceremonies, funeral services, and prayer for the sick. The collection also includes Bible readings to be read daily over the course of a month.

Readings for daily prayers are provided by reference, and canticles (songs) are included to be sung between the readings. About two-thirds of the content is derived directly from the Old and New Testaments.

In 1552, Thomas Cranmer—the editor of the original book—revised it, but the revision was never used. When Edward VI died, his half sister, Mary, a Catholic, took the throne. After her death in 1559, a modified version was published. The final version came in 1662, after the English Civil War. The official name of the 1662 version is *The Book of Common Prayer and Administration of the Sacraments* and other Rites and Ceremonies of the Church according to the use of the Church of England together with the Psalter or Psalms of David pointed as they are to be sung or said in churches and the form and manner of making, ordaining, and consecrating of bishops, priests, and deacons.

Churches of various denominations have adapted and revised *The Book of Common Prayer* for use in their services. It appears in fifty countries and more than 150 languages.

Notable Books

The Book of Common Prayer
Edited by Thomas Cranmer,
Archbishop of Canterbury (1662)

The 1662 version continues to be the official prayer book of the Church of England, though in the twenty-first century, a new prayer book, entitled *Common Worship*, has all but replaced it.

FACT

Do not be anxious about anything, but in everything, by prayer and petition, with thanksgiving, present your requests to God.
PHILIPPIANS 4:6

The author of this hymn text, Eliza Hewitt, wrote her songs with a heart of devotion for the Sunday school movement during the latter part of the nineteenth century.

During that time, hymn writers often focused on writing songs that would reach and teach children truths about the gospel. This hymn features a basic scriptural fact—that every believer in Jesus Christ, whether living or dead, will be caught up to instantaneously join the Lord in the air. It is considered to be a song of eternal hope and promise.

It was while attending a Methodist camp meeting in Ocean Grove, New Jersey, that Eliza Hewitt joined her writing efforts with those of Emily Wilson, wife of a Methodist district superintendent in Philadelphia, and composed this hymn that has been an endearing and generational favorite for all ages.

Because poetic license is often taken with hymns, the original title and chorus were changed in some renditions because of the feeling the old version implied that unsaved people would also go to heaven. The original title and verses are found in hymnals today.

Songs of the Faith

"When We All Get to Heaven"

Words by Eliza E. Hewitt (1897)
Music by Emily D. Wilson (1898)

Sing the wondrous love of Jesus,
Sing His mercy and His grace.
In the mansions bright and blessed
He'll prepare for us a place.

Refrain:
When we all get to Heaven,
What a day of rejoicing that will be!
When we all see Jesus,
We'll sing and shout the victory!

While we walk the pilgrim pathway,
Clouds will overspread the sky;
But when traveling days are over,
Not a shadow, not a sigh.

FACT

Eliza Hewitt's career as a public school teacher came to a screeching halt when she suffered a debilitating back injury—allegedly caused when a reckless student hit her with a piece of slate.

[Jesus said,]"In my Father's house are many rooms; if it were not so, I would have told you. I am going there to prepare a place for you."
JOHN 14:2

Dr. James Dobson began Focus on the Family (FOF) in 1977 with a twenty-five-minute weekly radio program broadcast from a two-room studio in Arcadia, California. Skip ahead three decades, and the FOF complex spans three office buildings in Colorado Springs, Colorado, with more than thirteen hundred employees. Heard on more than one thousand radio stations, Dobson reaches 3.4 million listeners each week nationally and internationally.

FOF's stated mission is to share "the Gospel of Jesus Christ with as many people as possible by nurturing and defending the God-ordained institution of the family and promoting biblical truths." The nonprofit organization works interdenominationally to support Christians and counter unbiblical cultural movements, especially those that threaten the family and the sanctity of life.

Dobson, an outspoken critic of humanistic social values, has garnered both praise and ridicule. Many evangelicals admire him for his unwavering reliance on the Bible to guide individual and family life. FOF radio programs, videos, on-line resources, and magazines for adults and children are a staple in many Christian homes. Dobson's public condemnation of the gay lifestyle, abortion, and same-sex marriage has brought down the wrath of practicing homosexuals and social liberals who label his views narrow and intolerant.

Miscellany

Focus on the Family

Over the years, Dobson has become a widely recognized and influential spokesperson for conservative political causes. He frequently initiates ad campaigns urging voters and congressional members to support family-friendly legislation. FOF has instituted special radio programs, publications, and seminars throughout the country to equip and encourage evangelical Christians to get involved in community, state, and national politics.

Focus on the Family's headquarters, an eighty-one-acre campus in Colorado Springs, boasts its own zip code. One of its three office buildings houses its largest segment of employees—those who answer telephone calls from listeners needing resources, counseling referrals, prayer support, and to make financial donations.

FACT

"As for me and my household, we will serve the LORD."
JOSHUA 24:15

Because German-born Dietrich Bonhoeffer was only twenty-one years old when he received his theology PhD from the University of Berlin, he was not eligible to be ordained. This gave him the opportunity to go abroad, so he spent a postgraduate year at Union Theology Seminary in New York City. There, he attended Abyssinian Baptist Church in Harlem, where he learned about social justice from the African-Americans who worshipped there. Hence, when the Nazi Party took over his native homeland, he had a strong affinity for the oppressed and afflicted minorities living there.

Bonhoeffer wasn't raised in a particularly political or religious environment. He came from an aristocratic family that had nominal religious leanings. However, when Dietrich wanted to enter the ministry, his parents didn't object.

Men of the Faith

Dietrich Bonhoeffer (1906–1945)

German pastor, theologian, and anti-Nazi activist

Throughout the 1930s, German pastors and theologians rallied behind Hitler, but Bonhoeffer couldn't stand the führer's anti-Semitic rhetoric. Bonhoeffer joined with likeminded theologians and launched the Confessing Church, whose members openly declared their allegiance to Jesus Christ alone. In the 1930s, he traveled to India to learn nonviolent resistance methods and he also penned his now famous book *The Cost of Discipleship*. He ultimately became convinced that Hitler must be removed from power, even if it meant assassinating the führer.

In 1943, Bonhoeffer was caught rescuing Jews. He was arrested and driven to Tegel Prison. Able to correspond with family and friends, he continued to write and outline his theological beliefs. Eventually, Bonhoeffer was transferred from Tegel to Buchenwald prison where he was hanged with six other resisters, just one month before Germany surrendered.

FACT

Dietrich Bonhoeffer wrote, "When Christ calls a man, he bids him come and die."

Jesus said to his disciples, "If anyone would come after me,
he must deny himself and take up his cross and follow me."
MATTHEW 16:24

Historians call Mary Lyon's achievement an "astonishing feat." At a time when most Americans viewed higher education for women as a silly, if not shocking, idea, Lyon founded Mount Holyoke Female Seminary (now Mount Holyoke College) in South Hadley, Massachusetts.

Mary Lyon's early life dealt her hard blows. Her father died when she was five, and her mother remarried when Lyon was thirteen, leaving the girl in the charge of her older brother on the family farm. Lyon left school to manage the home, though she had distinguished herself as a promising student. Four years later, she took a teaching job offered to her on the basis of her prior aptitude for learning.

Women of the Faith

Mary Lyon
(1797–1849)
Educator and American pioneer

Lyon yearned to continue her education, but fees at institutions of higher learning outstripped her budget. While continuing her teaching duties, Lyon attended lectures and classes as she could, picking up "knowledge by the handfuls." She not only established herself as a gifted teacher, but also an astute school principal and an authority on the education of women.

When Lyon decided to give full-time attention to her dream of opening a college for young women, she worked tirelessly to raise funds and gain supporters. She planned a challenging academic curriculum, set affordable rates, and put in place a rigorous entrance examination. In the fall of 1837, the doors of Mount Holyoke Female Seminary opened to eighty students, each required to bring a Bible, an atlas, a dictionary, and two spoons to school.

Mount Holyoke was the first academic institution of higher learning for women in the United States.

It's possible Mary Lyon referred to her institution as a "female seminary" because the term sounded less jarring to nineteenth-century sensibilities than "female college."

FACT

We consider blessed those who have persevered.
JAMES 5:11

Judea, Samaria, the Dead Sea, the Jordan River, Bethlehem, and even the city of Jerusalem (about thirty miles away) can all be seen from the top of Mount Nebo on a clear day. This panoramic view of the promised land is the one Moses glimpsed shortly before his death. Although the Bible states, "to this day no one knows where his grave is" (Deuteronomy 34:6), Christians have been coming here to visit the "grave of Moses" since the second half of the fourth century.

The handwritten accounts of these early pilgrims have helped modern archaeologists piece together the history of the structures built on this sacred site. The earliest record of the first church built here comes from the travel journal of a woman by the name of Aetheria in AD 394. In 531, a baptistery was added to the church. For the next two centuries, the basilica and baptistery were partially dismantled and then enlarged.

Important Sites

Mount Nebo

Abarim Mountain Range—
Eastern Shore of the Dead Sea

Today, what looks like an ancient church from the outside is really more of a protective structure built over the excavated ruins. Within the Sanctuary of Nebo lie layers of elaborate mosaics, some in geometric designs and some depicting animals and flowers, exposed for visitors to view. Beneath the white mosaic floor of the basilica, six tombs from different periods have been hollowed out from the bedrock. Outside, the Serpentine Cross, a modern metal sculpture by Italian artist Giovanni Fantoni, commemorates the bronze serpent carried by Moses, intertwined with the cross of Christ.

FACT

In 2000, a fifteen-foot stone monolith was erected in front of the Sanctuary of Nebo. Books are carved into its base, depicting the Bible, the Torah, and the Koran. The inscription GOD IS LOVE, carved in Greek, Latin, and Arabic, composes the central design.

Moses climbed Mount Nebo from the plains of Moab to the top of Pisgah,
across from Jericho. There the LORD showed him the whole land.
DEUTERONOMY 34:1

*A*d *majorem Dei gloriam*—"to the greater glory of God." The motto of the Society of Jesus proclaims the order's reason for being. Founded by Ignatius of Loyola in 1534 and confirmed by Pope Paul III in 1540, the Jesuits, as they came to be called, planned initially to travel to the Holy Land to convert the Muslims. The outbreak of war with the Ottoman Empire prohibited travel, however, so members of the order pledged to work under papal command.

Education proved the most urgent need. The growing strength and influence of the Protestant Reformation prompted an aggressive effort by the Roman Catholic Church to establish more schools, colleges, universities, and seminaries for the moral and religious instruction of the young. Jesuits sprang into action. In mission countries, they set up centers of learning and trade schools for the poor. Mission outreach included India, Japan, China, and the coast of Africa. Jesuits worked extensively in South America,

Groundbreaking Events

The Founding of the Jesuits

where they established settlements, headed by priests, where native peoples were taught Christianity, along with agriculture and other trades.

Jesuit history is not all rosy, however. Their loyalty to the pope brought about the ire of nationalistic, secular rulers. The Jesuits' push for reform within the church angered priests and other Roman Catholic leaders. By the end of the first centuries of the order's existence, Jesuits had been expelled from every country in Europe at some point.

Today, Jesuits work in more than a hundred countries worldwide. Their contributions to both religious and secular scholarship and education are incalculable.

At a chapel in Montmartre in Paris, Ignatius and six scholars pledged to live in holy poverty and selfless service to others. They were ordained priests in Venice in 1537 and offered their proposal to found a new religious order to the pope. The pope approved, and Ignatius became the first superior general.

FACT

The God of all grace, who called you to his eternal glory in Christ, after you have suffered a little while, will himself restore you and make you strong, firm and steadfast. To him be the power for ever and ever. Amen.
1 PETER 5:10–11

When Congregational minister Lloyd C. Douglas retired to pursue writing full-time, he was clear about his purpose—to present a Christian thesis in the form of a novel.

His first book, *Magnificent Obsession*, was a huge hit, which may explain why Douglas felt comfortable including some of the same elements in his second novel, *The Robe*.

Though one story is set in modern times and the other Bible times, both concern the conversion of an atheist hero to believing faith in Jesus Christ. The heroes, hearts encumbered with guilt, embark on journeys of spiritual discovery.

The Robe's title refers to the garment worn by Jesus during His trial. Marcellus, a young Roman soldier whose father is a powerful senator, has been denounced for offending Prince Gaius. As punishment, he's sent to Gaza, in Palestine, to carry out a gruesome order—the crucifixion of a Galilean named Jesus. Marcellus, drunk at the scene, throws the dice and wins the robe pulled from Jesus' body just before He was nailed to the cross. Later that evening, Marcellus puts on the robe and knows that he will never be well again until he learns all he can about the strange, tragic Galilean.

Notable Books

The Robe

By Lloyd C. Douglas (1942)

Along with his Greek slave, Demetrius, Marcellus follows the path before him, never suspecting that it will lead him finally to robust faith in Jesus and a martyr's death in the Colosseum.

In November of 1942, *The Robe* moved to number one on the *New York Times* bestseller list, where it remained for a year. To date, more than six million copies have been sold.

FACT

The film version of *The Robe*, released in 1953, was the first movie released in CinemaScope. Richard Burton played the part of Marcellus.

Dividing up his clothes, they cast lots to see what each would get.
MARK 15:24

James M. Black, a Methodist layman, music teacher, composer, and publisher of numerous gospel songs, found his inspiration for this hymn during a consecration meeting. He had invited a downtrodden fourteen-year-old girl to the meeting, and when members repeated scriptures as they answered the roll call, he noticed she was absent—and therefore did not respond. As he thought of how sad it would be if names were called from the Lamb's Book of Life without receiving a response, the first words to the first stanza of this hymn were birthed. Within a few minutes, he composed two more verses. When he sat down at the piano to compose a tune for the hymn, the notes formed the melody still found in hymnbooks today.

Songs of the Faith

"When the Roll Is Called Up Yonder"
Words and Music
by James M. Black (1894)

The girl who inspired those first words died of pneumonia shortly thereafter. Her death furnished the dramatic finale to the hymn and gives credence to the roll-call song.

Since its publication, the simple words have planted seeds of promise for a glorious future in the hearts of believers. After the hymn first appeared in Black's most popular hymnbook, *Songs of the Soul*, published in 1894—a hymnal that sold more than four hundred thousand copies in its first two years—it soon became widely used in evangelistic meetings in Great Britain and the United States.

When the trumpet of the Lord shall sound
And time shall be no more,
And the morning breaks, eternal, bright and fair;
When the saved of earth
Shall gather over on the other shore,
And the roll is called up yonder, I'll be there.

"When the Roll is Called Up Yonder" is harmonized with just four basic chords.

FACT

There shall by no means enter [New Jerusalem] anything that defiles, or causes an abomination or a lie, but only those who are written in the Lamb's Book of Life.
REVELATION 21:27 NKJV

How many candles flicker on planet earth's birthday cake? For evolutionists, the answer lies somewhere in the billions of years. Bible-believing creationists, however, find Earth a mere babe at around six thousand years old. The number reflects a plain reading of the Genesis account of God's six-day creation along with the historical information found throughout the Old Testament.

As the scientific community began promulgating the theory of evolution in public schools and the popular press, some within the Christian community set about to prove the Bible's accuracy. In 1970, engineering professor Dr. Henry M. Morris founded the Institute for Creation Research (IRC) devoted to countering the claims of evolutionists with physical, scientific evidence. Its research focuses on the fields of biology and geology, with particular emphasis on the creation of the world and the origins of humankind. Since its beginnings in Santee, California, IRC has established educational centers in Dallas, Texas, and Petersburg, Kentucky.

Miscellany

The Institute for Creation Research

As might be expected, evolutionists scorn research offered by the IRC in support of creationism (sometimes lumped together with intelligent design). Many go so far as to attack the motivations of creationists, claiming they're pawns of the "fundamentalist religious right," and therefore not speaking out of a concern for good science, but for political power.

Bitter Bible versus science fights are nothing new. Just ask Galileo, the seventeenth-century astronomer who ran afoul of the church for publishing the Copernican theory that the earth revolves around the sun. Clearly, neither science nor religion is ready to blow out the candles on the discussion anytime soon.

FACT

A proponent of intelligent design (ID) doesn't necessarily support the Bible's account of creation. ID merely rejects the evolutionary theory of chance determining the outcome of creation and, instead, favors the theory of purposeful creation by a higher power who may (or may not be) the Judeo-Christian God.

"Where were you when I laid the earth's foundation?
Tell me, if you understand."
JOB 38:4

F rom a very early age, Hudson Taylor seemed destined to be a missionary in China. His Methodist parents were fascinated by the Far East and they prayed over him as a newborn, "God, grant that he might work for you in China." During his teen years, Taylor studied medicine, the Bible, and the Mandarin language. At age twenty-one, Taylor was bound on a clipper ship for Shanghai.

Immediately, Taylor decided to make himself distinct from the Western missionaries he saw there. He decided to dress in Chinese clothes and grow the braid typical Chinese men wore. He also decided to venture into the Chinese interior, sailing down the Huangpu River, distributing Chinese Bibles and tracts.

Men of the Faith

Hudson Taylor (1832–1905)

Founder of China Inland Mission (CIM)

After the Chinese Evangelization Society said it couldn't pay him as a missionary, he decided to become an independent missionary, trusting God to provide his every need.

After an illness and a return to England, Taylor established an ambitious plan to bring missionaries to China. His own vision left him racked with doubt, but he was convinced of God's love for the Chinese. He formed a group called the China Inland Mission (CIM) and returned to China with even a greater fervor than he had on his initial trip.

For all his lifelong effort in China (fifty-one years), Taylor brought more than eight hundred missionaries to the country, who began 125 schools, which directly resulted in eighteen thousand Christian conversions. His work also established more than three bases and five local helpers in all eighteen provinces. All this occurred before his death in China at age seventy-three.

Hudson Taylor wrote, "You must first go forward on your knees."

FACT

To those who are weak, I became weak so I could win the weak.
I have become all things to all people so I could save
some of them in any way possible.
1 CORINTHIANS 9:22 NCV

Born in Charlottesville, Virginia, Frances Parkinson considered her formal education a bit sketchy. Her grandmother taught her to read from the Bible. Any other schooling was supplemented with lessons in French, Latin, and mathematics. She married Henry Keyes—a U.S. Senator—in 1903.

Frances's writing talents were recognized when a reputable publisher accepted her first book, *The Old Gray Homestead*. In the 1920s she wrote articles for *Good Housekeeping* magazine entitled, "Letters from a Senator's Wife." When her husband died in 1938, Frances began writing about her upbringing and travels.

In the 1950s Frances bought the historic Beauregard House in the French Quarter of New Orleans and restored it to its original Victorian elegance. It had once been the childhood home of Paul Morphy, a master chess player. His life and the home's history became the subject of her book, *The Chess Players*. It's interesting to note that during Hurricane Katrina, the house sustained only minor damage to the roof.

Women of the Faith

Frances Parkinson Keyes (1885–1970)

Author

All of Keyes's novels were a mixture of rich historical fact, real people, and fiction. Their subject matter revolved around sugar plantations, the Mississippi Delta, Creole culture, and southern social life. As a Christian, Keyes strongly believed in the virtue of chastity and furthermore believed that it was extremely important for a woman to be a virgin on her wedding night. Her morality of courtship and marriage are strong elements in her novels.

Frances Parkinson Keyes wrote twenty novels, five religious-based books, four nonfiction books, a cookbook, a children's book, and a book of poetry.

FACT

The last name Keyes rhymes with *skies* and not the word *keys* as most pronounce it.

Commit your way to the LORD; trust in him and he will do this:
He will make your righteousness shine like the dawn,
the justice of your cause like the noonday sun.
PSALM 37:5-6

In 1932, architect Marguerite Bruswig Staude was admiring the newly constructed Empire State Building in New York City. Staude noticed that from a certain angle, the image of a cross appeared to be the skyscraper's central support. That image inspired Staude to pursue building a modern skyscraper cathedral—one she envisioned would encompass an entire city block.

An accomplished painter, sculptor, and student of architect Frank Lloyd Wright, Staude traveled through Europe searching for further architectural inspiration and a suitable location. She found both and planned to build a cathedral in Budapest above the Danube. Then World War II and the death of her parents changed her plans. Staude's mother's dying wish was to leave behind a "spiritual trust," a monument that would draw people's hearts toward God. In turn, Staude's initial skyscraper-cathedral idea evolved into a small, ecumenical chapel perched in the rocky cliffs of Sedona, Arizona.

Important Sites

The Chapel of the Holy Cross
Sedona, Arizona

In a mere eighteen months, and at a cost of only $300,000, Staude completed the Chapel of the Holy Cross in 1956. Set between two red rock pinnacles, the central image of a cross is clearly visible in the modern-styled structure of glass, steel, and stone. Inside, the space is intimate, containing only two rows of seven pews and a floor-to-ceiling stained glass window. Though maintained by the Catholic Church, the chapel is open to people of all faiths as a place of prayer and contemplation. No weddings or services are held on-site, but Taizé-styled worship is celebrated weekly.

When Staude was flying over Sedona, she saw the letters *Rx* spray-painted on a rocky mesa. Since her father was a pharmacist, Staude felt this marked the perfect spot to build the Chapel of the Holy Cross in honor of her parents.

FACT

May I never boast except in the cross of our Lord Jesus Christ, through which the world has been crucified to me, and I to the world.
GALATIANS 6:14

Publisher Robert Aitken's American-produced Bible of 1782 left him close to bankruptcy. His little volume suffered in quality and measured only 5 x 7½ inches—definitely not for older eyes reading the Good Book by candlelight.

Almost ten years later, a highly successful and market-savvy Massachusetts printer, Isaiah Thomas, approached the project more strategically. He conducted, with the help of prominent clergymen, meticulous research of available King James Versions produced by different printers in various places to find the one with the best and most correct text. Thomas also commissioned four American artists to create a total of fifty copperplate engravings for his project. Then, in 1791, Thomas

Groundbreaking Events

The First Illustrated Bible Printed in America

came out with two editions of a Bible considerably larger in size than Aitken's. The first, a deluxe edition, was in two volumes and printed on the highest quality paper available. The second, a standard edition in one volume, was printed on ordinary paper. To save the publisher money, both editions of the Bible featured the same engravings. Thus, Thomas's two editions of the Bible became the first illustrated Bibles printed in America.

Thomas widely advertised his Bibles, calling attention to his low price. He also extended an easy payment plan, and, for the cash-strapped buyer, half could be paid in farm crops or produce, deliverable to the publisher's office. He also offered, for a widely affordable price, an edition without the engravings. Most buyers couldn't afford the high-end illustrated Bibles and opted for the one without pictures. For that reason, illustrated copies are very expensive and hard to find today.

FACT

Isaiah Thomas was a prolific printer and able businessman. He began printing the patriotic (and often radical) newspaper, the *Massachusetts Spy*, in 1770. Though the *Spy* enjoyed the largest circulation of any publication in New England, Thomas expanded his operation by publishing textbooks, children's literature, and general-appeal newspapers and magazines.

"Every word of God is flawless; he is a shield to those who take refuge in him."
PROVERBS 30:5

After only ten days of sales, *A Man Called Peter* landed on the bestseller list—and stayed there for more than three years.

A Man Called Peter is the biography of a Scottish immigrant who rose to Chaplain of the U.S. Senate. Written by his wife, Catherine Marshall, the book introduces readers to a young man who, after a profound religious experience, embraces the gospel of Jesus Christ and preaches it for the rest of his life.

The story follows Peter Marshall from his seminary days and ordination to his ministry in several congregations. A dynamic speaker, he believed sermons should be lively and fun. He inspired young people in particular to dedicate themselves to the Lord's service, and his ministry drew widespread attention. He assumed the position of pastor of Washington, D.C.'s Church of the Presidents, and was subsequently appointed to serve as spiritual counselor in the Senate.

Notable Books

A Man Called Peter
By Catherine Marshall (1951)

Catherine Marshall, a distinguished writer of inspirational books, allows readers a glimpse of her revered husband's private side, too. Marshall tells of their romance, their hardships, and their family life with honesty, humor, and tenderness. She quotes a dream she had shortly after her husband's death in which he said, "Tell it all, if it will prove to people that a man can love the Lord and not be a sissy."

He was no sissy. Indeed, *A Man Called Peter* has served as a reminder to generations of readers that the Lord enables, emboldens, and strengthens humble hearts and willing hands committed to doing his work.

The movie *A Man Called Peter* was released in 1955 and was nominated for several awards. It is now available on video.

*"You will go out in joy and be led forth in peace;
the mountains and hills will burst into song before you,
and all the trees of the field will clap their hands."*
ISAIAH 55:12

The Irish author of this hymn wrote from a heart plowed with pain. On the night before he was to be married, his fiancé drowned. From the depths of his grief, Joseph realized that he could only find true comfort from Jesus—his dearest Friend.

His life changed forever, Scriven moved to Canada and devoted his life to helping others. Soon he felt convicted to give away his possessions and help the poor without pay. Those who encountered him dubbed him "the Good Samaritan of Port Hope."

The words to this hymn were first written as a poem, enclosed with a prayer in a letter to his ailing mother in Ireland. In fact, he never intended "What a Friend We Have in Jesus" to be published. When he himself became ill some time later, a visiting friend spied a copy of the scribbled words on paper near his bedside. When the friend asked who wrote the beautiful words, Joseph Scriven replied: "The Lord and I did it between us."

Songs of the Faith

"What a Friend We Have in Jesus"

Words by Joseph Scriven (1855)

Music by Charles C. Converse (1868)

In 1875 Ira D. Sankey discovered the hymn just in time to include it in his collection, *Sankey's Gospel Hymns Number One*. Sankey later wrote, "The last hymn which went into the book became one of the first in favor."

What a Friend we have in Jesus,
All our sins and griefs to bear!
What a privilege to carry,
Everything to God in prayer!

O what peace we often forfeit,
O what needless pain we bear,
All because we do not carry
Everything to God in prayer.

> FACT
>
> Like his fiancé, Scriven also died of drowning—either accident or suicide. A concerned friend keeping vigil over the deeply depressed man from another room reported that he found Scriven's bed empty and his lifeless body floating in a nearby body of water.

There is a friend that sticketh closer than a brother.
PROVERBS 18:24 KJV

P ray together first. Fight to win second. The role of sports chaplains achieved prominence in the 1990s as para-religious men's movements brought the name of Jesus to macho lips.

Sports chaplains do for the soul what the coach does for the body—develop it, strengthen it, and help it reach its full potential. Typically, a team's chaplain leads a short service before a game, often inviting members of the opposing team to join. The chaplain makes himself or herself available to athletes at all times for spiritual direction and guidance in their professional and personal lives. An important part of the chaplain's role is to meet the spiritual needs of Christian and non-Christian athletes alike.

Miscellany

Sports Chaplains

It's win-win all around, though sports chaplaincy faces certain legal restrictions. Christian chaplains on public college campuses raise church-state conflicts—and in professional sports, the issue of employer-mandated worship. Coaches avoid the specter of state- or employer-sponsored religion by using volunteer chaplains and focusing on their advisory role. Their unpaid status gives them independence from management; consequently chaplains often hear the rants and gripes players would never voice to the coach.

Sports chaplains frequently gain the confidence of players who don't belong to a congregation, or church members who spend a great deal of time on the road. A trusting and confidential relationship between a chaplain and an athlete can help the athlete avoid emotional breakdowns, family tensions, and the pitfalls of sudden wealth and fame.

The Reverend Henry Soles, a sports chaplain, says: "As a sports chaplain, you're not to worship the players but to treat them as human beings and make sure that they understand you're not there just to put a blessing upon them for the game. Your goal is to equip them to live lives that glorify God."

---

*I press on toward the goal to win the prize for which
God has called me heavenward in Christ Jesus.*
PHILIPPIANS 3:14

Able to speak seven languages and proficient in Hebrew and Greek, William Tyndale was a priest with uncommon knowledge and ability. Compelled to teach English men and women that they were justified not by works, but by faith alone, he had a deep desire to translate the Greek New Testament into English vernacular.

Denied the opportunity to do the translation in his native land by the Bishop of London, Tyndale traveled to Europe looking for a hospitable environment, eventually landing in Worms, Germany. There he penned his New Testament. The manuscript was smuggled into England, where authorities bought up his copies, hoping to stop further distribution. Their efforts were futile. After settling in Antwerp, Belgium, the sale of his New Testament kept him financially afloat while he perfected the script and began the Old Testament translation.

Men of the Faith

William Tyndale (1494–1536)

First translated the Bible

in English

In translating the Bible, Tyndale coined several words and phrases still in use today. He introduced the words *Jehovah*, *Atonement*, *Passover*, and *scapegoat* in the English language. He also came up with the phrases *let there be light*, *the powers that be*, and *the salt of the earth*.

In 1535, Tyndale was betrayed by a confidant and handed over to soldiers on charges of heresy. Months later, Tyndale was condemned as a heretic, tossed from the priesthood, and delivered from papal to secular authorities for punishment. Then on October 6, he was strangled on a wooden post and burned at the stake. His dying words were, "Lord, open the King of England's eyes."

FACT

William Tyndale wrote, "The Church is the one institution that exists for those outside of it."

[Jesus said,] "Heaven and earth will pass away,
but my words will never pass away."
MARK 13:31

Born on January 20, 1669, to a London pastor, Susannah was the youngest of twenty-five children. Her father's many scholarly visitors created an atmosphere that enhanced her homeschooled education. Samuel Wesley, then a student and son of a minister, was one of those visitors. After attending Oxford University, Samuel Wesley was ordained in 1689, affiliated with the Church of England.

Susannah was twenty years old when she and Samuel married. In the following years, the couple had nineteen children. Only ten lived to become adults. A strong woman of faith, Susannah wrote in her diary that all her sufferings served to "promote my spiritual and eternal good. Glory be to Thee, O Lord."

During a time of great religious upheaval, Susannah's husband tried to remain with the Church of England, but he was arrested and taken to prison by his own congregation. His barns were burned and his cows were mutilated so his family wouldn't have milk to drink.

Women of the Faith

Susannah Wesley
(1660–1742)
Mother of John and Charles Wesley

Susannah and all but one child escaped when parishioners set fire to their roof. One child, John, was hurt when he jumped from a window to escape the flames. Later, he became a preacher and the founder of the Methodist denomination. Another son, Charles, is remembered for the hundreds of beloved hymns still being sung in churches today.

Susannah Wesley, a woman of courage, strength, devotion, and perseverance, had a clear vision of the influence a mother can have for good as she helped shape the destiny of two of the most important figures of the eighteenth century.

Susannah Wesley believed that for a child to grow into a *self-disciplined* adult, he or she must first be a *parent-disciplined* child.

FACT

The prayer of a righteous man is powerful and effective.
JAMES 5:16

The Mount of Olives is actually a ridge of four peaks rising about two hundred feet above the city of Jerusalem: The Mount of the Summit (where Jesus wept over Jerusalem), the Mount of the Ascension (where Jesus ascended to heaven), the Mount of Corruption (where Solomon allowed places of idol worship for his foreign wives), and the Mount of the Prophets (which contains catacombs housing the oldest remains of Jews who converted to Christianity, as indicated by the markings on their tombs). At the bottom of the main slope, across from the Temple Mount, lies the Garden of Gethsemane, where Jesus prayed before his arrest.

The Mount of Olives holds sacred significance for many reasons, not the least of which is the prophecy in Zechariah 14:1 that identifies this as the site where God will return to redeem the dead. For centuries, Jews have sought to be buried here for that reason. Though there are more than 150,000 graves on the Mount of Olives, hundreds of them have been destroyed or damaged through war or through the construction of the imposing Intercontinental Hotel.

Important Sites

Mount of Olives

Jerusalem

Several churches and shrines are scattered across the Mount of Olives, commemorating significant spiritual events. The Chapel of the Ascension (which was converted to a mosque in 1187 and remains so today) supposedly houses an imprint of Christ's right foot—left right where the disciples watched Jesus ascend to heaven. In the 600s, Christian pilgrims visiting this site were encouraged to take home dust from this rock as a souvenir.

FACT

Though tour guides often claim some of the Garden of Gethsemane's olive trees have been there since the time of Christ, it's unlikely because the Romans cut down all the olive trees in 70 AD during the Romans' siege of Jerusalem.

Then the LORD will go out and fight against those nations,
as he fights in the day of battle. On that day his feet
will stand on the Mount of Olives, east of Jerusalem.
ZECHARIAH 14:3–4

Frontier life in the late 1700s bred few churchgoers. In the newly admitted fifteenth state, the Commonwealth of Kentucky, for example, only 5 percent of the population claimed church membership. The Bluegrass State was ripe for the arrival in 1797 of frontier revivalist James McGready.

For years, McGready had astounded his hearers with his fiery oratorical style and calls for repentance, revival, and renewal. When word spread of a four-day Communion service to be held in the Red River Meeting House in June 1800, hundreds came from miles around to attend it.

Three days of meetings passed uneventfully. On the fourth day, however, emotions erupted as preacher John McGee exhorted the crowd, evoking the Holy Spirit to fill believers with ecstasy, which He apparently did. Members of the audience swooned and fell to the floor, "slain by the Spirit." Revival meetings, marked by similar emotional outbursts, spread rapidly throughout the

Groundbreaking Events

The First Camp Meeting Held in America

United States, attracting hundreds of converts and believers.

Presbyterian, Baptist, and Methodist preachers and speakers often came together in great tents to serve the faithful. Their brand of evangelicalism, dramatically expressed in Spirit-filled personal testimonies, assumed the status of a national religion. Combined with fervent patriotism, the conversion to Christianity quickly became the mark of any true patriot. As states ended tax support for churches in the early 1800s, evangelical Christians took on the role of enforcing public morality, reaching the lost, and sustaining Christian values in the community.

Revivals continued for some years, but gradually declined in influence and attendance over the following decade.

The Chautauqua Assembly, formed in 1874, stemmed from camp revival meetings. The assembly, convened initially to discuss issues pertinent to Sunday school teachers, expanded to religious, social, and cultural issues of the day. Soon, it attracted a growing middle-class populace eager to broaden its horizons and better itself through culture and education.

FACT

Never be lacking in zeal, but keep your spiritual fervor, serving the Lord.
ROMANS 12:11

That the president's powerful and influential "hatchet man" would end up in a prison cell surprises no one these days. In the decades since the Watergate debacle of the Nixon administration, we've seen one high-profile scandal after another. But that a formerly ruthless operative would emerge to prominence as a born-again Christian and humanitarian deserves notice.

During his four years of service to President Nixon, even the most powerful politicians feared Charles Colson, the president's "hatchet man." Colson had been willing to do just about anything for his political party and the president, including trying to cover up the burglary at the center of the Watergate scandal.

In *Born Again*, Charles "Chuck" Colson relates how, as Watergate investigations

Notable Books

Born Again

By Charles (Chuck) W. Colson (1976)

were unraveling the workings of the Nixon administration and revealing his illegal actions as special counsel to the president, he was thrown into a torturous search for hope and strength. In the office of a friend, he fell into tears of repentance. His friend prayed over him, and Colson, for the first time in his life, experienced the presence of God. At his trial, he pleaded guilty to obstruction of justice and was sentenced to one to three years as a guest of the U.S. government.

Colson was the first of the Nixon administration to go to prison for charges related to the Watergate scandal. He served seven months of his sentence, using his prison time to study the Bible, pray, and write the notes that became his autobiography, *Born Again*. The book was made into a movie of the same name in 1978.

FACT

Chuck Colson wrote, "All I knew was that I had a story I must tell, a story that might bring hope and encouragement to others."

"You brought my life up from the pit, O LORD my God."
JONAH 2:6

Well known as a fine gospel hymn of praise and adoration to God, "To God Be the Glory" was written and first published in a Sunday school collection, *Brightest and Best*, compiled by William Doane and Robert Lowry in 1875. It was also used by Ira Sankey in the British editions of his famous songbooks but not included in the U.S. editions.

In 1952, the Billy Graham team used the hymn with great response during a crusade being held in England.

Songs of the Faith

When they returned to the United States, they found American audiences received the hymn just as enthusiastically. It quickly became popular after Cliff Barrows sang it during a Billy Graham crusade in Nashville, Tennessee, in 1954. Since that time, it has become one

"To God Be the Glory"

Words by Fanny J. Crosby (1875)
Music by William Doane (1875)

of the most well known and loved of hymns.

In the first stanza, the message is clear: Jesus alone opens the door of salvation, everyone is given the opportunity to be saved, and it is grace rather than man's worth that grants eternal life.

To God be the glory, great things He has done;
So loved He the world that He gave us His Son,
Who yielded His life an atonement for sin,
And opened the Life-gate that all may go in.

Refrain:
Praise the Lord, praise the Lord,
Let the earth hear His voice!
Praise the Lord, praise the Lord,
Let the people rejoice!
O come to the Father, through Jesus the Son,
And give Him the glory, great things He hath done!

The hymn's composer, William H. Doane, was a frequent collaborator with Ms. Crosby in the production of spiritual songs. In his lifetime Doane composed more than two thousand tunes, many of which are still in common use today.

FACT

So that with one heart and mouth you may glorify the God
and Father of our Lord Jesus Christ.
ROMANS 15:6

Neeed Directions? No, that's not your spouse pointedly noting the circuitous route you've chosen to take on the way to the lake. It's God.

Through a Ft. Lauderdale advertising agency, an anonymous donor financed a series of billboards that appeared along south Florida highways in the fall of 1998. Large white letters on a black field proclaimed, in short, pithy statements, God's messages to travelers cruising along the road of life. The donor hoped to get people thinking creatively about God and their relationship with Him, the Bible, church, and each other. Eighteen different messages, ranging from no-foolin' serious to outright funny, were scheduled to run for three months.

Eller Media, one of the largest billboard agencies in the world, picked up on the idea and proposed to run the campaign nationwide. In 1999, the Outdoor Advertising Association of America offered to display the sayings as a public service. In total, God spoke in two hundred cities throughout the U.S. on roughly ten thousand billboards and on bus sides and bus interiors. No one had the nerve to charge Him for the space. The donated billboard real estate carried an estimated value of fifteen million dollars.

Miscellany

God Speaks

People listened, especially the media. Fascinated with the person who financed the initial award-winning campaign with neither fame nor gain for himself (or herself), they probed to find out the donor's identity. The donor chose to remain anonymous and let the attention remain on the Speaker.

FACT

Some of God's billboard messages included the following "signs":
LET'S TALK.
THAT "LOVE THY NEIGHBOR" THING. . . I MEANT THAT.
LET'S MEET AT MY HOUSE SUNDAY, BEFORE THE GAME.
WHAT PART OF "THOU SHALT NOT. . ." DIDN'T YOU UNDERSTAND?
HAVE YOU READ MY #1 BESTSELLER? (THERE WILL BE A TEST.)
KEEP USING MY NAME IN VAIN; I'LL MAKE RUSH HOUR LONGER.
I LOVE YOU. . . I LOVE YOU. . . I LOVE YOU.
—God

Your word is a lamp to my feet and a light for my path.
PSALM 119:105

History recognizes William Wilberforce as one of the key figures of influence in the Western world. However, his early life did not reflect morality or seriousness in his studies. While a student at Cambridge, he would spend late nights, playing cards, gambling, and drinking alcohol. Though he didn't apply himself to his education, at Cambridge he made a lifelong friend—William Pitt, the future prime minister of England.

During his first year as a member of Parliament, Wilberforce did very little. His own distinction was his pride and joy. Yet, as he reflected on his life over time, he began to regret his folly, abstain from alcohol, and turn back to his Christian faith.

Influenced by Thomas Clarkson, Wilberforce became obsessed with the abolition of slavery. He and Clarkson introduced twelve resolutions to Parliament against the slave trade, but all of them failed. Other bills over eight years were introduced and blocked primarily due to entrenched bigotry and political fear. Wilberforce began to write public essays on the topic, including "A Letter on the Abolition of the Slave Trade," which he used as the basis for the final phase of his campaign to Parliament. Finally in 1807, Parliament abolished slavery in the British Empire.

Men of the Faith

William Wilberforce (1759–1833)
British abolitionist

Wilberforce founded the African Institution, an organization dedicated to improving the lives of Africans living in the West Indies. He supported efforts taking Christianity into West Africa. In declining health, he worked his remaining days to ensure that the measures passed were enforced.

Wilberforce was a founding member of the Church Missionary Society (since renamed Church Mission Society), as well as the Society for the Prevention of Cruelty to Animals (now the Royal Society for the Prevention of Cruelty to Animals).

FACT

It is for freedom that Christ has set us free. Stand firm, then, and do not let yourselves be burdened again by a yoke of slavery.
GALATIANS 5:1

above the titles of wife and mother, which, although dear, are transitory and accidental, there is the title human being, which precedes and out-ranks every other." Mary Ashton Livermore's progressive views put her at the forefront of nineteenth-century feminism and social reform.

Born in Boston, Massachusetts, Mary Ashton Rice developed a deep love for the Bible and biblical principles of social justice. As a young woman, she tutored on a Virginia plantation, where she witnessed the treatment of slaves and became an abolitionist. Returning to Massachusetts, she managed a private school and eventually married Daniel Livermore, a minister and temperance advocate.

Women of the Faith

Mary Ashton Livermore (1820–1905)

Journalist, reformer, and feminist

When the Livermores moved to Chicago, Mary edited reform and religious periodicals and also published a collection of her essays. She campaigned for Abraham Lincoln in the 1860 presidential election. During the Civil War, Livermore volunteered in military hospitals and joined the U.S. Sanitary Commission, a war relief agency. She so successfully raised funds and secured needed food, clothing, and medical supplies that she was appointed an agent of the Commission. Her experience convinced her that social reform rested with the women's right to vote.

Livermore's interest in women's rights put her in league with suffragists Lucy Stone and Julia Ward Howe. She was a founding member of the American Woman Suffrage Association and a leader of the Women's Christian Temperance Union. In her later years, Livermore wrote several books about her activities during the Civil War and the ongoing battle for the rights of women.

> **FACT**
>
> Mary Ashton Livermore, a strong advocate of women's participation in war relief, facilitated the Great Northwestern Sanitary Commission Fair in 1863, which raised nearly $100,000 for soldiers.

To do what is right and just is more acceptable to the LORD than sacrifice.
PROVERBS 21:3

A fifteen-minute train ride from Amsterdam takes visitors to the Dutch city of Haarlem, home to the Corrie ten Boom House, nicknamed Beje (pronounced *bay-yay*). Refurbished to appear as it did in the 1940s, this living museum continues to bear witness to the love and sacrifice the ten Boom family extended to Dutch resistance fighters and Jews during World War II. The book and movie entitled, *The Hiding Place*, as well as the work of Corrie ten Boom's Christian ministry (after her release from a Nazi concentration camp), helped spread the story of the ten Booms' faith and courage worldwide.

In keeping with the ten Booms' spirit of hospitality, admission to their home has been free since it opened to the public in 1988. The main draw for visitors is the "hiding place" located in Corrie's third-story bedroom. This cramped, claustrophobic niche, accessed by a sliding door at the bottom of a linen closet, is where six people hid for forty-seven hours without food or water after the ten Booms' arrest by the Gestapo.

Important Sites

The Beje
Haarlem, Netherlands

It's estimated that the ten Booms saved the lives of eight hundred people during World War II. Before, during, and after the war, the ten Boom house was always open to those in need.

Founded in 1837, the adjoining ten Boom *Horlogerie* ("watch shop") where Corrie, her father, and grandfather worked remains open for business today. (Corrie was the first licensed woman watchmaker in the Netherlands.) Here visitors can purchase timepieces that still bear the ten Boom name.

Corrie ten Boom died in 1983 on her ninety-first birthday. According to Jewish tradition, only those specially blessed by God are allowed the privilege of dying on their birthday.

FACT

Be joyful in hope, patient in affliction, faithful in prayer.
Share with God's people who are in need. Practice hospitality.
Bless those who persecute you; bless and do not curse.
ROMANS 12:12–14

The man of dictionary fame took upon himself the formidable task of producing an American English translation of the Bible.

Noah Webster worked from the King James Version (KJV), which he revered for its accuracy and expressiveness. He planned to make no changes except where necessary: to replace obsolete words and words that had changed meaning over the previous two centuries; to update old spellings and exchange Britishisms for American idioms; and to substitute certain descriptive, but earthy, terms sprinkled throughout the King James Version with more gently stated euphemisms compatible with American sensibilities. In tone and format, however, Webster closely followed the KJV. So closely, in fact, that critics cited many areas where he could have made significant changes to promote American English usage. Nonetheless, Webster's accurate and readable translation retains its place as the first modern translation of the English Bible.

Groundbreaking Events

The First Modern Translation of the English Bible

Published in 1833, Webster's Bible offers lexicographers today a base for comparing nineteenth-century American English with the English of the King James Bible. His work influenced American translators who followed him fifty years later with the American Standard Version, the source of the Revised Standard Version of 1952.

While Webster's Bible never achieved great acceptance among the Bible-reading public of his day, it's realizing some degree of popularity now. Webster's translation ranks among the few modern English texts that, because of age, is in the public domain. Writers can quote the Bible without seeking permission from or paying royalty to the publisher.

FACT

Noah Webster wrote, "In my view, the Christian religion is the most important and one of the first things in which all children under a free government, ought to be instructed. . . . No truth is more evident to my mind than that the Christian religion must be the basis of any government intended to secure the rights and privileges of a free people."

Glory in his holy name; let the hearts of those who seek the LORD rejoice.
PSALM 105:3

In the struggle of Communism against Christianity, Brother Andrew played a key role on the side of the Christians. He tells of his exploits in his autobiography, *God's Smuggler*.

As a boy, Andy van der Bijl dreamed of being a spy. As a young man, he fought with the Dutch army and gained a reputation as a daredevil. Using the spying techniques learned while working for the Dutch Resistance in World War II, Brother Andrew found ways to get Bibles into Communist countries. *God's Smuggler* tells story after story of the miraculous ways God made it possible to get Bibles into places across closed borders. In Communist countries, possessing more than one Bible could quickly land you in prison, yet Brother Andrew took carloads of Bibles through border checkpoints where guards literally did not see them in plain view. His strategy was to pack Bibles as ordinary luggage and pray that guards would not see them. Brother Andrew confesses it was often easier to get Bibles past border guards than it was to put them into the hands

Notable Books

God's Smuggler
By Brother Andrew (1967)

of wary Christians living behind the Iron Curtain who could hardly believe it was possible to receive the Word of God. He trained others, and his efforts and the efforts of his companions helped keep the flame of faith alive in the dark decades of government repression and persecution.

By some estimates, *God's Smuggler* has sold more than twelve million copies in forty languages, encouraging millions of Christians in the free world to remember and help those who have no access to the Bible, Bible studies, and Christian fellowship.

Brother Andrew was honored as a legendary Christian by the World Evangelical Fellowship in 1997. **FACT**

[Jesus said,] "See, I have placed before you an open door that no one can shut."
REVELATION 3:8

The Reverend John Fawcett, pastor of the Baptist Church at Wainsgate, England, was an outstanding scholar and preacher. While watching over his small congregation of about a hundred souls, he founded a school for training young ministers, compiled a hymnal, and wrote a number of books to supplement his modest salary—often partly paid in potatoes and wool.

Orphaned at the age of twelve, Fawcett was used to working hard and living modestly. It must have been quite a surprise when representatives of King George III contacted him. The monarch had read an essay written by Fawcett on anger and was so impressed that he wished to confer a great honor on him—any benefit within the king's reach. Soon after, the humble preacher received a call from the mighty Carter Lane Church in London.

Songs of the Faith

"Blest Be the Tie That Binds"

Words by John Fawcett (1845)

Music by Hans G. Nageli (1845)

Fawcett accepted the call, but ultimately could not leave Wainsgate. As he went from house to house saying farewell—young couples he had married, children he had blessed, older people he had seen through trial and sickness—he decided to stay a little longer. In fact, he continued on until his death fifty-four years later. He has said that those humble people he served for so long were the inspiration for his great hymn "Blest Be the Tie That Binds."

Blest be the tie that binds
Our hearts in Christian love;
The fellowship of kindred minds
Is like to that above.

We share our mutual woes;
Our mutual burdens bear;
And often for each other flows
The sympathizing tear.

FACT

It has been estimated that John Fawcett's annual salary never exceeded the equivalent of two hundred dollars.

[Jesus said,] "A man's life does not consist in the abundance of his possessions."
LUKE 12:15

The battlefield—or the fort? Traditionally, American Christians chose the latter option. They fortified themselves with the gospel, held on to traditional morals and values, taught their children right from wrong, and clicked their collective tongues as they watched the rest of the country go to hell in a handbasket. Not so television evangelist Jerry Falwell. He chose the battlefield.

In 1979, Falwell and other Christian conservatives called for religious leaders to band together and fight America's cultural decline. They established the Moral Majority, a group committed to a pro-life, traditional family, patriotic, and pro-Israel agenda. Within a year, the Moral Majority boasted a membership of one hundred thousand evangelical ministers, Catholic priests, and orthodox rabbis, along with seven million families.

Miscellany

The Moral Majority

The organization hit the streets. It launched an aggressive get-out-the-vote campaign, mobilizing 8.5 million new voters in support of Ronald Reagan's candidacy in 1980. Reagan's landslide victory is largely credited to the efforts of Moral Majority voters, also known as the "religious right." The Moral Majority's political power in large part led to the defeat of more than a few liberal senators and representatives in Congress.

Falwell officially disbanded the Moral Majority in 1989 to focus his attention on the growth of Liberty University, a Christian center for political and church leaders. While evangelicals continued to make their voices heard in the political arena, the years of the liberal-leaning Clinton presidency softened their tone and effect.

Falwell died in May of 2007 in his office at Liberty University in Lynchburg, Virginia.

In 2004, Falwell established the Moral Majority Coalition. The Coalition committed itself to continued national get-out-the-vote campaigns in upcoming elections; the mobilization of social conservatives; and the promotion of private and corporate prayer to revitalize spiritual values throughout America. His sons continue to lead the organization.

FACT

You're here to be salt-seasoning that brings out the God-flavors of this earth.
If you lose your saltiness, how will people taste godliness?
MATTHEW 5:13 MSG

Despised by the Roman Catholic Church, English theologian John Wycliffe was not allowed to rest in peace. Forty-three years after his death, officials exhumed his body, burned his remains, and threw his ashes into the River Swift. John Wycliffe's influence, though suppressed, continued to spread.

In his own lifetime, Wycliffe was called "the master of errors" by the papal authorities. He told Parliament not to give money to Rome because Christ called his disciples to poverty. Such an opinion brought Wycliffe the charge of heresy, and he was brought to London before a court. The hearing ended in a physical brawl. Pope Gregory XI issued five papal bulls (or church edicts) condemning Wycliffe's opinions.

Men of the Faith

John Wycliffe
(c. 1325–1384)
The "Morning Star of the Reformation" and Bible Translator

While under house arrest, he continued to study the scriptures and began to believe that every Christian should be able to read the Bible in the vernacular. Hence, he began to translate the Bible into English with the help of his friend John Purvey.

Throughout his life, Wycliffe spoke on his convictions, preceding Martin Luther in the belief that people are justified by faith and not works. He wrote, "If a man believe in Christ, and make a point of his belief, then the promise that God hath made to come into the land of light shall be given by virtue of Christ, to all men that make this the chief matter."

Wycliffe died before the translation of the Bible was complete, but his friends and followers (called Lollards) continued to be an irritant to the Catholic Church until the Protestant Reformation arrived in the 1500s.

FACT

John Wycliffe wrote, "I believe that in the end the truth will conquer."

---

*Clearly no one is justified before God by the law, because,
"The righteous will live by faith."*
GALATIANS 3:11

Phoebe Worall's parents, Henry and Dorthea Worall, were devout Methodists, her father having had a religious conversion during the Wesleyan Revival. The couple emigrated from England to New York, where Phoebe was born.

In 1827, Phoebe married Walter Palmer. As a Methodist couple the Palmers became interested in the writings of Methodism founder, John Wesley, and his teaching about holiness and sanctification. During the 1830s they felt compelled to share with others what they had personally experienced.

Phoebe's sister, Sarah, began holding women's meetings in her home in 1835. Within two years, Phoebe was leading the Tuesday "Promotion of Holiness" meetings in her own home. In 1839 men began attending the meetings. Bishops, theologians, and prominent clergy became involved in the holiness movement that eventually influenced Methodist churches nationwide.

From this movement Phoebe and Walter became itinerate preachers and received countless invitations to preach at churches and various meetings in the

Women of the Faith

Phoebe Palmer
(1807–1874)
Revivalist and theologian

United States, Canada, and the United Kingdom, where they stayed for many years. While Walter did the preaching, Phoebe was better known and most influential in spreading the holiness concept throughout the world and preparing the way for the Pentecostal movement.

Phoebe wrote the foundational book *The Way of Holiness*, which became an invaluable tool for the spread of the movement. She wrote other books including *The Promise of the Father*, a book that defended a woman's role in Christian ministry.

In 1850 Phoebe Palmer led the Methodist Ladies' Home Missionary Society in founding the Five Points Mission—located in a New York City slum.

Phoebe Palmer wrote, "Holiness is a state of soul in which all the powers of the body and mind are consciously given up to God."

FACT

I urge you, brothers, in view of God's mercy, to offer your bodies as living sacrifices, holy and pleasing to God—this is your spiritual act of worship.
ROMANS 12:1

In the Old Testament, the Jordan River was the site of several miracles. In the book of Joshua, the flow of the river stopped to allow the Israelites, and the priests who carried the ark of the covenant, to cross. In 2 Kings, God empowered Elijah to stop the river's flow with a touch of his cloak, heal an army commander of leprosy by having him wash in the Jordan, and made an iron ax-head float on the river's surface. But the main reason people consider the Jordan River sacred is because it's the site of Jesus' baptism, recorded in the New Testament.

More than four hundred thousand visitors a year travel from all over the world to Yardenit—the spot where the Jordan flows out of the Sea of Galilee—

Important Sites

The Jordan River

Northern Israel

to follow Jesus' example. A visitors' center, held up by huge pillars in the shape of a cross, houses a souvenir shop resembling a Galilean-style bazaar. Here visitors can rent white baptismal robes and towels, pick up a certificate of baptism or rededication, or purchase a Jesus-shaped bottle to bring home water from the River Jordan, 364 days a year. (Yardenit is closed only on the Jewish holiday of Yom Kippur.) Participants can choose to be baptized by immersion or have a pastor or priest sprinkle them with water from a tree branch dipped into the river.

Other than the relatively clean water flowing through the Yardenit region (thanks to a nearby dam and hydraulic plant), today the remaining two hundred miles of the Jordan River is stagnant and polluted.

FACT

No swimming, fishing, picnicking, or boating is allowed in the area surrounding Yardenit. However, there is a dining hall and St. Peter's Fish Table buffet where visitors can enjoy a bite to eat.

Then Jesus came from Galilee to the Jordan to be baptized by John.
MATTHEW 3:13

B efore the days of CNN, instant communications, and adventure travel, few Americans had the vaguest notion of what life was like beyond the Western world. Tall tales and jungle legends constituted all most people knew about places like South America, Africa, and the Pacific Islands. The darkness began to lift at the dawn of the twentieth century, thanks in large part to evangelist Dwight L. Moody.

In 1886, Moody established the nondenominational Student Volunteer Movement for Foreign Missions (SVM) to attract and recruit college graduates to serve in foreign missions. "The Evangelization of the World in This Generation" was Moody's idealistic motto for an idealistic and energetic generation. During the next forty years, over thirteen thousand college-age men and women took up Moody's

Groundbreaking Events

The Student Volunteer Movement Launched

challenge and traveled to far-flung points on the map to evangelize the world. Many thousands more pledged to faithfully support missions and missionaries through their prayers and financial contributions.

The appeal of foreign missions intensified across denominational boundaries. Protestant congregations stepped up their efforts to support and send missionaries abroad and sent cash and resources to establish churches, schools, medical clinics, and orphanages in countries worldwide.

Missionaries brought back to their hometowns eyewitness accounts of mysterious peoples and their customs. Magazine articles about missionaries who had died in the field piqued the interest of both religious and nonreligious readers. A large percentage of missionaries were academically trained, so many contributed scholarly articles on linguistics, religion, and anthropology. The SVM opened the world to students and ordinary Americans alike.

Dwight L. Moody wrote: "I was born of the flesh in 1837. I was born of the Spirit in 1856. That which is born of the flesh may die. That which is born of the Spirit will live forever."

FACT

"Go and make disciples of all nations,
baptizing them in the name of the Father and of the Son and of the Holy Spirit,
and teaching them to obey everything I have commanded you."
MATTHEW 28:19–20

On the day a child is born, parents and friends celebrate. The growth of that child, however, takes place over the course of a lifetime. It happens gradually through daily nurturing, nourishment, and guidance. The same process, says world-renown evangelist Billy Graham, applies to new Christians. In his book *How to be Born Again*, Graham helps converts affirm their decision for Christ, then guides them toward a lifelong commitment to nurture and grow in their faith.

In accessible and dynamic language with plenty of relevant examples and observations from real life, Graham's book addresses the fundamentals of the Christian faith. Three sections take readers through the decision-making process. "Man's Problem," the first section, addresses the questions skeptics—and even many Christians—pose concerning the reality of God's interest in the lives and purpose of individuals. "God's Answer," the second section, presents God's plan of salvation and His grace in the person of Jesus Christ. "Man's Response," the third section, follows up on the commitment once made with practical advice on how to ensure that the first flame of faith becomes a lasting fire.

Notable Books

How to be Born Again
By Billy Graham (1977)

Overall, Graham makes the point that being born again is not just a personal decision, but a community affair. Like a new baby, new Christians need other Christians for continued growth, support, and fellowship.

How to be Born Again remains a popular and practical manual for new Christians and for growing Christians—that is, all believers in Jesus Christ.

FACT

Billy Graham's *How to be Born Again* boasts the largest first printing in publishing history with eight hundred thousand copies released.

Your new life is not like your old life. Your old birth came from mortal sperm; your new birth comes from God's living Word.
1 PETER 1:23 MSG

F irst published in leaflet form in 1855 by Frederick Whitfield, an Anglican clergyman, this hymn specifically revolves around the name of Jesus. The lyrics encourage believers to strive to know Christ personally through the study of God's Word and to express their love to God and acknowledge His love for them.

The simply worded stanzas along with the easy-to-remember refrain made the hymn a favorite for Sunday schools. It also found popular use during camp meetings and evangelistic crusades like those of D. L. Moody, and has become a classic for crusades worldwide, which probably explains why it has been translated into numerous languages and is found in many old and modern-day hymnals.

Songs of the Faith

"Oh, How I Love Jesus"

Words by Frederick Whitfield (1855)

Music: American Folk Melody

(Unknown)

Frederick Whitfield was born at Threapwood, Shropshire, England, and educated at Trinity College in Dublin. "Oh, How I Love Jesus" is one of at least ten hymns he authored. He originally wrote eight stanzas, only four of which are found in most current hymnbooks. His words are set to an anonymous nineteenth-century American folk melody.

There is a Name I love to hear,
I love to sing its worth;
It sounds like music in my ear,
The sweetest Name on earth.

Refrain:
O, how I love Jesus,
O, how I love Jesus,
O, how I love Jesus,
Because He first loved me!

It tells of One whose loving heart
Can feel my deepest woe,
Who in each sorrow bears a part,
That none can bear below.

The refrain is not part of Whitfield's original hymn. Its authorship is unknown.

FACT

We love because he first loved us.
1 JOHN 4:19

Is it constitutional to display the Ten Commandments on public property? Well, that depends on the motivation of those who erect the display, according to two 2005 Supreme Court decisions.

At issue were monuments in Kentucky and Texas. In Kentucky, the Ten Commandments—the Decalogue—was exhibited on the walls of two county courthouses. Why? To advance belief in God, ruled the Supreme Court, thus rendering the display in violation of the separation between church and state. The Court's ruling, however, fell in favor of the Texas display. The presence of the Ten Commandments on the Texas State Capitol grounds in Austin is legal. While identifiable as a sacred religious text, the Decalogue appears among other monuments and, as such, was motivated not by religion, but by historical interest.

Miscellany

Thou Shalt (or Not) Display Sacred Text on Public Property

Opponents of the Texas ruling take the view that the state's Ten Commandments are, indeed, in violation of church-state separation. After all, the text promotes the existence of a God and constitutes the government saying, "There is a God, and one God, at that." Proponents say the display is nothing more than an observance of the fact that Judeo-Christian values played a role in the lives of the Europeans who came to and settled in the New World.

Currently, it's legal to display the Ten Commandments in conjunction with other historical monuments and remembrances. You may set up a Nativity scene on public grounds at Christmastime, provided Santa Claus looks on in approval. Yet the case is far from closed.

FACT

The Ten Commandments appear in Hebrew scriptures (the Old Testament) and are summarized in the Koran. As such, they are accepted by the majority of Jews, Christians, and Muslims as binding moral law.

"I am the LORD your God. . . . You shall have no other gods before me."
EXODUS 20:1–3

A true philosopher and scholar, Francis Schaeffer believed Christianity presented a rational understanding of God that could be defended against objections. Very well educated, Schaeffer graduated *magna cum laude* from Hampden-Sydney College and then enrolled at Westminster Theological Seminary. After transferring to Faith Theological Seminary, he held pastorates in Pennsylvania and Missouri.

In 1948, Schaeffer and his family moved to Switzerland and in 1955 established the community called *L'Abri*. The tenets of belief at L'Abri are fourfold: (1) Christianity is objectively true; (2) it speaks to all of life; (3) God's grace allows us to live as fully human; and (4) until Christ returns, mankind will be disfigured by sin.

After gaining several honorary doctorate degrees, Schaeffer would go on to pen great Christian classics including *The God Who Is There; He Is There and He is Not Silent;* and his most famous work, *A Christian Manifesto.*

Men of the Faith

Francis Schaeffer (1912–1984)

Theologian, philosopher, and author

Within that final seminal work, Schaeffer argued that the decline of Western civilization is due to society's drift toward secular humanism, a worldview where "man is the measure of all things," not God. Schaeffer also criticized the church, saying Christians have not been salt and light to the culture as Christ commands. Others credit Schaeffer with contributing to the rise of today's Christian Right and Christian political activism.

In the decades since Schaeffer's death in 1984, his writings and work remain influential to Christian readers and seekers everywhere. His major works remain in print, and L'Abri Fellowship International still operates in Switzerland, encouraging Christian scholarship, fellowship, and debate.

Francis Schaeffer wrote, "Christianity provides a unified answer for the whole of life."

FACT

Who has known or understood the mind (the counsels and purposes) of the Lord
so as to guide and instruct Him and give Him knowledge?
But we have the mind of Christ (the Messiah)
and do hold the thoughts (feelings and purposes) of His heart.
1 Corinthians 2:16 AMP

Readers of the popular Left Behind novels will recognize her writer-husband's name, Tim LaHaye. Beverly LaHaye is equally known in Christian circles as a political activist and advocate of godly values in government. In 2005, *Time* magazine dubbed Tim and Beverly LaHaye "the Christian power couple."

In 1956, the LaHayes began a radio show, *LaHayes on Family Life.* Tim, a Baptist minister, and Beverly condemned social trends they saw as ruinous to traditional family life and threatening to Christianity. While Tim LaHaye went on to author a range of nonfiction and fiction books, Beverly LaHaye founded Concerned Women for America (CWA), a national organization to promote and protect family values.

Established in 1979, CWA responded to the proposed federal Equal Rights Amendment, which would grant women the same constitutional rights as men.

Women of the Faith

Beverly LaHaye
(b. 1926)

Activist and author

LaHaye, as well as other conservative Christian spokespersons, opposed the amendment because, she said, it would not be "interpreted in the light of scriptures by churches."

Other national campaigns launched by CWA, still under LaHaye's leadership, include opposition to condom and alcoholic beverage ads on television, federally supported research on teen sexuality and embryonic stem cells, and the abortion industry. CWA supported the Children's Internet Protection Act as well as the movement to impeach former president Bill Clinton and also led the public outcry that followed entertainer Janet Jackson's "wardrobe malfunction" during the 2004 Super Bowl.

LaHaye has authored and coauthored a number of books on marriage, family life, women's roles and spirituality, and a Christian fiction series.

FACT

Beverly LaHaye's CWA is the largest public policy women's organization in the nation.

Be very careful, then, how you live—not as unwise but as wise, making the most of every opportunity, because the days are evil.
EPHESIANS 5:15–16

T he original architects of Cappadocia's vast underground cities and "fairy chimneys" were volcanoes, wind, and water. Over time, erosion carved the otherworldly looking columns and cones from the porous *tuff* soil made of volcanic residue and compacted ash. According to historians, about four thousand years ago people began to take part in the process. They carved tunnels, staircases, windows, and air ducts in the bizarre outcroppings of tuff and relied on them for shelter and defense.

After the apostle Paul visited the area of Cappadocia (which is in modern-day Turkey, just north of Tarsus) small Christian communities began to sporadically inhabit, and expand, the Swiss-cheese-like network of tunnels and caves. Over the next several centuries, they carved more than three hundred fifty churches into the tuff and decorated many of them with vibrant frescoes depicting biblical scenes.

But Cappadocia was more than just a place of worship for the early Christians. It also became a refuge during times of persecution. The Christian community fashioned the labyrinth of tunnels in a manner designed to confuse invaders. Though outside entrances were easily camouflaged by the irregular landscape, they also could be sealed by large millstones wedged into place. This gave those inside time to escape through more obscure exits. In the Göreme region of Cappadocia, the churches, passageways, and personal dwellings of these cave-like communities were carved as deep as eight levels into the earth and housed tens of thousands of people for months at a time.

Today Cappadocia is one of Turkey's premier tourist destinations, with the Göreme Open Air Museum registered as an official World Heritage Site.

Important Sites

Cappadocia
Turkey

Descendents of Cappadocia's underground communities inhabited many of the region's fairy-chimney dwellings until 1923, when the government moved them out.

Being reviled, we bless; being persecuted, we endure.
1 CORINTHIANS 4:12 NKJV

Say "fundamentalist," and most people picture a televangelist calling down a shower of fire and brimstone on a godless nation. The Protestant fundamentalist movement, however, began with noble intentions in the early years of the twentieth century.

A series of twelve polemical pamphlets called *The Fundamentals* were issued in 1910 by a coalition of conservative Protestants. The pamphlets articulated ninety articles of belief defined as fundamental to Christianity. In the same year, the General Assembly of the Northern Presbyterian Church published "the five fundamentals" of Christian doctrine, including the inerrancy of the Bible, virgin birth of Christ, the authenticity of Christ's miracles, His sacrificial death, and His physical resurrection. Both *The Fundamentals* and "the five fundamentals" addressed specific points of doctrine conservative Protestant leaders believed were being challenged by science, liberalism, and modernism.

Groundbreaking Events

Publication of
The Fundamentals

Debate on the subject flared across mainline denominations. Many churches split over issues raised by fundamentalists and congregants who espoused more liberal views. Those who stood by fundamentalist principles broke off from their parent denominations to set up new denominations or independent congregations.

Fundamentalist influence increased as conservative Protestants lobbied state legislators for conservative social causes. In the last several decades of the twentieth century, influential conservative talk-radio stations and television ministries multiplied, pulling in audiences of fundamentalists, evangelicals, and Pentecostals, among others. Today, fundamentalists write books, produce movies, and set up Web sites to reach even broader audiences. Though a movement highly critical of popular culture, fundamentalism continues to enthusiastically adopt and deftly use the world's newest technology.

FACT

In the early years of the twentieth century, archaeologists in the Holy Land excavated the sites of cities mentioned in the Bible, such as the ancient walled city of Jericho. Some authors of articles in *The Fundamentals* used archaeological discoveries as proof of the Bible's authority as an accurate historical document.

Test everything. Hold on to the good.
1 THESSALONIANS 5:21

Gertrude Hobbs probably knew that one day her lightning-fast shorthand skills would come in handy. She had been clocked at 150 words per minute—for all intents and purposes unbeatable! But she couldn't have known that her skill would be used to preserve the powerful words of a Scottish minister.

Born in Aberdeen, Scotland, Oswald Chambers was converted as a teen under the ministry of Charles Haddon Spurgeon. He studied art and archaeology at the University of Edinburgh before answering a call from God to the Christian ministry. After studying theology at Dunoon College, Chambers began to travel to Egypt, Japan, and America to preach. In America he met and married Gertrude Hobbs.

In 1911, Chambers founded the Bible Training College in Clapham, England. His teachings on the life of faith and abandoning all to God could be heard during his scheduled classes as well as the college's devotional hour. Each one was recorded by Gertrude in her impeccable shorthand.

In 1915, Chambers suspended operations at the Bible College as World War I raged on. After being designated as a YMCA chaplain, he left for Egypt to minister to the troops. There, at the age of forty-three, Chambers died of a ruptured appendix.

Notable Books

My Utmost for His Highest
By Oswald Chambers (1935)

Grief-stricken, Gertrude turned to the verbatim notes she had so carefully compiled of her husband's many teaching sessions. Slowly and meticulously she translated those teachings into devotions, one for each day of the year. Published in England in 1927 and in the United States in 1935, *My Utmost for His Highest* has become one of the most popular religious books ever written.

My Utmost for His Highest has been in print in the United States continuously since 1935. It remains one of the top ten religious book titles.

FACT

The things you have heard me say in the presence of many witnesses entrust to reliable men who will also be qualified to teach others.

2 TIMOTHY 2:2

In May 1735, Charles and John Wesley went as missionaries to the new colony of Georgia. On board ship, they encountered twenty-six German Moravians, who impressed them with their hymn singing and preaching. Even during the fierce Atlantic storms, the men sang on, demonstrating to the Wesley brothers that hymn singing could be a spiritual experience and causing them to look beyond the legalistic and lifeless spirituality they had known before that time.

The mission was not deemed successful and the brothers returned within a year. Around that time, they encountered another Moravian, Peter Bohler, who expressed his spiritual joy and state of being concerning his faith by sharing the words: "Oh Brother Wesley, the Lord has done so much for my life. Had I a thousand tongues, I would praise Christ Jesus with every one of them!"

Songs of the Faith

"O for a Thousand Tongues"

Words and Music
by Charles Wesley (1749)

These encounters convinced both John and Charles that they should seek more from the Christian life. They both felt they had spent too many years engaged in zealous, religious activity without ever knowing God personally or experiencing His joy.

When Charles did enter a time of deeply personal spiritual awakening, he remembered the words of the Moravian and included them in the hymn commemorating the celebration of his own conversion.

O for a thousand tongues to sing
My great Redeemer's praise,
The glories of my God and King,
The triumphs of His grace.

My gracious Master and my God,
Assist me to proclaim,
To spread through all the earth abroad
The honors of Thy name.

FACT

Consisting of nineteen original stanzas, this hymn is one of the longest on record.

Let everything that has breath praise the Lord. Praise the Lord.
PSALM 150:6

Shopping for a bestselling Christian book? Go to your nearest Costco or Wal-Mart. Once relegated to the shelves of religious retailers, Christian books have crashed the genre barrier.

The crossover began in the early 1990s when the profitability of faith-based books attracted the attention of mainstream publishers. Evangelical views were becoming more generally accepted as secular Americans, disillusioned by the failed promises of materialism, sought spiritual wisdom and guidance. Inspirational titles surged into popular culture, followed by apocalyptic adventures and Christian romances. Christian titles began appearing regularly on the bestseller lists of the *New York Times* and *USA Today*. In the 1990s, Jerry Jenkins and Tim LaHaye's Left Behind series became the bestselling fiction series in publishing history. Rick Warren's *The Purpose Driven Life* was the first book to sell more than one million copies at Sam's Club, and was the fastest selling hardcover in publishing history up to that time. Currently, the Christian book category is one of the fastest growing categories in book publishing.

Miscellany

Christian Publishing

Growth isn't limited to the United States market. International sales of Christian books have seen phenomenal increases in the last several years. Translations of Christian English titles outsell those of any other category of book.

The Evangelical Christian Publishers Association (ECPA), an international nonprofit trade organization for publishers and distributors of Christian literature, attributes the extraordinary growth in readership to unprecedented access to markets. In addition, the ECPA cites the industry's recent advances in professionalism and production technology.

And the bestselling book of all time? The Bible. In all its various versions in English alone, the Bible accounts for upward of four hundred fifty million dollars in sales each year.

Despite dire predictions of the death of reading, surveys show Bible readership rising. In 2006, Barna Group research found that 47 percent of the U.S. population reported reading the Bible at least once in a typical week. Among evangelical Christians, the percentage rose to 96 percent.

FACT

Let love and faithfulness never leave you;
bind them around your neck, write them on the tablet of your heart.
PROVERBS 3:3

Portugal's King John III desired to send Jesuit missionaries to the colonies in the Orient. He asked Jesuit founder Ignatius Loyola for six, but Loyola could spare just two. After one turned ill, just Francis Xavier remained. He had only enough time to mend his cassock before he was shipped out.

Born a Spaniard, Xavier had been Loyola's roommate at the University of Paris, Western Europe's theological center. The two became fast friends and they, along with five others, dedicated themselves to poverty and celibacy, just like Jesus. The order was called the Jesuits and their fame for Christian service quickly spread across the continent.

Xavier's first stop was Goa, India, where he spent five months ministering to hospitalized Portuguese colonists. But Xavier quickly became discouraged with ministering to the Portuguese, reasoning that if God meant for him to reach these people, he could have done so in Portugal. Xavier's attention then turned to the Eastern natives.

Men of the Faith

Francis Xavier
(1506–1552)

First missionary to Japan

He sailed on, reaching Sri Lanka and possibly the Philippines, but his heart turned to Japan after meeting a man named Han-sir. Xavier witnessed to Han-sir and converted him to Christianity. Then after discussing the possibility of converting Japanese to Christ, Han-sir became Xavier's interpreter and guide. Another Japanese man, Anjiro, helped translate a few paragraphs of Christian doctrine into phonetic Japanese, which Xavier memorized. Though the Jesuits claim he converted seven hundred thousand people to Christ, modern scholars place the number closer to thirty thousand. Even so, his work has established him as one of the greatest missionaries of that era.

> **FACT**
>
> Xavier's right forearm, which he used to bless and baptize his converts, was detached by General Claudio Acquaviva in 1614, and has been on display ever since in a silver reliquary at the main Jesuit church in Rome.

The man brought me to the gate facing east.
EZEKIEL 43:1

Harriet Beecher Stowe was born in Litchfield, Connecticut, to Roxana Beecher and abolitionist Congregationalist preacher, Lyman Beecher. Unfortunately, Roxana died when Harriet was only four years old.

In 1832, Harriet moved with her father and two siblings, Isabella and Charles Beecher, to Cincinnati. While living in Cincinnati, Harriet experienced secondhand observations of slavery and became well acquainted with the Underground Railroad movement. She talked with former slaves as she began writing *Uncle Tom's Cabin*, the first American novel depicting an African-American hero.

Harriet married widower and clergyman Calvin Ellis Stowe in 1836 and moved to Brunswick, Maine. Four of their seven children preceded her in death.

When *Uncle Tom's Cabin*, her two-volume antislavery novel, was published in 1852, Harriet soon realized what her husband and readers of her articles and sketches had believed—her story had the power to change the mind. Her authentic writing about a mother's broken heart when her son was sold on the auction block came from remembering the heartache she felt when she lost her son Samuel.

Women of the Faith

Harriet Beecher Stowe (1811–1896)

Abolitionist and author of

Uncle Tom's Cabin

Her book sold ten thousand copies within the first week of its release and more than three million in the first year. Within two years it had been translated into thirty-seven languages and inspired thousands to become abolitionists. *Uncle Tom's Cabin* was also among the most popular plays of the nineteenth century.

Following the Civil War, Harriet established homes for newly freed slaves. Her cause touched prominent government officials, nobility, and common people from all walks of life.

When Abraham Lincoln met Harriet Beecher Stowe, he commented: "So you're the little woman who wrote the book that started this great war."

FACT

What does the LORD require of you?
To act justly and to love mercy and to walk humbly with your God.
MICAH 6:8

In the late 1800s, a movement toward Bible-based education swept through the Christian community of America. In response, the Presbyterian Church of Indiana sought a common location where ministers and church workers could join together to study the Bible and discuss church-related matters. They settled upon a tract of land surrounding Indiana's Eagle Lake. The Presbyterian Church changed the lake's name to *Winona*, which means "first born" in the language of the Potawatomi Indians who were the area's original settlers.

Within ten years, Winona Lake went from hosting thirty-five church workers to more than ten thousand. An Agricultural Institute, Technical Institute, and four-year liberal arts college were established. In the 1920s the Winona Lake School of Theology was founded—along with Billy Sunday's Tabernacle. The arrival of Sunday, a baseball-player-turned-evangelist, helped earn Winona Lake the nickname of "The World's Largest Bible Conference." The 7,500-seat Tabernacle was the site of revivals, church services, and special events led by Sunday and many other well-known speakers and personalities of the day. By the 1930s many prominent Christian organizations moved their headquarters to the surrounding area.

Important Sites

Winona Lake

Indiana

Though Christian conventions and conferences continued at Winona Lake through the 1950s and '60s, by the '80s the area's glory days were over. Today, Winona Lake is primarily a residential area. However, the Billy Sunday Home has been restored and is open to visitors. It chronicles the life of the evangelist. A visitor's center, built to resemble the original Billy Sunday Tabernacle, is also open to the public.

FACT

It is believed that Billy Sunday preached to more than one hundred million people during his lifetime—for the most part without the aid of a microphone.

It was [Christ] who gave some to be. . .evangelists,
and some to be pastors and teachers, to prepare God's people
for works of service, so that the body of Christ may be built up.
EPHESIANS 4:11–12

Though challenged by deep rifts between various Christian churches, many prominent Christian leaders have worked tirelessly to build bridges. In a spirit of ecumenism (from the Greek *oikoumene*, meaning "one world"), they have endeavored to highlight points of agreement and downplay the differences among Orthodox, Roman Catholic, and Protestant traditions.

The modern ecumenical movement emerged in the early decades of the twentieth century. Various Protestant denominations or groups of churches pooled resources for missionary projects and coordinated their mission activities. In some cities, congregations from different denominations planned joint community-wide ecumenical prayer services. In 1948, representatives from Orthodox and Protestant churches met in Amsterdam to further the cause of Christian unity. They established the World Council of Churches (WCC), not to promote a single Christian confession or standard method of worship, but to create a fellowship of churches across Christian denominations. Today, the WCC continues its role as a national and international voice for the Christian message, in addition to promoting peace, justice, tolerance, and understanding in the world.

Groundbreaking Events

The Ecumenical Movement

Though embraced and practiced by liberal Protestant church bodies, ecumenism has yet to gain the full support of conservative Christian groups and the Roman Catholic Church. Issues such as the inerrancy of scripture, the meaning of holy communion, the authority of the pope, the suitability of women's ordination, and the morality of the homosexual lifestyle preclude authentic unity with churches of opposing views. Despite major theological differences, however, local congregations often join in community and social projects for the common good and to foster fellowship and understanding among Christians.

The WCC has no provisions to excommunicate a church body from its ranks, although a few churches have given up their membership. In the early 1960s, three South African churches withdrew over apartheid; and in the 1970s, two churches withdrew in reaction to a WCC grant to support liberation movements in Africa.

FACT

Make every effort to keep the unity of the Spirit through the bond of peace.
EPHESIANS 4:3

Rees Howells started life in a Welsh mining village in the latter years of the nineteenth century. He left school at age twelve to work in the mines and was destined to spend the rest of his life unknown to anyone outside his family, neighbors, and coworkers. That is, until the Lord had His way with him. Through Norman Grubb's biography, *Rees Howells: Intercessor,* millions of readers know about him and his remarkable life's story.

Influenced by the Welsh Revival of the early twentieth century, Howells surrendered his life to God and soon realized he possessed a gift for intercessory prayer. He began by praying for conversion and healing of individuals. As his reputation grew, he expanded his spiritual work to include the needs of groups and nations. Howells and his wife traveled as missionaries to South Africa and were influential figures in the revival movement taking place there. Through vivid and dramatic examples, Grubb brings Rees Howells's gift of intercessory prayer to the forefront and shows how God worked miracles through him.

Notable Books

Rees Howells: Intercessor
By Norman Grubb (1952)

Grubb includes Howells's founding and early years of the Bible College of Wales at Swansea. Inspired by the Moody Bible Institute in Chicago, Howells envisioned a similar college in Wales. In 1924, believing God's promise to make his vision a reality, he established a college to train men and women for the mission field. The college was led by Howells until his death in 1950 and then by his son, Samuel, until Samuel's death in 2004. It continues its founder's great mission.

FACT

Rees Howells said, "I hadn't the faintest idea of the love of the Holy Ghost for a lost soul, until He loved one through me."

Pray in the Spirit on all occasions with all kinds of prayers and requests. With this in mind, be alert and always keep on praying for all the saints.
EPHESIANS 6:18

Sung today for almost every festive occasion in England, this particular hymn is considered to be one of the most beautiful in English hymnody, and is recognized as perhaps the finest of Isaac Watts's six hundred hymns. It was first published in 1719 in *The Psalms of David Imitated in the Language of the New Testament.* The lyrics depict a theme on the mystery of time and a paraphrased commentary from Psalm 90. To veer from anything other than exact scripture in hymn writing was considered an insult during Watts's day, but at his father's urging to create something with a more expressive style for congregational singing, he began creating more lively hymns using adapted paraphrases.

Songs of the Faith

"O God, Our Help in Ages Past"

Words by Isaac Watts (1719)

Music by William Croft (1708)

The original hymn contained nine stanzas, but the hymn sung from hymnals today consists of only five. The grand and majestic tune, originally entitled "St. Anne," was written in 1708 by a notable church musician, William Croft, to be used with a version of Psalm 62. The tune wasn't well recognized until several years later when George F. Handel borrowed the tune to incorporate into his own musical anthem entitled, "O Praise the Lord," and J. S. Bach used it in his *Fugue in E-Flat Major*—St. Anne's Fugue.

After two hundred and fifty years, Isaac Watts's hymn still reminds those who sing it of God's faithfulness throughout the ages.

> O God, our help in ages past,
> Our hope for years to come,
> Our shelter from the stormy blast,
> And our eternal home.
>
> Under the shadow of Thy throne,
> Still may we dwell secure;
> Sufficient is Thine arm alone,
> And our defense is sure.

John Wesley changed the first line of the text from "Our God" to "O God" in his 1738 hymnal, *Psalms and Hymns.*

FACT

Lord, you have been our dwelling place throughout all generations.
Before the mountains were born or you brought forth the earth
and the world, from everlasting to everlasting you are God.

PSALM 90:1–2

When God allotted brainpower, He must have given Isaac Newton a double dose. Born in 1642 to an illiterate woman in Woolsthorpe, Lincolnshire, England, he remains for many scholars the greatest scientist of all time.

Newton's observations led him to explain the workings of the physical world in mathematical terms. He formulated laws explaining gravity and motion, prompted, some claim, by his observation of an apple falling from a tree. Newton established the modern study of optics, the behavior of light, and he developed calculus (much to the chagrin of math-challenged students). His seminal published works, *Mathematical Principles of Natural Philosophy* and *Opticks*, set Newton at the forefront of the scientific community.

Newton, raised in a Protestant household, venerated the Bible. He read it daily throughout his life. Accepting the Book as true in its literal sense, he tested biblical accounts against physical observation and theoretical science, leaving copious notes on the subject. Biblical prophecies, particularly those in the books of Daniel and Revelation, held particular fascination for Newton, who considered these prophecies essential to the human understanding of God. He wrote prolifically on biblical and theological subjects, his manuscripts filling the equivalent of twenty volumes. Newton considered individual Bible study essential to understanding God and universal truth.

Miscellany

Sir Isaac Newton and the Bible

Nonetheless, Newton was not a traditional Christian. He believed religion veered from its true course in the fourth century, and he vigorously criticized the church's creeds and confessions, rejecting doctrines he considered irrational or superstitious. Before his death in 1727, he dared to refuse the Sacrament. He lies buried in Westminster Abbey, the first scientist given this honor.

FACT

Despite the abundance of notes Newton kept on his lifelong study of the Bible, only one book on the subject was published, and this not until six years after his death. *Observations upon the Prophecies of Daniel and the Apocalypse of St. John* examines end-times events described in the Bible.

"You, Daniel, close up and seal the words of the scroll until the time of the end. Many will go here and there to increase knowledge."
DANIEL 12:4

During his first professional baseball at-bat, Billy Sunday struck out! In that very same game, he would strike out two more times. He would go on to strike out seven times and see three more games before he finally got his first hit. Undeterred, Sunday became one of the most popular players in the game in the late 1800s. He played for the Chicago White Sox, the Pittsburgh Pirates, and the Philadelphia Athletics.

Sunday's start in life didn't predict success in anything. Five weeks after he was born, his Civil War veteran father died. When Billy was ten, his mother was forced to send him and his siblings to a Soldier's Orphanage because she couldn't afford to take care of them. Nevertheless, Billy gained a high school education and discovered great athletic skill.

Men of the Faith

Billy Sunday (1862–1935)

Baseball player and evangelist

While playing major league baseball, in 1886, Billy stopped by the Pacific Garden Mission in Chicago and there was converted to Christianity. He immediately began preaching in churches and at YMCAs. In fact, Billy would turn down a lucrative baseball contract to accept a position with the Chicago YMCA for two-thirds the pay—just to preach!

After conducting a revival in Iowa, Sunday held campaigns throughout the Midwest. After World War I, he preached in Boston, New York, and other major cities. Unorthodox in his style, he would often cuss, use colorful language, and prance around the stage—sometimes even throwing chairs. He firmly stood against card playing, moviegoing, and especially drinking alcohol. He remains one of the most colorful and successful evangelists in American history.

> Throughout his preaching career, Sunday remained prominent in baseball, umpiring minor league games and even attending the 1935 World Series two months before he died.
>
> FACT

I have strength for all things in Christ Who empowers me
[I am ready for anything and equal to anything through Him
Who infuses inner strength into me; I am self-sufficient in Christ's sufficiency.]
PHILIPPIANS 4:13 AMP

Poor harvests. Widespread hunger. A disintegrating social order. The Black Plague hanging in the air. The church embroiled in internal strife. In an age of conflict, fear, and unrest, Julian of Norwich was celebrated for her message of God's love and eternal hope.

Little is known about the English mystic's life except that she took the vows of a Benedictine nun in Norwich's St. Julian Church, from which she took her name. For the rest of her years, she lived as an *anchorite*—one who lives in a fixed place and in solitude for the purpose of attaining religious perfection. Julian resided in a small room attached to the church, where she devoted herself to prayer, meditation, and intellectual development. Though a recluse, she provided spiritual counsel to those who sought her out and became known for her gentle wisdom and

Women of the Faith

Julian of Norwich
(1343–1413)
Writer and Christian mystic

spiritual insights. Julian's keen religious perception led her to express genuine joy despite the hardships and uncertainties of her time. Her expressions of God's enduring love and friendship gave hope and encouragement to her followers, who heard nothing but God's condemnation and wrath from the pulpit.

The first known female writer in English, Julian penned *Revelations of Divine Love*. Written after her recovery from a life-threatening illness, *Revelations of Divine Love* is based on sixteen "showings," or visions, of Christ she received while ill. In lively and descriptive prose, she reveals a sound knowledge of church doctrine along with profound spiritual perception. *Revelations of Divine Love* is considered a masterpiece of English literature.

> **FACT**
>
> Julian of Norwich wrote, "Just as our flesh is covered by clothing, and our blood is covered by our flesh, so are we, soul and body, covered and enclosed by the goodness of God."

Give thanks to the Lord, for he is good. His love endures forever.
PSALM 136:1

From 1939 until 1962, the Eagle and Child Pub was more than just a good place in Oxford, England, to grab a pint. It was home to meetings of the Inklings, a group of Christians who met in a private sitting room, now known as the Rabbit Room, at the rear of the establishment. The Inklings met weekly, every Monday or Friday, before lunch. Gathered on worn armchairs and settees in front of the small fireplace, the Christian scholars discussed literature, theology, and life.

Though nineteen men are known to have been a part of the Inklings at one time or another, two names stand out from the rest—C. S. Lewis and J. R. R. Tolkien. A decade before the Inklings were established, Tolkien was instrumental in Lewis's conversion to Christianity. Though Lewis's subsequent books of Christian apologetics, including *Mere Christianity*, earned him the reputation of being one of the most influential Christian writers of the twentieth century, it was Lewis's and Tolkien's works of fantasy that captured the widest audience. To date, Lewis's Chronicles of Narnia and Tolkien's Lord of the Rings trilogies have sold more than one hundred million and one hundred fifty million copies, respectively.

Important Sites

The Eagle and Child Pub
Oxford, England

In 1962, the Inklings switched their long-standing allegiance from the "Bird and Baby" (as the pub is nicknamed) to the Lamb and Flag Pub across the street. But visitors from around the world continue to visit the renowned Eagle and Child Pub to remember the gifted men of faith who once met within its walls.

Although a plaque in the "Bird and Baby" commemorates the Rabbit Room as where the Inklings read drafts of their manuscripts to one another, this is a fallacy. This took place in C. S. Lewis's room on the university campus.

FACT

---

*[Jesus said,] "If there is no readiness,
any trace of receptivity soon disappears.
That's why I tell stories: to create readiness,
to nudge the people toward receptive insight."*
MATTHEW 13:13 MSG

In November of 1949, a little-known Baptist evangelist pitched a tent over a sawdust floor in downtown Los Angeles. His planned three-week revival lasted more than eight weeks.

The dynamic young preacher, Billy Graham, enthralled his hearers and caught the attention of William Randolph Hearst, the newspaper magnate. As a result, Hearst newspapers nationwide published Billy Graham headlines and photos. Graham's decades-long career was launched.

Graham's crusades continued to draw large to overflowing crowds and were routinely extended. A crusade in London lasted nearly three months, and one in New York City ran nightly for four months. Graham, who has held crusades in 185 countries and territories, has preached to more live audiences than anyone else in history. Through his radio broadcasts, televised crusades, films, Web casts, books, and magazines, Graham has reached untold millions of souls with the gospel of Jesus Christ.

Groundbreaking Events

Billy Graham's Los Angeles Crusade

Graham holds a unique place among evangelists. He has achieved prominence, respect, and influence in a variety of secular and religious spheres. U.S. presidents have invited him to the White House on numerous occasions. The evangelist has received awards from a range of organizations and honorary doctorates from institutions in the U.S. and abroad.

In November of 2004, fifty-five years after the sawdust-floor tent meetings in downtown Los Angeles, Graham held another crusade, this time at the 92,000-seat Rose Bowl in neighboring Pasadena. The four-day event drew 312,500 people to hear Graham preach, and more than fourteen thousand of them committed their lives to Jesus Christ.

FACT

Billy Graham said, "My one purpose in life is to help people find a personal relationship with God, which, I believe, comes through knowing Christ."

You have been born again, not of perishable seed, but of imperishable, through the living and enduring word of God.
1 PETER 1:23

Former investigative reporter and legal editor of the *Chicago Tribune*, Lee Strobel takes on the adventure of a lifetime in *The Case for Christ: A Journalist's Personal Investigation of the Evidence for Jesus*. In his compelling book, Strobel methodically searches for credible evidence of Jesus' divinity and historicity.

When Strobel began his project, he was an atheist. His wife's conversion to Christianity prompted him to scrutinize the claims, actions, and promises of Jesus Christ in an effort to debunk them. In *The Case for Christ*, Strobel interviews Bible scholars and experts in various fields—history, archaeology, science, and psychiatry—to determine what evidence exists to prove that Jesus Christ really is the Son of God.

During his tough examination of the "witnesses," Strobel asks the questions that have been lobbed at Christians by skeptics since the early days of the church: Did Jesus really do what His biographers said He did? Did He really claim to be the Son of God? If so, did He exhibit the attributes of God? Did He, in fact, die? Was His body missing from the tomb, and if so, does that prove He rose from the dead?

Notable Books

The Case for Christ
By Lee Strobel (1998)

Strobel pulls his findings together and discovers a compelling case for Jesus as the Son of God and the veracity of the biblical account of his life, death, and resurrection. Strobel was himself convinced of the truths of the Bible and became a Christian. In *The Case for Christ*, Strobel urges readers—especially skeptical ones—to objectively examine the evidence and reach their own verdict.

Lee Strobel followed *The Case for Christ* with a series of books on Christian apologetics, including *The Case for Faith*; *The Case for a Creator*; *The Case for Christmas*; and *The Case for the Real Jesus*.

FACT

They had Peter and John brought before them and began to question them:
"By what power or what name did you do this?"
ACTS 4:7

There are several legends surrounding the origin of this beautiful hymn. Some believe it was called the "Crusaders' Hymn," sung by twelfth-century German Crusaders as they made their long journey to the Holy Land. Other sources believe it originated in 1620 with a small group of peasant people who followed John Hus into Poland (known then as Silesia) after they were driven out of Bohemia during the anti-Reformation purge. While they were forced to keep their faith a secret, they openly sang their traditional folk songs and hymns.

The lyrics were first published in 1677 in the Roman Catholic *Munster Gesangbuch* as one of three new hymns. The most well-known rendition today is said to have come from Hoffman Fallersleben who heard the song in a service being sung by Silesians. He wrote down the words and published it in 1842 in his *Schlesische Volkslieder.*

Songs of the Faith

"Fairest Lord Jesus"

Words and Music: Traditional
Bohemian Folk Song (1677)
English Version
by Richard Storrs Willis (1850)

In 1850, the English version, written by Richard Storrs Willis, first appeared in his *Church Chorals and Choir Studies*. In that hymnal, it is noted that German knights on their way to the Holy Land sang the song. While few facts are known about the origin of this song, it has been used for centuries as a hymn that uses the glory of nature and creation to inspire believers in their praise and worship of the Creator.

Fairest Lord Jesus, ruler of all nature,
O thou of God and man the Son,
Thee will I cherish, Thee will I honor,
Thou, my soul's glory, joy, and crown.

FACT

The word *fair* has several definitions. In this case, it means pleasing to the mind due to fresh and flawless quality. Some commonly used synonyms for *fair* are "beautiful" and "lovely."

By him were all things created, that are in heaven, and that are in the earth, visible and invisible, whether they be thrones, or dominions, or principalities, or powers: all things were created by him, and for him.
COLOSSIANS 1:16 KJV

W ho works ten to twelve hours a day, six days a week? That's right, a workaholic—or the farm boys of nineteenth-century England who flocked to London to work in factories and mills. Far from home, they bunked together in their employers' crowded dormitories, or drifted into the city's tenements. Conditions stank—literally.

In 1844, George Williams, a draper (department store clerk) and a group of associates organized the first Young Men's Christian Association to enrich the lives of London's young workers. The first Y focused on Bible study, prayer, and fellowship.

By the early 1850s, Ys had spread throughout Great Britain and were well established in the United States and abroad. Ys thrived as religious and social centers and residences for young men. In the early twentieth century, influenced by evangelist Dwight L. Moody and others, YMCAs sent thousands of missionaries and workers overseas. The

Miscellany

The Young Men's Christian Association (YMCA)

Great Depression of the 1930s, however, saw a dramatic downturn in the fortunes of YMCAs. Membership and donations dropped, and many of the Y's social services were rendered redundant by government programs.

Even more devastating was the "Great Delusion" of the 1960s and '70s. Reaction to the Vietnam War, the disgrace of President Nixon's resignation, the assassination of political leaders, and widespread rebellion among the nation's youth lumped the YMCA together with all institutions to be distrusted. Yet winds shifted in the early 1980s. Interest in healthy lifestyles and wholesome values made people look again at the YMCA. Ys wisely refocused to meet current needs, and today offer a wide range of activities, pastimes, classes, and mentorship programs for all.

The founders of the YMCA welcomed boys of all Christian denominations and social classes, a revolutionary idea at the time when denominations and social classes rarely mixed socially. In the Unites States, women were Y members by 1860, and even before that worked as fund-raisers and teachers. Today, Ys welcome men, women, and children of all races, religions, and nationalities.

No discipline seems pleasant at the time, but painful. Later on, however, it produces a harvest of righteousness and peace for those who have been trained by it.
HEBREWS 12:11

DAY 288

By 1536, the Protestant Reformation had already begun to take hold in Europe. John Calvin was fleeing Catholic-led France and heading for the free city of Strasbourg, Germany. One night while traveling, he lodged in Geneva. Word quickly spread that the famed Protestant Reformer was in town. Local church leader William Farel was desperate to retain Calvin to gain his help in establishing a local Protestant church. Initially, Calvin balked, but then after prayer said these words, "I felt as if God from heaven had laid his mighty hand upon me to stop me in my course—and I was so terror stricken that I did not continue my journey."

Men of the Faith

John Calvin
(1509–1564)
Founder of Calvinism

By that same year, Calvin had written the seminal work *The Institutes of the Christian Religion*, which was intended as a primer for those interested in the evangelical faith, especially for those in his native France. The book detailed and explained godliness and the doctrine of salvation. He relayed his views on the church, the sacraments, justification, Christian liberty, and political government. Throughout it all, he spoke of God's sovereignty. The most developed and remembered aspect of the book is his defense of the doctrine of predestination, or election.

John Calvin believed God's grace could never be withdrawn from the elect. By defending election, John Calvin was offering Christian believers comfort and assurance that they no longer had to suffer or doubt their own salvation. Out of this doctrine, sprang the theology of Calvinism—a belief practiced the world over, which still emphasizes grace and preservation of the elect.

FACT

John Calvin suffered from migraines, lung hemorrhages, gout, and kidney stones. At times he had to be carried to the pulpit to preach and sometimes gave lectures from his bed.

To him who is able to keep you from falling and to present you before his glorious presence without fault and with great joy.
JUDE 1:24

Josephine's father, John Grey, was a strong advocate who campaigned for the 1832 Reform Act and repeal of the Corn Laws. Josephine inherited her father's love of justice, devout religious principles, and equality.

Josephine married George Butler in 1852 and had four children. The couple shared political viewpoints during the Civil War and encountered opposition for their anti-slavery stand.

When Josephine witnessed her six-year-old daughter's accidental fall to her death, she never fully recovered. She coped with grief through her commitment to charitable work, including rescuing prostitutes who were often snatched from the street and forced into their profession. Her involvement in the sex trade began very simply: She wanted to "rescue fallen women" for Jesus.

In 1867 Josephine helped prepare advanced educational study courses for women and contributed to the establishment of Newham College. She rallied for employment opportunities, better education, and women's suffrage, believing it vital to the welfare of the nation.

In 1885 Josephine campaigned along with Florence Booth of the Salvation Army to expose child prostitution. Her efforts resulted in the Criminal Law Amendment Act being passed in 1886.

Josephine Butler led the long

Women of the Faith

Josephine Butler (1828–1906)

British social reformer

and women's advocate

campaign against the British Contagious Diseases Act, which made it possible for any man to denounce any woman as a prostitute for any reason. Her husband was ridiculed for her speaking publicly about women's rights and sexual matters, but he supported his wife's successful attempts to have the law repealed.

Butler's writings and promotion of social reform for, as well as education and equality of, women were widely distributed. Her most famous publication, *Personal Reminiscences of a Great Crusade*, was written in 1896.

FACT

We are to God the aroma of Christ among those who are being saved and those who are perishing.
2 CORINTHIANS 2:15

On a rocky plateau, midway between Athens' Acropolis and the ancient Agora, lays Mars Hill. The Romans named this limestone outcropping after their god of war, Mars. The Greeks, who called the god of war Ares, called the site Areopagus, the Hill of Ares. But many simply referred to this site as the "Hill of Curses." That's because this arena-like setting was where the Murder Tribunal of Athens met to try those accused of some of the city's most heinous crimes.

When the apostle Paul visited Mars Hill, the summit was filled with philosophers, not magistrates—and it was Paul who put their gods on trial. If Paul arrived in Athens via the port of Piraeus, which would have been a logical point for him to enter the city, he would have passed temple after pagan temple on his way to the city center. An ancient proverb stated that Athens had "more gods than men." After passing statues of Poseidon, Athena, Zeus, Apollo, and Hermes on his way into town, Paul may have been inclined to agree.

Important Sites

Mars Hill

Athens, Greece

But it was the altar "to an unknown god" that Paul brought to the attention of the Stoic and Epicurean philosophers who spent their days debating the latest ideas. Using this altar as a sermon illustration, Paul introduced the one true God into the philosophers' debates. Paul's words on Mars Hill marked a shift in how he spread the gospel. This time he preached to strangers, instead of being invited to speak by friends.

FACT

In the fourth century, a pagan temple was dedicated to the mythological goddesses of vengeance at the foot of Mars Hill. Murderers who killed someone in their own family could find sanctuary here, legally escaping punishment for their crimes.

Paul then stood up in the meeting of the Areopagus and said: "Men of Athens! I see that in every way you are very religious. . . . I even found an altar with this inscription: to an unknown god. Now what you worship as something unknown I am going to proclaim to you."
ACTS 17:22–23

As the story goes, a young shepherd boy went looking for his lost goat among the caves near the ancient settlement of Khirbet Qumran on the shore of the Dead Sea. He tossed a rock into one of the caves and heard the crack of breaking pottery. He shimmied into the cave and found several jars of scrolls wrapped in linen. Had he won the antiquities lottery? The boy took the jars to a Bethlehem antiques dealer. The dealer returned them, thinking the scrolls stolen property. Two years later, in 1949, a few scrolls found their way through the antiquities market and into the hands of scholars. Excavation of the Dead Sea Scrolls commenced.

Over a period of seven years, archaeologists located jars of scrolls scattered among eleven area caves. Among the fifteen thousand fragments found, scholars have identified nonbiblical documents as well as every book of the Old Testament, with the exception of the book of Esther. Notable is the Isaiah Scroll, a relatively intact copy of the book of Isaiah, older than any known copy of the text. In addition, extra-biblical prophecies of Ezekiel, Jeremiah, and Daniel, and psalms of David were translated from fragments.

Groundbreaking Events

Discovery of the Dead Sea Scrolls

Though other theories abound, most scholars believe a community called the Essenes wrote the scrolls from about 200 BC to AD 68. The Essenes were a fundamentalist Jewish sect led by a priest, the Teacher of Righteousness. When the Romans approached the community following the Jewish revolt of AD 66, the Essenes hid their writings in nearby caves for safekeeping.

An advertisement in the *Wall Street Journal* on June 1, 1954, said, "The Four Dead Sea Scrolls: Biblical manuscripts dating back to at least 200 BC are for sale. This would be an ideal gift to an educational or religious institution by an individual or group. Box F206." Through intermediaries, the scrolls were purchased by Israel for $250,000.

FACT

"The grass withers and the flowers fall, but the word of the Lord stands forever."
1 PETER 1:24–25

For well over a century, *The Christian's Secret of a Happy Life* has opened the joy of Christianity to millions of believers worldwide. Its author, Hannah Whitall Smith, said that the idea for the book came as a response to someone who had noted the gloomy faces worn by most Christians. Smith set about to put a smile on those faces with a practical guide to all the things Christians have to be glad about.

Smith begins by differentiating God's part in Christian life (to make us holy through the work of the Spirit) and our part (to trust God). She then deals with a series of challenges that beset Christians of all eras, such as doubts, temptations, and failure. She illuminates the joy that comes to the Christian who obediently follows God's will and experiences union with God. Smith's views on suffering reflect her belief that God does not cause, but uses trials, to strengthen the soul, elevate faith, and deepen understanding.

Notable Books

The Christian's Secret of a Happy Life
By Hannah Whitall Smith (1875)

Throughout the book, Smith offers real-life examples to show how the Spirit of God works in the lives of believers. She repeatedly drives home the observable marks present in a Christian's attitude and actions that witness to an unbelieving world the transforming power of the Spirit.

The Christian's Secret of a Happy Life holds particular insight for today's Christians who live in a culture focused on human reason and emotions. Smith reminds readers that human feelings are notoriously changeable, whereas God's love remains eternally the same. For Christians then and now, that's something to smile about.

FACT

Hannah Whitall Smith wrote, "The God who is behind His promises and is infinitely greater than His promises, can never fail us in any emergency, and the soul that is stayed on Him cannot know anything but perfect peace."

I praise you because I am fearfully and wonderfully made;
your works are wonderful, I know that full well.
PSALM 139:14

William Walford, the author of the hymn "Sweet Hour of Prayer" was blind, but behind his unseeing eyes was a brilliant mind and remarkable memory. He was known to have memorized large portions of scripture, composed lines of verse, and engaged in a substantial prayer life, all while sitting in a chimney corner, whittling useful items. He served as a guest preacher in the rural English church he attended, and his sermons were carefully composed in his head and delivered flawlessly, quoting scripture as if he were reading it directly from the text.

The verse he composed was also stored in his head, since no one was present to write it down for him. That is precisely how this hymn was written. Tradition has it that Thomas Salmon became acquainted with Walford while living briefly in Coleshill, Warwickshire, England. Salmon has said that one day during a visit to Walford, the blind, uneducated preacher mentioned to him that he had composed several lines of verse. When asked to see them, Walford spoke the lines from memory as Salmon jotted them down. Salmon later submitted them to the *New York Observer* for publication in 1845. The music was added by William Bradbury in 1861.

Songs of the Faith

"Sweet Hour of Prayer"
Words by William Walford (1845)
Music by William Bradbury (1861)

Sweet hour of prayer! Sweet hour of prayer!
That calls me from a world of care,
And bids me at my Father's throne
Make all my wants and wishes known.
In seasons of distress and grief,
My soul has often found relief
And oft escaped the tempter's snare
By thy return, sweet hour of prayer!

So extensive was Walford's ability to quote scripture verbatim that many of his friends and acquaintances were convinced he had memorized the entire Bible, cover to cover.

FACT

Pray continually; give thanks in all circumstances,
for this is God's will for you in Christ Jesus.
1 THESSALONIANS 5:17–18

Supersize that, would you? No, not the greasy burger and bag of fries, but the Sunday morning (or Saturday evening) church service. Ever since the 1980s, megachurches have hugged suburban highways across America.

Megacongregations typically begin with a core group of evangelicals around a dynamic pastor. Denomination rarely plays a part in the church's identity, if the congregation claims a particular denomination at all. A large tract of land on the fringes of suburbia is purchased, and up goes an auditorium-like sanctuary surrounded by classrooms, meeting rooms, offices for the ministerial staff, and acres of parking spaces. Within two to five years, weekly worshippers gather in the thousands.

The churches' strength stems from their numbers. Popular programs, the promise of relaxed, user-friendly worship services, and a reputation for having something for everyone brings in more members and guests. Most churches preach a conservative Christian message, often with a Charismatic or Fundamentalist orientation. Less concerned with doctrine than with practical living, attenders come with the expectation of taking away an applicable how-to, enabling them to more fully live the Christian life. Elaborate theatrical dramas, musicals, and dance presentations often accompany festival services and holidays.

Miscellany

Megachurches

In light of late-twentieth-century American experience, megachurches are hardly an anomaly. Most Americans shopped for food in warehouse-like mega-markets and many worked for large corporations housed in sprawling office complexes. Children attended consolidated schools, and families saw movies in multiplex theaters. Why not a big church? Besides, it's nothing new. St. Peter's in Rome can accommodate sixty thousand worshippers.

FACT

Many megachurches have mushroomed into megaorganizations. World Changers Ministries includes a music studio and its own record label, plus a publishing house. The Potter's House broadcasts a talk show and operates a prison satellite network. Lakewood Church, housed in the former home of the Houston Rockets, spends twelve million dollars on television airtime each year.

They will celebrate your abundant goodness and joyfully sing of your righteousness.
PSALM 145:7

One of Christianity's most beloved devotional authors, Oswald Chambers, originally found God's Word unimpressive. Born in Scotland to devout Baptist parents in 1874, he described the Bible at Dunoon College as "dull and uninspiring." He, instead, gravitated toward the works of Robert Browning, even starting a study society dedicated to exploring this poet.

After four years of spiritual emptiness, Chambers ultimately came to the conclusion that he couldn't make himself holy. He eventually realized that only Christ could redeem him from his depravity and give him strength and peace. Chambers was then born anew into a condition he described as a "radiant, unspeakable emancipation." Those who knew him said he was fond of saying, "Beware of reasoning about God's word—obey it."

Men of the Faith

Oswald Chambers (1874–1917)

Author of *My Utmost for His Highest*

In 1908, on board a ship bound for America, Chambers met Gertrude "Biddy" Hobbs, a stenographer, who would become his wife two years later. Together, they ran the Bible Training College in Clapham, London. After only a few years, Chambers suspended operations at the college because he believed he should serve as a chaplain during World War I. He was stationed in Egypt.

Oswald Chambers died as a result of a ruptured appendix in 1917 in Egypt. He endured the pain of appendicitis for three days before seeking medical help because he didn't want to take a hospital bed needed by a wounded soldier. Biddy announced his passing with a simple telegram, "Oswald; In His Presence."

The only book that Oswald Chambers actually penned is given the enigmatic moniker *Baffled to Fight Better*.

FACT

[Jesus said,] "The one who speaks on his own authority seeks his own glory;
but the one who seeks the glory of him who sent him is true,
and in him there is no falsehood."
JOHN 7:18 ESV

Christina Rossetti was born into an artistic and highly educated London household. Her father, the poet Gabriele Rossetti, taught at King's College, her brother became the famed painter Dante Gabriel, and all four children of the household were writers. Christina and her sisters followed in their mother's commitment to the Anglican Church.

The Oxford or Tractarian Movement influenced Rossetti's spiritual development. The popular nineteenth-century movement tried, among other things, to recreate Anglican traditions of the previous century and protect the church against modern reforms and government intervention. The movement revived an interest in medieval literature, architecture, and culture. Rossetti's religious poetry, often marked by a sense of melancholy and yearning for a lost past, reflects the romanticism of her time.

While Rossetti composed nonreligious poems, ballads, love lyrics, and songs for various journals, her best-known work, *Goblin Market and Other Poems*, takes up biblical themes in a fairy tale ostensibly for children. "Goblin Market," the title poem, tells the story of two sisters tempted to "come buy" luscious fruit. One sister does, while the other does not. The refraining sister saves her nibbling sibling in a noble act of self-sacrifice.

Women of the Faith

Christina Rossetti (1830–1894)

Writer and poet

Rossetti remained unmarried, having refused two gentlemen's proposals for religious reasons. Never in good health, in her later years she suffered from increasingly debilitating bouts of Graves' disease—a thyroid disorder. Though she continued to write poetry, prose, and devotions, study scriptures, and read religious classics, she rarely left the sanctuary of her home.

FACT

Christina Rossetti wrote, "Obedience is the fruit of faith."

[Jesus said,] "If you obey my commands, you will remain in my love,
just as I have obeyed my Father's commands and remain in his love.
I have told you this so that my joy may be in you and that your joy may be complete."
JOHN 15:10–11

The history of Canterbury Cathedral begins beneath the floor of the nave. That's where the ruins of the original church, founded by St. Augustine in AD 602, can be found. But the cathedral built atop those ruins is the one Christian pilgrims have flocked to for 350 years, beginning in the late twelfth century. Pilgrimages to this site were so popular that they inspired the fourteenth-century poem "Canterbury Tales," which is still considered to be one of the finest works of literature ever written.

What inspired pilgrims to make the journey to Canterbury, however, was anything but poetic. In 1170, three overzealous knights, trying to impress King Henry II by eliminating the archbishop of Canterbury whom the king was known to be at odds with, murdered Thomas Becket near the cathedral's Trinity Chapel. The spot of the murder soon became known as a place where miraculous healings occurred. People left behind gifts, such as gems, brooches, golden goblets, and what's been described as a "forest" of crutches, where a shrine to Becket was erected. When the shrine was destroyed by King Henry VIII in 1538, twenty-six wagons were required to haul away the treasures pilgrims had left behind.

Important Sites

Canterbury Cathedral
Kent, England

Modern-day pilgrims to Canterbury will find the East Chapel of the cathedral dedicated to more contemporary martyrs, such as Dietrich Bonnhoeffer and Martin Luther King Jr. A simple binder displayed on a lectern holds the biographies of fifteen twentieth-century Christians who died for living a life in line with what they believed.

Although the church's library was destroyed during World War II, Canterbury Cathedral remained intact thanks to a team of "fire watchers" who patrolled the roof and disarmed incendiary bombs.

FACT

"You will be betrayed even by parents, brothers, relatives and friends, and they will put some of you to death."
LUKE 21:16

Adopted by the United States on December 15, 1791, the first ten amendments to the Constitution confirm basic civil liberties. Known as the Bill of Rights, they guarantee: freedoms of speech, the press, association and assembly, and worship; the right to bear arms; freedom from unauthorized search; freedom from forced self-incrimination; the right to a timely and public trial; and freedom from disproportionate, cruel, or unusual punishments.

The First Amendment forms the foundation of individual freedoms enjoyed by citizens, immigrants, and visitors to the United States. It allows people the right to worship according to their conscience—or not worship at all. It forbids government-funded or state-sponsored religion. Along with the other freedoms articulated, the First Amendment ensures a free flow of ideas, the protection of minority viewpoints, and an intellectually lively, diverse society.

Groundbreaking Events

The Bill of Rights

While religion is protected from government interference, clashes between church and state inevitably occur. Controversy continues to stir over the issues of school vouchers that assist needy students with tuition for parochial schools; proper accommodation of Muslim students' religious practices; and government aid to religious charities.

In total, the Bill of Rights upholds a cherished American ideal—an individual's right to live lawfully and peaceably without undue government interference. In the ensuing decades, the United States has continued to add amendments to the Constitution that broaden individual rights, including a ban on slavery (1865) and women's suffrage (1920). To date, twenty-seven amendments have been added to the Constitution.

FACT

Despite civil liberties articulated in the Bill of Rights, slave trade was permitted through 1808. Blacks were not emancipated until the end of the Civil War, and even then, racial segregation and discriminatory laws prevented African-Americans from enjoying freedoms guaranteed by the Bill of Rights.

Live as free men, but do not use your freedom as a cover-up for evil; live as servants of God.
1 PETER 2:16

Wₕₐₜ happened on the streets of New York City's toughest neighborhoods held no personal interest for David Wilkerson, pastor of a rural church in Pennsylvania. One picture, however, changed his perspective.

The brutal murder of a polio victim by members of a New York street gang led to one of the most sensational trials in 1950s America. Seven boys stood accused of the crime, all members of a Coney Island gang. A *LIFE* magazine portrait of one of the boys—young, confused, angry—caught the pastor's attention. Wilkerson felt prompted by the Holy Spirit to help the boy, but he pulled back, having never been to the city before and without personal knowledge of gang culture.

The Lord prevailed, however, and Wilkerson went to New York. *The Cross and the Switchblade* tells what happened when he took the simple message of the gospel into the violent world of criminal gangs. Cowritten with Elizabeth and John Sherrill, the book describes Wilkerson's highly publicized but failed effort to visit the jailed gang members. The fiasco earned him the street credentials that won him the trust and acceptance of their friends still on the street.

Notable Books

The Cross and the Switchblade

By David Wilkerson (1962)

Wilkerson resigned his ministry in Pennsylvania and went on to work with young drug addicts, alcoholics, gang members, and troubled teens who called the violent streets of New York's inner city their home. He established Teen Challenge, an outreach program and shelter, and has brought untold numbers of teenagers to Christ through his ministry.

The Cross and the Switchblade, now translated into thirty-five languages, has sold more than fifteen million copies and continues to inspire readers the world over. The 1969 movie of the same name debuted to sold-out theaters.

FACT

[Jesus said,] "I was in prison and you came to visit me."
Mₐₜₜₕₑw 25:36

All that's known of the writer and composer of the hymn "There Is Power in the Blood" is that he was a classmate of evangelist Billy Sunday while attending Moody Bible Institute. After graduating, Lewis Jones went to work for the YMCA in Davenport, Iowa; Fort Worth, Texas; and Santa Barbara, California.

Lewis, a hymn writer by avocation, is said to have written this hymn while attending a camp meeting at Mountain Lake Park, Maryland.

The hymn's strong beat, straightforward melody, and didactic lyrics have caused it to be described by some as a song advertising where to go to get your sins forgiven and your life changed. These elements also make it an enduring favorite for congregational singing. It is also well loved for its message. The blood of Jesus shed on the cross of Calvary is the ultimate, power-filled remedy for sin. It provides life, victory over sin and Satan, and power for service for those who trust in its purity and purpose.

Songs of the Faith

"There Is Power in the Blood"

Words and music
by Lewis E. Jones (1899)

Would you be free from the burden of sin?
There's power in the blood, power in the blood;
Would you o'er evil a victory win?
There's wonderful power in the blood.

Would you do service for Jesus your King?
There's pow'r in the blood, pow'r in the blood;
Would you live daily His praises to sing?
There's wonderful pow'r in the blood.

Refrain:
There is power, power, wonder working power
In the blood of the Lamb;
There is power, power, wonder working power
In the precious blood of the Lamb.

FACT

Lewis Edgar Jones also wrote hymns under the names Edgar Lewis and Mary Slater.

"They have washed their robes and made them white in the blood of the Lamb."
REVELATION 7:15

I f it's true for you, it's true." The postmodernist's skepticism (and often outright dismissal) of universal truths puts all religions, values, and belief systems on the same level. A patchwork of beliefs and nonbeliefs is a difficult concept to build a church around, yet the emerging church movement of the twenty-first century is making an attempt.

Emerging church communities vary and defy a clear-cut definition, but can be identified by several common teachings and practices. Adherents seek to engage the culture at large by integrating the assumptions of postmodernism into Christian thinking. While some adherents immerse themselves in postmodernism in an effort to better relate to postmoderns, others become postmoderns. They shy away from universal truths in favor of personal narratives that may include some elements of truth.

Miscellany

The Emerging Church Movement

Adherents place a great deal of emphasis on how the Christian life is lived out by the individual Christian and aim to pattern life on the earthly ministry of Jesus Christ. With Jesus, they believe, they can redeem society with a return to authentic Christianity based on love for others and practical help to heal social ills.

Community worship is fluid and experimental. It includes sensory elements such as candles and incense and looks for ways the actual practice of worship can enhance its meaning. The preacher seated among the people, for example, could visually foster the concept of the priesthood of all believers and Christian fellowship. Or a dialogue instead of a sermon might articulate the message in a natural and more meaningful way.

Controversial? You bet. And that's the truth.

The *emerging church* describes the movement overall, which has no central hierarchy and varies in beliefs and practices among communities. *Emergent church*, on the other hand, refers to a U.S. and UK organization, the Emergent Village.

FACT

[Jesus said,] "In everything, do to others what you would have them do to you,
for this sums up the Law and the Prophets."
MATTHEW 7:12

A large and jovial man, writer G. K. Chesterton often exercised verbal sparring with his friends and fellow academics. Once while talking with George Bernard Shaw, Chesterton said, "To look at you, anyone would think there was a famine in England."

Shaw retorted, "To look at you, anyone would think you caused it."

Born in London, Chesterton was initially educated to be an artist. He produced paintings and illustrations throughout his writing career.

Misunderstood and labeled controversial, he often wrote paradoxes like the phrase, "Anything worth doing is worth doing badly." He believed that such turns of speech were an excellent vehicle for communicating great truth. None of his works gained prominence as a definitive work, but various writings (or the entire collection) influenced such luminaries as Mahatma Ghandi, George Orwell, T. S. Eliot, and C. S. Lewis. In fact, his Christian apologetics were instrumental in Lewis's conversion.

Men of the Faith

G. K. Chesterton (1874–1936)

English writer of Christian apologetics

Though he was raised in the Church of England, he called himself an "orthodox Christian." Later in life, as he became more and more comfortable with Catholicism, he converted to the Church of Rome.

Not long after writing his autobiography, Chesterton fell ill and died. Following his funeral, Pope Pius XI declared Chesterton, "Defender of the Faith—a title as true for Protestants as it is for Catholics."

Chesterton wrote about eighty books, several hundred poems, two hundred short stories, four thousand essays, and several plays. He wrote the biography of *Charles Dickens* (1903), and authored works such as *The Man Who Was Thursday* (1907), *Orthodoxy* (1908), and the *Father Brown* short stories.

FACT

G. K. Chesterton said, "The Bible tells us to love our neighbors, and also to love our enemies; probably because they are generally the same people."

[Jesus said,] "I say, love your enemies! Pray for those who persecute you!"
MATTHEW 5:44 NLT

After graduation from Methodist-founded Northwestern Female College in Evanston, Illinois, Frances Willard began her career in education. As she gained experience and recognition, she moved from teaching positions in one-room schoolhouses to secondary schools and finally to the presidency of the newly established Evanston College for Ladies. Evanston College merged with Northwestern University, and Willard became Dean of Women at the women's college. A professional fallout with the university president, with whom she already had had a romantic fallout, ended her stint at the college.

Willard joined Chicago's fledgling temperance movement and, with others, founded the Woman's Christian Temperance Union (WCTU). On behalf of the WCTU, she traveled throughout the United States to garner support and form local Unions. Willard was instrumental in broadening the WCTU's cause to include women's suffrage, women's rights, and reforms in education and labor. She was elected president of the organization in 1879. Under her leadership, the WCTU became a powerful voice in social reform and attracted a membership of more than one hundred fifty thousand women.

Women of the Faith

Frances Willard
(1839–1898)
Reformer and educator

In the early 1890s, Willard traveled to England and worked to establish a world WCTU. She inspired and motivated women across nations to involve themselves in effecting social change, and she was successful in persuading men to support women's rights.

By the late 1890s, Willard's health had declined precipitously, and she died of influenza in New York City in 1898. While she was lying in state in the WCTU headquarters in Chicago, some twenty thousand mourners paid their respects. Her remains were placed in her mother's grave in Chicago.

Willard and five other women were elected as lay delegates to the 1888 General Conference of the Methodist Church. Though Willard didn't attend, the other women were denied seats. Willard advocated for women's full participation in church affairs in her influential treatise, *Women in the Pulpit*.

FACT

They all joined together constantly in prayer, along with the women and Mary the mother of Jesus, and with his brothers.
Acts 1:14

The sounds of cackling chickens, neighing horses, and a talking cow may seem an unlikely backdrop for any site with the word *library* in its name, but the Billy Graham Library was designed with a greater purpose in mind than just housing Reverend Graham's books and personal papers. In keeping with the focus of Graham's life, this dairy-barn-styled library was built with an eye on evangelism. And if barnyard sound effects and an animatronic cow can help draw more families to Charlotte, North Carolina, to hear God's Word, then perhaps the unique displays this library/museum holds should simply be considered "creative evangelistic tools."

Visitors to the forty-thousand-square-foot library are invited into the story of "a country boy's journey of faith." The early years of that story began on a dairy farm only four miles from where the library is located. Graham's family farmhouse has been reconstructed on the library grounds using many of the original building materials.

Important Sites

The Billy Graham Library

Charlotte, North Carolina

Within the library walls, visitors find a variety of reconstructed scenes, including a portion of the Berlin Wall (commemorating Graham gaining permission from the Communist government to evangelize behind the Iron Curtain) and the "canvas cathedral" (recreating Graham's 1949 Tent Revival in Los Angeles). Exhibits, such as a set of handguns turned over by gang members touched by Graham's message during a 1957 crusade, and multimedia presentations are also on display. A visitor's trip to the library concludes, in true Billy Graham fashion, with a videotaped altar call.

FACT

Though the animatronic Bessie the Cow was designed to appeal to small children, it was also included as a reminder that Billy Graham practiced his first sermons while milking the cows on his family's farm.

[Jesus] told them. . . "The Christ will suffer and rise from the dead on the third day, and repentance and forgiveness of sins will be preached in his name to all nations."
LUKE 24:46–47

Street banners, lemonade stands, and performing chimpanzees. Over a thousand onlookers, in addition to reporters and journalists from far and wide, swarmed the streets of Dayton, Tennessee, in July of 1925, to witness a trial billed as a showdown between good and evil, truth and ignorance.

High school biology teacher John T. Scopes was accused of presenting Darwin's theory of evolution in a public school classroom in violation of the Butler Act, an antievolution state law. The "Monkey Trial," catering to the popular understanding of evolution as meaning human beings descended directly from apes, was in full swing. Criminal lawyer Clarence Darrow represented Scopes, and former U.S. Secretary of State William Jennings Bryan appeared for the prosecution. Darrow argued for the validity of evolution and the unconstitutionality of the Butler Act. Bryan spoke passionately in defense of the biblical account of creation.

Groundbreaking Events

The Scopes Trial

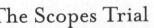

The trial was far from an intellectual, or even religious, debate. Darrow, Bryan, and Judge John T. Raulston, each for his own reasons, craved publicity and encouraged monkeyshines. Through day-by-day radio broadcasts, the Monkey Trial and its colorful courtroom antics sparked debate in cafes, beauty salons, and barbershops from coast to coast. The trial ended when the jury found Scopes guilty and the court fined him one hundred dollars.

The state supreme court reversed the verdict on technical grounds, though the Butler Act remained on the books until 1967. Debate on the teaching of evolution in public school classrooms versus the creation account in the book of Genesis continues in state legislatures and courtrooms to this day.

The 1920s were a time of social upheaval. Young progressive thinkers, relying on human reason, science, and Freudian theories, challenged the spiritual verities and traditional values cherished by older members of society. Fundamentalists and social conservatives, especially in the South, aggressively fought the threat through the courts and state legislation.

FACT

God created man in his own image,
in the image of God he created him;
male and female he created them.
GENESIS 1:27

Countless numbers of European Jews desperately searched for a hiding place during Hitler's reign of terror, and more than a few found refuge in the ten Boom home in Haarlem, Netherlands. A secret room about the size of a medium wardrobe and about thirty inches deep had been added to one of the bedrooms. The room, accessible by one small sliding panel, contained a mattress, biscuits, vitamins, and a jug of water.

The Hiding Place tells the story of the room in the home above Caspar ten Boom's quiet watch shop, and how it was constructed and used by Caspar and his daughters, Corrie and Betsy. All three were part of the Dutch Resistance after the Germans took control of Holland in 1940. Corrie relates how her family took in Jews—and others sought by the Nazis—spiriting them away to the hiding place until they could be supplied with false papers and ration cards and escorted out of the country.

Notable Books

The Hiding Place

By Corrie ten Boom (1971)

In February of 1944, all three of the ten Booms were arrested by the Gestapo in a night raid on their home. They had been betrayed by a friend, a Dutch countryman. Corrie and Betsy never saw their father again. The middle-aged women were imprisoned in camps in the Netherlands until they were transferred to Ravensbruck in Germany in 1944. Betsy died there, but Corrie survived and wrote this powerful and moving story documenting the efforts of courageous Dutch Christians who gave all they had to come to the aid of their Jewish neighbors.

FACT

So deftly was the secret room hidden that it was not discovered during the raid on the ten Boom home. The six people hiding inside escaped with the help of the underground Resistance.

[Jesus said,] "Greater love has no one than this,
that he lay down his life for his friends."
JOHN 15:13

Originally written in the Netherlands, "We Gather Together" appeared in a Dutch hymnal in 1626. Though the Pilgrims had already sailed for Massachusetts by that time, they probably knew the song, which had been floating around since it was written by Adrianus Valerius in 1597.

The Pilgrims may have known it, but they would not have sung it—at least not as a church hymn. The Pilgrims sang only words from the book of Psalms in their worship services and even those were without musical accompaniment. The song was probably brought to the United States by Dutch settlers who kept it alive in their tight-knit communities.

The song was first called *"Wilt Heden Nu Treden"* and was meant to celebrate victory over religious oppression as demonstrated by the Dutch victory over the Spanish at the Battle of Turnhout. The modern arrangement was published in Leipzig, Germany, in 1877 by Viennese choirmaster Eduard Kremser. In 1894, an American student studying in Leipzig translated the hymn into English. Theodore Baker called it his "prayer of Thanksgiving."

Songs of the Faith

"We Gather Together"
Words by Adrianus Valerius (1626)
Music: Dutch Folk Melody
(16th century)

The hymn's popularity increased significantly after 1937, when the Christian Reformed Church, which began with Dutch immigrants, changed its long-standing policy of singing only psalms and allowed for other hymns to be sung at church. "We Gather Together" was chosen as the opening hymn in their new hymnal. Thirty years later, it has become America's quintessential Thanksgiving hymn.

> We gather together to ask the Lord's blessing.
> He chastens and hastens His will to make known;
> The wicked oppressing cease them from distressing:
> Sing praises to His name, He forgets not His own.

Just a few decades ago, this song was sung in classrooms around the country as Thanksgiving Day approached. Its mention of God, however, has rendered it an unavailable choice for America's schools.

FACT

They gathered the church together and reported all that God had done through them.
ACTS 14:27

So what did Eve bite into on that fateful day in the Garden of Eden? The Bible says, "fruit," tradition says, "an apple," and now botanists say, "probably an apricot." Whatever the name of the edible in question, fruits, trees, vegetables, herbs, and flowers flourish throughout the scriptures.

Tended by gardeners in home backyards and on church properties across the country, Bible gardens display some or most of the more than 125 kinds of plants cited in the Old and New Testaments. In Song of Songs, the poet extolled the beauty and excellence of his beloved in terms of precious spices found in a private garden. The prophet Isaiah mentioned the heathen who cut down a pine tree and from it "fashions a god and worships it" (Isaiah 44:15). Botanists believe modern mugho pines are descendants of the pines so used.

Miscellany

Bible Gardens

Many names of plants in popular Bible translations are inaccurate, the Bible translators being experts in linguistics, not botany. Modern scholarship has led to revisions, and debate still exists on the correct identification of various plants, such as those Jesus mentioned when He said, "See how the lilies of the field grow" (Matthew 6:28). Some botanists say Jesus was referring to lilies, while others claim the Lord was pointing to anemones or wildflowers that adorned the hills of the Holy Land.

From a small plot of herbs to an elaborate gated paradise, Bible gardens remind us of God's abundant creation and His eternal green thumb.

FACT

A Mary Garden is an enclosed garden devoted to the Virgin Mary. In the Middle Ages, readers of the Bible associated the enclosed garden mentioned in Song of Songs with the Virgin Mary. Artwork from the time often depicts the Virgin Mary standing in the center of a gated garden.

You are a garden locked up, my sister, my bride;
you are a spring enclosed, a sealed fountain.
SONG OF SONGS 4:12

Max Lucado is one of the best-loved authors living today. For all his accolades, his early life was anything but Christian. During his high school years in Texas, even after his baptism, Lucado was a womanizer, a tough guy, and a heavy drinker. He claimed he could drink a whole six-pack of beer and not feel it.

During his years at Abilene Christian University, Lucado wanted to be a lawyer. But a Bible course and a mission trip turned his mind to missions. After graduating, he moved to Miami, Florida, where he ministered to singles and wrote a church newsletter. His short columns were favorably reviewed, so he compiled them and put them into book form called *On the Anvil*. He showed the manuscript to fifteen publishers before Tyndale House published it.

God eventually used him as a missionary in Rio de Janeiro. In 1988, he accepted a pastoral position at Oak Hills Church in San Antonio. As his writing became more successful, Lucado stopped taking a salary from the church. Though he preached regularly, he took the time he needed to put out one book a year. In early 2007, Lucado told his congregation he was stepping down due to a heart condition.

Men of the Faith

Max Lucado (b. 1955)

Author and pastor

Max Lucado was named "America's Pastor" by *Christianity Today* and "The Best Preacher in America" by *Readers Digest* in 2005. Eleven of his first twelve books landed on the Christian Booksellers Association (CBA) bestseller list. More than thirty-three million copies of his books have been sold worldwide.

Max Lucado wrote, "There is a time for risky love. There is a time for extravagant gestures. There is a time to pour out your affections on one you love. And when the time comes—seize it, don't miss it."

FACT

The LORD replied: "Write down the revelation and make it plain on tablets so that a herald may run with it."
HABAKKUK 2:2

Evangelical philanthropist Hannah More started out life near Bristol, England, in straightened circumstances. As a young woman, she earned her living as a teacher at her sister's girls' school and wrote plays for students to perform. Her interest in theater drew her to the Theatre Royal Bristol, where she became acquainted with actors and playwrights.

Obviously a patient sort, More broke with her fiancé after a six-year wait for him to set a wedding date. In compensation, the man paid her an annuity that enabled her to devote herself to writing. She moved to London and immersed herself in London's theater scene. More had a few of her plays produced, but lost interest in the theater when her works weren't well received.

Women of the Faith

Hannah More
(1745–1833)

Author and philanthropist

Around 1785, More experienced a religious conversion. She began moving in evangelical circles and supporting social causes. She wrote pamphlets in support of French clergy who were under attack during the French Revolution and took a conservative stance on other religious and political issues. One of a series of moralistic tracts More penned was satirized by Thackeray in *Vanity Fair*. Her tracts, however, were widely read and formed the foundation of the Religious Tract Society.

With a younger sister, she founded the first of nine Sunday schools in the Somerset area and worked to further the cause of the working man. She spoke out on (and wrote about) the failings of women's education.

More's book sales gave her a comfortable income, and she donated generously to charity over the course of her lifetime.

FACT

Hannah More wrote, "Genius without religion is only a lamp on the outer gate of a palace; it may serve to cast a gleam of light on those that are without, while the inhabitant sits in darkness."

Let the word of Christ dwell in you richly as you teach and admonish one another with all wisdom, and as you sing psalms, hymns and spiritual songs with gratitude in your hearts to God.
Colossians 3:16

Rising 16,945 feet, Mount Ararat is the tallest mountain in Turkey—taller than any peak found in the continental United States. But Mount Ararat is not only tall; it's considered the largest mountain in the world when categorized by sheer mass. Also, the top three thousand feet of the peak are covered by an ice cap that in places reaches three hundred feet thick.

According to any scale, Mount Ararat is noteworthy. However, what puts it into the important-site category is the long-held belief that this is where Noah's ark landed after the flood. The earliest known eyewitness account comes from Josephus in AD 70. Josephus noted that the remains of a boat were so visible on the mountain that there was really no need for exploration to confirm his find. But for centuries, explorers from Marco Polo to James Irwin (the U.S. astronaut) have searched for evidence of the ark on the mountain's slopes.

Since 1701, over 175 documented expeditions have searched the mountain, but none have turned up any conclusive proof. A French explorer found a piece of ancient cypress wood in 1978, but carbon dating determined the wood was from the eighth century AD. Scientists also note that a boat built of wood to the specifications noted in the Bible would be almost the size of the Titanic. If a wooden ship, even one that large, had landed on the ice cap, the movement of glacial ice would have crushed it to bits centuries ago.

Important Sites

Mount Ararat
Turkey

In the Near East where wood is often scarce, it's believed that many famous structures can no longer be found because the wood was recycled to build other necessary structures. Some theologians believe this could have been the fate of the ark.

FACT

At the end of the hundred and fifty days the water had gone down,
and on the seventeenth day of the seventh month
the ark came to rest on the mountains of Ararat.
GENESIS 8:3–4

What would Jesus do? Walter Rauschenbasch, a Baptist minister, was asking that question long before the advent of WWJD bracelets and key chains. Conditions in New York slums of the late nineteenth century had convinced Rauschenbasch that Jesus, Healer of the sick, would have taken action to relieve the plight of the poor.

Rauschenbasch and fellow clergyman Washington Gladden founded the Social Gospel Movement in reaction to the side effects of unabashed capitalism: underpaid and overworked employees, child labor, abusive management practices, and a dearth of employee rights. In 1908, the Federal Council of the Churches of Christ in America (a forerunner of the National Council of Churches) formally articulated the fundamental principles of the Social Gospel Movement.

Besides labor, other contemporary concerns dovetailed into the movement, such as women's suffrage and civil rights for former slaves. Shelters for the urban homeless were being established in major cities, and the Chautauqua Movement was offering education and culture to all comers. The ideology of the Social Gospel Movement attracted the support of progressive politicians of the early twentieth century and many of its goals served as the foundation of future legislation, most notably the New Deal programs of the 1930s. Organized labor unions, too, found their foundation in the aims and ideals of the movement.

Groundbreaking Events

The Social Gospel

While the term *Social Gospel* fell into disuse, the movement continues to influence religious and nonprofit agencies. Its voice echoed in the civil rights demonstrations of the 1960s and the peace protests of the Vietnam era. Food pantries, homeless shelters, and calls for immigrant justice stem from the early twentieth-century movement.

FACT

The Social Gospel Movement contrasted with other religious reform movements by focusing on the salvation of society over individual salvation. To "save" society, Social Gospel advocates promoted a Christian, compassionate, and harmonious welfare state where everyone received just rewards for labor and full civil rights. While never reaching its lofty goals, it did give impetus to Christian concern for the downtrodden.

Faith by itself, if it is not accompanied by action, is dead.
JAMES 2:17

W hy does God allow evil to continue in the world? Why is there suffering? Why wars and famine and violent death? Is there a purpose in all of it? Paul E. Billheimer's book *Destined for the Throne* sheds light on these questions that have perplexed Christians since the beginnings of the Christian faith more than two thousand years ago.

Billheimer contends that God's eternal purpose has always been to prepare an eternal companion (a Bride) for His Son, and this preparation takes place as Christians engage in spiritual warfare and practice believing prayer in the midst of conflict, confusion, and suffering. As Christians grow and mature in their faith, they become fit for the task of reigning and ruling the universe alongside God's Son, Jesus Christ.

Destined for the Throne is still popular with readers who appreciate its down-to-earth style, biblical insights, and an unveiling of Billheimer's concept of God's eternal destiny for believers—as the Bride.

Billheimer and his wife began their ministry by holding tent revivals in Anderson, Indiana, in 1936. But soon *preaching* gave way to the *teaching*, and Billheimer built a Bible Institute. Later he added a Christian high school and day school. In 1957, he established a Christian television station.

Notable Books

Destined for the Throne

By Paul E. Billheimer (1975)

Other books by Billheimer include, *Don't Waste Your Sorrows; Love Covers; Destined to Overcome;* and *Destined for the Cross. Destined for the Throne*, however, stands apart for its unique description of the Church as the glorious Bride of Christ.

Paul Billheimer wrote, "As the Lord of history, God is controlling all of its events, not only on earth but in all realms, to serve His purpose of bringing to maturity and eventually to enthronement with His Son, not angels or archangels, but the Church, His chosen Bride."

FACT

"Let us rejoice and be glad and give him glory!
For the wedding of the Lamb has come,
and his bride has made herself ready."
REVELATION 19:7

In 1856, Reverend William Cushing wrote a beautiful little song taken from Malachi 3:17. A year later, George Root wrote an equally lovely melody to accompany Cushing's song.

Cushing pastored churches in Auburn, Brooklyn, Buffalo, Searsburg, and Sparta, New York. After his wife died in 1870, Cushing's own declining health forced him to retire. It was then that his love for composing hymns was revived. He wrote more than three hundred hymns before his death in 1902. George Root's musical giftedness was evident even as a child. In 1838, he moved to Boston to study music. He soon became a successful composer, especially of religious and patriotic music.

An interesting story involving the song states that a minister, returning to America on an English steamer, visited the steerage and suggested a sing-along to encourage the beleaguered passengers. Since most of the people on board were European emigrants, the minister knew he would have to choose an easy tune—probably American. The steerage master suggested "Jewels." Soon the poor, half-fare passengers were singing along. They sang the song again and again, night after night. When the steamer docked in Quebec, the passengers moved from the ship to the trains. As they rolled away, the words of the song could be heard coming from every car.

Songs of the Faith

"Jewels"

Words by Rev. William O. Cushing (1856)

Music by George F. Root (1856)

When He cometh, when He cometh
To make up His jewels,
All His jewels, precious jewels,
His loved and His own.

Refrain:
Like the stars of the morning, His bright crown adorning,
They shall shine in their beauty, bright gems for His crown.

FACT

William Orcutt Cushing also wrote the hymn "Ring the Bells of Heaven, There Is Joy Today."

They shall be mine, saith the LORD of hosts, in that day when I make up my jewels.
MALACHI 3:17 KJV

Ezekiel, like many Old Testament prophets, issued dire warning to an unheeding audience. Unlike other prophets, however, Ezekiel showed rather than told his message. In the years preceding the fall of Jerusalem in 586 BC, God commanded Ezekiel to perform a series of vignettes depicting the privations that awaited the population of Jerusalem during the siege of the city by the Babylonian army. One of Ezekiel's symbolic activities included making bread, but not just any bread. God provided the recipe for these loaves.

"Ezekiel bread" is made with the six ingredients God ordered his prophet to store in a jar for use during the next 390 days, the length of the performance. Ingredients included no sugar, flour, or yeast, but did include sprouted grains. The amount for Ezekiel to eat each day demonstrated the meager rations of a near-starvation diet, a diet everyone was forced to adopt during the siege of the city.

God's further instructions startle the squeamish: "Bake it in the sight of the people, using human excrement for fuel" (Ezekiel 4:12). Ezekiel had an issue with the fuel, and not simply because it sounded disgusting to him. Handling

Miscellany

Ezekiel Bread

human waste rendered a Jew unclean according to Levitical Law, and Ezekiel's conscience caused him to protest the suggestion of using it. The prophet's objection proved God's point: During the siege, Jews would be forced to defile themselves. Taken captive by the Babylonians, they would live among and live like pagan people. For the purpose of Ezekiel's skit, God relented on the human excrement and allowed him to substitute cow manure.

You need be neither a prophet nor a drama major to make a loaf of Ezekiel bread. Christians with a culinary bent have given the recipe a try, usually to illustrate the Bible story for children. A staple of health-food stores, the bread's reputed dietary and nutritional value appeals to health-conscious buyers.

[God said,] "Take wheat and barley, beans and lentils, millet and spelt; put them in a storage jar and use them to make bread for yourself."

EZEKIEL 4:9

One of the most influential Chinese Christians ever, Watchman Nee was made famous by his book *The Normal Christian Life*. Based on talks he gave in Europe in the late 1930s, the work outlines his views on the book of Romans and describes what daily life should be for the Christian.

At the age of seventeen, Nee consecrated himself to Christ. He read as many as three thousand books to absorb and learn Christian doctrine and practice. From the early 1920s to the late 1940s, the Christian church flourished and grew in China, thanks in no small part to Nee's influence.

In 1952, Nee was arrested and imprisoned by Chinese authorities for his faith. His friends had advised him not to stay in China because of the persecution of Christians there, but Nee compared his homeland to a house on fire. He couldn't leave it. He had to stay and rescue as many as possible. During his incarceration, only his wife was allowed to visit him. Though he was forbidden to share about Christ in his letters, his final letter written on the day of his death, said, "In my sickness, I still remain joyful at heart." He remained in prison for twenty years.

Men of the Faith

Watchman Nee
(1903–1972)
Minister, author, and martyr

His English name *Watchman* is a literal translation of his Chinese name. Pronounced "pinyin tùo," it means Chinese knocker or plaque that sounded out to mark the hours of the night. Watchman Nee believed it was his duty to stay up through the dark of night to awaken men to the coming of Christ.

FACT

Watchman Nee wrote, "Our old history ends with the cross; our new history begins with the resurrection."

I have been crucified with Christ; it is no longer I who live,
but Christ lives in me; and the life which I now live in the flesh
I live by faith in the Son of God, who loved me and gave Himself for me.
GALATIANS 2:20 NKJV

Contrary to "funny Sunday school answers," Joan of Arc was *not* Noah's wife.

Jeanne la Pucelle, Joan the Maid, was born in Champagne, a region of northeastern France that had been embroiled in conflict between French loyalists and the English for more than one hundred years. Though an illiterate peasant girl, Joan exhibited piety and intelligence as a child. In her early teens, she discerned inner voices accompanied by a blaze of light that invited her to save France from the English.

Joan gained an audience with King Charles VII and convinced him of her God-sent purpose. An assembly of churchmen examined her and found her to be deeply devout and consecrated to God, adding credibility to her claims. The girl was provided with a suit of armor, and she joined a campaign against the English army besieging the town of Orléans. The French victory at Orléans led to further successes, but political intrigue, apathy, and deceit led to Joan's capture and imprisonment under English command.

Women of the Faith

Joan of Arc
(c. 1412–1431)
Martyr and military leader

The English, beaten in battle by the wisp of a girl, wanted to get rid of the source of their embarrassment in short order. A tribunal of politically motivated churchmen tried Joan for witchcraft, found her guilty, and sentenced her to die by fire in the marketplace of Rouen. Twenty years after her death, Pope Callistus III held a second trial and Joan was cleared of all charges.

Historians credit Joan of Arc—both her military skills and her martyrdom—with uniting and invigorating the French to eventually drive the English from their country.

More has been written about Joan of Arc than any other person of the Middle Ages—male or female. She has been portrayed as a saint, a heretic, a religious zealot, a seer, a demented teenager, a feminist, a faithful and godly woman, a Marxist liberator, and the savior of France.

FACT

Brethren, give diligence to make your calling and election sure:
for if ye do these things, ye shall never fall.
2 PETER 1:10 KJV

Christ Church in Oxford, Great Britain, is unique in that it is the only college in the world that is also a cathedral. Christ Church houses both the seat of the bishop of Oxford and one of Oxford University's largest and most visited colleges. It is considered improper to say "Christ Church College" or "Christ Church Cathedral," as the two cannot be separated. Christ Church is a one-of-a-kind college-church community that has existed for almost five hundred years.

In the ninth century, a monastery stood on this site. But King Henry VIII broke away from the Catholic Church, reorganized the Church of England, and asked his chaplain, Cardinal Wolsey, to tear down the existing monastery. The Cardinal had a college and cathedral built there, which he named Cardinal College. When the Cardinal died, Henry renamed the site Henry VIII's College. But in 1545, Henry integrated the church and college, renaming the site Christ Church.

Important Sites

Christ Church
Oxford, England

Often referred to simply as the House (because its Latin name means the house, or temple, of Christ), Christ Church has housed many famous students over the years, including religious leaders John Wesley and William Penn, mathematician Charles Dodgson (better known as the author of *Alice in Wonderland*, Lewis Carroll), physicist Albert Einstein, and thirteen British prime ministers. As for the religious aspects of Christ College, tradition dictates that the dean of Christ Church be a clergyman and that the grace recited together by students before meals in the dining hall continues to be a long-established Latin prayer.

FACT

Every evening at 9:05, Great Tom (the seven-ton bell in Christ Church's bell tower) tolls 101 times, once for each of Christ Church's founding class of students.

Start with GOD—the first step in learning is bowing down to GOD;
only fools thumb their noses at such wisdom and learning.
PROVERBS 1:7 MSG

Like the fragrant spring breeze after a cold and grueling winter, the Edict of Milan brought the winds of freedom to Christians throughout the Roman Empire. The era of state-sanctioned persecution and killing of Christians had come to an end. At last, Christians could worship without fear for their lives.

The Edict of Milan was issued in 313 after the two Roman emperors, Constantine, ruling the West, and Licinius, ruling the East, had come to an agreeable (though temporary) peace. Their main focus and first concern was the stability of the empire. Religious freedom for all—Christians and non-Christians alike—not only curried divine favor (whoever or whatever the deity), but assured the contentment of the populace.

Groundbreaking Events

The Edict of Milan

The edict lifted legal sanctions against the church and released imprisoned Christians. It even returned property confiscated during the years of persecution.

Though the Edict of Milan was not the first proclamation of religious tolerance, it was the first one that actually encouraged the church. Church buildings were exempt from taxes. The edict granted the church state support and gave public status, special privileges, and increasing authority to the clergy. The Christian church grew, spread, and prospered as a result.

Not everyone, however, rejoiced in this newfound freedom. Some Christians objected to the church's state sponsorship, fearing that it would dilute and compromise the gospel. While the Edict of Milan set the stage for an era of harmony, it actually worked to divide Christians. In protest, many left the church to become hermits in the desert or join small communities of like-minded believers.

The Edict of Milan said in part, "[W]e thought, among other things which we saw would be for the good of many, those regulations pertaining to the reverence of the Divinity ought certainly to be made first, so that we might grant to the Christians and others full authority to observe that religion which each preferred."

FACT

[Jesus said,] "If the Son sets you free, you will be free indeed."
JOHN 8:36

I forgive you." Pope John Paul II spoke these words to his would-be killer, and the event made headlines around the world. Similar stories of victims who express unconditional forgiveness to those who have grievously harmed them or a loved one still make news. Philip Yancey explores why in his book, *What's So Amazing About Grace?*

Yancey leads his readers to understand biblical grace in action through true stories of people who have extended grace to their fellow human beings under wrenching circumstances. He compares grace to *ungrace*, a word he uses to describe the expected and predicable response to victimization—anger, revenge, and condemnation.

Unflinchingly, he pits grace against the seemingly unforgivable people—child abusers, serial killers, perpetrators of the Holocaust. Yancey explores controversial subjects, such as contemporary politics and alternative lifestyles, in light of grace. While grace never excuses sin, nor does it release the sinner from the earthly consequences of his or her actions, it does extend mercy to the sinner. Grace, Yancey explains, has the life-changing power to transform a suffering world. He challenges all Christians to become grace-full and live as the world's living answers to the question, "What's so amazing about grace?"

Notable Books

What's So Amazing About Grace?

By Philip Yancey (1997)

In 1998, Yancey received the Gold Medallion Christian Book of the Year Award from the Evangelical Christian Publishers Association. He is also the author of bestselling titles *Finding God in Unexpected Places, The Jesus I Never Knew,* and *Where Is God When It Hurts?*

FACT

Philip Yancey wrote, "There is nothing we can do to make God love us more. There is nothing we can do to make God love us less."

[God] does not treat us as our sins deserve or repay us according to our iniquities.
PSALM 103:10

T oday's audiences know "Oh Happy Day" from the Edwin Hawkins Singers' 1969 hit recording. What many fans may not realize is that Hawkins's popular arrangement comes from a hymn written in the eighteenth century, "O Happy Day, That Fixed My Choice."

Philip Doddridge, a member of the dissenting clergy in England, pastored a congregation in Northampton and taught at a seminary for nonconformist ministers. He wrote a number of hymns, including "O Happy Day," that were published posthumously in a book titled *Hymns Founded on Various Texts in the Holy Scriptures.*

Doddridge set "O Happy Day" to an early eighteenth-century melody attributed to J. A. Freylinghausen. Later, Edward F. Rimbault, a church organist in London, composed a new melody for Doddridge's text. Throughout nineteenth-century Britain and the United States, the Doddridge/Rimbault "O Happy Day" became a popular choice for baptisms and confirmation ceremonies.

Songs of the Faith

"Oh Happy Day"

Words by Philip Doddridge (1755)

Music by Edward F. Rimbault (1854)

When Hawkins arranged the hymn in 1967, he took the refrain and set it to 4/4 time for solo and chorus. The foot-tapping song reached new audiences, has been recorded by other artists, and remains a gospel music standard.

O happy day that fixed my choice
On Thee, my Savior and my God!
Well may this glowing heart rejoice,
And tell its raptures all abroad.

Refrain:
Happy day, happy day, when Jesus washed my sins away!
He taught me how to watch and pray, and live rejoicing every day.
Happy day, happy day, when Jesus washed my sins away.

The Northern California State Youth Choir, later renamed the Edwin Hawkins Singers, recorded an album, *Let Us Go into the House of the Lord.* The track "Oh Happy Day" unexpectedly reached the top of the charts and won a Grammy award.

FACT

Philip began with that very passage of Scripture
and told him the good news about Jesus.
ACTS 8:35

When evangelicals spend money, marketers notice. During the last decades of the twentieth-century, retail shelves groaned under the weight of Christian-themed books, candles, plaques, bracelets, and breath mints. Yes, breath mints.

In 1996, M&M/Mars's former vice-president of marketing Alfred Poe invested in Testamints, a candy manufacturer and distributor. Packaged in small tin boxes, each Testamint came wrapped in a Bible verse and embossed with a cross. Poe expanded the product line by designing collectors' tins for Christmas and Easter and other occasions. The company committed itself to donating 10 percent of its profits to not-for-profit Christian shelters. Testamints sold mainly in Christian bookstores and other retail stores amenable to Christian-themed merchandise.

Seen as a fun and winsome way to share the message of Jesus Christ by many evangelicals, Testamints couldn't avoid being added to the already burgeoning array of Christian kitsch. Proponents say that T-shirts bearing testimony in the words of ad slogans, bumper stickers expressing faith in five words or less, and similar products are viable ways to witness to the culture on its own terms. The messages reach people where they are and can get them thinking about religion. They also provide a way for Christians to publicly identify themselves and remind each other of their fellowship in Christ.

Miscellany

Testamints

Christian critics find these outbursts of religious capitalism an embarrassment. Some messages, while well intended, oversimplify the gospel or give a negative or erroneous impression of it. They also put Christians on display, and when public behavior proves less than Christlike, the witness is worse than a bad case of halitosis.

FACT

Mint and other herbs have been used throughout history to sweeten breath and disguise food (and alcoholic beverage) odors. In the early 1950s, American Chicle introduced Certs, a combination candy and breath freshener. The breath freshener market turned sweet and remains so to this day.

May my prayer be set before you like incense.
PSALM 141:2

George Whitefield was known as the "Great Itinerant." Traveling from town to town, he emphasized the concept of saving grace and the emotional experience of conversion. Basically, he reduced Christianity to its lowest common denominator. Those sinners who love Jesus will go to heaven, other distinctions notwithstanding.

Whitefield became a principal figure in the Great Awakening, surprising since he was raised in a gin house—a hotel tavern run by his parents in England—that served highway robbers. Listening as these miscreants sat around the tables, planning their crimes, young George developed a vivid imagination and a dramatic speaking voice.

When he was seventeen, Whitefield attended a meeting with Charles Wesley, and what he heard there caused him to come under conviction. He tried in a legalistic way to become a better person, but finally embraced the concept of grace and his divine calling as a preacher. His animated presentation was a stunning contrast to the cold, rational religion that

Men of the Faith

George Whitefield (1714–1770)

American evangelist

dominated the church scene at the time and his popularity soared.

In the course of his lifetime, Whitefield held open-air meetings in almost every town in England, Scotland, and Wales. He also made at least seven trips to America, where he preached in many towns and cities along the eastern seaboard. He preached his last sermon from the staircase of a parsonage in Newburyport, Massachusetts. Asked by visitors to say just a few more words, he paused on the stairs and with the drama of a great actor, preached until the candle he was carrying burned out. Then he retired to bed and died. He was just fifty-six years old.

It is said that Whitefield could pronounce the word *Mesopotamia* in such a way that it would mesmerize audiences. He liked to use the word at least once in every sermon regardless of the topic.

FACT

When I preach the gospel, I cannot boast, for I am compelled to preach.
Woe to me if I do not preach the gospel!
1 CORINTHIANS 9:16

One dive into deceivingly shallow water took Joni Eareckson from fit, athletic, and energetic to wheelchair-bound for life. Only seventeen, she faced a bleak future.

As with many American teens, Joni's Christian religion played little part in her life outside of Sunday services. It's just not something she gave much thought to—until her 1967 swimming accident, that is. Learning how to live as a quadriplegic drew Joni to her only hope, the God in whose hands she committed herself and her life.

The story of her slow, often painful, physical rehabilitation and spiritual development has given encouragement and inspiration to untold numbers of people. She has written more than two dozen books, the first being her autobiography, which was made into a feature film. In addition, she has written magazine articles, recorded songs, and appeared on numerous television shows.

Women of the Faith

Joni Eareckson Tada

Author and advocate
for the disabled

In 1979, Joni founded Joni and Friends, a worldwide organization devoted to Christian ministry to the disabled and their families. The organization trains church leaders how to more effectively serve disabled members and include them and their families in the life and activities of the congregation. She held a presidential appointment to the National Council on Disability when the Americans with Disabilities Act became law. She has received numerous awards and honors.

Joni Eareckson's husband, Ken Tada, is commended for his support for and commitment to his wife. The couple travels throughout the world with their message of God's enduring goodness and love in spite of tragic circumstances.

FACT — Joni Eareckson Tada said, "The greatest good suffering can do for me is to increase my capacity for God."

It is God who works in you to will and to act according to his good purpose.
PHILIPPIANS 2:13

Once the trade center of the ancient world, the port city of Ephesus was renowned for its wealthy and well-educated population. It was also home to the Artemesium, a colossal temple to the goddess Artemis and one of the Seven Ancient Wonders of the World. Within this extensive shrine complex, thousands of Ephesians made a very profitable living.

Then the apostle Paul settled into Ephesus for a few years. He took up preaching in a local synagogue and later in a public lecture hall. The spread of Christianity throughout Ephesus was so pervasive that those involved in trades related to idol worship staged a riot against Paul in the main theater of the city. The ruins of the Ephesus theater, built to seat twenty-four thousand spectators, is one of the few specific locations pinpointed in the Bible which is still visible today.

As for the Artemesium, it has long since disappeared from view beneath a layer of mud. Today a single stone column, excavated from the swampy ground, marks the spot where one of the wonders of the world once stood. (However, other excavated columns from the site are on display in London's British Museum, and a major statue of Artemis can be found in the nearby Selcuk Museum.) Today, Ephesus remains one of the premier tourist attractions in Turkey, although it is no longer found on the coast, but 6¼ miles inland. When silt from the Cayster River eventually landlocked the city, it was abandoned.

Important Sites

Ephesus
Turkey

According to tradition, both the apostle John and Jesus' mother, Mary, spent their final days in Ephesus. Many modern-day pilgrims visit the Basilica of St. John, supposedly built over the spot where John was buried and the home where Mary allegedly lived.

FACT

[Paul] had discussions daily in the lecture hall of Tyrannus.
This went on for two years, so that all the Jews and Greeks
who lived in the province of Asia heard the word of the Lord.
ACTS 19:9–10

In AD 323, Constantine defeated his co-emperor Licinius and ordered his execution. Licinius's death made Constantine sole ruler of the Roman Empire, a vast area divided by various political allegiances, ethnic loyalties, and religious differences. Christians, split over matters of doctrine and church authority, further threatened the unity of the empire.

Constantine convened the Council of Nicea in 325 to achieve harmony in the Christian church. He gathered bishops from all points of the Roman Empire, some three hundred in all. The Council drafted the Nicene Creed to address the Arian heresy, which had arisen in Alexandria, Egypt. Arius, a priest, claimed that Jesus Christ, being begotten of the Father, must have had a beginning. The Council condemned the heresy, declaring that the Son was "one in being with the Father."

The Council addressed other issues of doctrine and practice facing the church. Constantine is credited with keeping the debates civil and orderly and bringing the contentious bishops to agreement. Scholars do not believe, however, that Constantine voted with the bishops or forced their decisions.

Groundbreaking Events

The Council of Nicea

Though Constantine supported the bishops' condemnation of the Arian doctrine, years later he changed sides. Arius, excommunicated by the bishops at Nicea, redefined his position and asked for readmittance to the fold. The church refused, whereupon Arius took his plea to the emperor. Constantine's sister spoke on Arius's behalf, but before Constantine could force the bishops to accept the erring brother back, Arius died.

The words of the Nicene Creed are regularly recited in orthodox and liturgical Christian churches today.

FACT

The Nicene Creed states, in part: "I believe in. . .one Lord Jesus Christ, the only-begotten Son of God, begotten of His Father before all worlds, God of God, Light of Light, very God of very God, begotten, not made, being of one substance with the Father, by whom all things were made."

In the beginning was the Word, and the Word was with God,
and the Word was God.
JOHN 1:1

First things first. Theologian and lecturer James Innell Packer's book, *Knowing God*, explores the Christian's primary goal in life: to strive for intimate knowledge of God. In clear and accessible language, Packer engages the reader with doctrinally sound and theologically focused chapters dealing with topics such as the Trinity, God's sovereignty, and God's will.

First written as essays to counter the trend toward easy answers to complex questions of faith, *Knowing God* quickly gained an enthusiastic following. The book clarifies for readers not versed in theology the meaning of terms heard in church, but not readily understood.

Packer divides his book into three sections. In the first part, he calls Christians to personally commit themselves to study the character of God. Then, the book examines the attributes of God as revealed in the Bible. In its conclusion, *Knowing God* describes the happy consequences of a Christian's serious and continuing commitment to knowing God. Packer shows how the pursuit of God guides, comforts, and encourages believers through the changes and chances of life. Packer leads Christians to more fully realize the awesome attributes of God, the astonishing fact of being God's child, and the extraordinary joy of living life as a Christian.

Notable Books

Knowing God
By J. I. Packer (1973)

Packard has penned other books and essays, yet he is best known in Christian circles for the one title, *Knowing God*. Now considered a modern classic, the book was recognized in the year 2000 by the Evangelical Christian Publishing Association for achieving more than one million copies sold in North America.

As a young man, Packer committed his life to Christian service and was ordained a priest in the Church of England, where he became an influential leader of the evangelical movement.

FACT

Skilled living gets its start in the Fear-of-God,
insight into life from knowing a Holy God.
PROVERBS 9:7 MSG

Julia Ward Howe and her husband, Samuel, were prominent abolitionists in their day. Their efforts on behalf of the North during the Civil War brought them to the White House for a visit and a tour of a Union Army camp. During their walk-through, they were treated to a rousing rendition of "John Brown's Body (lies a'mouldering in his grave)." Had the couple walked through a Confederate camp, they would have heard the same song. Northern soldiers sang to commemorate the martyrdom of a freedom fighter; Southern soldiers to celebrate the death of an insurrectionist.

A clergyman asked Julia Ward Howe, a published poet, if she could come up with a more elevating text for the popular tune. According to her autobiography, she did so the next day. The *Atlantic Monthly* bought the anthem, named it "Battle Hymn of the Republic," and printed it in its February 1862 issue. Howe received a grand total of five dollars for her work.

Songs of the Faith

"Battle Hymn of the Republic"

Words by Julia Ward Howe (1862)

Music: Traditional Melody

"John Brown's Body," the song that provided the tune, was written by John William Steffe, an abolitionist who led a short-lived insurrection to free the slaves. "Battle Hymn of the Republic" is frequently heard at the funerals of statesmen and presidents, and at national events and commemorations.

Mine eyes have seen the glory of the coming of the Lord;
He is trampling out the vintage where the grapes of wrath are stored;
He hath loosed the fateful lightning of His terrible swift sword;
His truth is marching on.

Refrain:
Glory! Glory! Hallelujah! Glory! Glory! Hallelujah!
Glory! Glory! Hallelujah! His truth is marching on.

FACT

Julia Ward Howe wrote, "I awoke in the grey of the morning, and as I lay waiting for dawn, the long lines of the desired poem began to entwine themselves in my mind, and I said to myself, 'I must get up and write these verses, lest I fall asleep and forget them!'"

"Brother will fight against brother, neighbor against neighbor,
city against city, kingdom against kingdom."
ISAIAH 19:2

B y the side of the highway, three white crosses stand as a solemn testament to the fragility of life.

The tradition of erecting roadside memorials for the dead is far from new. The Spanish brought to the New World their custom of using stones to mark the places between church and cemetery where pallbearers rested. Gradually, crosses replaced the stones. Within the last twenty years, roadside memorials have become an increasingly common sight along U.S. highways where fatal auto accidents have occurred, usually those involving the death of a young person. Crosses, often decorated with flowers, personal messages, teddy bears, and balloons, stand as a public expression of private grief—and a flash point for controversy.

Miscellany

Roadside Memorials

Though intended as a marker of mourning for family and friends, a memorial also can pose a distraction for motorists and an obstruction for highway maintenance crews. In addition, a vocal minority decries the presence of religious symbols on public land. States have taken various measures to meet the challenge of honoring citizens' grief and to ensure the safety and civil rights of all. A few states have banned roadside memorials altogether, while others encourage them or place a thirty-day limit on them. Other solutions to mark the scene of a fatal accident include state-sanctioned markers; wildflower gardens; an engraved brick added to an accessible state-maintained highway memorial; size and placement regulations; or restriction to alcohol-related crashes only.

Passing a roadside memorial, not a few drivers remind themselves to get off the cell phone, pay attention to the road, and drive safely.

In New York City, "ghost bikes" stand as memorials for cyclists who have died in crashes involving motor vehicles. They're old bicycles painted white and placed near the scene of the accident, along with a plaque bearing the name of the deceased.

FACT

Rejoice with those who rejoice; mourn with those who mourn.
ROMANS 12:15

Though his Christian faith has been called into question by some modern historians, no one can deny that God dramatically worked through Constantine and changed the face and practices of the Roman Empire forever. He was born the son of a Roman official. On his father's death, Constantine assumed his father's property and power. By the time he was thirty-one years old, Constantine was in line to rule the entire Western world.

In the year 311, with forty thousand troops at his disposal, Constantine bore down on Rome to face an enemy whose numbers were four times his own.

Men of the Faith

Constantine (280–337)

The first Christian emperor

His challenger was the pagan ruler Maxentius, who believed he had been told in a dream that the "enemies of Rome" would perish. When he confronted Constantine at the Milvian Bridge, however, he met his doom. Constantine, boosted by a vision of the cross, drove Maxentius into a river, where he drowned.

As emperor, Constantine ordered the Edict of Milan, which banned the persecution of Christians. The move also restored stolen church property to its rightful owners. Constantine gave his sons an orthodox Christian education and supported the church financially. He conferred with bishops, offering testimony to His faith in Christ, and moved the seat of power to Byzantium, then named Constantinople, now named Istanbul.

Just before his death, Constantine was baptized as a Christian. Although many of his actions as emperor cannot be defended, he got rid of the old Roman gods and made the cross an emblem of his reign.

> FACT
>
> Constantine I said: "I have experienced this in others and in myself, for I walked not in the way of righteousness. . . . But the Almighty God, who sits in the court of heaven, granted what I did not deserve."

Every person is to be in subjection to the governing authorities.
For there is no authority except from God, and those
which exist are established by God.
ROMANS 13:1 NASB

At a revival meeting, fourteen-year-old Kathryn Kuhlman accepted Jesus Christ as her Lord and Savior. Two years later, Kuhlman joined her sister and her sister's husband, an evangelist, on the revival-meeting circuit. She gave testimony during services and commenced preaching several years later. By that time, the revival meetings included a faith-healing component.

In the late 1920s, preacher Kuhlman and pianist Helen Gulliford launched their own traveling ministry. They started out in humble surroundings—pool halls, tents, and barns throughout the Midwest. As Kuhlman built name recognition, she opened her own church in Colorado. She attracted well-known evangelists to her church and revival took root in the community. All progressed well until the evangelist Burroughs Waltrip Sr. came to preach. To pursue Kuhlman, he abandoned his wife and children. Their own marriage lasted only six years, but gossip followed both evangelists for the rest of their lives.

Women of the Faith

Kathryn Kuhlman
(1907–1976)
Evangelist and faith-healer

Kuhlman's growing celebrity as a healer brought her to Carnegie Hall, where she held services for twenty years. She appeared on talk shows, at times confronted by medical doctors who challenged her ability to heal physical ailments. Other experts sided with Kuhlman, at least to the point that she was sincere and true to what she believed in.

In the mid-1960s, Kuhlman moved her ministry to Pasadena, California, where she held healing meetings for the next ten years. Her popular ministry put her at the forefront of the growing charismatic movement. Kuhlman never took credit for the healings that surrounded her prayers, always insisting that they were the work of God alone.

When Kuhlman prayed for the sick, they were often "slain in the Spirit." Ushers would catch recipients as they fell backward, sometimes entering a semiconscious state. This was thought to be an ideal state in which to receive healing.

---

*To one there is given through the Spirit the message of wisdom,
to another the message of knowledge by means of the same Spirit,
to another faith by the same Spirit, to another gifts of healing by that one Spirit.*
1 CORINTHIANS 12:8–9

Known in the British Isles as the "cradle of Christianity," the spiritual heritage of the Scottish isle of Iona began with the arrival of Columba and twelve fellow monks from their native Ireland in 563. The monastic community Columba founded on the 3½-mile-long island, and Columba's widespread evangelistic journeys, are credited with spreading Christianity throughout Scotland, Northern England, and into Europe.

Columba believed the faith of a people often followed the faith of their leader. So he journeyed north to visit King Brude of the Picts. As the story goes, the king wouldn't let Columba in. But Columba made the sign of the cross, knocked on the door, and the door flew open. Impressed by both Columba's "miracle" and his persuasive gospel teaching, the king converted to Christianity.

Though Viking raids in the ninth and tenth centuries were responsible for the deaths of many monks on the island, the spiritual influence of Iona continued throughout the twelfth century. In 1203, an abbey was built on the site of Columba's original wooden church. But as Catholicism overshadowed Celtic Christianity, the spiritual influence of Iona faded.

Important Sites

Iona
Scotland

In 1938, an ecumenical Christian group called the Iona Community refurbished the ruins of the abbey and helped reestablish the island's heritage. The vision of the Iona Community is to "seek new ways of living the gospel of Jesus Christ in today's world." Today, visitors continue to tour the refurbished abbey and adjoining chapel built over the traditional site of Columba's grave.

FACT

On August 22, 565, one of Columba's followers was attacked by a "monster" while swimming across a loch. Columba commanded the beast to release the man and leave, which it did. This is believed to be the first recorded sighting of the Loch Ness monster.

"Everyone who calls on the name of the LORD will be saved."
But how can they call on him to save them unless they believe in him?
And how can they believe in him if they have never heard about him?
ROMANS 10:13–14 NLT

Several popular authors of fiction have incited great interest in "lost" or "secret" Gospels. These sacred writings, they suggest, didn't make it into the canon, because churchmen of the time wanted to conceal certain truths. As beguiling as these claims appear, history tells a much more complex story.

The New Testament books in today's Bible were collected from eyewitness accounts of Jesus' earthly ministry and from the letters of St. Paul and others. The formation of the canon—those books of the Bible recognized as authoritative—happened over the course of time. No one person or church council made the decisions. Instead, scholars and clergy studied a wide range of sacred writings dating from the earliest years of Christianity. At first, only the Gospels (the sayings of Jesus and accounts of His ministry as related in the books of Matthew, Mark, Luke, and John) were regarded as authoritative and worthy of equality with Old Testament scriptures. Acceptance widened to include books and letters of apostolic origin, that is, written by an apostle, someone associated with one of the apostles, or a member of the Lord's family. In addition, the writings were required to date from the apostolic age and have been accepted

Groundbreaking Events

Recognition of the New Testament Canon

by and used in the worship life of several of the earliest Christian communities.

In 367, Athanasius of Alexandria made a list of all the books in use and accepted as authoritative in the church at that time. The Catholic Church approved his list. Although the book of Revelation was disputed as late as the eighth century, the New Testament canon was essentially fixed.

The world's oldest known Christian Bible dates from the days of Constantine, who ordered fifty volumes of scripture copied onto fine vellum. A sufficient quantity of vellum would have required the skins of around forty-five hundred animals. Fragments of one of those Bibles are housed in various museums and monasteries.

FACT

All Scripture is God-breathed and is useful for teaching, rebuking, correcting and training in righteousness, so that the man of God may be thoroughly equipped for every good work.

2 TIMOTHY 3:16–17

Isaac Watts's *Hymns and Spiritual Songs* may well have been the first pew-edition hymnal of the Christian church. A prolific hymnist, Watts wrote songs of prayer and praise that appear in the hymnals of numerous Christian denominations to this day.

Watts grew up in England and attended independent congregations with his father, a dissenter from the Anglican Church. In public worship, the people sang only a few rather lackluster hymns, and the gifted lyricist decided to do something about it. Over the course of his adult life, Watts wrote around six hundred hymns and spiritual songs based on passages from scripture. He composed his text in "hymn meter," a quatrain common in English folk ballads, combining his words with chants, sacred music, and familiar folk tunes.

Notable Books

Hymns and Spiritual Songs
Isaac Watts (1707)

Ministers introduced Watts's hymns into their worship services to mixed reviews. While many congregants found joy in singing the words of the Bible, others found offense in giving voice to rewritten Bible verses. To accommodate those who disdained the new songs as "Watts's whims," some ministers saved the singing to the end of the service when those who so chose could leave.

In 1729, Benjamin Franklin introduced *Hymns and Spiritual Songs* to the American colonies. Watts's hymns became the songs of the Great Awakening in the 1740s, and were generally enthusiastically received by American churches. As a child, Emily Dickinson heard the hymns sung in her church in Amherst, Massachusetts, and was inspired by their compelling meter and biblical allusions. Many of her poems reflect the influence of the great hymnist, Isaac Watts.

FACT

The preface to *Hymns and Spiritual Songs* reads, "While we sing the Praises of our God in his Church, we are employed in that part of Worship which of all others is the nearest a-kin to Heaven: and 'tis pity that this of all others should be performed the worst upon Earth."

Sing to the LORD a new song; sing to the LORD, all the earth.
PSALM 96:1

DAY 335

"America, the Beautiful" has been called "an expression of patriotism at its finest." Indeed, its poetic, descriptive language has created a picture of America's grandeur and expanse for all those who call her dear.

In the summer of 1893, English professor Katherine Lee Bates was traveling by train from her home in Wellesley, Massachusetts, to Colorado Springs, Colorado. Along the way, she was deeply moved by her country's obvious beauty and diversity—from the World's Columbian Exposition in Chicago to the wheat fields of Kansas to the majestic view

Songs of the Faith

"America, the Beautiful"
Words by Katherine Lee Bates (1893)
Music by Samuel A. Ward (1882)

from the top of Pike's Peak that awaited her at her destination. In her hotel room at the Antlers Hotel, she penned the words, which were published two years later by the *Congregationalist* to commemorate the Fourth of July. A revised version was published in the *Boston Evening Transcript* in 1904.

The melody for the hymn, composed in 1882 by Samuel A. Ward, was added in 1910. Ward, a church organist and choirmaster, composed the tune as he traveled by ferryboat from Coney Island to his home in New York City on a leisurely summer day. Is it any wonder that the lyrics and music, though composed ten years apart and not united until 1910, fit together so perfectly? Ward died before he knew the national stature his music had reached.

> *O beautiful for spacious skies*
> *For amber waves of grain,*
> *For purple mountain majesties,*
> *Above the fruited plain!*
>
> *Refrain:*
> *America! America!*
> *God shed His grace on thee,*
> *And crown thy good with brotherhood*
> *From sea to shining sea!*

At various times during the past century, efforts have been made to give "America, the Beautiful" legal status, either as the national hymn or a replacement for "The Star-Spangled Banner."

FACT

In the beginning God created the heavens and the earth.
GENESIS 1:1

Long before Christians affixed fish symbols to the bumpers of their cars, they were chiseling them into the rock walls of Rome's catacombs. The catacombs provided a relatively safe place for third-century Roman Christians to meet during periods of persecution, and the fish marked the spot. Brave believers also found a place near the doors of their homes to etch in a fish symbol, thus letting other Christians know they were welcome. Presumably, the symbol provided bait for knowledgeable officials, too.

The fish symbol is a natural sign for Christianity. Many of Jesus' disciples made a living as fishermen, and fish and fishing are mentioned repeatedly in the four Gospels. There's also a Greek angle, Greek being the original language of the New Testament. The simple fish outline α resembles the first letter of the Greek alphabet, alpha. In the book of Revelation, Jesus refers to Himself as the Alpha and Omega—something like the Greek A to Zed. The Greek word *ΙΧΘΥΣ* (transliterated to "ichthus") means *fish*. The five Greek letters also form an acrostic, where each letter stands for a word: In English, the acrostic spells out "Jesus Christ God's Son Savior." Since most Christians today converse in keyboard rather than biblical Greek, the fish symbol has taken on a distinctly modern look: ⋉.

Miscellany

The Fish Symbol

The fish marking cars, key chains, businesses, and personal stationery, has reeled in parody. The Darwin fish sprouts "evolved" legs with Darwin's name inside, continuing the debate of humankind's origins. Jumping out of the whole creationism-evolution net, the Trek fish sports the tail of the USS *Enterprise*.

May the fish be with you.

> FACT
>
> It's said that when an early Christian met a stranger who might be a believer, he would discreetly trace one half of the simple fish symbol in the dirt with his foot. If the stranger completed the fish, the two recognized one another as fellow followers of Christ. If not, the Christian quickly stepped over the evidence.

"Come, follow me," Jesus said, "and I will make you fishers of men."
MARK 1:17

Though called "The Prince of Preachers," Englishman Charles Spurgeon was criticized for his crude and vulgar style. Behind the pulpit, he would pace the platform, act out Bible stories, and fill his sermons with melodrama about dying children, grieving parents, and repentant harlots. Spurgeon didn't listen to his critics. He said, "I must and will make people listen. My firm conviction is that we have had enough polite preachers."

His convictions created controversy along with his style. He was unwavering on theological matters and condemned ritualism, hypocrisy, and modernism. He particularly didn't like Darwinism and biblical criticism that "downgraded" the faith. The controversy took its toll on his delicate health—he experienced weight gain, bouts of gout, and depression.

Once, while Spurgeon preached to a large crowd, an audience member shouted "Fire" and some spectators were trampled to death. Spurgeon was emotionally devastated by the event, and it had a sobering effect on his life. His faith and action kicked into high gear. He opened the massive Metropolitan Tabernacle, wrote several hymns, and challenged and befriended fellow pastors including Hudson Taylor and D. L. Moody. His sermons grew in popularity and were often published fully in the *London Times* and the *New York Times*.

Men of the Faith

Charles Spurgeon (1834–1892)
The "Prince of Preachers"

Charles Spurgeon left such an impression on his fellow Englishmen that when he died, nearly sixty thousand people came to pay homage to "the preaching sensation of London" as his body lay in state. And some one hundred thousand people lined the streets during his funeral parade.

Charles Spurgeon said, "If we cannot believe God when circumstances seem to be against us, we do not believe him at all."

FACT

Jesus answered them, "This is the work of God,
that you believe in him whom he has sent."
John 6:29 esv

Madeleine L'Engle, author of the beloved children's book *A Wrinkle in Time*, was born in New York City and educated in Switzerland. At an early age, she wrote stories and poems, developing a rich and imaginative inner life. Later, she graduated from Smith College and moved to New York to work in the theater and write. There she published two novels and met her actor-husband, Hugh Franklin.

After the birth of a daughter, the couple decided to move to Connecticut, but later moved back to the city so Franklin could pursue his acting career. L'Engle began work as a librarian at the Cathedral Church of St. John the Divine and came under the tutelage of the Cathedral's scholarly subdean, Edward Nason West. She recognized his influence in her spiritual development by modeling her character "Canon Tallis" after her gifted spiritual advisor.

Women of the Faith

Madeleine L'Engle (1918–2007)

Author

Her interest in quantum physics inspired her first commercially successful book, *A Wrinkle in Time*. Like her many subsequent books, the award-winning sci-fi-fantasy novel *A Wrinkle in Time* reflects L'Engle's deep thinking on questions of Christian theology and her firm belief in the victory of goodness over evil. Though aimed at young readers, the book's profound insights and religious subtext engage readers of all ages. She also penned poems, essays, devotionals, and personal reflections.

L'Engle was a sought-after speaker, inspiring audiences with her messages of joy, comfort, encouragement, and spiritual fulfillment. She conducted spirituality retreats and wrote what has become a classic for Christian artists, *Walking on Water*.

The beloved author died at age eighty-eight in 2007.

FACT

Madeleine L'Engle said, "A book comes and says, Write me. My job is to try to serve it to the best of my ability, which is never good enough, but all I can do is listen to it, do what it tells me and collaborate."

"The eternal God is your refuge, and underneath are the everlasting arms. He will drive out your enemy before you, saying, 'Destroy him!' "
DEUTERONOMY 33:27

The *Awakening* is a prayer carved in wood and painted in vibrant hues. Stylized depictions of the Last Supper, the Resurrection, and the glories of heaven cover eight thousand square feet of walls, doors, and ceiling in this single exhibit museum in Santa Fe, New Mexico. But this work, inspired by the artist Jean Claude Gaugy's personal awakening of wonder and his desire to connect with God and his fellow man, was first created in a remote, abandoned high school gymnasium in the hills of West Virginia.

Working without an overall plan or sketch, Gaugy would begin each morning with prayer and then start carving. Thirteen years and four hundred panels later, the walls and ceiling of the gymnasium were covered with Gaugy's seamless artistic expression of worship. When Gaugy moved to Santa Fe in 1998, his wife, Michelle, suggested he move his masterwork to New Mexico as well. In 2000 the panels were dismantled and transported to the historic center of old town Santa Fe.

Described as "the Sistine Chapel in a contemporary idiom," the *Awakening* is a fusion of sculpture and painting, rendered in a distinctive style of art known as Linear Expressionism. Other work by Gaugy is found in museums and prominent architectural structures throughout the world. It could be said that Gaugy is simply following in the footsteps, or brushstrokes, of his ancestors. For the last four hundred years, members of Gaugy's family have worked as artisans in the Jura region of France. Gaugy emigrated to the United States in 1966.

Important Sites

The *Awakening*
Santa Fe, New Mexico

At the age of fifteen, Gaugy was painting portraits in an upscale Parisian club when Salvador Dali happened to see his work. Dali was so taken by Gaugy's talent that he arranged a one-man show for the artist at a local gallery.

FACT

> " 'Love the Lord God with all your passion and prayer and intelligence and energy.' "
> MARK 12:30 MSG

With freedom of speech comes controversy. In the early Christian church, debates between priests and bishops, and bishops among bishops, forced the need for frequent councils to reach consensus on matters of faith and belief.

In 451, the Emperor Marcian convened the fourth ecumenical council, the Council of Chalcedon, to address a popular and growing controversy concerning the personhood and divinity of Jesus Christ. Because the issue is fundamental to the Christian faith, the Council of Chalcedon is regarded as the most important of the four early ecumenical councils.

At the time, the heresy of *monophysitism* was rapidly gaining acceptance throughout religious circles. Monophysites taught that Jesus possessed a single, divine nature (*mono* = one; *physite* = nature). The Council of bishops flatly condemned monophysitism and clearly defined the church's orthodox doctrine that Jesus Christ, though He was a single person, is true God, begotten of the Father, and also true man, born of the Virgin Mary. The Council's decision left Eastern bishops unhappy, a large number of whom supported the monophysites.

Groundbreaking Events

The Council of Chalcedon

The Council held additional sessions to address other matters of dispute and questions concerning church discipline and jurisdiction. In one such session, the bishops decreed that the city of Constantinople, being the seat of the emperor and the senate, ranked second only to Rome in importance and privilege within the church. Understandably, the decree upset the patriarchs of Alexandria, Antioch, and Jerusalem, as well as Pope Leo I himself. In response, Pope Leo ratified only those acts of the Council concerning matters of faith and doctrine.

FACT

The dual nature of Christ is a fundamental issue. If Jesus were man only, He would have been a liar in His claims of divinity. If Jesus were God only, He could not have experienced human suffering and death. Thus the church affirms, in accordance with scripture, the dual nature of Jesus Christ.

The Word became flesh and made his dwelling among us.
JOHN 1:14

In the tradition of *The Pilgrim's Progress,* Hannah Hurnard's *Hinds' Feet on High Places* dramatizes the soul's journey to God through symbolic characters and situations. Readers follow Much Afraid, Sorrow, and Suffering as they wend their way to the High Places in search of strength and courage. Their journey is fraught with dangers, temptations, and stumbling blocks, yet they reach their goal under the leadership of their loving Shepherd.

Hinds' Feet on High Places reflects its author's torturous journey to faith. Born to a wealthy Quaker family in England, Hurnard found herself unable to share her parents' enthusiasm for worship. She was a shy, self-conscious girl who was beset with a stammer and failed to find peace or happiness in the words of the Bible. She contemplated suicide, resigning herself to hell. At nineteen years of age, enlightenment came to her through a Bible reading, and she realized she lived in a hell of her own making. She surrendered herself to God and at last experienced the joy of His presence.

Notable Books

Hinds' Feet on High Places
Hannah Hurnard (1955)

Hurnard's faith matured. She overcame her fears and anxieties, taking on the roles of evangelist and servant of the poor and infirm. Then, in 1955, she wrote *Hinds' Feet on High Places,* the partially autobiographical allegory that continues to encourage and inspire Christian readers. Hurnard authored a number of other titles, though none reached the high places in the bestseller lists as *Hinds' Feet on High Places* did and continues to do.

> While *Hinds' Feet on High Places* reflects biblical teachings, Hurnard's later books became increasingly mystical. In the last years of her life, she stopped attending church, relying instead on direct communication with Jesus Christ. Hurnard died in 1990.
>
> FACT

The Sovereign LORD is my strength;
he makes my feet like the feet of a deer,
he enables me to go on the heights.
HABAKKUK 3:19

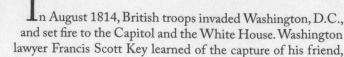

In August 1814, British troops invaded Washington, D.C., and set fire to the Capitol and the White House. Washington lawyer Francis Scott Key learned of the capture of his friend, Dr. William Beanes.

In an effort to rescue Dr. Beanes, Key and the American agent for prisoner exchange boarded the ship where Beanes was being held. The Brits agreed to release the prisoner, but were unwilling to let any of the men leave right away. It was feared that they had overheard too much about the British plans to bomb Fort McHenry and would warn their countrymen.

Songs of the Faith

"The Star-Spangled Banner"

Words by Francis Scott Key (1814)

Music attributed to

John Stafford Smith (18th century)

On September 13, 1814, British vessels began shelling. The bombardment lasted until the early morning hours of the next day. By the rays of the rising sun, the detained men gazed at a glorious sight: The American flag still flew over Fort McHenry! Moved beyond measure, Keys wrote a poem, "Defense of Fort M'Henry."

In October of 1814, a Baltimore actor sang Key's words to an existing tune and named the song "The Star-Spangled Banner." In 1931, Congress proclaimed it the national anthem of the United States.

O say, can you see, by the dawn's early light,
What so proudly we hail'd at the twilight's last gleaming?
Whose broad stripes and bright stars, thro' the perilous fight,
O'er the ramparts we watch'd, were so gallantly streaming?
And the rockets' red glare, the bombs bursting in air,
Gave proof thro' the night that our flag was still there.
O say, does that star-spangled banner yet wave
O'er the land of the free and the home of the brave?

FACT

The American flag that inspired Key's poem is on display at the Smithsonian's National Museum of American History.

We will shout for joy when you are victorious
and will lift up our banners in the name of our God.
PSALM 20:5

J ohn 3:16 is commonly cited as "the Bible in a nutshell." Jesus spoke the words of God's action on behalf of humankind to Nicodemus when the temple leader visited Him in the dark of night. Rollen Stewart took these same words to one of the most well-lighted places in America—nationally televised football games.

It all began in 1980 with Stewart's conversion to Christianity. Already familiar to sports fans as the Rainbow Man who popped up in front of cameras wearing a colorful Afro wig, Stewart exchanged the wig for signs bearing Bible verses, such as John 3:16. Media savvy, he positioned himself so he'd be seen by viewers as cameras followed team plays.

Stewart had no occupation other than appearing in front of television cameras. He traveled with his wife, who also held up signs, and both of them lived out of their car. Stewart and his signs showed up at football games, golf tournaments, World Series games, the summer and winter Olympics, political conventions, the Indy 500, World Cup soccer championships, and even the wedding of Princess Diana and Prince Charles. He drew a small cadre of fellow sign flashers, giving the desired impression that they were "everywhere."

Miscellany

John 3:16 and Football

In the late eighties, television and stadium officials started making it harder to capture on-camera attention. Other adversities struck: Stewart's wife left him; a drunk driver totaled his car; his money dwindled. Broke and homeless, Stewart wandered the streets of Los Angeles. Convinced the end was near, he set off stink bombs in several locations to punctuate his point. He was later convicted on more serious charges and is now serving three life terms in prison.

A kidnapping charge stemmed from Stewart's taking a hotel maid hostage in his room. A standoff with police and a SWAT team ensued. When the police went through Stewart's belongings after his arrest, they found his multicolored Afro wig, a pistol, incendiary devices, a supply of food, Bibles, and religious tracts.

FACT

[Jesus said,] "God so loved the world that he gave his one and only Son, that whoever believes in him shall not perish but have eternal life."
JOHN 3:16

Those who are in most need of grace are often those who can best understand its wonder and power after they have received it. Such was the case with John Newton, a "wretch" of a sailor with a long list of sins and transgressions. He lost his first job at a merchant's office for "unsettled behavior and impatience of restraint." As a teen, he rebelled against the discipline of the Royal Navy and deserted. He remained freethinking and insubordinate, even after he was relegated to working on a slave ship. He prided himself on moral abandonment and later wrote, "I sinned with a high hand and I made it my study to tempt and seduce others."

During a thunderstorm at sea, Newton, fearing death, converted to Christ. Though he continued working aboard the slave ships, he hoped he could restrain cruelty to the slaves and the worst of excesses on board among the crew.

Soon, Newton left the sea life and took a desk job in Liverpool. He began to hold Bible studies for his friends and became increasingly disgusted with the slave trade. After becoming an Anglican minister, he wrote hymns with William Cowper, including his now famous "Amazing Grace." He then wrote *Thoughts Upon the African Slave Trade* to help William Wilberforce's campaign to end the practice. Even as an old and feeble man, Newton would not stop talking about the wrongs of slavery, convinced it was by grace alone that he could stand forgiven, and hence was compelled to speak out against the injustice.

Men of the Faith

John Newton
(1725–1807)

Author of hymn "Amazing Grace"

FACT

John Newton wrote, "If the Lord be with us, we have no cause of fear. His eye is upon us, His arm over us, His ear open to our prayer—His grace sufficient, His promises unchangeable."

By grace you have been saved through faith,
and that not of yourselves; it is the gift of God.
EPHESIANS 2:8 NKJV

M arjorie Holmes's success as a writer of Christian fiction rested in her ability to bring familiar Bible stories to life. Her bestselling trilogy—*Two from Galilee*, *Three from Galilee*, and *The Messiah*—recounts the story of Mary, Joseph, and Jesus in descriptive, conversational prose. For millions of readers, Holmes's trilogy infused faraway people of a distant land and time with lifeblood, immediacy, and relevance.

Holmes showed a flair for writing while growing up in her home state of Iowa. She sold her first story during the Depression. After graduation from Cornell College (now University) in New York, she married, and she and her husband moved to Virginia where they reared four children.

During her years in Virginia, Holmes wrote long-running columns, "Love and Laughter"and"AWoman'sConversations with God." She contributed numerous articles that appeared in popular women's and family magazines, as well as inspirational journals. One of her stories was purchased and produced for film by MGM. She penned radio scripts, as well.

Women of the Faith

Marjorie Holmes
(1910–2002)
Author

Her first novel, *World by the Tail*, was published in 1943. Holmes went on to write dozens more books and short stories in Christian fiction, family life, inspiration and devotion, self-help, creative writing, and Christmas holiday categories. Like her popular trilogy, many of her stories were written for young audiences, yet appeal to readers of all ages.

Holmes received awards from the Freedom Foundation, the National Federation of Press Women, and other organizations. Her pioneering style—bringing Bible characters to life—has helped to open doors for wider acceptance of fiction in the Christian community.

Marjorie Holmes wrote, "I find the great thing in this world is not so much where we stand, as in what direction we are moving: To reach the port of heaven, we must sail sometimes with the wind and sometimes against it, but we must sail, and not drift, nor lie at anchor."

FACT

Mary said, "My soul glorifies the Lord and my spirit rejoices in God my Savior, for he has been mindful of the humble state of his servant."
LUKE 1:46–48

The Sea of Galilee has been known by many names throughout history, including Lake Kinneret, the Waters of Gennesaret, and Lake Tiberius. Actually a harp-shaped lake and not a sea, this body of water measures 13 miles long by 7 miles wide and reaches a depth of more than 150 feet. The largest freshwater lake in Israel and lowest freshwater lake in the world, the Sea of Galilee has many claims to fame. But it is most well known as the epicenter of Jesus' ministry.

On the shores of the Sea of Galilee, Jesus preached the Sermon on the Mount (commemorated by the Church of the Beatitudes). He fed five thousand followers with five fish and two loaves of bread in the narrow valley of Tabgha (site of the Church of the Multiplication). At least five of Jesus' twelve apostles called the ancient fishing village of Capernaum home. (Capernaum was rediscovered in the 1800s on the Galilean shore.) And on the surface of the lake itself, Jesus calmed a violent storm and urged His disciple Peter to join Him as He walked on the water.

Important Sites

The Sea of Galilee
Israel

During Byzantine times, this area was a very popular destination for religious pilgrimages. The area surrounding the Sea of Galilee is dotted with Byzantine shrines, monasteries, and churches. One of the most noteworthy is in Tabgha, known for its exquisite mosaics, making it unique among Byzantine churches in the Holy Land. Today, the Sea of Galilee remains a popular destination for Christian pilgrims and a holiday resort for Israelis.

FACT

The Sea of Galilee is known for its unpredictably violent and often deadly storms, caused by winds sweeping off the Golan Heights to the east. In 1992, a storm sent waves ten feet high into the shoreline city of Tiberias, causing significant damage.

[Jesus] replied, "You of little faith, why are you so afraid?"
Then he got up and rebuked the winds and the waves,
and it was completely calm.
MATTHEW 8:26

Christian or Muslim? The outcome of the Battle of Tours determined the subsequent religious history of Europe. Victory fell to the Christians.

After the breakup of the Roman Empire in the fifth century, the struggling states of Western Europe lay open to invaders from all directions. Though the feudal system provided some amount of political organization and military protection, the loose conglomeration of states seemed easy prey for the Moors, vast armies of Muslims sweeping through Syria, Egypt, North Africa, and Spain. In October of 732, under the command of Abd-er Rahman, governor of Spain, the Moors crossed the Western Pyrenees.

The invading army was met outside the city of Tours by the Frankish ruler Charles Martel and his army. The Moors, on horseback and armed with large swords and lances, plowed into the ranks of Frankish foot soldiers. The Franks, however, had four distinct advantages. First, the foot soldiers' flexibility worked in their favor to navigate the heavily wooded areas where the battle took place. Second, the Franks were dressed in warm clothing. The weather had turned bitterly cold, and the invading Moors still sported their summer attire.

Groundbreaking Events

The Battle of Tours

Third, while traveling through France, the Moors had captured quite a bit of booty, which further hampered their mobility. And fourth, Moorish spies had significantly underestimated the size of Martel's force.

The fighting—two days or seven days, depending on the source—ended on October 10, when Abd-er Rahman was killed. Leaderless and in disarray, the Muslim army withdrew and never returned. Victory fell to the Christians.

The captured loot proved the Moors' weak spot. They stood on the brink of victory when the Franks captured their treasure carts. In panic, the Moors broke formation to reclaim the carts. While Abd-er Rahman tried to rally his scattered forces, a Frankish lance killed him.

FACT

[Jesus said,] "When you hear of wars and rumors of wars, do not be alarmed. Such things must happen, but the end is still to come."
MARK 13:7

When Moses and the Israelites fled from Egypt, God offered them an interesting proposition. Follow my instructions to the letter and you will be free of the diseases you saw in Egypt (see Exodus 15:26). He then gave them the Levitical Law, which included many prohibitions and recommendations, including quarantine for sicknesses like leprosy and simple acts of sanitation such as hand washing. There were also instructions concerning how to prepare food and what foods to avoid. With advances in medical science, we now see the inherent wisdom in much of what we read in Leviticus.

Not only is it interesting to note that the scriptures predate modern medicine by thousands of years, but McMillen in *None of These Diseases* contends that our own lives can be vastly improved, spiritually, mentally, emotionally, and physically, by paying attention to the instructions provided in the entirety of God's Word.

Notable Books

None of These Diseases
By S. I. McMillen, MD (1974)

We already know that elevated stress hormones overload our systems, grief and bitterness are toxic, and anger and depression can send our bodies and minds reeling. Unhealthy habits like gossip, sexual promiscuity, and smoking are prime movers for a wide variety of diseases. On the flip side, if we were today to follow the instructions stated in the Bible, could we improve our ability to fight off disease and aging? McMillen thinks so.

None of These Diseases, released in 1974, has sold more than a million copies worldwide. Dr. McMillen's grandson, Dr. David E. Stern, has added updated materials in two revised editions published in 1984 and 2000.

FACT

Dr. S. I. McMillen wrote, "God guaranteed a freedom from disease that modern medicine cannot duplicate."

"I am the LORD, who heals you."
EXODUS 15:26

A *doxology* is simply a short hymn of praise to God, used regularly in worship services. A number of doxologies are known, but two are most often used in churches.

The first—known as the *"Gloria Patri"*—is used by Catholics, Orthodox, and many Protestant churches. Considered both a hymn of praise and a short declaration of faith, it is said to be based on Ephesians 3:21 and Isaiah 45:17 in the King James Bible. The musical arrangement most often used with the "Gloria Patri" was composed by Henry Wellington Greatore in 1851.

> *Glory be to the Father and to the Son*
> *And to the Holy Ghost.*
> *As it was in the beginning, is now, and ever will be*
> *World without end, Amen.*

The second doxology—widely used in English in Protestant churches—was originally the seventh and final stanza of the hymn entitled "Awake My Soul, and with the Sun." Thomas Ken, a bold, outspoken, seventeenth-century Anglican bishop, was the author of this evening worship hymn sung to the tune of "Old Hundredth." This was a sixteenth-century melody attributed to the French composer Loys Bourgeois and best known by the hymn "All People That on Earth Do Dwell" by William Kethe. It is credited with being the most famous of all Christian hymn tunes.

Songs of the Faith

The Doxologies

"Gloria Patri" (1851)

"Praise God from Whom all Blessings Flow" (1674)

> *Praise God, from Whom all blessings flow;*
> *Praise Him, all creatures here below;*
> *Praise Him above, ye Heavenly Host;*
> *Praise Father, Son, and Holy Ghost. Amen.*

The apostle Paul used doxologies constantly in the New Testament. They are addressed to God the Father, to Him through the Son, or with the Holy Spirit. Examples are found in Romans 11:36; Jude 25; Ephesians 3:21.

FACT

You will be blessed when you come in and blessed when you go out.
DEUTERONOMY 28:6

Cartoonist Al Hartley converted to Christianity in 1967. His new commitment led him to drop much of his existing comics work because of the salacious nature of certain publications. The religious themes emerging in his work led a few publications to drop him. Income relief came with an invitation from an editor at Archie Publications to draw the popular Archie characters. Hartley attributed the editor's contact to God's hand in his life, in that at no other time had an editor sought him out. "I ought to point out that during my 20 years as a cartoonist, no one had ever called me this way," he later wrote. "Every relationship I had with a publisher, I had developed. No one had ever come to me."

When Hartley began writing stories that touched on matters of faith, Archie editors took notice—and not all of it positive. Positive consumer response, however, satisfied the skittish editorial board, and Hartley gained control over the text of his stories. His chance to work on a purely religious line came in 1972 when the Fleming H. Revell Company asked Hartley to write

Miscellany

Spire Christian Comics

a comic book version of *The Cross and the Switchblade*, an up-from-the-streets conversion account by David Wilkerson. From there Hartley began to create a new line, Spire Christian Comics. Based on Bible stories and Christian novels and movies, Spire comics were frequently populated by various Archie characters.

In 1982, after Hartley stopped creating new stories, Barbour Publishing reprinted Spire Comics, under the name Barbour Christian Comics, for several more years. Overall, more than forty million Spire Christian Comics have sold worldwide.

FACT

Hartley and Archie publisher John Goldwater, who was Jewish, collaborated on the production of the Spire Comics line. Despite their religious differences, the evangelical Christian Hartley praised Goldwater as a deeply spiritual man dedicated to his family and home. Hartley's skills at storytelling, cartooning, and character development influence Christian cartoonists today.

Rejoice in the LORD and be glad, you righteous; sing,
all you who are upright in heart!
PSALM 32:11

An everyman with a common touch, Dwight L. Moody believed that God could and did use average people for His glory. A simple man himself, Moody was never encouraged to read the Bible as a child in Northfield, Massachusetts, and he only acquired a fifth-grade education. Moody, instead, took to business and declared his goal of amassing one hundred thousand dollars, a fortune by 1800s standards. At seventeen, Moody moved to Boston to work in his uncle's shoe store, where he proved himself to be a gifted salesman. It was also in Boston that he gave his heart to the Lord.

In 1856, Moody moved to Chicago to continue his sales career. Soon after arriving, Moody joined the Plymouth Congregational Church and began to invite the people he met while recruiting new customers for his business. Later he moved to the First Methodist Church, but the traditional church school did not seem compatible with most of Moody's converts. In response to this, he found an abandoned shanty and began his own Sunday school. When it was simply overflowing, he received permission from the mayor to move into a large hall over North Market.

Within a year's time, the average attendance at his Sunday school was six hundred fifty. Sixty volunteers from various churches served as teachers. Becoming famous all over America, newly elected President Lincoln visited and spoke at the school.

Men of the Faith

D. L. Moody
(1837–1899)

American evangelist and publisher

In 1886, Moody addressed the church about establishing a school for young evangelists and church leaders. The result was the Chicago Evangelization Society, renamed Moody Bible Institute after Moody's death.

Moody promoted cross-cultural evangelism using "The Wordless Book," a teaching tool with red, black, white, and gold colors on it, representing various aspects of the gospel message.

FACT

Jesus said, Make all the people recline (sit down).
Now the ground (a pasture) was covered with thick grass at the spot,
so the men threw themselves down, about 5,000 in number.
JOHN 6:10 AMP

Helen Barrett Montgomery has been referred to as "a woman of ten talents, who used them all." The consummate churchwoman, she gave liberally of her money and herself.

Her greatest contribution, however, is her translation of the Greek New Testament into English, first published in 1924. She is the first woman to ever publish such a translation.

Montgomery's translation is innovative, translated in the language of everyday life, and formatted to indicate elements such as dialogue and quotations. Each book includes a brief summary, and there are paragraph headings to help the reader follow. Montgomery also designed her New Testament to be easily carried in a pocket or handbag.

Helen Montgomery felt that her love of scholarly pursuits came from her father,

Women of the Faith

Helen Barrett Montgomery (1861–1934)

Translator of the New Testament,

minister, author

Adoniram Judson Barrett, a noted professor of Latin and Greek. Her father and paternal grandmother—a great woman of prayer—also greatly encouraged her faith in God. When she was fifteen, her father took the position of pastor at Lake Avenue Baptist Church in Rochester, New York. She joined the church and gave herself fully to the work of the church until her death at age fifty-eight.

Helen Barrett married William Montgomery in 1887. He was said to be 100 percent a partner with her in her many enterprises, which included Greek and Latin studies, translation, preaching, and teaching. She served as the first woman president of the Northern Baptist Convention and was president of the American Baptist Foreign Mission Society for ten years. She was an ordained Baptist minister and a prolific writer of Christian books.

FACT

Helen Barrett Montgomery said, "It is the only way to keep money or land or talent, or happiness—give it away. If only everyone had studied the divine arithmetic, what a world it would be."

Give freely and spontaneously. Don't have a stingy heart.
The way you handle matters like this triggers GOD, your God's,
blessing in everything you do, all your work and ventures.
DEUTERONOMY 15:10 MSG

Modern-day Mount Zion may not actually be Mount Zion at all. Early Byzantine pilgrims mistook the larger, flatter hill of the two "mounts" of Jerusalem to be the site of the original city of David. Most biblical scholars believe the true Mount Zion is one-in-the-same as the Temple Mount. Nonetheless, the hill that people refer to as Mount Zion today remains a sacred site for visitors, and has been considered sacred from as early as the fifth century.

Though the Bible does not give a specific location for the upper room where Jesus and his disciples celebrated the Last Supper, a site on Mount Zion known as the *Coenaculum* (Latin for "the room where one ate") has been venerated as the location for centuries. It is a small two-story structure within a larger complex of buildings that is believed to be in the general vicinity of where the Last Supper was probably held. Some people hold that this is the same upper room where Christ's followers experienced Pentecost as recorded in Acts 2.

Important Sites

Mount Zion
Jerusalem

On the first floor of the building below the Coenaculum, visitors can see the tomb of King David—though once again this location may be more traditional than historical. Along with David, the bones of Stephen, Christianity's first martyr, are said to be housed here. Adjoining this structure, built by the Crusaders, is the Franciscan Church of the Coenaculum, which was converted into a mosque in 1523 and remains so to the present day.

Oskar Schindler, the German businessman who saved the lives of hundreds of Jews during the Holocaust (as depicted in the movie, *Schindler's List*) is buried in the Christian cemetery on Mount Zion. Jews whose lives Schindler saved arranged for his burial here.

FACT

[Jesus said,] "Go into the city, and a man carrying a jar of water will meet you. Follow him. . . . He will show you a large upper room, furnished and ready. Make preparations for us there."
MARK 14:13, 15

Priest, theologian, and Bible translator John Wycliff (or Wycliffe) invented bifocal eyeglasses, a fact not lost on anyone who has pored for any amount of time over lengthy biblical texts.

Wycliff and his fellow translators worked from the Latin Vulgate, the fourth-century Bible translated from the Greek and Hebrew by St. Jerome and long held as authoritative by the Roman Catholic Church. The church, however, never approved Wycliff's English Bible, but not because it was written in English. Translations into local spoken languages already existed on the Continent, and parts of the Bible written in Early English were available in England at the time. But Wycliff had earned papal rebuke with his insistence on scripture alone to determine matters of faith, as opposed to the church's reliance on church tradition in addition to scripture. Wycliff had attacked several points of Roman Catholic doctrine, the same points disputed by later reformers. His translation of the Bible, therefore, was denounced and, in 1408, condemned and ruled unacceptable for use in the Roman Catholic Church.

Groundbreaking Events

The First English Bible Completed

Wycliff's Bible did, however, spur interest in biblical translation and scholarship. Theologians sought out copies of Hebrew and Greek manuscripts in a desire to get at the original meaning and intention of scripture, adding momentum to the push for church reformation.

The Wycliff Bible was handwritten, the last handwritten Bible before Gutenberg invented the printing press nearly a hundred years later. A Wycliff Bible is housed in the British Museum in London, England.

FACT

Like his contemporary, Chaucer, Wycliff wrote using the Middle English dialect spoken in London and southern England. This particular dialect became the foundation of Modern Standard English.

Utterly amazed, they asked: "Are not all these men who are speaking Galileans? Then how is it that each of us hears them in his own native language?"
ACTS 2:7–8

One of the most dearly loved and bestselling devotionals in history, *Streams in the Desert* reads like a daily journal filled with rich insights into God's provision, purpose, and plan. Perhaps its timeless emotion stems from the fact that this masterpiece was written during a time of genuine heartbreak for the author.

L. B. (Lettie) Cowman and her husband, Charles, began their service as pioneer Wesleyan missionaries to Japan and China in 1901. For the next sixteen years, the American couple devoted themselves to the work, helping to found the Oriental Missionary Society. But in 1917, Charles's health issues made it necessary for them to return to the United States. For the next six years, Lettie Cowman cared for her husband's every need. When he died, she was brokenhearted. To heal her own wounded heart, she began to compile devotionals taken from sermons, readings, writings, and even poetry that brought her comfort. The result was a heartfelt devotional with 366 daily readings for dry spiritual seasons. These readings include scriptures, inspirational anecdotes about missionaries and faith workers, interesting analogies, and first-rate Christian writing focusing on the veracity of God's promises.

Notable Books

Streams in the Desert
By L. B. Cowman (1925)

Before her death on Easter Sunday, 1960, Lettie Cowman published seven other books, including a companion text entitled *Springs in the Valley*. Her writing also inspired several nationwide scripture distribution campaigns.

In 1997, Mrs. Cowman's script was updated by James Reimann. His work allows younger generations to discover for themselves the wisdom and comfort provided by this fine devotional.

Lettie Cowman never coveted the limelight. She preferred to be known as L. B. Cowman or Mrs. Charles E. Cowman.

FACT

As the deer pants for streams of water,
so my soul pants for you, O God.
My soul thirsts for God, for the living God.
PSALM 42:1–2

This much-loved benediction, taken from Numbers 6:24–26, was set to music by composer and conductor, Peter C. Lutkin, while he served as church organist at St. Clements and St. James in Chicago in the 1880s and '90s.

Peter Lutkin, the son of Danish immigrants, was born in Thompsonville, Wisconsin, in 1858. He showed an early aptitude for music. He started singing in the church choir when he was just nine years old and became the chief organist at St. Peter and St. Paul's Episcopal Church in Chicago when he was a mere fourteen years old. Throughout his education, Lutkin showed a strong interest in church music, composing many hymns, some included in the *Methodist Sunday School Hymnal* for which he served as musical editor.

Dwight L. Moody in *Notes from My Bible* described the simple compelling song in these words: "Here is a benediction that can give without being impoverished. Every heart may utter it, every letter may conclude with it, every day may begin with it, every night may be sanctified by it. Here is a blessing—keeping—shining—the uplifting upon our poor life of all heaven's glad morning. It is the Lord Himself who gives us this bar of music from heaven's infinite anthem."

Songs of the Faith

"The Lord Bless You and Keep You"

Words and Music by Peter C. Lutkin

(20th century)

The Lord bless you and keep you;
The Lord lift His countenance upon you,
And give you peace, and give you peace;
The Lord make His face to shine upon you,
And be gracious, and be gracious;
The Lord be gracious, gracious unto you.

FACT

Numbers 6:24–26, the basis for this song, is called "The Priestly Blessing" and is one of the most read passages in the Bible.

May the grace of the Lord Jesus Christ, and the love of God,
and the fellowship of the Holy Spirit be with you all.
2 CORINTHIANS 13:14

M el Gibson's 2004 movie *The Passion of the Christ* became what Hollywood analysts call a "cultural event." Theaters teemed with church groups eager to see a biblical story produced by a professed Christian believer, and movie discussion panels sprang up in church basements and classrooms across the country. It remains the highest grossing religious film of all time.

The Passion of the Christ, referring to the events of the week preceding Jesus' death on the cross, opens with His prayer in the Garden of Gethsemane and ends with His crucifixion. The graphic violence of Jesus' scourging shocked many Christians into realizing the extent and brutality of the Lord's treatment at the hands of the Romans. (Viewers with sensitive stomachs declined to see the original movie, in favor of an edited version released later.) Because the Bible is brief or silent on particular details surrounding the Passion, Gibson added events, scenes, and characters for the sake of drama and artistry. Dialogue in Aramaic, Latin, and Hebrew with English subtitles

Miscellany

The Passion of the Christ— the Movie

lent authenticity to the story. Overall, the movie was deemed historically factual, artistically satisfying, and true to the scriptural account.

Critics decried the movie's portrayal of Jews, claiming it made all Jews responsible for Jesus' crucifixion. Defenders denied any such intention or inference, pointing back to the Bible account, where only a small group of Jewish leaders plotted Jesus' death. The film's Christian fans found its central theme—Jesus Christ suffered and died for the sins of all—courageous for a Hollywood film, but regretted Gibson's omission of Jesus' resurrection from the dead.

Mel Gibson said, "I want to show the humanity of Christ as well as the divine aspect. It's a rendering that for me is very realistic and as close as possible to what I perceive the truth to be."

FACT

I am poured out like water, and all my bones are out of joint.
My heart has turned to wax; it has melted away within me.
PSALM 22:14

Author John Milton, still considered one of the greatest masters of English prose, suffered some of the most debilitating personal setbacks to befall a man of such achievement.

At St. Paul's school, young John Milton fell behind his classmates and was considered "slow" in learning. At age seventeen, he was teased by his classmates at Christ's College at Cambridge and called "the Lady" because of his delicate features. Shortly after admission, he was expelled for clashes with his tutor. Despite some initial success as a writer, he was silenced by the death of his friend, fellow student Edward King, who drowned in the English sea. A year later, another close friend, Charles Diodati, died and the personal loss struck him deeply.

Men of the Faith

John Milton
(1608–1674)
Author of *Paradise Lost*

One month after their marriage, Milton's young bride left him and returned to her parents. Though she came back to him three years later, she died giving birth to a son. Not long after this tragedy, Milton, only forty-three years old, became totally blind. Milton remarried, but his second wife also died during childbirth. Then, his life was in danger from a new king who hated his political views. Authorities issued a warrant for his arrest, so the writer went into hiding.

After all these events, Milton produced his masterpiece, *Paradise Lost*, and his follow-up five years later, *Paradise Regained*. His subject was the fall of man from God's grace, and God's work to restore man to his former place. His essays on Republicanism are also source materials for the Constitution of the United States of America.

> **FACT**
>
> Helen Keller founded the John Milton Society for the Blind in 1928 to develop an interdenominational ministry that would bring spiritual guidance and religious literature to deaf and blind persons.

Jesus stopped and said, "Call him."
So they called to the blind man, "Cheer up!
On your feet! He's calling you."
MARK 10:49

Direct me in Thy service, and I ask no more. I would not choose my position of work, or place of labor. Only let me know Thy will, and I will readily comply." God took Ann Hasseltine at her word, and she took His Word halfway around the world.

In 1812, Ann Hasseltine Judson and her missionary-husband, Adoniram, sailed to Calcutta, India, where the couple intended to preach the gospel. She was the first American woman missionary to work overseas.

When the Indian government ordered the couple out of the country, the Judsons proceeded to Rangoon, Burma (now Yangon, Myanmar). Ann Judson learned the local languages, enabling her to translate scripture, teach girls, and organize a prayer circle for women. The couple's mission work continued until 1824, when war broke out between the British and the Burmese army. Western missionaries, including Adoniram Judson, were rounded up as spies and imprisoned. Ann Judson fared only slightly better, being allowed to stay in her house, but under guard and subject to the whims of her keepers.

Women of the Faith

Ann Hasseltine Judson (1789–1826)
Missionary and Bible translator

With bribes, Ann managed to gain freedom of movement so she could visit her husband, who lived under recurring threats of execution. Judson wrote in vivid detail an account of her sufferings and privations during this time in her life. After eighteen months, Adoniram was released and the Judsons returned to America.

Letters from the Judsons motivated the Baptist church in America to give increased attention and support to missions in foreign lands.

Ann Judson wrote of the plight of Burmese girls who were denied even a primary education and were forced into early marriages. As women, they held no rights or privileges, save those their husbands chose to allow them. Her descriptions elicited the help of American women, who sent donations to the Judsons' ministry.

FACT

A great door for effective work has opened to me,
and there are many who oppose me.
1 CORINTHIANS 16:9

The word *Malta* means "refuge." According to Acts 28, the island of Malta certainly lived up to its name for the apostle Paul. The Maltese people consider the three months Paul spent shipwrecked on their island as the single most significant event in Malta's history.

Every February 10 all of Malta celebrates a public holiday commemorating the island's "spiritual father." On this day, church services are held at St. Paul's Shipwreck Church in Valletta and a gilded, wooden statue of the apostle is carried through the city's streets. Inside the church, and its ten domed chapels, are paintings depicting Paul's life and an altarpiece portraying the shipwreck. The church also houses two venerated relics: a piece of the apostle's wrist bone and the block of stone Paul is believed to have been beheaded on in Rome. Way back in AD 60, a small memorial niche was dedicated to Paul on the spot where the present church stands today.

Important Sites

Malta

Mediterranean Sea

But there are many sites dedicated to Paul scattered over the island of Malta (which is the largest of three islands that make up the island nation of Malta). A small chapel in St. Paul's Bay commemorates the bonfire where Paul encountered a viper. In Rabat, visitors can see St. Paul's Grotto, where the apostle supposedly lived and preached while shipwrecked on the island. Nearby, St. Paul's Catacombs holds a labyrinth of passageways and tombs hewn out of the rock. During World War II, the Maltese used the catacombs as an air-raid shelter.

FACT

Because of Paul's "harmless" experience with a poisonous viper as recorded in Acts 28, the Maltese people perpetuate the belief that poisonous snakes cannot exist on the island. If one is brought to Malta, it supposedly is rendered nonpoisonous as soon as it touches land.

Once safely on shore, we found out that the island was called Malta. The islanders showed us unusual kindness.
ACTS 28:1–2

While many hippies of the sixties tuned out in drug-induced oblivion, many others turned on to Jesus. Scorned as "Jesus freaks" by the over-thirty crowd, Christian hippies and enthusiastic converts ignited a religious revival of sorts called the Jesus Movement. Clearly, their parents' traditional hymns wouldn't do in this vibrant new spiritual environment. Believers blended the music they grooved to—folk, blues, and rock and roll—with the spontaneous expression of street poetry and a heartfelt gospel message. The combination became known as Jesus Music, and it changed the sound of Christian worship.

Originating with Christian street musicians in California's coastal communities, Jesus Music shunned the form and formula of Christian hymnody for plainspoken and passionate expression of faith. It was sung in communes, on street corners, in parks, and was soon picked up by young ministers eager to reach and relate to the sixties generation. Liberal-leaning churches opened their doors to hippies and others with "contemporary services," in which the booming

Groundbreaking Events

Jesus Music

organ gave way to a lone guitar, the pulpit sermon to an informal chat, rows of pews to a circle of beanbag chairs, and the liturgy to freestyle prayer, praise, and worship.

Christian coffeehouses and Jesus rock festivals featured Christian groups such as Love Song, Agape, and the All Saved Freak Band. Magazines materialized to track the doings of Jesus artists and promote their music and the gospel.

Jesus Music, despite the scorn of conservative Christians, morphed into big business as contemporary Christian music. What began as the personal testimony of a few California street musicians is regarded by many Christians as a positive alternative to the vulgar and violent rock music scene.

Jesus Christ Superstar, Tim Rice and Andrew Lloyd Webber's rock opera, debuted in 1971. As with Jesus Music, many conservative Christians found the juxtaposition of rollicking rock music and the solemn theme of Jesus' crucifixion blasphemous. In addition, the story's omission of the Resurrection rankled religious sensibilities.

FACT

Sing for joy to God our strength; shout aloud to the God of Jacob!
Begin the music, strike the tambourine, play the melodious harp and lyre.
PSALM 81:1–2

"Why on earth am I here?" That's the question mega-church pastor Rick Warren sets out to answer in his mega-selling book, *The Purpose-Driven Life*. With more than eighteen million copies sold since its publication in 2002, the book has become an influential force in contemporary-Christian thinking worldwide.

In forty chapters, intended to be read on forty consecutive days, Warren challenges readers to take each inspirational thought he offers and make it their own. He leads readers to conform their lives around God's plan for them as individuals, as opposed to trying to manipulate God into granting personal favors. The book's program of discovery and discernment is founded on Warren's discovery of five God-given purposes for each person's life. He cites these purposes as to: love God with all your heart; love your neighbor as yourself; make disciples (evangelism); join and participate in a church; and teach others.

Notable Books

The Purpose-Driven Life
By Rick Warren (2002)

In each concise chapter, Warren expounds on a single aspect of Christian living in positive, upbeat language. With references to contemporary culture, the Southern Baptist pastor reaches out to Christians who may not be versed in biblical imagery and doctrinal arguments. Critics complain that Warren avoids some of the more difficult truths of Christianity, such as sin, hell, and judgment. While certainly not a complete course on Christianity, *The Purpose-Driven Life* achieves its purpose of getting the general reader and ordinary Christian to interact with his or her faith in a personal, observable, and meaningful way.

FACT

A spate of associated journals, study guides, meditations, and calendars followed the success of *The Purpose-Driven Life*, in addition to sequels targeting specific groups of readers.

They asked him, "What must we do to do the works God requires?"
Jesus answered, "The work of God is this: to believe in the one he has sent."
JOHN 6:28–29

What would Easter be without the much loved hymn "Christ the Lord Is Risen Today"? Three manuscripts dating from the fourteenth century contain the Latin hymn on which the text is based. The familiar tune called "Easter Hymn" and the English translation were part of a collection of hymns entitled *Lyra Davidica* published in 1708. The original three stanzas of "Christ the Lord Is Risen Today" have undergone various revisions and refinements through the centuries.

Around 1735, the great hymnologist Charles Wesley wrote a fourth stanza for the hymn to be sung at the inaugural service of the Foundry Meeting House, London's first Wesleyan chapel. His fourth stanza completes the hymn in doxological verse. It appeared in 1739 in *Hymns and Sacred Songs* by Charles and John Wesley as "Hymn for Easter Day."

Some hymnals provide the three original stanzas with the Wesley stanza appended. Others include both hymns separately. Here are the three original verses and the fourth verse by Wesley:

Songs of the Faith

"Christ the Lord Is Risen Today"

Words by Charles Wesley (1739)
Music from "Lyra Davidica" (1708)

Jesus Christ is risen today, Alleluia!
Our triumphant holy day, Alleluia!
Who did once, upon the cross, Alleluia!
Suffer to redeem our loss, Alleluia!

But the pains which He endured, Alleluia!
Our salvation hath procured, Alleluia!
Now above the sky He's king, Alleluia!
Where the angels ever sing, Alleluia!

Hymns of praise then let us sing, Alleluia!
Unto Christ, our heavenly king, Alleluia!
Who endured the cross and grave, Alleluia!
Sinners to redeem and save, Alleluia!

Sing we to our God above, Alleluia!
Where the angels ever sing, Alleluia!
Praise him, all you heavenly host, Alleluia!
Father, Son, and Holy Ghost, Alleluia!

The "alleluia" at the end of each line was not written by Wesley but added by an editor to fit the text to the tune.

FACT

"Hallelujah! For our Lord God Almighty reigns.
Let us rejoice and be glad and give him glory!"
REVELATION 19:6–7

Wﾟhat's the big idea? The gospel as told by a tomato, Bob, and a cucumber, Larry, that's what. Computer animator Phil Vischer's first half-hour episode, *Where's God When I'm S–S–Scared?* debuted in late 1993 as the nation's first completely computer-animated video. The kids—and parents—loved it.

Vischer founded his media company, Big Idea, with the goal of creating family-friendly films with Christian themes. He and his cocreator Mike Nawrocki produced a series of half-hour videos based on biblical themes, many of them suggested by letters from fans. Episodes begin as Bob and Larry ponder a moral dilemma and talk it over with other vegetables. When no one can come up with a firm answer, everyone agrees to discover what the Bible says about the issue and they "roll the video." Bob and Larry close the show with a moral and an applicable Bible verse.

Miscellany

VeggieTales—
Verbal Vegetables

In 2002, Big Idea came to the big screen with *Jonah—A VeggieTales Movie*, one of the most successful general audience films of the year. Lively animation and deft screenwriting supported goofy humor and catchy songs kids and adults could enjoy. The creators, through their choice of voices and vegetables, brought in a broad diversity of races, ethnic origins, accents, and body shapes.

Despite the remarkable growth and sunny sales of Big Idea productions, the company died on the vine in 2003. It has since been purchased by other media companies. In the fall of 2006, *VeggieTales* episodes were released on national television.

FACT

When NBC took the *VeggieTales* episodes, the network edited episodes, deleting all mention of God and other specifically religious words. After strong criticism from Vischer, fans, and the conservative Christian group, the Parents Television Council, NBC stopped snipping after the first batch of episodes aired.

As the soil makes the sprout come up and a garden causes seeds to grow,
so the Sovereign LORD will make righteousness
and praise spring up before all nations.
ISAIAH 61:11

Though regaled as a national hero upon his death and buried in Westminster Abbey, missionary, explorer, and abolitionist David Livingstone was no example of Christian warmth and kindness. Within Africa, he didn't get along with other Westerners. He fought with other missionaries and explorers. White Afrikaners drove him out whenever he spoke out against racial intolerance. He even had problems with the London Missionary Society, who felt his explorations were a distraction to his mission work.

Whatever he did in Africa, however, David Livingstone always thought of himself first and foremost as a missionary. One of his primary objectives was to open a "Missionary Road," or "God's Highway" as he called it—a trail fifteen hundred miles into the interior to bring Christianity and civilization to the unreached peoples there. He wished to make the Zambezi River passable, so that Christian commerce could reach deep into the heart of the continent.

Men of the Faith

David Livingstone (1813–1873)

Missionary to Central Africa

Livingston went on to find the source of the Nile and was the first Westerner who saw Victoria Falls. Throughout it all, he stirred up public support, through his books and letters, for the abolition of slavery.

In 1871, *New York Herald* newspaper reporter Henry Morton Stanley found Livingstone in the town of Ujiji on the shores of Lake Tanganyika and greeted him with the now famous words, "Dr. Livingstone, I presume?" Stanley urged Livingstone, now late in his life, to leave Africa, but Livingstone would not budge. He was determined to stay until his mission was complete.

David Livingstone said, "Without Christ, not one step; with Him, anywhere!"

FACT

Ye came near unto me every one of you, and said,
We will send men before us, and they shall search us out the land,
and bring us word again by what way we must go up,
and into what cities we shall come.

DEUTERONOMY 1:22 KJV

Index

Men of the Faith

Women of the Faith

Important Sites

Groundbreaking Events

Notable Books

Miscellany

Other popular Bible reference books
from Barbour Publishing

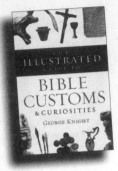

The Illustrated Guide to Bible Customs and Curiosities
6" x 9" / Paperback / 256 pages / $9.97
ISBN 978-1-59310-703-1

If you've ever wondered why Bible people did such strange things, *The Illustrated Guide to Bible Customs and Curiosities* will answer your questions.

Who's Who and Where's Where in the Bible
6" x 9" / Paperback / 400 pages / $14.97
ISBN 978-1-59310-111-4

Here's a Bible dictionary that's actually fun to read! Dig deeply into the stories of five hundred people and places that make the Bible such a fascinating book.

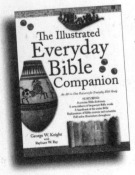

The Illustrated Everyday Bible Companion—
An All-in-One Resource for Bible Study
7" x 9½" / Paperback / 704 pages / $24.97
ISBN 978-1-59310-905-9

Open the door to better Bible study with *The Illustrated Everyday Bible Companion*! You'll find a dictionary, concordance, handbook, and more—plus more than 200 full-color illustrations.

Available wherever Christian books are sold.